MANUAL OF SPANISH-ENGLISH TRANSLATION

Kelly Washbourne
Kent State University

Prentice Hall

Boston Columbus Indianapolis New York San Francisco Upper Saddle River
Amsterdam Cape Town Dubai London Madrid Milan Munich Paris Montréal Toronto
Delhi Mexico City São Paulo Sydney Hong Kong Seoul Singapore Taipei Tokyo

Library of Congress Cataloging-in-Publication Data

Washbourne, R. Kelly.

Manual of Spanish-English translation / Kelly Washbourne.

   p. cm.

ISBN-13: 978-0-13-159297-1 (pbk.)

ISBN-10: 0-13-159297-1 (pbk.)

1. Spanish language—Translating into English. 2. English language—Translating into Spanish.
3. Translating and interpreting—Handbooks, manuals, etc. I. Title.

PC4498.W38 2009

428'.0261—dc22

2009026680

Acquisitions Editor: *Donna Binkowski*
Sponsoring Editor: *María F. García*
Editorial Assistant: *Gayle Unhjem*
Executive Marketing Manager: *Kris Ellis-Levy*
Senior Marketing Manager: *Denise Miller*
Marketing Coordinator: *William J. Bliss*
Senior Media Editor: *Samantha Alducin*
Media Editor: *Meriel Martinez*
Development Editor for Assessment:
  Melissa Marolla Brown
Senior Managing Editor: *Mary Rottino*
Associate Managing Editor: *Janice Stangel*
Production Supervision: *Manuel Echevarria*

Composition/Full-Service Project Management:
  Jill Traut, Macmillan Publishing Solutions
Senior Operations Supervisor: *Brian Mackey*
Operations Specialist: *Cathleen Petersen*
Publisher: *Phil Miller*
Printer/Binder: *Hamilton Printing Co.*
Cover Printer: *Demand Production Center*
Manager, Rights and Permissions: *Zina Arabia*
Manager, Visual Research: *Beth Brenzel*
Manager, Cover Visual Research & Permissions:
  Karen Sanatar
Image Permission Coordinator: *Fran Toepfer*

This book was set in 10/12, Palatino.

Credits and acknowledgments borrowed from other sources and reproduced, with permission, in this textbook appear on appropriate page within the text.

Copyright © 2010 Pearson Education, Inc., publishing as Prentice Hall, 1 Lake St., Upper Saddle River, NJ 07458. All rights reserved. Manufactured in the United States of America. This publication is protected by Copyright, and permission should be obtained from the publisher prior to any prohibited reproduction, storage in a retrieval system, or transmission in any form or by any means, electronic, mechanical, photocopying, recording, or likewise. To obtain permission(s) to use material from this work, please submit a written request to Pearson Education, Inc., Permissions Department, 1 Lake St., Upper Saddle River, NJ 07458

This work is protected by United States copyright laws and is provided solely for the use of instructors in teaching their courses and assessing student learning. Dissemination or sale of any part of this work (including on the World Wide Web) will destroy the integrity of the work and is not permitted. The work and materials from it should never be made available to students except by instructors using the accompanying text in their classes. All recipients of this work are expected to abide by these restrictions and to honor the intended pedagogical purposes and the needs of other instructors who rely on these materials.

10 9 8 7 6 5 4 3 2 1

Prentice Hall
is an imprint of

www.pearsonhighered.com

ISBN 13: 978-0-13-159297-1
ISBN 10: 0-13-159297-1

To the *chaparritos* of Northeast Ohio.
Grow up proud of speaking Spanish.

BRIEF CONTENTS

CONTENTS

PREFACE

Manual of Spanish-English Translation is designed to be a lively, student-centered introduction to translation practice, maneuverable for the student and nonspecialist professor alike, and with a view to making translation accessible (though not oversimplifying). The text is envisioned to serve junior and senior undergraduate students of Spanish in North American university language programs and master's programs in translation. The level is introductory but challenging enough to be appropriate for advanced translators, thorough enough that it can stand alone as the primary text for use in a 14- to 16-week course, and extensive enough that it can be used over two semesters. The activities presuppose at least intermediate knowledge of Spanish.

PROGRAM OVERVIEW

The text's scope is necessarily modest: It aims to create not industry-ready practitioners but pre-professionals, though it does seek to simulate or replicate many industry realities and circumstances in which the translator must weigh important choices. For example, with few exceptions, students are given *translation briefs*, situational features, and target-audience information that condition their approach to a given translation as if it were a professional assignment. *Manual* strives to create frameworks for self-directed learning in which the student takes a leading role in consciously defining problems, goals, and procedures—as Savery and Duffy (1996, 139) term it, *ownership of the process*, part of which is the students' uncovering of a task's relevance to their own lives.

Experience in the classroom has illustrated overwhelmingly that students of translation want and need to be *producers of translations* and not simply consumers of translation studies. This text provides a level-appropriate framework for individual and group translation activities in Spanish-English translation. *Manual* is designed to help organize an entire course and explain the rudiments of praxis, allowing the student to engage language creatively, critically, and sensitively and build skill sets and competences organically through the strategic resolution of pragmatic problems. Translation is considered in its entire process: preparation, translation, diagnosis. It is also considered beyond its merely linguistic dimension, the limitation of almost every translation activity book to date. Encouraging cross-cultural and dialogical thinking, this work engages the indispensable cultural dimension of language as a *negotiation* of meaning transfer, which empowers the student to articulate and refine strategies when faced with ambiguities and discrepancies, a key to confidence building, critical thinking, and metacognitive knowledge. Tasks and activities are built around inductive and deductive learning, and convergent and divergent thinking, rather than on generating unproblematic solutions to complex problems. A text of this sort can help trainers reach the next generation of potential translators, and set students on a course toward professionalization so they do not have to resort to learning the trade vicariously, or receive too late or too unsystematic a start.

Manual of Spanish-English Translation is the only task-based activity manual on the market for the Spanish-English language combination at this level, and it is designed as a *worktext*. Balanced in theory and practice, it has been piloted and refined at both the undergraduate and graduate levels. Introduced skills are scaffolded and recycled into subsequent integrative tasks, and learning is built on students' previous knowledge. Vocational information is presented—particularly in Chapter 1 and the Appendices (see the Companion Website™ at http://www.pearsonhighered.com/manual)—to give the apprentice translator a grounding in the industry culture and norms of the discipline. *Manual*'s primary goals include supporting the development of students as both independent workers and team players: autonomous learners who are both socialized into the norms of the field and self-motivated, intentional, lifelong learners.

CHAPTER ORGANIZATION

Manual is designed to be modular for ease of customization: pair or group activities can be assigned for homework, pair activities can become "think-pair-share" activities in class, thought questions can become prompts for written reflection, and tasks herein can be substituted by Companion Website tasks.

The *Manual* is level appropriate in content (theory, activities, pedagogical design):

- Technologically engaged and relevant, including activities for electronic bulletin boards and Internet research.
- Timely, considering projected growth of the field.
- Focused on activities using key translation tools and skills such as *parallel texts, collocation, précis writing, corpora, editing*, and coverage of such domains as Internet marketing.
- Based on up-to-date discussion of market conditions and research.
- Centered on texts of varied subject areas, sizes, skill levels, and duration (within the novice translator's* range).
- Modeled on a communicative approach to translation, accounting for linguistic and cultural factors, the multiple stakeholders in the translation cycle, process (decision making, documentation, outcomes), "top-down" and "bottom-up" approaches, open and closed tasks, and individual and shared learning.

Types of written activities in *Manual* include:

- Models and exercises: terms, phrases, sentences, genres/text types
- Terms in context (distinguishing nuances)
- Prereading activities: guessing meaning, identifying keywords, gisting
- Short workshop texts (in class): computer-aided ("blitz texts") and unaided ("prepping" or "glossing")
- Longer workshop texts (weekly)
- Select or fill in possible translation ("guided translations")
- Documentation (e.g., finding, comparing, and evaluating parallel texts or neighboring texts)
- Individual edits and group edits
- "Metaedits" (mastering from more than one translation)
- Evaluating translations holistically
- "Translation Teasers" (translation games, conundrums, or humor)
- "Case studies": read, research, and solve information, reasoning, or opinion gaps (see Willis 2004, 21)
- Comparing translations: bitext columns ("ST/TTs") for comparisons
- Glossary building
- Updating a translation
- Self-surveys: self-knowledge and self-assessment

---

*What I am calling the *novice translator* should not be confused with the ACTFL scale use of the terms *novice, intermediate, advanced,* and *superior,* in that here, intermediate to superior source language skills are assumed; in other words, for our purposes a novice translator is not a novice language student.

Reading and oral discussion activities include:

- Brainstorm questions (small groups)
- Translation Traps: cautionary tips and common errors
- Translation Tips: practical and vocational advice
- Cultural Notes: contexts in which texts are embedded
- Linguistic Notes: fine points of language
- ¿? (Thought question): issues for awareness-raising

A GUIDE TO *MANUAL* ICONS

Brainstorming Activity

Editing Task

Group Activity

Pair Activity

Workshop Text

Web Activity

COMPANION WEBSITE™

The Companion Website, http://www.pearsonhighered.com/manual, is organized in chapters that correspond to those in the *Manual*. The site features learning goals for each chapter, links corresponding to and supplementing activities in the chapters and other suggested sites that will help students with their research assignments. The appendices are a supplemental resource in Chapter 1 of the *Manual* Web site that features translation-related organizations, electronic databases, and professionalizing tasks for students to become more attuned to the working life of language mediators and to develop strategies of self-presentation for the market.

INSTRUCTOR'S RESOURCE MANUAL

The Instructor's Resource Manual features teaching tips and methods for presenting, extending, varying, and evaluating the materials in *Manual*.

ACKNOWLEDGMENTS

I am grateful to María F. García, Sponsoring Editor at Pearson Education, Manuel Echevarria, Donna Binkowsi, Gayle Unhjem, Phil Miller, Jennifer Murphy, Aleksandra Tomich, and many others in the organization for their support of this project and their hard work toward its success. My gratitude also goes to Jill Traut, Napolean Panneerselvam and the composition team at Macmillan Publishing Solutions for their meticulous work, and Heather Dubnick and Araceli S. Popen for the careful proofreading and editing. To Paul Grens, many thanks for the invaluable reviewing and research. I also want to recognize the support of Michael Scott Doyle, whose *Éxito comercial* provided me a model of communicative methodology. All those individuals and corporations who allowed their materials to be used in this book—text, photos, realia—are much appreciated. And Camelly, without whom this would have been impossible: thank you; and my mother, of course.

Finally, the attentive suggestions offered by the following reviewers made this a better book. I recognize the following individuals for sharing their expertise: Claudia V. Angelelli, San Diego State University; Ruy Burgos-Lovèce, University of North Carolina at Chapel Hill; Olgierda Furmanek, Wake Forest University; Eduardo González, University of Nebraska at Kearney; Daryl R. Hague, Brigham Young University; Susan G. Rascón, University of Wisconsin-Milwaukee; Michael Scott Doyle, University of North Carolina at Charlotte.

K. Washbourne

An Introduction to Translation: Translation as a Profession, Theory and Practice

IMAGINING TRANSLATORS

Consider the following two images, which are representations of two legends of translation, St. Jerome and Martin Luther, respectively. How do the images characterize the translator and the translator's labors?

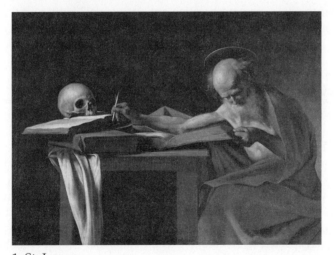

1. St. Jerome

Source: Galleria Borghese, Rome, Italy / The Bridgeman Art Library International

2. Martin Luther

Source: Corbis / Bettmann

1. Now critique the images. Are they limiting? Are they accurate for all circumstances and eras? Are they made by translators? Which one appeals more to you? Which is more harmonious with your personality or style of work? Your instructor will pass out a montage of images of contemporary translators at work. How do these compare?
2. Do you know any sayings about translation? Are they flattering to translators? From what you know about it, how would *you* describe translation metaphorically (i.e., using a comparison without the use of "like" or "as")?

In pairs, brainstorm some apt metaphors and analogies for the act or product of translation.

Follow-Up

1. The phrase "lost in translation" is an old warhorse of an expression, now rather tired. Sometimes upon hearing it translators reply with the idea of what is "gained" in translation. What do you think of these concepts? What do *loss* and *gain* presume about a given piece of writing? Can you think of a better, or more productive, way of seeing translation? Do you think a fixed meaning exists in all texts that must be preserved or recovered, or is meaning something in flux, negotiated and contingent upon circumstance? Discuss.
2. Laypeople, and even many clients, tend to underestimate the difficulty of translation. Discuss some reasons why this may be and what translators could do to educate people. What are the consequences if translators cannot sufficiently educate clients?
3. What role do translators play in society? Across societies?
4. How visible are translators in human events? Why do you think that is? Think of the last translation you read. Did you know it was a translation? Was the translator's name attached to it somehow? Featured prominently?
5. Can a translator have a recognizable *style*? A *voice*? Do you think you would recognize your own translations long after doing them? How?
6. Make a short list of the reasons you would like to enter the profession. Would you consider your translation goals to be more idealistic (e.g., to foster understanding) or more pragmatic (e.g., to earn a livelihood)? More personal (e.g., to master a craft) or more professional (e.g., to earn prestige and influence)? How will these goals condition the types of texts that appeal to you and the range of skills you wish to develop?

WHAT IS EXPECTED OF TODAY'S TRANSLATOR?

The job profile for the translator has changed, and is changing, rapidly. One translator, Don Kiraly, details some of the conditions of his work environment. Read his account, taking note especially of how the image of the translator that he paints is highly *collaborative*. The translator works and networks within and between communities; the reach of translation, and faster-moving time lines, have widened the definition of the translator, who serves a wider constituency in a wider migration of knowledge than in years past, with all the technological proficiency and adaptability this entails; translators are expected to acquire new subject knowledge as well as to stay abreast of changes in their present subject domains. Also, translators are expected to be able to execute databases and spreadsheets, learn new tools and programs "on the fly," and manage terminology on the desktop. As Kiraly notes, translators can now work together with subject area specialists

> to collect terminological and contextual data in a common database that can be used for various purposes by personnel with different tasks within a company, or by a set of freelancers working on projects in a team. The translator can be expected to know what software is available, how to use it and how to best exploit its advantages to serve the terminology and knowledge management needs of the firm or client.
>
> Technological advances have contributed to the crumbling of barriers in international communication and the global market. This in turn has led to an

increased awareness of cultural and textual differences as well as the implications of these advances for the translator's work. A decade ago, software was simply translated; now it is also 'localized', or adapted to the textual and cultural conventions of the target markets. Multi-cultural technical writing, involving the production of parallel texts in different languages, has become a more cost-efficient alternative to simply 'translating' a culturally embedded technical text from one language to another. Whereas in earlier days, translators might have been expected to 'just translate what's on the paper', today there is much greater awareness of the importance of creating an appropriate effect on a reader, particularly within the translation profession itself. Translation studies as an academic field has matured greatly over the past fifty years, and has gradually liberated itself from the domination of contrastive structural linguistics; most contemporary perspectives in the field view the translator's professional activities essentially in terms of social and cognitive processes and intercultural communication, rather than primarily as a process of linguistic transfer.

When it comes to subject matter knowledge, it is now less of matter of mastering one specialized field prior to beginning work as a translator. Rather, it is one of having the ability to acquire adequate knowledge in new areas as needed, and of developing a finely tuned sensitivity to norms and text types in preparation for tackling a variety of new language-related tasks and challenges. It is impossible to predict years in advance what particular topics one will work on after graduation or over the course of one's career. A well-developed ability to adapt to ever-changing market demands is crucial. Thus, knowing how and where to research new topics adequately and efficiently is an essential skill for translators to acquire.

Translators today cannot afford to be linguistic hermits, sitting alone behind a typewriter and surrounded by dusty tomes. Translators are embedded in a complex network of social and professional activity. They should not be considered anonymous language lackeys, passively transferring a message from one language to another. Translators are professional text interpreters and communicators. They do not transfer meaning: they make meaning as they work. They must have a professional 'self-concept', a profound awareness of their responsibility as active participants in a complex communicative process where they serve a key role that can significantly affect the degree of success of commercial contacts, legal interaction, medical treatment, and technical operations.

(Kiraly 2000, 11–13)

 Given the preceding description of the translator and the state of the field, and adding your own ideas, brainstorm as a class (on an overhead, a whiteboard, or a blackboard) the **qualities of an ideal translator today**. Focus on personal *qualities* rather than *skills*. Then take an honest look: How does your own self-concept compare with the class's ideal? (Granted that the ideal translator is an abstraction and that in different environments, certain qualities and certain proportions of them will be more or less predictive of success than a general "ideal.")

Text translation is increasingly seen in the wider sense of including not only words. As Yves Gambier and Henrik Gottlieb note (2001, ix–x):

It is also easy to notice the great diversity of expectations and representations related to the concept of translation, hence the different labels existing today in some professional fields: localization, language transfer, adaptation, editing, revision, documentation management, co-authoring, technical writing, multilingual text creation and design, versioning, language mediation, language-service provision, language management, proofreading, copywriting, language consultancy, etc. There are at least two reasons for this: 'translation' remains synonymous with transcoding . . . while the concept of 'text' is no longer seen as a string of sentences, partly because language is seen as being integrated with images, sound, graphics, etc. . . . This double explanation shows how the concepts of translation and the translator's world are generally considered archaic.

Research

1. Find out more about the implications of developments in multimedia and hyper-media for translation today. Give a summary of what tasks translators are now called on to do and how the market trends are widening and redefining the translator's role.

2. Translation is sometimes considered both an *art* and a *craft*. What translation theory or history can you find to account for each part of this twofold conception? Which—art or craft—describes translation as you see it?

CULTURAL NOTE

The Tower of Babel

One of the key foundational narratives about our profession centers on the lesson at Babel: that language diversity arose *as a punishment* for hubris. Some translators see themselves as rebuilders of the Tower of Babel, which was demolished when the people, who all spoke one language, aspired to rise too high toward heaven by means of the tower (actually thought to have been a ziggurat, or pyramid-like structure). Today many people and cultures (though by no means all) can at least partially overcome geographical dispersal and the "confusion of tongues" through multilingualism, advanced technology, the accessibility of travel, and the labors of translators and interpreters.

Today, a "Tower of Babel" refers to a linguistically chaotic situation—Babel stands not for the harmony achieved before the scattering, but for the confounding of mutual comprehension.

Source: Towneley Hall Art Gallery and Museum, Burnley, Lancashire/The Bridgeman Art Library International

COMPETENCE

Many competing models of competence exist. Competence might be simply called "what it takes to be a translator." One useful model sees competence as referring to the "*combination of skills, knowledge, aptitudes, and attitudes*" and the "*disposition to learn as well as know-how*" of the translator (González and Wagenaar 2003, 10). Citing Roberts (1984), Delisle (1993, 42) delineates five components of translator competence:

> *Linguistic competence:* "being able to understand the source language and to produce acceptable target language utterances"
>
> *Translation competence:* "the ability to express the meaning of the source text appropriately in the target text without unwarranted changes in form"
>
> *Methodological competence:* "the ability to research and select the right terminology"
>
> *Disciplinary competence:* "being able to translate texts in given discourse areas, such as medicine, law and so on"
>
> *Technical competence:* "knowing how to use translation aids like word processors and databases"

A more nuanced model (the EU Tuning Project) identifies *instrumental*, *interpersonal*, and *systemic* competences (Kelly 2005, 35), which include the process-related features of translation that bear not only on abilities but on translator qualities that are not always objectively measurable but are consistent with good practice (e.g., teamwork, adaptability, commitment). This model is as follows:

Generic Competences

Instrumental Competences

Oral and written communication in the native language

Knowledge of a second language

Capacity for analysis and synthesis

Capacity for organization and planning

Basic general knowledge

Grounding in basic knowledge of the profession

Elementary computing skills

Information management skills (ability to retrieve and analyze information from different sources)

Problem solving

Decision making

Interpersonal Competences

Critical and self-critical abilities

Teamwork

Interpersonal skills

Ability to work in an interdisciplinary team

Ability to communicate with experts in other fields

Appreciation of diversity and multi-culturality

Ability to work in an international context

Ethical commitment

Systemic Competences

Capacity for applying knowledge in practice

Research skills

Capacity to learn

Capacity to adapt to new situations

Capacity for generating new ideas (creativity)

Leadership

Understanding of cultures and customs of other countries

Ability to work autonomously

Project design and management

Initiative and entrepreneurial spirit

Concern for quality

Will to succeed

Source: Reprinted by permission of González and Wagenaar, 2003

What do you think is the *single most important* competence for a translator or translator-in-training to have or to develop?

Do you think translators are *made* or *born*? If you say they are born, explain how one is born with the capacities and attitudes listed in the table.

NORMS

What governs how translators guide their choices (production) and how translations (product) are judged? Although far from agreed upon in their specifics, **norms** are in operation and are an important feature, whether implied or stated, of the translational landscape. They essentially offer frameworks for gauging the "assumptions and expectations about correctness and/or appropriateness" of a translation for a situation (Schäffner 1999, 1), "internalized behavioural **constraints** which embody the values shared by a community" (5, emphasis mine). A *norm*, in other words,

> is a notion of what a particular community regards as correct or proper. The directive force of a norm is there to secure and maintain these notions as *values*. The assumption is roughly that norms serve as the active ingredient by means of which general values are transmuted into guidelines and prompters of concrete action. The dominant values, and hence the dominant norms, of communities tend to reflect the hierarchies of power in those communities. If norms, understood in this sense, are relevant to acts of translation, then translation can never be value-free.
> (Hermans 1998, 59)

Three main theorists who have debated norms are Gideon Toury, Theo Hermans, and Andrew Chesterman. Norms within the earlier **normative linguistic approach**—a weakness of which was that it focused almost exclusively on the level of sentence or phrase—are giving way to **textlinguistic norms**, which focus on communicative function and genre and, on the production level, the retextualization—reuse—of textual conventions from the target language repertoire (Schäffner 1999, 3–4). In this book we strive to present both, though recognizing the trend toward the latter, and the prevailing preference for descriptive rather than prescriptive norms. At bottom, it is now quite difficult to deny that translation is, as Toury notes, a *sociocultural activity*—that is, a norm-governed, negotiated, conventional one (Toury 1999, 13). We should observe that by now the concept of **equivalence**—a major concept in translation studies over the last several decades—has fallen mostly into disrepute.

Tasks

1. Print out a brief exchange (several threaded postings) from a translators' forum that demonstrates the acquisition and negotiation of a translation norm. Share in small groups.
2. Find out more about *constraints* in translation, in particular as they relate to our language pair (Spanish<>English). Are constraints variable by text type and audience, are they assumed to be inherent to the contrastive differences between English and Spanish syntaxes, or are they germane to the translator's task in general?

LINGUISTIC RELATIVITY AND TRANSLATION: SAPIR-WHORF

Linguist Benjamin Lee Whorf (1897–1941) had a tremendous impact on twentieth-century linguistics in general and on discussions of translatability in particular. Read the following paragraph, which distills the essence of one of his and his teacher Edward Sapir's most influential thoughts.

The grammar of each language does not merely *express* ideas but in fact *shapes* ideas. As he notes in "Linguistic Relativity and the Relation of Linguistic Processes to Perception and Cognition" (1961, 464–5): "We dissect nature along lines laid down by our native languages." Our minds organize the world linguistically: "We cut nature up, organize it into concepts, and ascribe significances as we do, largely because we are parties to an agreement to organize it in this way." Different speakers' ways of categorizing the world in thought, in other words, determines their reality. Each language, as a natural corollary to this view, has a worldview that cannot be reconciled to any other.

 What do you think of Whorf's idea? If he is right, what are the implications for translation? Must he be wrong for translation to be possible? Is there a middle ground?

Follow-Up

What schools of thought since Whorf have challenged Whorfian thinking that posits the incommensurability of languages? What kinds of data or evidence have theorists used to convince others?

LINGUISTIC NOTE

THE FIVE STAGES OF EXPERTISE

Chesterman (1996, 67), following Dreyfus and Dreyfus (1986), relates the five steps, proceeding from novice to expert:

Stage one: that of the novice, "who learns to recognize relevant facts and situational features and acquires objective rules for determining actions based on these."

Stage two: that of the advanced beginner, who "begins to recognize relevant facts and situational features that have not been previously defined and presented, by perceiving their similarity with others experienced earlier."

Stage three: that of competence, "the ability to develop a sense of priorities between all the relevant situational features, in order to reach a decision-making capability, a conscious problem-solving skill."

Stage four: that of proficiency; "intuition begins to play more of a role here, as the learner reacts more holistically, without consciously analysing, unless the situation turns out to be exceptional."

Stage five: that of expertise; in this stage, "non-reflective involvement is dominant: intuition becomes the driving force, but 'deliberative rationality' plays a part as a way of testing and fine-tuning intuitions when necessary."

Chesterman adds: "These steps illustrate how rules and strategies for action are first consciously recognized by the novice and beginner; then internalized and applied consciously, analytically, at stages of competence and proficiency; and finally used automatically, unconsciously. At the highest stage of expertise, action is shaped by intuition but is always accessible to monitoring by deliberate rationality: strategies and principles can be recalled to consciousness if required." Note that experts know the principles behind what they do, even if they don't call them consciously to mind—working from intuition alone is not enough to qualify one as an expert. And clearly, in any field, some experts can articulate better how they work than others can.

 Think of something of which you have learned the process that took the path outlined previously whether or not you have become an expert. Could you teach it to others step by step?

WHAT SHOULD BE TRANSLATED?

(Un)translatability is a long-standing issue in translation, however unsatisfying, academic, or subjective its defenses tend to be. Perhaps just as relevant a question as "What is translated?" and "What is translatable?" is a third question, *"What should be translated?"*

Discussion

In groups of three, come to a consensus about what should be translated. Perhaps you can start by defining your answer negatively: What *should not* be translated or *need not* be translated? Is there anything unworthy of translation but *is* translated because it has to be or simply because someone translates it? Break into your groups now and discuss.

. . . .

Follow-Up

Some students like to answer instinctively that *everything* should be translated. Although in some respects this is admirably completist, (1) it is impossible pragmatically, and (2) it ignores a fundamental truth: An audience or a need may not exist for the translation and, thus, neither a patron, nor a context, nor possibly even an interested translator. Would a 1941 primer on young women's table etiquette normally need translating in whole or in part? How about literature on an obsolete technology? Or health certificates for products to be sent to a country still under embargo (for example, Cuba)? What if the original audience has completely different needs from those of any new imagined audience—for example, English as a Second Language (ESL) textbooks written in English *in order for students to be exposed to English*? How about highly nationalistic propaganda for an election in which outsiders could not vote, or the language of which is itself politicized (think of Castilian and Catalan)? What about old political tracts now illegal or deemed hate speech? Someone's terrible, self-published PhD dissertation? Highly sensitive documents at a financial institution or ministry of defense? A third-rate pulp romance half-plagiarized from a foreign author and sold at news kiosks? *Quality* is a factor; *relevance*, another. (In Chapter 4 we will study the all-important *translation brief*, the commission that signals the *why*, the *for whom*, and the *what for* of a translation.)

Does a new audience justify the credo that everything should be translated? The question put another way is: Can or should a text be transformed indefinitely, or are some texts meant to be ephemeral?

. . . .

Challenge

1. In pairs, search the phrase "must be accompanied by a translation" in a search engine. How many different types of documents can you find? To speed your search, guess keywords to include with the phrase (e.g., "+ adoption").
2. Read the Fort Worth, Texas, city newsletter article that follows, which is aimed at preventing gunshots during New Year's Day celebrations. Do you think the same article would appear in an English-language edition of the gazette? Discuss.

Siga a Salvo este Año Nuevo, No Dispare sus Armas al Aire

De acuerdo con las leyes de física, lo que sube siempre baja. Esto incluye balas que caen al haber sido disparadas al aire, las cuales han matado gente en pasadas celebraciones de Año Nuevo.

Daños en los techos y vehículos también son abundantes durante esta temporada debido a disparos que se hacen en el aire.

Cada año, cientos de residentes de Fort Worth celebran el Año Nuevo disparando balas al aire. Esta práctica ilegal ha aumentado en los últimos años y es extremadamente peligrosa.

Una bala disparada al aire puede viajar por dos millas y volar por más de un minuto. Al caer, la bala alcanza velocidades de 300 a 700 pies por segundo. Una velocidad de 200 pies por segundo es suficiente para penetrar el cráneo humano.

El Departamento de Policía de Fort Worth le advierte a los residentes que las personas que sean vistas disparando armas al aire serán arrestadas. Esta es una violación y tiene una sentencia de un año en la cárcel y una multa de $4,000—esto si nadie ha sido herido o ninguna propiedad ha sido afectada por las balas.

Los residentes deben reportar los disparos llamando al 9-1-1. El Departamento de Policía anticipa 1,000 llamadas en la noche de Año Nuevo reportando disparos de armas de fuego.

La Policía afirma que aunque muchas personas que disparan balas al aire no saben que las balas caen a velocidades mortales, disparar armas al aire dentro de los límites de la ciudad está en contra de la ley, aunque sea una tradición.

Así que mantenga sus armas guardadas durante la celebración de Año Nuevo.

Pólvora Prohibida por el Condado esta Temporada

La pólvora también es usada como parte de la celebración de año nuevo.

Es por esto que la Corte de Comisionados del Condado de Tarrant ha prohibido la venta y el uso de pólvora dentro del condado en Diciembre—Diciembre 2 al 1 de Enero. Esto es debido a las áreas extremadamente secas esta temporada. Violación de esta orden es clase C con multas de hasta $2,000.

Para reportar la violación llame al **817-922-3000**. **No** llame al 9-1-1.

Recuerde, que la ignorancia sobre leyes no es una excusa.

Source: Article courtesy of the City of Fort Worth, Texas

Source: Michael Newman/PhotoEdit Inc.

What photos of bilingual signs and labels can you find online? "Do-it-yourself," or "DIY" translation—translation undertaken by nonspecialists—can be risky.

Discussion

In what circumstances do translations appear side by side with their source texts? Do they appear consecutively, in bitext (aligned columns), in facing page ("*en face*") format, or as *hypertext translations* online? What kinds of texts are they, where do they appear, how do they appear (what medium), and for what communicative goals? Can you think of a case in which texts appearing with their translations would be useful for more than one group of end users (e.g., even the dominant-language speakers)?

In what circumstances does a translation seem to replace or efface the source? Could there be a translation without an original? If the original is lost, does a translation gain the status of an original?

· ·

Follow-Up

Can you find multiple versions of a text the source language of which is indeterminate? In other words, multiple apparent target texts without a clear source? Bring them to class.

· ·

TRANSLATION TEASER

Determine a text type that is not translated or not widely or regularly translated but *should* be. Research thoroughly. Make your case to the class, identifying your ideal readership and speculating as to why translations have been "behind the curve" with your proposed text type.

TRANSLATION LENGTH: THE SPANISH WILL BE LONGER THAN THE ENGLISH

Note how the Spanish title in a Monterey Park Fire Department emergency service flyer is considerably longer in Spanish than in English, a typical phenomenon that must be planned for in layout, because text can run 30% longer in Spanish:

Paramedic ambulance membership   *Cómo hacerse miembro del programa de servicio de ambulancias paramédicas*

Some clients are surprised and wary upon first receiving Spanish target texts longer than their sources. These clients can be educated briefly in contrastive syntax with a simple illustration: "Roberto's house" (two words), "*La casa de Roberto*" (four words). Or consider this pairing of industrial signs (Bonet 2002, 20): "Staff only > *Prohibida la entrada a toda persona ajena a la Administración*."

THINKING ABOUT TRANSLATION

As a warm-up to some of the debates of translation, answer instinctively. Remember your responses and compare at the end of the semester. These prompts serve also to introduce you to a few of the main issues central to the translator's task.

1. Who needs and uses translations? Who commissions translations? What translations have you used (read)?
2. Should a translation sound like a translation? (Should an exchange student from the Ukraine sound like one? Is the analogy valid?) Do you read a translation the same way you would an "original"? Is "original" merely a figure of speech? Is a translation necessarily inferior to the original?
3. a. In whose service is the translator?
   b. What is *fidelity*?
   c. Is it possible to have a translation that is both beautiful and faithful?
   d. The most infamous cliché in translation, in case you have not come across it yet, is from the Italian, *Traduttore, traditore*, "The translator is a traitor." Comment in light of 3a, b, and c.

4. Is everything translatable? (On the textual level? On the lexical level? Are entire cultures untranslatable to others?) Who do you suppose might be attracted to the doctrine of untranslatability? What nonlinguistic reasons might a person have for claiming that a work or writer is untranslatable? Is untranslatability something useful to keep in mind while translating or not?

5. How can you tell if a translation is adequate or skillful? (Who can adequately judge a translator's work? Only those skilled in the source and target languages? Other translators?) How would you react if a translation of a text you find meaningful were shown to actually be a poor translation?

6. Does translation weaken its users' will to learn other tongues? (i.e., does translation foster dependency?)

7. Does translation "colonize" or appropriate texts of other cultures? How does translation serve the relationship between identities, gender, national literary histories, political ideologies, economic systems, and so on?

8. Is self-translation possible? How might it differ from translation proper?

   a. Think of the metaphors and analogies you thought of earlier for the act and/or product of translation. A famous one you may not have heard of, and one that disparages the success of the product, is that of *translation as the reverse side of a tapestry*, in which the work and the craft are revealed but not the colors, the delineation, or the fullness of the "artistic" side. (This image comes from Cervantes's *Don Quixote*.) Another, explored in Doug Robinson's *Becoming a Translator*, is *translator as actor*. Why actor? What do successful actors do that translators must do as well? (Hint: Think not only of the performance, but of the preperformance.) Another way that one could see the translator is as *dramaturge* (the person who researches, advises, adapts, revises, and translates plays, assesses textual problems and reconceptualizes a work for new stagings or different audiences, and "advocates for the playwright").

   b. How practical is your conception of the translator? Do you hold any ideas of the translator as mystic, medium, alchemist, and so forth? Hold these ideas up to scrutiny (yours and others').

9. Do you think machines can and will replace human translators?

CULTURAL NOTE

Not every end user of a translation is a monolingual or unacquainted with the source language. Sometimes using a translation in one's mother tongue helps the user feel more comfortable, better informed, and more socially connected, even if he or she has a passing command of the source language. The distinctions "**Spanish-dominant**" and "**Spanish-preferring**" acknowledge this reality. Lipton (2002, 51) offers the caveat to marketers that it is a mistake to try to "force feed English to those who want to hear and read Spanish. It's a myth that people who prefer Spanish will get over it when they become acculturated. Advertisers used to think they didn't need to advertise in Spanish because Hispanic immigrants all learn English eventually. But although many do, that doesn't mean they'll prefer it. [According to Daniel Nance,] language preference isn't a function of binguality, income or education."

For some text types, such as those in the arts and sciences, bilingual readers have long read translations as an intellectual exercise or to appreciate the artistry of the translations themselves. And sometimes translations occur simply because an official translation in a certain language is mandated, independent of what individual needs may be. Other times a translation may provide a common language for an international business meeting or deal for the benefit of only a few of the participants. The above notwithstanding, millions of translation users depend on translations for access to a language they do not know at all.

TRANSLATION AND THE BROKEN HAMMER

Philosopher Martin Heidegger wrote that a hammer is most fully a hammer when it is broken, because then the function of the hammer is forced into our awareness. Is the same true of translation? Do we notice that languages exist, and that they are not mechanically interchangeable only when flaws, gaps, or outright communication breakdown occur? What else makes us aware of different languages and their (in)accessibility? Is it fitting that we often do not notice translations? *Should* we always notice when we are reading a translation? Why or why not? Can you think of other things, professions or activities, that are least conspicuous to the average person when they are least effective?

What infamous cases of flawed translations have you heard about? What consequences could result from a poor translation in various arenas (international politics, construction, business, legal arbitration, tourism, informatics, literature, etc.)?

LINGUISTIC NOTE

DOMAINS

Broad subject areas in translation—legal, medical, literary, technology, and others—are called **domains**.

In practice, domains are frequently overlapping, that is, just as texts are often—or always—hybrids in register, so too do they frequently cross over to other domains. For example, a hospital intake form—for which the patient fills out his or her medical history and personal information—might qualify as "medical-legal" (or "medico-legal").

 What other overlapping domains can you think of? Brainstorm text types that fit in more than one category.

SPECIALIZATION

Whether or not a translator-in-training should specialize is the source of ongoing debate. Yet for many people the desiderata for a novice translator, in descending order, would probably look like this:

1. Formal translation training + a previous and concurrent specialization
2. Formal translation training + a previous specialization
3. Formal translation training + no specialization
4. No formal translation training + a previous and concurrent specialization
5. No formal translation training + a previous specialization
6. No formal translation training + no specialization

These, of course, are abstractions and assume that other variables are fixed (exceptional accomplishment in any of the previously mentioned metrics would clearly increase that person's marketability). And long work experience in a particular field may prove invaluable—some might even rank a nonlinguist subject specialist (#4) ahead of a formally trained translator with no specialization (#3). Others value above all the ability to learn new specializations in an ever-changing marketplace and the capacity for developing *transferable skills* (one of the buzzwords of the twenty-first century, and justifiably so). Still others fret about fledgling translators specializing too soon, putting *subject competence* ahead of *transfer competence* (the general ability to convey messages across languages). Common sense would indicate that both can and should coexist, and subject competence must be *maintained* to truly constitute a specialization. (The American Translators Association has a continuing education requirement that must be met to keep certification current.) The reality you want to avoid is having only a very partial understanding of the texts you translate—this will only lead to self-doubt, guilt, and problems producing convincing texts. It is in your best interest (ethically, economically, and psychologically) to claim only those subject areas you can work in with at least the potential for superior competence every time out. Simply put: If you cannot do a job, you should turn it down.

¿?

> Do you have a specialization you don't even realize? (Perhaps you're a sports nut, a tech junkie, a history buff, a nature enthusiast, a music lover, a gearhead, a video game fanatic, a cat fancier, a cigar aficionado, an art connoisseur, or a fashion maven.)

NOTE One may achieve success in translation without being formally trained, as one could in music, art, business, or virtually any endeavor. *However*, resistance has built up against those who one fine day wake up and call themselves translators, hang out their shingle, and proceed to undermine industry standards and practices. Fundamental misunderstandings—that to be bilingual is to be a translator—persist. A depressing number of people are called on to translate and interpret for the sole fact of their standing nearby—the infamous *ad hoc interpreters* (sometimes they are even children). One could speak, too, of "ad hoc translators"—someone near at hand who the author or translation initiator knows or knows of and who is hired (or imposed upon) to translate. This practice, although convenient, only proliferates the idea that translation is something that does not require background knowledge, text interpretation skills, and a whole host of competences.

Some untrained translators *have* made their way as professionals of the first order. Yet training is the ideal. Many—if not most—agencies recognize the competitive advantage of an individual with a formal background in translation studies versus another individual without it, assuming equal work experience for both.

Follow-Up

1. Research the most in-demand specializations in translation right now for Spanish<>English. Compare your findings. How might your own specializations or potential specializations fit in?
2. List your potential fields of specialization from the strongest down. Look on the ProZ profiles for ideas about how broadly or narrowly to classify them.

HINT Don't list 15 areas on a profile or curriculum vitae (CV)—you are better off *knowing fewer fields well*. Credibility is strained when subject areas start multiplying.

3. Which do you think is better prepared for translation—a lawyer who translates or a translator who knows law? How about a doctor who translates or a translator who knows medicine? Which would you rather *hire*?
4. What is meant by "LSP translation"?

LINGUISTIC NOTE

"Easy" and "Hard" Languages and Texts

On occasion you will hear such remarks as "Chinese is a hard language," "Spanish is an easy language," and so forth, even from highly educated people. Linguists have long known that these are unfounded and breezy generalities—the "difficulty" of a language depends on the language from which a person is starting. (Is Chinese "hard" for a Japanese speaker? *Relative to what?*)

Moreover, for translators, the *commission* is what is determinant: how dense the writing, how quick the turnaround, how straightforward the research, how difficult the client; in short, how reasonable the job expectations and constraints. Or think of the issue of difficulty this way: Is translating a Chinese menu harder for the average translator than translating a Uruguayan essay on plate tectonics would be for the average translator? Regardless of the variables (translators' specialties, the time lines involved, etc.), we can say confidently that *some texts are simply harder to translate* than others. Text density in particular can be a prime factor in difficulty (perhaps even beyond the degree of technicality). And the most difficult source texts of all, as many translators will attest, are poorly written ones. One might say that as one gains in expertise, one learns to recognize (and protect oneself from) such jobs. Difficult texts, however, are inescapable at all levels.

If Spanish<>English translation doesn't pay as well as, say, Urdu<>English, it has nothing to do with difficulty, but rather with *supply and demand*: the availability of translators; there may be costs, too, associated with support of different character sets and personnel for proofreading. However, this difference in pay is more than compensated for by the relatively massive amount of work for Spanish <> English translators.

TRANSLATION TIPS

The Translator's Preparedness and Continuing Education

- Do word puzzles in both languages of your combination.
- Sight translate short texts as you come across them in your everyday life.
- Keep a journal of interesting problems and solutions you see or devise.
- Read! Not only on the Internet, but journals, books, and documents germane to your field(s) and in your languages. Join a book circle if that keeps you on task. Set reachable reading goals, and start with material of your greatest interest. *Plan* reading time—don't hope for idle time to appear. The greatest detriment to the would-be translator is to have rusty or poorly developed reading skills.
- Subscribe to and read a newspaper such as *The Wall Street Journal* or *The New York Times*. Reading with pen in hand, circle concepts, phrases, collocations, text types, neologisms, regionalisms, acronyms, and allusions that are new to you. Read news magazines (*The Economist*) and journals (*The New England Journal of Medicine*) faithfully. For legal texts, for example, find and read contracts, forms, treaties, indictments, police reports, political science, international agreements, legal theory, and case histories. For *all* fields, read the latest textbooks.
- Stay organized and current. Label and update your glossaries and bookmarks.
- Take continuing education courses or workshops to strengthen those computer skills in which you are weakest.
- Read journals that publish in both English and Spanish formats, such as *Americas*. Compare and critique.
- Collect and share translation "howlers" (outrageous mistranslations).
- Read and *buy* translations, habits that support translators and encourage translators' patrons to continue their patronage. Collect translations you would like to emulate.

(Continued)

- Correspond with established working translators and novices alike.
- Attend regional and national translation and localization conferences at least yearly. Sometimes there are student scholarships to defray conference travel costs.
- Join Espalista, the listserv for the ATA Spanish Language Division members, or a similar group.
- Look into ATA's Mentoring Program, a way to accelerate your professionalization under an established translator's tutelage.

 Connect with your **Manual** Web site to find invaluable databases in Spanish of newspapers, magazines, radio, and Internet.

THE DEFINITIVE TRANSLATION: "THREE INTERPRETATIONS"

Indries Shah tells a story of three dervishes who seek the truth. Their great teacher strikes the blooms off the tallest flower with a stick, and asks what his actions mean; whoever interpreted correctly would be accepted for the Teaching. Shah relates:

> The first dervish said, 'My interpretation of the lesson is "people who imagine that they know more than others may have to suffer a leveling in the Teaching."'
>
> The second dervish said, 'My understanding of the action is "things which are beautiful in appearance may be unimportant in the totality."'
>
> The third dervish said, 'I would describe what you did as indicating "a dead thing, even a stick of repetitious knowledge, can still harm what is alive."'
>
> The Master said, 'You are all enrolled, for between you meanings are shared. Not one of you knows all; what all of you have is not complete; but what each of you says is correct.' (Shah 1991)

The definitive translation is as elusive as the "perfect language" sought by the linguists of old. Language is too chimerical, too changing, and too connotative for a single rendering to capture every facet of a source text. Multiple translations can appear almost simultaneously, or over the years, as each successive generation renews its reading of a major text, such as *The Odyssey*. Land deeds, for example, are not given in multiple, variant versions for economic reasons, naturally, and because the superstition reigns that everyday language has a single, unmistakable, transparent, fixed meaning. Further, the average language user feels that what he or she has said or written is readily comprehensible; we are quick to attribute misunderstandings to the *other* person's failure to decode our meaning. Virtually everyone wishes to be understood; *what* is understood, however, is often quiet variable and depends on culture, the receiver's predisposition, surrounding verbal cues, and previous interactions between the interlocutors. A mistake in reading that some novice translators make is actually one of perspective: adhering to the "anything goes" school of translation in which meanings are assembled promiscuously into a ragtag whole without regard for coherence or other constraints. *Not all translations are equally valid.*

By the same token, one point of the preceding parable may be that multiple readings need not be mutually exclusive but, in fact, can contribute to a full, or fuller, understanding. Two wildly different translations of a source text can be equally excellent. Each translation contributes, but none exhausts.

Discussion

1. How do you think translation quality is measured? Is there a "last word" on quality? Can a translation be of expert quality and still fail? Do you think quality control measures are put in place to ensure *perfection*?

2. Assuming you had unlimited funds, which work procedure or model would you put in place as the basis of quality assurance—a translation team, each responsible for a different facet, or a series of independent translators, each producing a version of the text for an editor to choose the best final product from among them? Discuss, proposing other models.

3. Is conceding that multiple translations can or should exist for a given source text tantamount to confessing its untranslatability?

4. One overlooked quality of the expert translator is having a *tolerance for ambiguity*. This means that sometimes there is no final, definitive test for the quality of a particular translation solution the way one would test, say, a fuse or the emissions levels of an engine. How comfortable are you with ambiguity? Do you become impatient if no absolute, definitive answer is available to something, or can you work with occasional consensus, improvisation, educated guesses, good-faith documented research, and negotiated solutions (sometimes overridden by a more powerful stakeholder in the translation chain)? Remember that negotiation involves concessions—gaining or resolving by conceding something. Do you hold fast to the idea of absolute meanings? If so, explain your distaste for the idea of negotiating meaning.

LINGUISTIC NOTE

COMMON TERMS AND DISTINCTIONS

Translators often make the distinction between **highly technical** and **semitechnical** language in determining the density and difficulty of a text. Obviously this is a subjective, sliding scale to some extent.

Other distinctions you will become aware of include **literary** and **nonliterary translation** (a binary formed unmistakably from the literary translators' point of view!). Many use the term *pragmatic texts* or **pragmatic translation** to refer to those general texts that are not primarily in the expressive mode, but instead have a predominantly "transparent" communicative function; for example, interoffice memos, living wills, patents, police reports, or bills of sale. Delisle and colleagues (1999, 169–70) estimate that this type of translation accounts for 90% of all translation, and that texts in this type are "for generally immediate, short-term use [,] designed for utilitarian communication and are frequently anonymous."

TRANSLATION TRAP

Transliteration

Translation is not the same as transliteration. **To transliterate** means to spell, often by sound, with the characters of another alphabet; for example, between Roman and Cyrillic scripts, or Arabic and Greek. Neologisms can appear as a result of transliteration, because simple "equivalents" may not exist. Proper names frequently receive this treatment.

Translation and transliteration can actually be competing strategies. Can you think of cases where this might be so?

CULTURAL NOTE

Reading

"Pleasure reading" in the United States is in crisis, particularly literary reading, but so is nonfiction. In September 2004, various media reported on the alarming rise of "aliteracy": the state of being able to read, but not reading. The usual suspects are, namely, the digital age, new ways of processing information, competing demands on our time combined with shorter attention spans, and increased competition, all having led us to pursue informational recreation in a way one commentator has called "amusing ourselves to death." A 1999 Gallup poll noted that only 7% of Americans are avid readers (defined as reading one book or more per week). Reading to cull information—which is primarily what happens today—arguably disrupts the facility to create, and the ability to process, sustained argumentation and erodes analytical abilities and critical thinking.

This is the gauntlet that translation throws down to the "visual-learner" generation: New and alternate literacies are invaluable, but good old-fashioned reading—widely, deeply, and habitually—must occur as well.

TRANSLATION TIP

Quality and Publication

Don't assume that an accepted or published translation is equal or superior in every way or is the best possible translation. A healthy skepticism will help you to demythify published work. Remember that those who commission translations—even publishers—have vastly different benchmarks for what constitutes good translation. Everything from highly dubious to brilliant translations, judged by different criteria, coexist on the same library shelves. In the virtual world it may be even more nebulous and lawless: On the Web, an appalling homemade translation can make the rounds theoretically forever. Consider too that what was once considered a great translation may have aged badly—"dated" translations abound, thus it is said that retranslation is necessary every generation. Near-contemporary versions of a masterwork, representing different emphases, strategies, and skill levels, can appear within a mere few years of one another (since the 1990s, renderings of Dante have mushroomed, for example). Often a publisher will want to stay with an aesthetically poor, but money-making, translation.

In the business world, where a text may be for one-time use and read only by a single user (or even *no one* may use it, as can happen in international organizations where translations are required but not always ultimately used), quality can vary greatly, particularly if the users have no experience working with translators, and *most* particularly if they underestimate (in time, money, or effort) what the translation process entails.

Simply put, one will see more quality where *quality controls* are in place—excellence is rarely an accident and often a team effort. Don't underestimate the influence—for good or sometimes ill—that an editor can have on a translation in the prepublication phase of a text.

LINGUISTIC NOTE

THE OFFICIAL LANGUAGE OF THE UNITED STATES

By now you've become aware that English is *not* the official language of the United States. At the federal level, there is no provision for the language that must be used (often at the state and local levels there is, however). English is what is called the de facto official language of the United States—the language that is used but nowhere mandated. In fact, many of the Civil Rights gains of the 1960s brought legislation that put safeguards in place to prevent discrimination against those of other national origins—including based on language.

(Continued)

Spanish, with more than 30 million speakers (estimated), is the most commonly spoken language in the United States other than English. Note the distribution of speakers of languages other than English in the home in the map that follows.

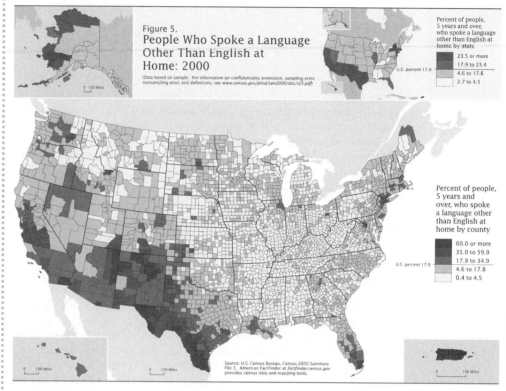

Figure 5.
People Who Spoke a Language Other Than English at Home: 2000

(Data based on sample. For information on confidentiality protection, sampling error, nonsampling error, and definitions, see www.census.gov/prod/cen2000/doc/sf3.pdf)

Percent of people, 5 years and over, who spoke a language other than English at home by state

- 23.5 or more
- 17.9 to 23.4
- 4.6 to 17.8
- 2.7 to 4.5

U.S. percent 17.9

Percent of people, 5 years and over, who spoke a language other than English at home by county

- 60.0 or more
- 35.0 to 59.9
- 17.9 to 34.9
- 4.6 to 17.8
- 0.4 to 4.5

U.S. percent 17.9

Source: U.S. Census Bureau, Census 2000 Summary File 3. American FactFinder at factfinder.census.gov provides census data and mapping tools.

Source: <http://www.vistawide.com/languages/us_languages2.htm>

Considering the changing U.S. demographics, does it make sense to speak of Spanish as a foreign language? Do you use the word "foreign" or "foreigner"? Applied to what or whom?

CULTURAL NOTE

New U.S. Legal Rulings and Their Effect on Translation

The Translation Center at the University of Massachusetts Amherst reports that new rulings and legislation are increasing demand for translations. Title VI of the Civil Rights Act, for example, prohibits discrimination based on "race, color, or national origin." In 2000, the Office of Civil Rights issued a policy guidance against discrimination based on national origin, which included people without English proficiency or with limited English proficiency (LEP). Thus, government agencies are increasingly *required* to provide interpreting and translation in education, health and human services, and many other areas. (Connect with your **Manual** Web site to learn more about the U.S. Department of Health and Human Services and the Office for Civil Rights.) The center adds: "In addition, new laws such as the Sarbanes-Oxley Act require translations of audit proceedings of all international business units. Private and public firms providing services to the federal government or receiving federal funds will have to comply." Thought question: Have you seen instances of noncompliance despite the mandate just described?

Source: University of Massachusetts Web site

THE AMERICAN TRANSLATORS ASSOCIATION CODE OF PROFESSIONAL CONDUCT AND BUSINESS PRACTICES

I. As a TRANSLATOR, I stand between two languages and act as a bridge for the free passage of ideas from one side to the other. Because my knowledge, skill, and discretion are essential to intellectual commerce, I commit myself to the highest standards of performance, ethical behavior, and sound business practice.

I will endeavor to translate with utmost accuracy and fidelity, so that I convey to the readers of the translation the same meaning and spirit the original conveyed to me. I acknowledge that level of excellence requires:

1. Mastery of the target language equivalent to that of an educated native speaker;
2. Up-to-date knowledge of the source language and the subject area sufficient to understand the message;
3. Continued efforts to improve my professional skills and to broaden and deepen my knowledge.

I will be truthful about my qualifications and business and will not accept any assignment for which I am not fully qualified, without the express consent of my client.

I will safeguard the interests of my clients as my own and divulge no confidential information.

I will derive no personal profit or financial gain from confidential information I receive in my professional capacity.

I will clarify all aspects of my contractual relationship with my client, preferably in writing, prior to performing any assignment and will strictly adhere to the agreed terms.

I will notify my clients of any unresolved difficulties I may encounter in the performance of the assignment.

I will use a client's name as a reference only if I am prepared to direct the prospective client to the individual who can attest to the quality of my work.

I will respect and refrain from interfering with the business relationship that exists between my client and my client's client.

II. As an EMPLOYER of translators or as one who contracts assignments to translators, I will uphold the above standards in conducting my business. I further commit myself to the following fair practices in dealing with translators.

I will clarify all aspects of my contractual relationship with the translator and state my expectations regarding the assignment from the outset, preferably in writing.

I will strictly adhere to the agreed terms of this relationship, including the payment deadline and will not capriciously change the job specifications after the translator's work has begun.

I will not require translators to do unpaid work against the prospect of a paid assignment; if we fail to resolve the problem, we will seek an arbitrator.

I will deal directly with the translator in the event of any dispute about an assignment; if we fail to resolve the problem, we will seek an arbitrator.

I will not use the translators' credentials in bidding for a job or promoting my business without the translators' consent or without the bona fide intention to use the translators' services.

In the case of translations intended for publication or performance, I will grant translators recognition of the kind traditionally granted authors, including mention of their names on the title page and jacket of the published translation or in the theater program and in the advertising of the work.

In the case of commercially published or produced works, I acknowledge the translators' rights to approve or reject any substantial changes in the translated text, or, alternatively, to have their names removed from the work without prejudice to the agreed payment.

(*Source:* American Translators Association)

Discussion: Ethics

The following situations, which are modeled on real occurrences and are designed to introduce you to some of the field's ethical issues, offer few clear-cut answers. With your instructor's guidance, and considering others' answers carefully, work your way through the scenarios to come to your own responses.

1. The Federal Bureau of Investigation (FBI), U.S. Customs and Border Protection, and Internal Revenue Service (IRS) all tend to be leading entry-level employers. How willing would you be to work in a language-related capacity for each if the opportunity presented itself? How comfortable are you with having a security clearance—an extensive background check—performed before you can translate classified materials?

2. Once established, would you *donate* your language services ("volunteer translation" or "pro bono translation") to any of the following? If so, under what circumstances or conditions? Be specific. If not, why not?

the local Little League	the League of Women Voters
the local Chamber of Commerce	a graduate student low on funds
a political activist organization	a family member
a friend's online business	a community food pantry
your alma mater	a retail chain manager of your acquaintance
a restaurant	a community health clinic
your local newspaper	a telethon for charity
a disaster relief organization	a current professor
a former professor	your religious organization or group
a nongovernmental organization (NGO)	a nonprofit organization (NPO)
a human rights defense organization	an in-law's boss
a migrant worker camp	a Wiki page
your own company (press releases)	
a stranger calling for a "quick" (by implication, free) translation over the phone	

3. Suppose that, once you are fairly well established, a high-profile university press contacts you about a translation for a new book series they are launching. The topic is something you have great interest in, and you are certain you could do a good job. You could clear your calendar in the mornings for 6 months and have enough time to meet the demands of steady-paying work you have lined up for that period. The source text is 75,000 words of academic prose. You will be guaranteed publication with your name on the cover under the author's. Your only payment will be 10 hardbound copies of the work. The series editor tells you up front that with the state of affairs in academic publishing, they have nothing in the budget for a translator's stipend, but that the publication would be a "nice credit" for your CV. How would you respond?

4. An agency owes you nearly $1000 for services rendered. You do not have a long-standing relationship with them. After 30 days—the typical industry grace period for receipt of payment—you contact them politely and are told that they will remit when the client pays *them*. What is your reply?

5. a. A new client has a 100-page prospective job for you. While previewing the text you notice that 20 pages of it are virtually identical except for a particular item or two such as a name or invoice number. For how many pages should you charge?

   b. Can recycled text from *earlier* translations for a client be billed at 100% of your going rate?

6. You worked 2 years for a well-known agency in your area. After the 2 years you want to strike out on your own. You've built up a good reputation as a staff translator and you know many of the agency's clients' parameters, terminology, and even their quirks and business style. It is an open secret that they have stayed with the agency because of you. Can you bring their business with you as you start freelancing?

7. You find whole sections—verbatim—of an assignment online. Is a posted and/or published translation fair game for you to use?

8. You realize you are in over your head on a particular job. You were screened and hired for the translation but are now woefully behind. At 1 a.m. the morning of the drop date, you call in reinforcements— bilingual friends who are not professional translators. You tell yourself that you had to in order to meet the tight deadline. You will have a chance to proofread their work but not as closely as you normally do your own. Is this ethical?

9. You've taken a job sight unseen that turns out to be a fiancé visa for some kind of mail-order bride service. You realize this to your horror. You are even more indignant at what you suspect, the further you get into the work, is a scam—legal fraud. You consider missing the deadline in protest. Would you be within your rights?

10. You are on a Usenet group ranting that a Colombian software giant, MicroBlandito, has treated you shabbily. You "name names," consign the client to the devil, and generally vent your spleen over a host of abuses, real and imagined. You feel super, almost gleeful. Have you done well to do this?

11. A Cuban play you are working on for publication is full of machista innuendo and language that your friend, a specialist in feminist theory, finds degrading and misogynistic. She urges you strongly to neutralize the language and offers strategies for subverting the text, including expurgating and "ironizing"; in short, she gives you a blueprint for appropriating the text for what she calls "more enlightened ends." None of these issues she raises had occurred to you before, and your middle-of-the-road publishing house, which is not used to dealing with translations, had not specified any kind of translation strategy. In fact, you wonder if they would even realize that translators use strategies. What would you tell your friend? If, upon reflection, you share her concerns about the text's message or means, what other options are ethically open to you?

12. There is an error in a source text that could potentially embarrass the client were the text published. Your options include, but are not limited to, perpetuating the error in the spirit of "faithfulness," adding "[sic]," or giving a long footnote explaining the error and the reasons you are changing the target. What would you do, and what other factors would affect your decision?

13. You have turned in your translation and the client refuses to pay, not because he or she is a deadbeat, but because the client finds your translation far too literal. You reread it objectively and find it quite adequate; in fact, you are left wondering about the client's fitness to judge translations. What should be done about this?

14. Your good friend is slightly younger than you and less experienced in the translation field. You are on your feet but only a few years into the profession. He comes to you

and over the course of a few months asks for back copies of invoices you've sent, your TRADOS (translation memory) terms, templates of your translations done in various fields, lists of useful reference works, Web sites where you have found work, and the names of your contacts to see if they have extra work (providing, he says, they have gone to you first, because he "doesn't want to be a sponge off your success"). The friend is not untalented, lives in the same area, has similar subject fields in his repertoire, and just may cut into your bottom line if successful. How comfortable are you with giving him the materials mentioned, things that you feel to some degree constitute your competitive edge in your field(s)?

15. You are offered the job of translating a U.S. senator's pro-English Only Web page in Spanish (they exist!). Do you take the work?

16. a. You will be hired for a certain job on the condition you not use machine translation (MT) or computer-assisted translation (CAT) tools. Is the client's request reasonable? Ethical?

    b. You will be hired for a certain job on the condition you *must* use a certain memory software. Is the request reasonable? Ethical?

17. You have a long list of queries for your translation initiator but are deathly afraid of seeming like a novice. You work them out willy-nilly on your own, hoping you guessed right at such issues as your author's meaning here and there, where he got a certain quote, exactly what that passage in the last paragraph really said (it was smudged on the fax), what the agency's in-house style sheet calls for on the writing of numbers with numerals or letters ("18" or "eighteen"), and the use of graphs, fonts, and margins. You'll surprise them and show your independence. Right. . . ?

18. You are translating a sacred text. Which is more appropriate to use, a source-oriented approach ("faithfulness" to the spirit or letter of the source) or a target-oriented approach (the creation of texts meaningful for particular users' needs or expectations)?

19. Imagine that you've been offered a job that has been partially translated already. What would you need to know about the job before accepting or rejecting it? Delimit your conditions.

20. Much to your surprise, the translation you've done appears in print, vastly changed—edited—from the final version you delivered. Describe what your reaction would be, or what recourse you might have, depending on the different possible scenarios (credited or uncredited work, text type, short- or long-term relationship, valid or questionable edits, etc.) Variation: The end client has used your target text for a purpose far different from what she had told you (you expected to produce it for information only, but it winds up on flyers, press materials, banners, and exhibits at a political rally).

21. A fan group from Japan has brought you into their *scanlation* team to translate manga Japanese>English and then English>Spanish for direct download from a mirror site. Scanlation is illegal. Are you troubled ethically by participating?

TRANSLATION TRAP

Ethics and Online Help

If you are doing an assignment for school or a test for an agency, many online forums will obligate you to label your queries up front as such. Some see querying online for professional translation tests as ethically gray at best—although consulting colleagues and experts is part of the job, it may cloud the view of an assessor in an exam situation.

What do you think translators and interpreters should do when faced with duties that fulfill professional obligations but that go against individual or collective ethics (e.g., the harsh interrogation of prisoners)?*

DIRECTIONALITY

The languages a translator works into and from are called the **language combination** or **language pair**. Most translators work into their mother tongue (or "A" language or "L1"), rather than into their primary adopted language (or "B" language or "L2"). Insisting on this practice becomes problematic sometimes, however, because of the following:

1. It is usually a self-policed rule—some people claim two "A" languages when more accurately they are likely to have two "Bs" or an "A" and a "B"; moreover, the boundaries of "A" and "B" are becoming blurred, particularly for people with multicultural, multilingual heritages.
2. In the popular imagination, translating both directions is not posited as any more problematic than one direction; clients absorb this belief (Baker 1998, 64).
3. Limited client budgets, the demands of the marketplace, or self-delusion (see #1) often lead people to work A > B or even C > B, B > C, or A > C.
4. Highly skilled translators with a good editor have been known to circumvent the rule.
5. Beeby Lonsdale (1996, 65) notes that because English is an international language, demand into English is high, and though a shortage of competent translators into mother-tongue English around the world is common, incompetent translators are not discouraged from translating.

The bottom line is probably that translating into one's "B" language becomes an issue when it compromises quality or hampers workflow. It is frowned upon—even *vehemently opposed*—in some circles (and in many organizational ethics). Many agencies will not even let you do it, and many translators resent other translators who practice it. The tolerance for working into one's "B" language varies by country. Yet most translator training courses and programs will do at least *some* work into the nonnative language, and some will expect it as a matter of course, and even hold this work to the same standards, regardless of one's primary direction. The distinction in academia is usually termed **direct** translation (into the mother tongue) and **inverse** translation (out of the mother tongue). Wherever you, or your instructor, stand on the issue, realize that disagreement exists, and it lies mainly in practice—the gulf between the intentions of theory and what happens in reality. The author of this book does not presume to try to enforce one practice or the other but merely is reporting this polarizing issue as he sees it. That said, the take-home lesson is to follow best practice: *plan and expect to work predominantly into your most active language.*

Why do you think some countries are more tolerant of working into the nonnative language? Try to think of more reasons apart from those suggested.

---

*Author's note: My thanks to an anonymous reviewer who suggested this topic be included.

Discussion

1. Translator 1's "B" language is stronger than Translator 2's "A" language; both have equal subject competence for the job in question. All else being equal, which would you hire if you were in that position?

2. Suppose you are a translation vendor. A perfectly matched translator is not available for a job, only an equally competent translator who is happier working the other direction. What are ways you could try to solve this situation? Under what circumstances would you forego the job?

3. A translation bureau in Spain balks at a nonnative English speaker's attempts to work for them as an into-English translator (assume that they already have a sufficient but not an ideal stable of into-English translators). The translator argues that the bureau should use her because its texts are for international audiences who will not notice or need the native fluency of an English native speaker and that her strengths are in such tasks and fields as human resources, birth certificates, automated weather report postediting, and tax returns, so the quality, she reasons, will largely remain unaffected. On what conditions, if any, should the bureau lift its unofficial ban on inverse translators?

4. If you are against the idea of a translator working into his or her "B" language, how do you reconcile your objection with the community interpreter's task, which is inescapably bidirectional on a daily basis? Or is the comparison unequal?

TRANSLATION TIP

Collaboration

One way around the directionality problem is to work closely with someone in your language pair who works the way opposite that you do. Some of the best translations are produced with this kind of "checks and balances" system.

Discussion: Awareness of Translation Traffic on the Cultural Level

1. Translations occur in both directions (en<>es) but not in the same proportions. In some domains (subject areas), the outflow is heavier. In pairs, come up with a list of subject areas that you think are frequently translated from en>es and another from es>en. Contrast your lists. Discuss why each might be the case. For example, do you think information technology is heavier in en>es or es>en?

2. Do you think the United States makes full use of others' cultural storehouse, or do we tend to export more than we import culture? Argue your case.

3. Is there a ready market for others' cultural production, or does a market—a demand—have to be *created*?

LINGUISTIC NOTE

The languages of your combination are sometimes called your **working languages**. The same term is used in international organizations to refer to the language(s) in which they conduct business.

TRANSLATION TIPS

Procedure

One's first reading of a text can bring valuable intuitions. Try to preserve these thoughts as they occur. When "glossing" the source text this way, *circle* term possibilities you have written in the margins as you confirm they are viable; use a *check mark* (right on top of the source) for valid cognates. This type of consistent code to yourself helps you remember what research you have done when you are inputting text. Also, draw lines between related terms and concepts, structural cues, and key ideas, even using a concept map if that helps you. Brainstorm multiple possibilities without censuring yourself or straining to finalize anything—use your mind's "reflexes"; the time to mull things over comes later.

Leave multiple electronic term banks, dictionaries, and glossaries *open* on the desktop, toggling back and forth between them as needed.

Try color-coding your translation difficulties: for example, yellow automatic highlight for unsolved passages.

It's a *bad habit* to use brackets "[ ]" or slash marks "/" for unsolved terms—especially in longer texts because these marks can go unnoticed, and wind up in the final draft as amateurish "multiple choices." For big jobs, translators have recommended using unusual, searchable symbols, for example, "@@." Or you can put unfinished work in double parentheses: "(( ))." Their use will minimize the risk of unsolved terms getting through. *Avoid at all costs* delivering final drafts with lines like this: "The corpse/body/cadaver lay there for days."

Date and label (name) your translation drafts for easy version control: "Washbourne/Neruda/EDIT3" or " . . ./DRAFT3."

Some translators find it good practice to overwrite (input the translation directly into the source text electronic file). Although this assumes certain risks, you may want to experiment with it to see for yourself how you like it. Back up the original source file(s).

Don't leave off translating for the day at a trouble spot. It is more motivating to begin a translating session with a passage that is not excessively problematic.

Set translations down and return to them, allowing them to "ripen." Often after a night's rest, the subconscious mind will solve certain problems that seemed insoluble the day before. It follows, then, that translations should be done in "waves" or layers, *never at the last minute*, unless they are "rush" jobs (i.e., given to you last-minute and acknowledged as such). What is "rush" depends on the size of the text, but usually it is a function of time; anything 24 hours and under definitely qualifies but 48 hours or even longer for some tasks demand above-average speed. This should *always* be determined up front, never in the billing phase.

Translations can always be improved, but deadlines, although not immutable, are taken *very seriously* in this industry. Real people with real objectives for your text are waiting in real time. Remember, then, especially if you are a perfectionist (and good for you if you are), that you sometimes are finished simply because the clock says so. As Jorge Luis Borges (1960) quipped, "We publish so we are not correcting drafts forever."

TRANSLATION TIPS

Work Environment

Use a bookstand to hold your translation assignments upright so they are in your line of sight as you word process; use an ergonomic keyboard if you are prone to repetitive stress disorders; have good back support.

Turn off all potential sources of electronic distraction, especially telephones and music (particularly music with lyrics).

Organize your workspace so that everything you need is within reach.

Figure out where you work best, when you work best, and how you work best. At peak performance the translator finds "flow" (or "the zone," whatever you may call it): some kind of loss of self and gain of total focus that allows for his or her most dynamic work.

THE TRANSLATION AGENCY: PRODUCTS AND SERVICES TYPICALLY OFFERED

Translation   Quality assurance
Interpreting   Layout
Transcription   Graphic design
Desktop Publishing (DTP)   Project management
Voiceovers, subtitles, and multimedia   Intercultural consulting
Web site translation   Copywriting
Software localization   Web content management
Proofreading and editing   Notarization

1. Which of these products or services would you like to learn more about?
2. What software do you know? Is it listed on your CV? What software would you like to learn next?

TRANSLATION TIPS

Translators Are Writers

One inescapable fact is essential to internalize: **Translators are writers**, not stenographers (with all due respect to stenographers). Everything that a writer has to do well, a translator has to do well. You already love languages. Love to write, too.

Translators Are Rewriters

A project can call for a one-time translation, but booming e-commerce (for "e-tailers") is driving the need for simultaneous availability of products in all markets, and thus a premium is placed on timely content delivery into languages that consumers are most comfortable buying in—*their own*. This means that translators are *updaters*.

> Most professional Web sites contain continuously updated and revised content, sometimes referred to as streaming content. Most of today's professional Web sites are updated frequently, are provided in multiple languages, and offer a high degree of personalization. The main challenges in maintaining multilingual (or global) Web sites are internationalizing the site architecture, balancing global/translated versus local content, automating translation workflows, and keeping multilingual content in sync with the source language. (Esselink 2000, 16)

Research: The Translation Agency

Go online and search 20 to 25 translation agencies and/or translators in some detail. Survey the basic **strategies used to market translation**. Consider many of the following prompts in your survey: What priorities are given (or required for freelancers to be desirable)? What vocabulary is most common to describe services ("fast turnaround"? "reliable"? "versatile"? etc.)? Is money brought up? What features distinguish one from another? What clichés in promoting products and services can you spot? Is there much variance in the target market? What about variance in Web site design? Do you see any information that seems dubious or misleading? Do they list clients or client testimonials? (If they don't list clients, what conclusions, if any, can you draw from that?) Do they offer free samples? Can an agency really be a "one-stop" source for any language need? Do you see discussions of ethics? Importantly, what kind of client education is offered (e.g., warnings about substandard practices)? What differences in presentation can you find here? Organize your information as you like. Give *specifics* in your study when appropriate, though you need not give Web addresses. Use statistics or charts in your answer and/or write a succinct composition, but either way be sure to *analyze* your findings in the form of (at least) tentative conclusions regarding trends. Finally, give an encapsulation of what you think are effective marketing strategies for an agency's or freelancer's Web page, whether in content or design.

 Connect with your **Manual** web site to find out much more on the vocational side of translation.

Research: Roles

1. Deduce the definition and role of each of the following participants in the translation cycle/workflow: initiator, commissioner, translator, addressee, and user. (Note: Nord (1997), *Translating as a Purposeful Activity*, will be useful for this task.)
2. What overlap of the preceding functions can you imagine as plausible? (e.g., Can the initiator be the commissioner? Can the commissioner be the user? etc.)
3. You will be individually assigned one of the following actors in the translation production chain on which to report back to the class. What are their primary responsibilities on a given job? Consider especially their role relative to the others in this list—how does each participant's work *interrelate* with the others'? If necessary, students may be paired up for this task. (Students: Don't simply print out a Web page and read it for this task—compare information, weigh it, analyze it, verify it, and put it in your own words. The class should be held accountable for the information presented.)

| Project manager | Editor/proofreader | Localization engineer |
| Translator | Terminology manager | |

Follow-Up

1. Who is responsible for quality assurance?
2. From what you can ascertain from the roles played by each of the participants, what is the *client*'s role?
3. What do the terms "upstream" and "downstream" refer to in the language industry?
4. Discuss *the logic of the division of labor* in translation—why is there a project manager, what does the terminology manager do that translators working separately cannot, and so on?
5. What other names for any of the preceding roles have you found? What about combined roles? What other participants besides those on this list may be in the chain of production?

WORKFLOW

Find flowcharts of the translation process and compare different agencies' systems. What seem to be commonalities? Where and when do reviewers usually come into the picture? Can you find what you consider an ideal system for ensuring quality and one that is also practical, or can you modify any flowcharts that you find to suit how you would conceive it?

According to Suzanne Mescan, a multilingual management system automates the process: "[W]hen an author finishes writing a piece of content, the system can automatically send an email notification to the correct editor to let him/her know that the content is ready for review. The editor's comments can be automatically sent back to the author for revision, and once the revisions are made, the content can be automatically flagged as approved and sent off for translation. The system administrators should be able to easily set up the workflow, ideally with a graphical layout, and all system users should have access to it to check the project's status. Managing multilingual content is a complex process with many steps involved. Strong workflow capabilities can go a long way to minimize mistakes and errors."

TRANSLATION TIP

Speed

A professional translator can usually average 2,000 to 3,000 words of output a day, sometimes more or less, depending on various factors. Sometimes entire days are needed for bidding, correspondence, research, editing, querying, formatting, or technical troubleshooting, and the word count may be zero. Other days, one may yield twice one's normal production. Truly prodigious outputs, however, should be suspect—2,000 excellent words are far more valuable than 6,000 barely decent ones. A short, challenging text that is four words in length (AOL Travel's ad, "Spring fever? No sweat.") can take hours for a convincing final draft, so it should not be paid by the word but by the hour or by the project as a whole.

In the training phase of your career—now—don't put speed ahead of accuracy in your priorities. Do keep speed in mind, though, and work to improve it but never at the expense of quality work. Speed comes with experience, when problems can mostly be solved without dropping pace. There are economically successful translators who work without racing. One caveat: If you can't work fast enough to meet a particular deadline, pass on the job.

FREELANCE OR IN-HOUSE? WEIGH SOME PROS AND CONS

Larger companies often have translation departments. They can also outsource their work (send it to be done externally). Many translators and localizers start out as an **in-house** translator or staff translator (*traductor de plantilla*) in agencies (or bureaus). The other major option is to be a **freelance** translator (*traductor externo* or *traductor independiente*). Given the realities of the industry today, in-house positions are becoming more scarce, and so most new translators of necessity will be freelance. See how the two different paths compare, as shown in the table that follows, and discuss as a group. Note that these are not immutable prophesies but *general characteristics* of professionals' experience with each.

	Freelance		In-house
Pro	Opportunity for higher salary; business and negotiating skills prosper; low overhead	Pro	Security and benefits; paid by time; no start-up costs
Con	Paid by volume; financial uncertainty; possible lean times; success may depend on business acumen; some expenses; start-up costs; self-employment taxes	Con	May not learn the business industry as quickly; lower salary for equal volume; may be less prestige
Pro	Can develop niche market and specialize	Pro	May develop into jack-of-all-text-types
Con	May not have consistent work flow; may not have opportunity to work with many key sensitive documents	Con	Not as much leeway, or none, on choice of texts, demanding high adaptability; may spend much time editing work of others; may not master one domain
Pro	Can solicit and expand own client base	Pro	Ready-made client base
Con	Must depend on own customer service skills (client/vendor relations)	Con	Constrained on expansion, often cannot recruit outside; may not find time to freelance on the side (or even be allowed to)
Pro	Independence; deadlines negotiated	Pro	Access to linguistic team, mentoring and role modeling, human and informational resources (glossaries, Web designers, proofreaders); feedback loop
Con	Choices sometimes overruled without one's knowledge, or one is not present to defend; not given as much feedback on the fly; psychological isolation; need to requalify or be tested with each new potential client	Con	Sometimes overruled upstream; sometimes independence or innovation discouraged; deadlines assigned; may be difficult to free oneself of a disadvantageous contract or exploitative situations
Con	Cannot make contacts without sustained effort to network	Pro	Can make steady contacts; can start career with less training and experience
Con	One is not as familiar with in-house culture	Pro	Familiarity with style sheet, in-house terms and procedures

Follow-Up

1. What can you find out about *offshore outsourcing* and translation today? Does translation work lend itself to this phenomenon? What does it mean for translators based in the United States? Explain.
2. On balance, do you think it is an asset or a liability for a translator to live and work in the country of his or her "B" language? Brainstorm pros and cons and, in groups, render your judgment to the class as a whole. Debate.
3. What are the apparent advantages and disadvantages of working with large translation agencies (e.g., Berlitz)?
4. Compile short lists and Web addresses of the major providers, producers of products/ services, facilitators, and translation tool makers.
5. Suggest reasons that a client would go to an agency rather than a freelancer for a given job.

6. What is the difference, if any, between a translation bureau and a translation agency?
7. What is professional liability insurance? Is it relevant to translation?
8. What does "insourcing" mean in relation to translation? Is this term borrowed into Spanish or explicitated (translated with an explanatory phrase) generally?

CLIENT EDUCATION

Client education refers to the diplomatic, informational role that translators play in their relationships with clients or potential clients. For example, if a client wants an 80-page report by the next business day, the translator might go into client education mode, explaining the research and labor-intensiveness involved in meeting such a deadline. Client education may be preemptive, but the practice is particularly called for when a client professes some received wisdom that is in no way wise—for example, that translation is merely bilingual typewriting, that hiring a professional is an extravagance, or that any text type can be translated by any given translator on any given day, including holidays. These are extremes but very common presuppositions. *Translation is a decision-making activity*, and thus translators must learn to convey not only the fact of their mediation, but the many facets and processes of problem solving.

The purpose of client education is both immediate and long term: to create a climate of understanding so that the translator's services may be given fair market value and that the translator's working conditions be such that expectations are harmonized with reality, thereby minimizing the potential for miscommunication. Client education is not limited to the language industry.

LINGUISTIC NOTE

TRANSCRIPTION

Transcription is the conversion process of a written or an oral source into typewritten form. It frequently involves video tapes or audio tapes. The domains in which transcription is most typically used are legal, medical, technical, and advertising. Transcribers may find themselves working on a wide range of audio source texts, from undercover recordings from a body wire to depositions to product testimonials. Transcription is also used to create subtitles for DVDs in the entertainment industry. The transcriber, in some legal and medical instances, accepts extreme liability, even that of perjury, in the course of his or her duties. In that sense, and in many others, the transcriber is akin to the interpreter.

Transcription and translation are often seen together in job listings. In these cases some practitioners transcribe then translate. Some translate directly from the tape, the disadvantage of which may be obvious to you: The source text becomes unavailable as one inputs text, because it is steadily "unspooling" past, and thus one depends entirely on the editing phase to catch errors. Sometimes one worker will transcribe, and, subsequently, another will be hired for the translation. The translator who wishes to transcribe must be extremely patient, aurally inclined, and exacting.

The transcriptionist's tools include a *transcriber*, which allows for rewinding passages with the use of a pedal called a *foot switch* or *treadle switch*; a tape counter; and a console for playing mini or standard cassettes (frequently mini). Some translators have their own equipment, whereas others borrow or rent. Some serious transcribers have audio enhancement equipment that eliminates background noise. Now voice recognition technology is sometimes used, and software that turns a PC into a transcriber is available, but the need for editing transcriptions is inevitable, whatever the means of execution. Difficulties of this work often center on sound—quality may be uneven, various registers are heard, and after several hours on the job the transcriber can begin to hear "mirages," which is detrimental because transcriptions should not be interpretive in the least,

(Continued)

especially when entered into evidence in court. The transcriber may use the notations "Inaudible" and "Unintelligible" but usually will listen to the passage many times over first, which makes the process extremely time-consuming and occasionally frustrating. One hour of recording is generally equal to 4 to 8 hours of transcribing time, depending on the difficulty and other variables.

At some point in a translator's career, the call to transcribe will come. Listen to the source in advance if you can, weigh all the variables (including the complex issue of remuneration), and err on the side of caution, at least at first.

TRANSLATION TEASER

Going Global, Local, and International

Internationalization, **localization**, and **globalization** all have different meanings in the field. Distinguish these terms. Here's a head start: *In part* they have to do with at what level of the development of a product the process takes place—*during* or *after*.

HINT Research the Localisation Industry Standards Association (LISA, pronounced "Lisa") Web site. And if you have access to it, Bert Esselink's (2000) *A Practical Guide to Localization* offers a solid overview.

Software Localization

1. What do the abbreviations "L10n" and "i18n" stand for? What about "Xlation"?
2. **Web site localization**, which we will look at in some detail in Chapter 6, may be distinguished from **software localization**. What is software localization? What, specifically, are some of the tasks involved? What parts of the software are localized? Define the following terms:

user interface	resource files	help files
text string	DTP files	GUI files ("gooey" files)

3. What are some of the *difficulties* of software localization?
4. What are some of the primary *tools* of the software localizer?
5. What is a "fuzzy match" in the parlance of translation memory (TM) software?

TRANSLATION TIP

See PowerPoint slides offering an overview of this sector of the industry in the "Students" menu (> "Courseware and Course Resources") of the Institute for Applied Linguistics page on the Kent State University Web site (connect with the **Manual** Web site for the specific link).

LANGUAGE CONSULTANCY

Frequently you will find **language consultancy** or **language consulting** listed on providers' Web sites. What does this term mean? It tends to be something of a catch-all category, but its common denominator is assistance to the client to bridge a linguistic or cultural gap. Much like the ubiquitous "language solutions," language consultancy is broad enough—and perhaps vague enough—to refer to any of the following services related to translation:

- Coaching clients through presentations or preparation for court appearances
- Consulting on the cultural and situational appropriateness of texts
- Developing or improving cross-cultural strategies for a company or project
- Advising on country-specific business protocol
- Working up distance-learning course materials
- Delivering language-related speeches
- Performing audits or linguistic needs analysis
- Interpreting in Language for Special Purposes (LSP) situations, particularly commercial and legal
- Providing online or phone support for language queries
- Recruiting, examining, and assessing language professionals
- Brokering language-related jobs
- Proofreading, revising, and updating
- Compiling and standardizing terminology

TRANSLATION TRAP

"T & I"

Translation involves *written* communication. **Interpreting** involves *oral* communication. Don't call interpreters "translators."

CHAPTER

2

Determining Context: Negotiating Meaning

THREE KINDS OF TRANSLATION

Roman Jakobson (2004, 114) distinguishes **three kinds of translation**:

1. **Intralingual** (or *rewording*), whereby verbal signs are shifted to other verbal signs in the same language ("Come hither" to "C'mere" or vice versa).
2. **Interlingual** (*translation proper*), verbal signs interpreted between languages; for example, *Dime con quien andas y te diré quien eres* (an English rendering, "Birds of a feather flock together.").
3. **Intersemiotic** (or *transmutation*), or a shift from verbal to nonverbal sign systems. Examples might be a Shakespeare play transformed into a ballet, a pantomime, a painting, or a musical score; or to a partial extent, a theater performance of a word-based text (e.g., Uruguayan writer Horacio Quiroga's short story "Juan Darien" transformed into a Broadway show).

Can you think of occasions where it is necessary to self-translate or self-interpret intralingually? Why are some signs nonverbal? What would be a good process to accustom end users to a nonverbal sign or symbol—a visual translation—used by a particular company or economic bloc?

SEMANTIC AND PRAGMATIC APPROACHES

The primacy of the **semantic**, or meaning-based approach to translation, which focuses on the level of concepts and signs, has been ceding ground in recent decades to **pragmatic** approaches, which focus on the *use* to which a target text is to be put in a given set of circumstances, or its *communicative situation*. One approach need not come at the expense of the other, however.

As an example of pragmatics, consider: If a text reads "Say cheese" (let's suppose it's an ad, a title of an article, or a bit of dialogue), a pragmatic approach into Spanish (in industry shorthand, en>es) will consider the purpose as well as the propositional (semantic) content. A translator would quickly rule out the possibility that Spanish-speaking cultures say *queso* in picture-taking scenarios, in part because saying *queso* physiologically doesn't elicit smiles for the camera as "cheese" is intended to. Knowing or learning the target culture's norms and pursuing the pragmatic goal of making this text function with the same communicative goal, the translator chooses *[Diga(n)] patata* or "whisky" or the like, depending on *what a text receiver from the appropriate target country would respond to in the desired way.* Pragmatic approaches thus are not restricted to linguistic equivalency: They consider and understand how speech acts *work* within the target culture.

TRANSLATION TEASER

Nonverbal Signs

Nonverbal signs don't need translation because they're universal, or are they? In the African port of Stevadores, boxes arrived with the symbol meaning *fragile*—the broken wine glass. Staff assumed they were boxes of broken glass and threw them into the sea. The symbol was later replaced with that of an *intact* wine glass.

CULTURAL SIGNS

The meaning of symbols that one person takes for granted may be obscure to outsiders. Try to see the following signs as if you had no preconceptions about what they stood for, had never seen them, and had no cultural experience to lead you to the intended message. "Mistranslate" them either "literally" or with another meaning or meanings.

1.

Source: Bill Aron/PhotoEdit Inc.

2.

Source: Thomas J. Abercrombie/ National Geographic Image Collection

3.

Source: © Dorling Kindersley Media Library

4.

Source: Ed Homonylo/© Dorling Kindersley Media Library

5.

Source: Jonathan Massie/ Prentice Hall School Division

Do you think there are cultural universals? If so, are they represented the same way in all cultures? Discuss.

Oral Exercise: Intralingual Translation

Octavio Paz tells us that all communication *is* translation. Let's look at how we translate every day from context to context intralingually (within our own language).

"Translate" these phrases or sentences into everyday, nonfigurative English of the sort you would use with a speaker with limited English proficiency (LEP). Stress semantic transmission (meaning).

1. A squall line is approaching and we're looking at a major precipitation event for your overnight.
2. We live in a global village.
3. What's good for the goose is good for the gander.
4. Its space-age polymers act as a revolutionary antioxidizing agent.
5. The first party, failing to observe posted transit regulations, unlawfully accessed the path of the second party, occasioning the latter to apply the brakes and depart the roadway at 22.00 hours at a nondesignated point of egress.
6. IMHO: gj ^^. Ttyl @_@
7. Bless your heart!
8. I am seeking this position to fulfill my potential in sanitation engineering. I hope to utilize my ample physical assets in securing career stability within the ranks of your worthy firm.
9. *Been Down So Long, It Looks Like Up to Me* (book title)
10. Son, what is your major malfunction?
11. You have to step up to the plate, think outside the box, and take it to a whole new level.
12. Ain't she the cat's pajamas?
13. Zounds!
14. The bloomin' bobby wouldn't let me pram on the tube, the sod.
15. I was the canary in a coal mine on this one.
16. Dag nabbit! Mama's agwine lose her religion when she sees you'ns.
17. Ingredients: sucrose, sodium chloride, trimethylxanthine
18. The *sine qua non* of entertaining is a fully appointed kitchen, but the gourmand's true *raison d'êtrê* lies with the *vivacité* of his tableside manner.
19. We've had a negative patient-care outcome.
20. Intelligence activity was ordered, a surreptitious entry into the hotel was effectuated, attempts were made to contain the situation. Mistakes were made.

Follow-Up

Intralingually translate (en>en) the following written passage for the same audience as indicated previously:

> Translation is . . . shown to be a primary form of utterance and articulation in which discrimination and selection are always constitutive factors. Indeed, intentional articulation and utterance are manifestly inventive and validational, plural in their achievements and ramifications. The requirement that translations be similar to their originals is a condition of all articulation, not to be fulfilled in many particular respects, but pregnant at all times with alternative realizations to

be attained, as in representational art, by invention, creation, and discrimination, a profound manifestation of human capacities. (Wilss 1996, 21)

TRANSLATION TIP

If You Don't Get It, You Don't Get It Across

Two axioms:
> If you can't understand something, you can't translate it.
> If your translation can't be understood, you probably didn't understand the source.

Genre Expectations: Translating Text Types

Find or write *two* of the following text types. Then rewrite them in the text type indicated; study the textual conventions called for and attempt to reproduce them in your versions. Each should be at least one-half page.

Model: Find or write a *nursery rhyme* and rewrite it as if it were an *accident report*.

Accident Report

The party of the first part, hereinafter known as "Jack," and the party of the second part, hereinafter known as "Jill," ascended or caused to be ascended an elevation of undetermined height and degree of slope, hereinafter referred to as "hill." Whose purpose it was to obtain, attain, procure, secure, or otherwise gain acquisition to, by any and/or all means available to them, a receptacle or container, hereinafter known as "pail," suitable for the transport of a liquid whose chemical properties shall be limited to hydrogen and oxygen, the proportions of which shall not be less than or exceed two parts for the first mentioned element and one part for the latter. Such combination will hereinafter be called 'water.' On the occasion stated above, it has been established beyond reasonable doubt that Jack did plunge, tumble, topple, or otherwise cause to lose his footing in a manner that caused his body to be thrust into a downward direction. As a direct result of these combined circumstances, Jack suffered fractures and contusions of his cranial regions. Jill, whether due to Jack's misfortune or not, was known to also tumble in similar fashion after Jack. (Whether the term "after" shall be interpreted in a spatial or time passage sense has not been determined.)

(*Source:* "Jack and Jill - Accident Report", from *The Legal Guide to Mother Goose* by Don Sandburg, copyright © 1978 by Don Sandburg, text. Used by permission of Price Stern & Sloan, A Member of Penguin Group (USA) Inc., 345 Hudson Street, New York, NY 10014. All rights reserved.)

1. Find or write a **tourist itinerary** and rewrite it as if it were a **strategic plan**.
2. Find or write a **historical monument inscription** and rewrite it as if it were a **real estate listing**.
3. Find or write **driving directions** and rewrite them as if they were a **graduation speech**.
4. Find or write **a loan rejection letter** and rewrite it as if it were a **parent's lecture**.
5. Find or write a **recruitment letter** and rewrite it as if it were a **Valentine's Day card**.
6. Find or write a **Valentine's Day card** and rewrite it as if it were a **recruitment letter**.
7. Find or write a **package insert** and rewrite it as if it were a **UN Assembly address**.
8. Find or write a **recipe** and rewrite it as if it were a **romance novel**.
9. Find or write an **interoffice memo** and rewrite it as if it were a **children's book**.
10. Find or write a **White House press release** and rewrite it as if it were a **movie trailer**.
11. Find or write a **memoir entry** and rewrite it as if it were **prescription instructions**.

12. Find or write a **to-do list** and rewrite it as if it were a **prenuptial agreement**.
13. Find or write a **parking ticket** and rewrite it as if it were a **science textbook**.
14. Find or write a **wedding invitation** and rewrite it as if it were an **automated teller script**.
15. Find or write a **sports rulebook** and rewrite it as if it were a **parent permission waiver**.
16. Find or write a **gossip column** and rewrite it as if it were a **livestock auction**.
17. Find or write a **book review** and rewrite it as if it were a **customer satisfaction survey**.
18. Find or write a **family holiday letter** and rewrite it as if it were a **stock report**.
19. Find or write a **country western song** and rewrite it as if it were a **haiku**.
20. Find or write a **birth certificate** and rewrite it as if it were a **packing list**.

On which of the two genres did you have to focus more, the first or the second? What did this exercise show you about the link between form and purpose? Did you find this exercise liberating or constraining? Explain.

TEXTUAL CIRCUMSTANCES

In what medium or environment would you expect the following texts or text excerpts to appear?

1. "*¿Qué son las muelas del juicio? Las muelas del juicio son los últimos molares ubicados a cada lado de los maxilares. Además, son los últimos dientes en aparecer o erupcionar y esto, generalmente, ocurre cuando la persona tiene entre 16 y 20 años*".
2. "Let Conversation Cease. Let Laughter Flee. This Is the Place Where Death Delights to Help the Living."
3. "Please wait while the list is being populated."
4. "*Se ratifica la inconveniencia de la opción 'ninguna de las anteriores' porque al hacerlo, la CPI invalidaría la representatividad del Encuentro, y su soberanía para incluir opciones de contenido, se agrega que siendo éste un voto difícil se va a inducir esa opción*".
5. "*Si no hay más bicicletas en el porta-bicicletas, después de bajar la suya, por favor levante la parrilla hasta que el seguro se tranque en su lugar y quede asegurada*".
6. "a. *Balance hasta la fecha de sus cuentas*
    b. *Determinar si un cheque especifico ha sido canjeado*
    c. *Obtener información acerca de los intereses de sus cuentas*
    d. *Transferir fondos entre sus cuentas de Metropolitan Bank*
    e. *Recibir un estado de cuenta hasta la fecha actual por fax*"
7. "000   01031cz a2200229n 450
    001   5874705
    005   20030405000308.0
    008   030224 ‖ anannbabn ‖a ana
    151   __ ‖a Argentina ‖x History ‖y Dirty War, 1976–1983
    450   __ ‖a Dirty War, Argentina, 1976–1983
    670   __ ‖a Work cat.: 2002447852: Documentos, 1976 a 1977, 2001.
    670   __ ‖a Argentina, a country study, 1985: ‖b pp. 66–68 (1976–1983: Military in power; political structure of the military regime was legitimized by a constitutional amendment: the Statute for the National Reorganization Process of March 31, 1976; undertook a war against subversion, which became known as the "dirty war")
    952   __ ‖a 50 bib. record(s) to be changed
    953   __ ‖a lc07"

8. "This letter shall serve as your notification that 9th U.S. Bank will guarantee payment of any check being presented by Mr. Big Bidder to purchase items at your auction up to the amount of $75,000.00."

9. "angelheaded hipsters burning for the ancient heavenly connection to the starry dynamo in the machinery of night,"

10. "Set the joists so the crown, or bowed side, faces up. Add any required blocking for stability."

11. "Consuming raw or undercooked meats, poultry, seafood, shellfish, and eggs may increase your risk of foodborne illness."

12. "Preferred embodiments of the method comprise four steps:"

TRANSLATION TEASER

Guess the Context

Can you identify in what context these words are usually found together?

> **HINT** They are translations.

gruñón   *tímido*   *mudito*   *perezoso*   *mocoso*   *feliz*   *dormilón*

CONNOTATION AND DENOTATION

Denotation refers to the concrete referent intended by a word or phrase. **Connotation** refers to the secondary meanings, ideas, or overtones that adhere to a word. For instance, one may gladly accept another's *generosity* but reject his or her *charity*; one may balk at living in an *old folks' home* but embrace a *retirement community*; or one may be feeling stuck on a *dead-end street* but living the high life in a *cul-de-sac*.

Misunderstandings often arise where connotations are inferred in the sender's unintended use of a word for its denotative properties. Social changes in recent years have led to active attempts to avoid the connotations of "loaded" words—for example, many objected to "housewife" as a word because it portrays a wife as married to a house, and so the terms "homemaker" and "stay-at-home mom" gained currency. Hormel Foods, the maker of SPAM tinned meat, is concerned about confusion arising from its product and unsolicited commercial e-mail (UCE), popularly known as "spam"; naturally, it has expressed concern about the degradation of its trademark that may result from the association of "junk mail" and its meat. Sometimes two terms may coexist, each with different connotational charges: "Illegal aliens" has connotations that may reveal the user's disapproval of "undocumented laborers," sometimes even if the user does not realize it.

A word can acquire negative (or positive) connotations in language transfer—note the Spanish word "*peón*" (an unskilled farm laborer); in English, a "peon" is a drudge, one who is lowly or subservient. The Spanish *condescendencia* does not have the negativity of the English "condescension"; the English conveys a consciousness of superiority, whereas the Spanish is closer to a tolerance of someone of a lower station. A visitor to the Peruvian Amazon (and elsewhere) would do well to avoid calling the locals *nativos*—the word evokes the indigenous disrespectfully ("native" to a place is usually expressed *natural de* in Spanish). Connotations of cognates can be diametrically different: *algas marinas* in Spanish sounds lovely to the hispanophone, whereas "seaweed" in English is tainted by "–weed," whose connotations are negative (some might say "weed" is a word without a fixed denotation, having only connotations; a weed is any unwanted plant or any plant that grows to the detriment of a valued plant). "Gypsy" in English is often linked to travel, the exotic, and the romantic; in continental

Spanish, more often than not the stigma of thievery and conniving attaches to the word (though curiously in English the remnant slur of "to gyp" someone has its origin in "gypsy").

Connotations can accrue to a word due to its use in competing or conflicting contexts. A job applicant wishing to stress his intensity writes in his cover letter of his "full-frontal" approach to teaching—he is thinking "attack," but his bewildered readers may be collocating the phrase with "nudity." (Semanticists call this a "frame-shift.") Connotations have to do with rhetorical impact, language's power to motivate; for example, "Medication provided at no cost to you" has far less coercive connotations than "free treatment" (Cornelio 2002, 27), or, for that matter, "free drugs"! In literature, of course, particularly poetry, attention to connotations is of the essence even in translating names. In Gregory Rabassa's 2005 memoir, *If This Be Treason*, he recounts how, for a novel by Mario Vargas Llosa, he translated the name of a blond soldier called *El Rubio* as "Blondy." He had flirted with and rejected "Whitey" because the epithet conjured up the racial tensions then brewing in the United States (76). Hervey, Higgins, and Haywood, following Leech, term this "associative meaning" (1995, 99). This type of association helps explain why we might be unnerved to hear someone say "Rest in peace" as we head off to bed. For the same reason, men of a certain age in the United States would be distraught to receive any letter beginning "Greetings"—this was the U.S. government's formulaic opening for draft notices.

Connotations can also create unintentional humor. One sympathizes with the bar owner in an area of Thailand where many trees grow; he advertised his business as "the shadiest cocktail bar in Bangkok" (Ricks 1983, 81). In September 2006, Venezuelan leader Hugo Chávez gave a speech on the floor of the UN General Assembly in which he called George W. Bush "the Devil" and noted that the hall smelled of "sulphur." Many were confused at this strange insult. The link between the Devil and sulphur is rather tenuous for Americans, for whom sulphur is the smell of rotten eggs. The (interpreted) Spanish from Chávez was "*azufre*," which would have been better rendered as "brimstone." Intentional humor, too, often depends on connotations. Because Spanish distinguishes many human body parts from the homologous animal ones, for example, *pie/pata* (foot), *garganta/pezcuezo* (neck), and *uña/pezuña* (fingernail or toenail), the word for "snout" in Spanish (*hocico*) is used for humorous effect when referring to a person's face or nose.

Not only words and phrases but whole statements and even texts are connotative—Premier Khrushchev's declaration of "We will bury you" was inferred as a violent threat by millions of people although the intent was actually a metaphor; to wit, "Our system (Communism) will outlive yours (capitalism)" or "We will be alive after you're dead and gone." Similarly, when a Spanish speaker says *Parece mentira*, the Anglophone should understand surprise, not a literal accusation of untruthfulness. To sway witness testimony, a lawyer can manipulate reality by biasing witness recollection: It was shown that subjects asked "About how fast were the cars going when they smashed into each other?" reported a much higher speed than those asked "About how fast were the cars going when they hit each other?" (Berk-Seligson 2002, 25).

Language, even of the nonliterary variety, rarely escapes connotation. One reason many scientists prefer the more objective classification system of binomial nomenclature (e.g., the genus and species *Homo sapiens* for "man") is that Latin does not "contaminate" as the vernacular does. Connotation should not be seen as a flaw of language, however—good writing is often powerfully connotative. Unconsciously we have a storehouse of cultural connotations. Language very easily accommodates metaphorical dimensions. Witness "square," which we link to both conformity (square houses) or its opposite, social maladjustment ("Be there or be square"); perhaps unconsciously, we realize that the square does not occur in nature and that our language reflects our attitude toward it. Culture is inescapable: When Shakespeare wrote "Shall I compare thee to a summer's day?" he could not imagine the dilemma posed for translators in places where summer is not warm and lovely.

Many text types demand exact denotation in translation: manuals, contracts, prescription instructions, and medical inserts. Arguably, however, we sometimes misjudge the role of denotation in communication. Consider part of a simple nursery rhyme:

> Little Miss Muffet
> Sat on a tuffet
> Eating her curds and whey.

How many twenty-first-century children (or adults) could tell you what "curds and whey" are exactly? Who would know to even guess with a cultural substitution "something like cottage cheese"? And a "tuffet"? If a child imagines that it is the name for a makeshift cushion or a stool or a mythological beast, what matter? How many generations of children never even bothered to imagine what these words refer to! To the child, these details are subordinate to the action (the spider's dramatic appearance) and to the reassurance of rhyme. Of course this does not advocate for randomness or sloppiness in writing or translating but simply proposes this: *Readers (and listeners) can make sense of texts without knowing every denotation.* Corollary: Not every denotation contributes equally to overall meaning. Moreover, it is enough to reflect on the language of advertisements or a poem such as Lewis Carroll's "Jabberwocky" to realize that we frequently respond to the sounds, the implied meanings, and the emotional triggers set off by language as much as its actual denotations.

TRANSLATION TEASER

Cognates and Product Names

An anti-itch topical lotion called "Sarna" is on the market in the United States. Assume the role of cultural consultant for the product's maker and give your assessment of this product name's potential resonance among Spanish-speaking consumers. Is there a clear identification between the product name and its use in Spanish?

Research: Determining Connotations

1. Research to determine whether the connotations of each of the words on the list that your instructor will pass out to you are *positive, negative, neutral,* or *"depends"* (i.e., you can find or imagine a plausible context, including idiomatic expressions, for any combination of positive, negative, or neutral—e.g., "ambitious"). In cases where a series of related words appears, compare and contrast to arrive at your solutions. Discuss.

2. a. Connect with your **Manual** Web site and use the link to find the *Oxford English Dictionary* (OED) and the *Real Academia Española* (RAE) sites and look up "notorious" and *"notorio,"* respectively. Contrast their connotative weight in different contexts. Discuss the extent to which they are true or false cognates or situationally false.
   b. Do the same for "intervention" and *"intervención."*

Activity: Recognizing Euphemisms

> Martha, will you show her where we keep the ... uh ... euphemism?
> George, in Edward Albee's *Who's Afraid of Virginia Woolf?*

Whether the writer is using abrasive language or more socially acceptable forms of expression, the translator must recognize it in order to react accordingly.

In the list that follows, adapted from Lechado García (2000), circle the term or phrase in each pair that is *euphemistic* (mild or polite speech substituted for language perceived as offensive, discriminatory, or blunt). Give a corresponding English euphemism alongside the pair in the space provided. The impact of context will be low.

1. *hijo natural*   *bastardo*   _____
2. *prostituta*   *acompañante*   _____
3. *indispuesto*   *enfermo*   _____
4. *manicomio*   *institución*   _____
5. *inodoro*   *retrete*   _____
6. *¡miércoles!*   *¡mierda!*   _____
7. *campaña aérea*   *bombardeo*   _____
8. *compañera*   *novia*   _____
9. *adulterio*   *aventura amorosa*   _____
10. *drogadicto*   *drogodependiente*   _____
11. *gordura*   *envergadura*   _____
12. *subdesarrollado*   *en vías de desarrollo* _____
13. *pornográfico*   *verde*   _____
14. *tripulante de cabina*   *azafata*   _____
15. *estar viejo*   *estar en la tercera edad* _____
16. *morir*   *entregar el alma*   _____

Discussion

Suppose you had to translate something that you suspected could deeply offend your target audience. How would you handle the assignment, assuming the client were your author? What if the client were someone besides the author? What if you were translating something by a writer from an earlier era, when in many cases cultural sensitivities were quite different? Weigh your competing responsibilities to your immediate audience (your client and your author) and to your wider target audience. Then think of subject matter you would be uncomfortable translating in almost all scenarios. What would you do if presented it commercially?

LINGUISTIC NOTE

Translations have real effects. Many translators believe in not translating against their core beliefs or in support of something that contradicts their values, in part so as not to validate the thing in question, but also because they recognize the (even unconscious) temptation to censor. (It has been proven that as readers, we process better those materials that are in line with our philosophies.) Correspondingly, many translators seek out texts with which they have an affinity. What do you think?

CONNOTATION: THE DICTIONARY'S BLIND SPOT

How would you go about translating the phrase "Yankee ingenuity" into Spanish, for example, for the coverline (cover caption) of the international edition (all over Spanish America, in this case) of a computer magazine on which American innovations from Silicon Valley are featured? Suppose you're not aware of the problems with the word "*Yanqui*" (as you may not in fact be because we all have gaps in our experience). If you relied on *dictionaries* to warn you about the word *"Yanqui,"* you would have to read between the lines: *Larousse Unabridged* (Yankee: *yanqui*); *Simon and Schuster's International* (Yankee: *s. yanqui. a. propio o característico de los yanquis*); *El pequeño Larousse ilustrado* (Yankee o Yanqui: *n. m. y f. y adj. Apodo dado por los ingleses a los colonos rebeldes de Nueva Inglaterra, posteriormente por los sudistas a los nordistas, y actualmente aplicado a los habitantes anglosajones de E.U.A.*). Only in the *Vox Internacional* are the pejorative overtones to *Yanqui* (*"con cierto matiz despectivo"*) noted. And this probably understates the case because *Yanqui* is usually seen in graffiti in the collocation *Fuera yanquis*, a strong anti-imperialist formula. By contrast, some southerners may find "Yankees" an antagonistic word (and reality), but most speakers in the United States (except, perhaps, Boston Red Sox fans) usually use the word affectionately by now. One must know something of North American history to see the word in enough of its dimensions to negotiate it properly or else compensate with research. What if you had to translate "Welcome to Yankee Candle" (a U.S.-based company in New England) as this author once did? In short, *dictionaries will seldom provide sufficient context (i.e., usage and connotations).*

Realize too that neither words nor set phrases occur one to one between languages. Stop and think about it: Why would a Chilean, for example, have a collocation for "Yankee ingenuity"? Does every culture in the world have the concepts of a mixed blessing, no-man's land, a fool's paradise, beginner's luck, Dutch treat, or Mexican standoff? Or "tingo," which in Easter Island means "to borrow objects from a friend's home one-by-one until there is nothing left." (See Adam Jacot de Boinod's (2005) amusing *The Meaning of Tingo* for more culture-specific words of this sort.) Similarly, the author of *The Astonishment of Words* muses (Proetz 1971, 168), how would the French, a country without a whaling tradition, render the line "There she blows!" from *Moby Dick*? Denotations, too, are subject to lacunae (gaps): What would they call "mittens" in Mexico, where the hot sun shines almost year round?

Another example is *madre*. In matriarchal societies (which Hispanic and Spanish-American societies predominantly are, despite, or perhaps commensurate with, machismo), the importance of the *madre* is paramount. Hence its strength as a swear word (*"Me vale madre"*: "I couldn't give a ****"; the underclass of disaffected youth are sometimes called *valemadristas*, representatives of *valemadrismo*). *Cassell's Colloquial Spanish* notes that in Mexico the word is explosive and so should be softened by nearly always using *mamá* (1993, 150). The same is true in the Caribbean.

Not illogically, in Mexico, the word *"padre"* colloquially has come to mean "great" (*"Está padre ese coche, 'mano."*). This perhaps is from the perception of dominance and lineage (subtext: what has come before is superior). There is another insult in this vein that is common: *"¡Yo soy tu padre!"* It means, "I own you/I am tougher (more manly) than you/I can take you on/Who's your daddy?" (For more on this topic, see Octavio Paz's discussion on *machismo* in *El laberinto de la soledad* [1986].)

Some dictionaries have a section called *"Observ"* ("Observation"). An example from Larousse (*Gran diccionario*): "In some Latin American countries *coger* is not in decent use. It is replaced by either *tomar* or *agarrar*" (García-Pelayo y Gross et al. 1984, 155).

DIMINUTIVES AND AUGMENTATIVES

Diminutives on occasion create great challenges for the translator. Spanish speakers, particularly those from certain countries, use them more frequently than English speakers. Women are more likely to use them than men. Some of the most common suffixes used with the diminutive are: *-ito, -illo, -cillo, -uelo, -zuelo, -ezuelo, -ico, -cico,* and *-ecico*. The translator should draw a clear distinction between diminutives and those words that merely end with the diminutive suffix but are not true diminutives; for example, *maquinilla* (razor). Experience and context usually show when *casita* is more likely to be "little house" versus "home, sweet home." Augmentative endings include *-ucho* and *-acho*, which denote largeness, but with great frequency are used for negative characterizations, even denotatively: Whereas an *encuentro* is neutral or positive, an *encontronazo* is a crash or run-in.

The difficulty arises in conveying the nuances of attitude of the speaker or writer. *Feito* and *feucho*, to give one example, convey a difference of aggression toward the object as much as of degree: "homely" versus "seriously ugly." *Enfermito* and *solito* invariably show empathy. A *preguntita* might be a *quick* question, rather than a little one; English will sometimes abbreviate attenuations (*Momentito* > "Just a sec"). *Un poblacho* might be "this dump of a town." Endearment or familiarity is shown in diminutive forms of names: *Pedrito, Juanito, Marquito, Pablito* (Petey, Johnny, Markey, Pauly). The use of the diminutive can tone down any perception of insult or confrontation (in Peru the phrase "*No seas malito*" is commonly used where one would expect "Please" in English). Exceptions exist: *un señorito*, formerly "young master," is not simply an unmarried young man in today's usage (if it is used at all), but a "rich kid" with overtones that insult his manliness. English sometimes has words or phrases ("Comfy?" or "Hi, nana") to show affection the way "*¿Estás comodita?*" or "*Hola, abuelita*" do. English can also use formulas such as "Nice and . . ." or other idiomatic phrases: *Mi carro está arregladito* ("My car's all fixed up how I like it"). Even a gerund has been known to take a diminutive occasionally: *Vine corriendito* ≈> "I came as fast as I could." One final diminutive deserves special mention here, because it is one of the most often confused words in the language: *ahorita*. Depending on the country, the speaker, and the linguistic context, it can mean "right away," "a little later," "now," "right now," or even "a short while ago." Both an augmentative and a diminutive may appear together: *feuchito* (*feo>feucho>feuchito*) or *orejoncito* ("adorably big eared").

Spanish has one use of the augmentative that is added formulaically to personages or places in certain historical contexts. Two examples from recent history are "*bogotazo*" and "*fujimorazo*." These two terms are reminders of the need (1) for background research in translation; (2) that often a word belongs to a local context and, thus, will not appear in a general dictionary. Many novice translators look in dictionary after dictionary for words (particularly diminutives and augmentatives) they will never find there or which need context in order for them to be understood.

Activities

1. Using reliable Internet sources find three instances of "*bogotazo*" and "*fujimorazo*"; paste them and their contextual environment (at least a few sentences) into a word document and discuss briefly how you might translate them for a U.S. audience with little background on the subject matter. Offer a version of the whole sentences in which the terms appear. What audience or end use can you posit for the text that would justify your decision for each? Compare your solutions with those of your classmates. Which is the most general (widest) term of the following three: *golpe, autogolpe*, or *fujimorazo*?

2. a. What is a *semaforazo*? Find enough examples in which you understand the concept then use it in a Spanish sentence in your own words. Imagine a context, then translate the sentence es>en.
   b. Do the same for *golazo*.
   c. Finally, try *paquetazo* (in the political-economic sense).

3. Who are *los muertitos* in Mexico? Research this lexeme and report on how you would render it in English in different situations.

4. Describe what *dedazo* is based only on your understanding of the concept from this passage from an editorial describing a phenomenon common in the Mexican electoral practice ("La encrucijada de la paradoja azteca" [Camero 2000]):

   El peso de la magistratura presidencial en el proceso de selección del nuevo candidato, seguramente nuevo presidente, se demuestra en el mote popular con que se conoce la selección: 'el Dedazo'. Antes de que la Opinión Pública conozca al designado, a este último se le nombra 'El Tapado'.

CASE STUDY: TRANSLATION AND CONNOTATION IN GEORGE ORWELL'S *1984*

In George Orwell's novel, *1984*, the subversive parable of Oldspeak features translation as the confrontational mechanism wielded by a totalitarian state. In the work, *the entire language* of Oldspeak is translated into Newspeak, a language free from thought that is designed to *eliminate* the original (Oldspeak), which suffers the "flaw" of having connotations. Newspeak, an intralingual translation, purges and restricts rather than expands. In such essays as "Politics and the English Language," Orwell himself championed unencumbered, honest prose, noting that it was the product of clear thought and that clear thought, in turn, made thinking clearly easier.

Read the following excerpts and discuss the issues of **language**, **power**, and **translation** they raise.

The purpose of Newspeak was not only to provide a medium of expression for the world-view and mental habits proper to the devotees of Ingsoc, but to make all other modes of thought impossible. It was intended that when Newspeak had been adopted once and for all and Oldspeak forgotten, a heretical thought—that is, a thought diverging from the principles of Ingsoc—should be literally unthinkable, at least so far as thought is dependent on words. Its vocabulary was so constructed as to give exact and often very subtle expression to every meaning that a Party member could properly wish to express, while excluding all other meanings and also the possibility of arriving at them by indirect methods. This was done partly by the invention of new words, but chiefly by eliminating undesirable words and by stripping such words as remained of unorthodox meanings, and so far as possible of all secondary meanings whatever. To give a single example: The word *free* still existed in Newspeak, but it could only be used in such statements as "This dog is free from lice" or "This field is free from weeds". It could not be used in its old sense of "politically free" or "intellectually free" since political and intellectual freedom no longer existed even as concepts, and were therefore of necessity nameless. Quite apart from the suppression of definitely heretical words, reduction of vocabulary was regarded as an end in itself, and no word that could be dispensed with was allowed to survive. Newspeak was designed not to extend but to *diminish* the range of thought, and this purpose was indirectly assisted by cutting the choice of words down to a minimum . . . .

Some of the B words [the class of compound words] had highly subtilized meanings, barely intelligible to anyone who had not mastered the language as a whole. Consider, for example, such a typical sentence from a *Times* leading article as *Oldthinkers unbellyfeel Ingsoc*. The shortest rendering that one could make of this in Oldspeak would be: "Those whose ideas were formed before the Revolution cannot have a full emotional understanding of the principles of English Socialism." But this is not an adequate translation. To begin with, in order to grasp the full meaning of the Newspeak sentence quoted above, one would have to have a clear idea of what is meant by *Ingsoc*. And in addition, only a person thoroughly grounded in Ingsoc could appreciate the full force of the word *bellyfeel*, which implied a blind, enthusiastic acceptance difficult to imagine today; or of the word *oldthink*, which was inextricably mixed up with the idea of wickedness and decadence. But the special function of certain Newspeak words, of which *oldthink* was one, was not so much to express meanings as to destroy them. These words, necessarily few in number, had had their meanings extended until they contained within themselves whole batteries of words which, as they were sufficiently covered by a single comprehensive term, could now be scrapped and forgotten.

(*Source: Nineteen Eighty-Four* by George Orwell, © George Orwell, 1949, by permission of Bill Hamilton as the Library Executor of the Estate of the Late Sonia Brownell Orwell and Secker & Warburg Ltd.)

UNDERSTANDING AND COMPARING DICTIONARIES ✓

Source: © Jim Meddick/Dist. by Newspaper Enterprise Association, Inc.

Dictionaries are excellent "memory-joggers." To use another image, they are maps, not the destination. Novice translators often do not realize that dictionaries offer purely *potential*, not actual, translations. Dictionary blurbs that claim the reference "translates" are akin to claims that a hammer does home repair—the active, indispensable decision maker is always you, the translator. The dictionary, like all muses, does not do the actual work.

Context is of paramount importance in translation, and the translator must be on guard constantly against seeing words only in their familiar roles. For example, perhaps you learned the word "*mancha*" with its common English "translation," "*stain*". But you will need to be aware of "spot" (astronomy), "blot" (ink), "flaw" (on a diamond), "bruise" (on fruit), "patch" (of vegetation), and "stigma" (figuratively, a stain on one's honor). Perhaps in context there also is a pun or allusion (implicit or explicit reference) to La Mancha, the region in Spain, or the English Channel (Canal de la Mancha). All these possibilities of word choice revolve around the word's core meaning of *something blemished or made imperfect in a small way*. Each choice is determined by context. Sometimes you will find two words that fit equally well or seem to. This is normal, and rejecting a good possibility for a slightly better one is a far better thing than having no possibilities to reject!

For all their strengths, all dictionaries have gaps. Lexicographers (dictionary makers) try to update their work, but dictionaries are inevitably "behind the curve"—language is a living, evolving entity used by real people, whereas the dictionary is a frozen picture. And yet many artists, entertaining the romantic idea we had as children that all possibilities lie dormant there in the "infinite" book, have found inspiration in the dictionary as a life-giving force. Pablo Neruda's "Oda al diccionario" is just such an homage; the poet defends the book as the "*perpetuidad viviente*" of language. Some dictionaries are controversial for different users in that they take a *prescriptivist* position, which means they try to enforce how language *should* be used, rather than how it actually *is* used (the *descriptivist* position). So, for example, the swear words or substandard speech might be expurgated (removed) in a prescriptivist work.

Biases and stereotypes also exist in dictionaries and in ways few readers suspect. Ideology, race, class, and gender bias frequently are perpetuated through the many editions of a work despite the hard work of editors to catch such distortions. Almost at random, we open the bilingual Larousse (an excellent dictionary, we should stress, but one not immune to these problems). On page 622 we find under the headword *"sentido,"* the meaning "sense," and an example: *"Los negros tienen un buen sentido del ritmo"* (!)

In general, dictionaries list the most *concrete* and *basic* meanings first, followed by the more abstract (figurative) and obscure and by nuanced contextualizations such as idiom and collocation. It is important to read *around* an entry as well as the entry itself; for example, if you want to find *"dejar a uno plantado,"* you will want to generate ideas by searching not only *"plantado"* (adj.) but also the infinitive *"plantar."* Think of using the dictionary as exploring a crime scene—no potential clue should be missed if you want to "solve the case."

Novice translators are frequently mystified upon realizing the limits of dictionaries. But real-life usage trumps the dictionary every time. (This sounds heretical until you stop and think: You may check the dictionary to see if something is correct, but if something sounds "wrong," you will not use it anyway just because a dictionary said it should sound right.) Speech and writing as we use them lie ultimately with the people, the grand architects of language. Walt Whitman:

> Language, be it remember'd, is not an abstract construction of the learn'd, or of dictionary-makers, but is something arising out of the work, needs, ties, joys, affections, tastes, of long generations of humanity, and has its bases broad and low, close to the ground. Its final decisions are made by the masses, people nearest the concrete, having most to do with actual land and sea. It impermeates all, the Past as well as the Present, and is the grandest triumph of the human intellect. (Whitman 1998, 77–8)

Gabriel García Márquez, who sees dictionaries skeptically—as playthings more than repositories of lasting truths—in a similar vein, wrote of dictionaries' belatedness:

> [L]as palabras no las hacen los académicos en las academias, sino la gente en la calle. Los autores de los diccionarios las capturan casi siempre demasiado tarde, las embalsaman por orden alfabético, y en muchos casos cuando ya no significan lo que pensaron sus inventores. ("Prólogo", Diccionario clave de uso del español [Maldonado 1996])

Generally, dictionaries that include multiples languages are not as useful—not as thorough or even accurate—as monolingual and bilingual ones. Moreover, it is virtually unthinkable for a professional translator to work without a monolingual dictionary in the languages of his or her combination(s). The vast majority of bilingual dictionaries seek to offer "equivalents" (as a glossary does) rather than definitions, hence the importance of using the monolingual ones. Finally, monolingual dictionaries are far more likely than bilingual ones to give the search word in context, historical usage, and thorough coverage. Also, their overall margin for error is smaller. Try using two monolingual dictionaries side by side, one in English and one in Spanish.

A good rule of thumb: Have an approximate idea of a word's meaning *before* consulting the dictionary.

Activities

1. a. In three different bilingual dictionaries, find five different headwords, Spanish or English, whose senses are very different, particularly if they involve usage or if primary meanings in one source are secondary or nonexistent in another. Be aware

of connotations and whether the dictionaries address them. Draw a table comparing them.

    b. In class, write up the meanings on the board and have the class guess the word and what order the meanings came up in the dictionaries.

2. Examine your own assumptions about dictionaries. If you were compiling a dictionary, which of the two camps, prescriptivist or descriptivist, do you think you would be inclined? Stage a debate with two teams, each defending its choices.

3. How would you assess the quality of a dictionary (online or paper) on first sight? Describe the steps you might take to determine if it's a worthwhile tool.

4. Compare two similar dictionaries, general or specialized, on CD-ROM after reading *dictionary reviews* of them. Test them out on the same brief text or passage.

TRANSLATION TIP

Cross-Checking and "Trapping"

When you use bilingual dictionaries, look up words in both directions to cross-check. For example, if you're working en>es and when you look up "riddle," suppose that you find "*acertijo*" and "*adivinanza*"; look up both in the es>en side (and other dictionaries, including monolingual) to check which one you need—if either. In time you will have to look up fewer words; don't be discouraged by having to use dictionaries—it is not a failing. It *is* an error, however, to depend exclusively on them, or to assume that any reference work has final authority on the job you're working on! The dictionary is only one tool of many.

    When verifying a term online, don't simply go to the first site and consider the matter settled. Check *multiple reliable sources* one against another—open the pages and really check. And don't just count hits—a raw hit count may reflect very high redundancy or other "noise."

    Try trapping **term candidates** (potential terms) by searching for a thematically related word you are certain of in your target language: For example, say for a text on radio production, you want to know possibilities for "casting" in Spanish; try <*casting + voces*>. The *voces* will bring up pages in Spanish (it turns out that Spanish borrows the English word!). Try to trap definitions by calling up content-rich pages. Say you want to know about dubbing: Try <*doblaje + técnica que*>. This will give you the basic information you need for background on any given assignment. Remember to use quotes to search for exact phrases.

DICTIONARIES AND GLOSSARIES: WHAT'S THE DIFFERENCE?

A **dictionary** is more comprehensive and more general than a glossary and includes definitions, one of the main features that distinguish it. It may also include such information as pronunciation and etymology. A **glossary**, by contrast, lists "equivalents" rather than definitions. (The danger is clear: If you used only a glossary you theoretically might never gain thereby in subject competence, because glossaries don't necessarily aid understanding; on the other hand, subject area experts need very few concepts defined.) Also, a glossary, unlike most dictionaries, is restricted to a particular subject field or semantic field and its specialized vocabulary. Unlike a dictionary, a glossary may accompany another document in an explanatory role; in this sense, glossaries more frequently are, as the word implies, *glosses*, that is, explanations or translations of an *actual* text, though they may also be compilations from many similar texts, or even hyperglossaries, which are from many contributors (and, thus, texts). Glossaries are probably more frequently customized (enlarged) than are dictionaries, for obvious reasons.

The following are random excerpts from a glossary.* Can you guess who produced it or what it relates to?

G

geriatric	*geriátrico*
gestational	*gestacional*
gift	*regalo, obsequio, donación*
glasses (*optical*)	*lentes, anteojos, espejuelos, gafas*
gold	*oro*
golden	*dorado*
good cause	*razón justificada*
government Pension Offset	*ajuste por pensión del gobierno*
grant	*concesión, subvención*
gratuitous military wage credits	*créditos a título gratuito por servicio militar*
gross earnings	*ganancias brutas*
Growth Domestic Product (GDP)	*producto doméstico bruto*
guidelines	*guía, normas, pautas*
gums	*encías*

H

handicap	*impedimento, desventaja*
handicapped individual	*individuo con impedimento, con desventaja*
handle (*verb*)	*atender, manejar*
harassment	*hostigamiento, acoso*
hard of hearing	*problemas de audición*
hard disk	*disco duro*
hardship case	*caso de privación, de dificultad económica*

(The glossary or term list excerpt is from the "Glossary of Social Security Terminology." <http://www.ssa.gov/espanol/glossary_es.htm#g>, Accessed May 1, 2009)

 Discussion and Research

1. The preceding glossary excerpt does not sort by country. Give an example of an entry on which you would have to do further research to determine regional use.
2. There are also **lexicons**, **term banks**, and **multilingual vocabularies**. Can you sort out the features of each? (If you can, you're ahead of the translation community, which hasn't come to a consensus!) Can you find examples of these designations used to refer to different tools?
3. Do a search of **specialized dictionaries**. Give examples that are relevant to es<>en. How do you think they compare to general monolingual and bilingual dictionaries? What can they offer the translator? Do they appear to have any drawbacks?

---

*A colleague at Kent State University objects to this designation here (not mine)—for him, this sample is a *term list*, and a glossary would include definitions and other information.

Making Glossaries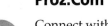

You can make your own glossaries with Microsoft Excel, for example, and save them as Web pages (in HTML) for others to use.

Proz.Com

Connect with your **Manual** Web site and use the link to find access to extensive searchable glossaries. This tool browses KudoZ, a term help network; Glosspost, an online glossary database; and other useful resources. Also, you can always try Google™ Book Search (Beta), where long excerpts of some print glossaries are accessible for viewing.

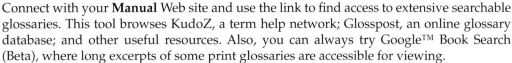

Tasks — *Discussion Board*

1. These days, intelligent "spiders" or "spidering software" can be used to find glossaries online. Find out more and report back to the class.
2. Software exists for creating glossaries. What can you find out about examples of these tools and their capabilities? Can you download demonstration versions of any? How steep does the learning curve seem to be for a first-time user?
3. Research to find out what companies maintain glossaries. Learn what you can about what format they are in, how they are managed, what tool is used to update and store them, and what kind of compatibility they have. How are terms imported?
4. Create a Web page with links to useful online dictionaries, glossaries, and other resources. Sort it to create a maneuverable user interface. Demonstrate it for the class.

"What Dictionary Should I Get?"

Eventually, try to have many different unabridged print (and electronic) dictionaries readily available. Meanwhile, many translation students overlook the "stacks" (the circulating books) in their home institution's library as a source of dictionaries. Also, consider buying dictionaries an *investment* rather than a cost (many are useful for years, though it is true that other specialized dictionaries, e.g., those in the technology industry, can be obsolete or of dubious worth in a few short years). Each dictionary has strengths and weaknesses depending on one's point of view and the domain in which one is working. With that in mind, following are some recommendations:

Bilingual:

Larousse: *Gran Diccionario Español-Inglés: English-Spanish Dictionary* [Unabridged]. Ramón García-Pelayo y Gross, ed. México, D.F.: Larousse Kingfisher, 1999.

HarperCollins: *Spanish-English, English-Spanish Dictionary*, 4th ed. Colin Smith, ed. Glasgow, UK: HarperResource; New York: HarperCollins, 2002. (Note: It tends toward British English.)

Oxford: *The Oxford Spanish Dictionary: Spanish-English/English-Spanish*, 3rd ed. Beatriz Galimberti Jarman and Roy Russell, eds. Oxford and New York: Oxford University Press, 2003.

Simon and Schuster: *Simon and Schuster's International Dictionary: English/Spanish, Spanish/English*, 2nd ed. Roger Steiner, ed. New York: Macmillan, 1997.

Monolingual:

Students might consider *El pequeño Larousse* for Spanish-Spanish, and a good English-English dictionary such as *Webster's Third New International Dictionary, Unabridged* (2002) or the CD-ROM 3.0. If you would like to have a few *specialized dictionaries*, try *Oxford's Business Spanish*, which is very efficient and affordable in paperback. For law, *McGraw-Hill's Spanish and English Legal Dictionary*, and the Wiley's series is also good (for business as well). A good dictionary of collocations (*The BBI Dictionary of English Word Combinations*, Benson et al., Amsterdam/Philadelphia: John Benjamins, 1997) and perhaps a thesaurus (*Roget's* in dictionary form) are a start. Marina Orellana's *Glosario internacional para el traductor* (Santiago de Chile: Ed. Universitaria, 2003) and Jean-Claude Corbeil and Ariane Archambault's *The Spanish/English Visual Dictionary* (Montréal: Firefly Books, 2004) are also highly recommended. Many dictionaries are becoming available on CD-ROM for working from the desktop. Here's what dictionary you should *not* get for translation work: any "pocket" dictionary, however portable. Often even the adequate "abridged" editions of dictionaries you likely have had until now will no longer quite meet your needs.

NOTE A fascinating, demystifying book that translators and translators-in-training tend to enjoy is Simon Winchester's *The Professor and the Madman: A Tale of Murder, Insanity, and the Making of the Oxford English Dictionary* (New York: Harper Perennial, 1999).

Activity: Word, Phrase, Text (Recognizing "Untranslatables")

1. Think of three *lexemes* (minimal linguistic units of language with semantic content) in both Spanish and English that would resist a one-to-one translation.

   Model 1: *tertulia*   **Model 2:** wellness   **Model 3:** *secuestro express*
   Model 4: troubleshooter   **Model 5:** *duende*

2. Think of phrases es<>en that would resist translation. Explain why and in what contexts.

   Model 1: *Buen provecho* ≠ *Bon apetit* (used in English) [different in frequency, register]
   Model 2: *¡Viva!*   **Model 3:** *si Dios quiere*
   Model 4: *en mala hora*   **Model 5:** "Welcome back"

3. Can you think of an *entire text type* that would resist translation, >en or >es? Explain.

TRANSLATION TEASER

"English As She Is Spoke"

One of the most notorious—and amusing—sustained mistranslations of all time is the book *English As She Is Spoke* (1883), originally a language learners guide by José da Fonseca. Pedro Carolino undertook a translation of the Portuguese original, armed with no English, and only a Portuguese-French phrase book and a French-English dictionary. The Parisian printer then added errata to the mix. Mark Twain was an early enthusiast of the work and even wrote an appreciative preface to this unintentional contribution to American humor.

POLYSEMY

Polysemy means having many meanings (lit. "many signs"). The adjective for such a word is *polysemous* or *polyvalent* (valence = meaning). Entire phrases can be polysemous as well. The word "set", with nearly 200 meanings, is the most polysemous word in the English language.

Polysemy in part accounts for translation's difficulty. The word "mean," for instance, in Spanish may call for *medio, inferior, mezquino,* or *despreciable,* all of which are different meanings; as a verb, "mean" can be *tener la intención, dirigir, querer decir,* or *suponer,* depending on context.

CASE STUDY: CHOOSING PLAUSIBLE MEANINGS

Consider closely each of the following potential meanings of *entraña(s)* from the Real Academia de la Lengua (each entry is paraphrased). Using only these entries as resources, render the source text passages in bold into a plausible English for the situations given. Write the number (1–6) of the definition(s) most closely related to the one you need for each translation regardless of part of speech. Each may be used more than once or not at all; in the latter case, write "Ø."

entraña.
(*Del sustantivo plural* interane˘a, *intestinos.*)

1. *f. Los órganos contenidos en las grandes cavidades del cuerpo.*
2. *f. La parte más esencial de algo; lo más íntimo.*
3. *f. pl. Algo oculto, retirado o secreto.* Las entrañas de la tierra.
4. *f. pl. El centro; en medio.*
5. *f. pl. Voluntad, afecto.*
6. *f. pl. Carácter, genio (de una persona).* Persona de buenas entrañas.

entraño, ña.
(*Del latín* interane˘us, *interior.*)

1. *adj. ant. Interior, interno.*

ST1: "**Somos amigos entrañables desde que estamos en el colegio.** *Temo que se haya perdido debido a la confusión ocasionada por los últimos huracanes en la región*". (for a bilingual online forum for contacting missing persons)

ST2: "**El Reino Unido, amigo entrañable de la paz**" (headline in *UN Chronicle*)

ST3: "**Trabajar con productos químicos entraña riesgos de salud**" (consumer alert posted on company bulletin board)

ST4: "**Saludo entrañablemente a mis hermanos del Opiscopado**" (remark from transcript of comments made by the Pope during a meeting with the world press)

ST5: "**Mi danza empieza en la entraña y toma forma en la cabeza**" (interview headline of a dancer, in the arts section of *El País* [12/31/2005])

ST6: "**Martí en las entrañas del monstruo**" (title of academic study of the presence of the United States in the Cuban intellectual's work, *Encuentro de la cultura cubana*, 1999/2000

ST7: "*Hay una amplia gama de actividades en que participar en esta zona fascinante de Chile.* **Ud. puede internarse en las entrañas de la tierra como los grandes exploradores**". (from an eco-resort's brochure for vacation packages for foreign travelers)

ST8: "**La entraña es un corte muy especial y es muy típica de la cocina local**". (line from a parrillada menu to be produced bilingually)

TRANSLATION TEASER

Words can "split" from language to language to make distinctions that the other language doesn't make; for example, "corner" in Spanish splits into *rincón* or *ángulo* (= inside corner) and *esquina* (= outside corner) (Singh and Pereira 2005, 37). Can you think of other examples en<>es?

Disambiguating Puns

Explain the source of confusion in the puns in these newspaper headlines.

1. Farmer Bill Dies in House
2. Milk Drinkers Are Turning to Powder
3. Red Tape Holds Up New Bridges
4. Kids Make Nutritious Snacks
5. Two Convicts Evade Noose, Jury Hung
6. Reagan Wins on Budget, But More Lies Ahead
7. Quarter of a Million Chinese Live on Water
8. Stud Tires Out
9. Teacher Strikes Idle Kids
10. Grandmother of Eight Makes Hole in One
11. Lack of Brains Hinders Research
12. Some Pieces of Rock Hudson Sold at Auction
13. Steals Clock, Faces Time
14. British Left Waffles on Falkland Islands
15. Eye Drops Off Shelf

Connect with your **Manual** Web site and use the links to find the principal sources for the puns listed.

TRANSLATION TEASER

Homographs

Connect with your **Manual** Web site and use the link to test out an online machine translation program such as Babelfish with these two time-honored phrases:

Time flies like an arrow.

Fruit flies like a banana.

CASE STUDY: PUNS

Source: Reprinted by permission of BP

A mainstay of advertising language is the pun. Why do you think this is so? Can you preserve the pun in translation (en>es) in the ad? Assume it is an online ad for a general news service and in U.S. Spanish.

LINGUISTIC NOTE

"HORNS" VERSUS "RAYS OF LIGHT": *PEGÁNDOLE CUERNOS*

St. Jerome, the patron saint of librarians, scripture scholars, students, and translators and interpreters, was not immune from problems of polysemy.

Look at the picture that follows. No, it's not Jupiter (as one flea market purveyor tried to assure a would-be customer interested in a replica of this sixteenth-century Michelangelo statue). It's Moses. Exodus 34-5 tells of Moses coming down from Mt. Sinai "radiating" (*karan*). Unfortunately, the Hebrew word also means "horns." St. Jerome chose "horns" for his Vulgate translation, and Michelangelo stayed true to the saint's version. The "intersemiotic mistranslation" is ironic in that horns have long associations with the pagan tradition, not the holiness of a saint. However, some have theorized that Jerome chose the meaning "horns" over "light" deliberately.

International Translation Day is St. Jerome's saint's day, September 30.

Statue of Moses by Michelangelo. The tomb of Julius II.
Source: Gianni Dagli Orti/Corbis/Bettmann

COGNATES

The word "cognate" when applied to languages means that the languages are descended from the same parent—for example, Italian and Spanish are *cognate languages* (Latin is the parent). When we speak of cognates on the level of words, we mean that due to common parentage, they are similar in appearance or structure.

Following are examples of kinds of cognates that the translator must distinguish constantly:

(True) cognates: *divorcio* and divorce

False cognates ("false friends"; *"falsos amigos"*; *"faux ami"*): *destreza* and distress (*destrezas* are *skills*)

Partial false cognates (or what we might call "situationally false cognates"): *entretener(se)* can mean entertain (though *No te entretengo más* features *entretener* in a partially false relationship with "entertain"—it's to distract, retain, hold up, keep busy)

Even the word "translation" is partially false (*trasladar* means to move); the cognate of *traducir*, to traduce, unfortunately means "to betray."

Long experience teaches which cognates give the most problems and in what ways. Moreover, it is not simply a case of learning the "true" from the "false"—often there are degrees of falsity with which to contend that are extremely slight ("false" is used here in the sense of *deceptive*, as in the expression *to play a person false*). Even obvious cognates such as *entrar* and "to enter" can be partially false in a way if the cognate would be in an inappropriate target text register compared to the source text (quotidian <> *cotidano*) or if the context calls for different usage (for this example, a shift from "enter" [an intransitive verb] to "bring in" [a transitive verb—i.e., one that admits an object]: "*Entra el correo, por favor*" ≈> "Please <u>bring</u> the mail <u>in</u>").

False cognates may be false for many reasons, including the natural drift of language. (The translator is not generally concerned with etymology—word origins—but may look to a word's history for clues to present meaning.) If, for example, we look into the notorious cliché that *embarazada* ≠ "embarrassed" but rather "pregnant," we find that *embarazada* is actually related to the Italian *imbarrazzo*, "to be surrounded by bars," and the limited prospects for expectant women centuries ago were described with this word that literally and metaphorically connoted barriers, burden, and hindrance. In other words, some words originally were not false cognates but came to be because we have forgotten their connections. (Others simply are borrowed into an instantly false relationship with their pairs.) Frequently a false or partial false cognate presents a case of the other language in the pair preserving only one, frequently secondary, meaning that is more predominant in the first language: for example, *matrimonio* ≈> "matrimony," but more likely to refer to the married partners. It may help, then, to think of some partial false cognates as occasionally or *situationally false cognates*. Everyone knows the difficulty of learning where these "landmines" are when learning to speak the language. They can be even more troublesome if not caught in writing; some of the worst translations owe their disastrousness to missed cognates. Witness these instructions given to Anglophone auto racers at an event in Mexico City: "The drivers will defile themselves on the Plaza at 10 a.m. They may relieve themselves on each other's convenience."* ("To defile," of course, is to desecrate or debase, to dirty; the translator or nonnative English speaker almost certainly was working from "*desfilar*," to file out, to line up.)

CASE STUDY: SITUATIONALLY FALSE COGNATES

The New York Times (April 8, 2003) contributor Erin N. Marcus, MD, reminds us that language has consequences: "In 1984, a 22-year-old man won a $71 million settlement after he asserted that a group of paramedics, doctors and emergency room workers at a South Florida hospital had misdiagnosed a brain clot. The patients' relatives used the Spanish word 'intoxicado' to describe his ailment." The staff took the word to mean intoxicated, a possible interpretation of the word, and so they treated him for a drug overdose. By *intoxicado*, however, his family had only meant he was nauseated.

Alternatives to the Cognate

Choosing Latinate words judiciously can greatly improve a writer's—and a translator's—style in English. The best translators develop a balance of words of Anglo-Saxon origin and those of Romance origin in order to suit the situation. If the proportion veers too much toward the Anglo, the style can seem choppy or harsh; if too Romance, it can seem abstract and bloodless. However, some domains use—even expect—higher proportions of Romance words, which nevertheless can hamper the reader's understanding.

This exercise will help you realize that Latinate words are not necessarily more elegant, more expressive, or even the best diction (word choice). Alternatives—particularly phrasal verbs (which we will see in more detail in Chapter 3)—should be considered as a matter of

---

*Willard R. Espy. *An Almanac of Words at Play*. New York: C. N. Potter, 1975, 40.

course. A phrasal verb is a (usually) two-part verb (verb + adverb or verb + preposition; e.g., "to run around"). Here are two recommendations, particularly if you are a nonnative user of English: the *Cambridge International Dictionary of Phrasal Verbs* or the *Oxford Dictionary of Phrasal Verbs*. A review of the monument to simplicity, Strunk and White's brief classic, *A Manual of Style*, would also serve the translator-in-training in this connection.

It should be stressed **that the cognate is perfectly appropriate—even preferable—at times** (e.g., *oxidado* is commonly "rusted" or "rusty," but "oxidized" may be preferable, even more precise, in certain technical texts). Regardless, it is best to exercise vigilance, particularly at first.

◀ NOTE ▶ *Don't go to the extreme of automatically replacing every cognate when translating text* (a habit that often betrays amateurishness as much as unwittingly using false cognates).

Task ✓

For each word (1–20), determine a phrase in English that avoids the cognate while conveying the semantic content (meaning); you may change registers (levels of formality of discourse). Each word is followed by a context with the word in question used in a way that might be improved with better word choice. These may be seen as first drafts in translations or as original creations; the sentence alone will be context enough to cue your edit.

Model: transpire (Success will transpire through hard work.) >>
(*possible solution*: come / come about / arise)

1. **convene** (The meeting will now convene.)
2. **equivocate** (He equivocated on the issue of his wrongdoing.)
3. **perturb** (Your humming perturbs me.)
4. **tranquilize** (Tranquilize your mind with music.)
5. **desire** (She desired him.)
6. **converse** (Let's converse about our options.)
7. **distinguish** (I can't distinguish your twins.)
8. **communicate** (It is hard to communicate this idea to you.)
9. **illuminate** (See if you can illuminate this issue for me.)
10. **depart** (What time do you depart?)
11. **discover** (I wonder what you'll discover in your search at the library.)
12. **encounter** (I don't expect to encounter problems.)
13. **necessities** (My necessities are few.)
14. **vitiated** (Civilization is a vitiated garden.)
15. **corroded** (Time has corroded my iron will.)
16. **abandon** (He abandons his work at 6.)
17. **extend** (Don't extend your cards flat on the table.)
18. **advance** (The bounty hunter was advancing on me.)
19. **ingest** (Who doesn't like to ingest a few extra calories now and then?)
20. **review** (The mother reviewed her child's homework.)

¿?

Which of the sentences in 1 to 20 would have connotations probably not intended by the writer or speaker? Can you find five full names (or parts of full names) of historical figures that are frequently translated into Spanish?

COGNATES IN CONTEXT

Tracking the logic of the text, translate the phrase *"hombres en razón y urbanidad"* from the following passage (El Inca Garcilaso de la Vega, Perú, 1539–1616, *Comentarios reales*). Context: El Inca, a descendent of an Incan princess and a Spanish nobleman, is relating the origin myth and genealogy of the Incas. Translation brief: Your target audience consists of the readers of a scholarly anthology of Colonial texts in the present year).

Prepare to discuss your process (your reasoning and findings) and why you discarded other possibilities than what you had chosen. What clues does the text give for rendering *urbanidad*? What contrast with the word *"razón"* is present in the text? Avoid bilingual dictionaries, though you may use monolingual dictionaries in conjunction.

> *Adviértase, porque no enfade el repetir tantas veces estas palabras: "Nuestro Padre el Sol", que era lenguaje de los Incas y manera de veneración y acatamiento decirlas siempre que nombraban al Sol, porque se preciaban descender de él, y al que no era Inca no le era lícito tomarlas en la boca, que fuera blasfemia y lo apedrearan. Dijo el Inca:*
>
> *—Nuestro Padre el Sol, viendo los hombres tales como te he dicho, se apiadó y hubo lástima de ellos y envió del cielo a la tierra un hijo y una hija de los suyos para que los doctrinasen en el conocimiento de Nuestro Padre el Sol, para que lo adorasen y tuviesen por su Dios y para que les diesen preceptos y leyes en que viviesen como* **hombres en razón y urbanidad***, para que habitasen en casas y pueblos poblados, supiesen labrar las tierras, cultivar las plantas y mieses, criar los ganados y gozar de ellos y de los frutos de la tierra como hombres racionales y no como bestias. Con esta orden y mandato puso Nuestro Padre el Sol estos dos hijos suyos en la laguna Titicaca. . . .* (de la Vega 1985)

Activity: Negotiating Cognates

Read the apartment ad that follows. Give a translation for each unit of translation in italics, assuming that the target text will be for an English-language newspaper in Colombia.

Source: Mary Lee Bretz, *Pasajes*, 3/e © 1992. Reproduced with the permission of The McGraw-Hill Companies.

punto de venta ≈>	*centro de Medellín*≈>
que sí tiene detalles ≈>	*unidad cerrada*≈>
Calidad-Economía-Ubicación≈>	*Zonas verdes*≈>
Entrega Inmediata≈>	*Mucho ojo*≈>
Sepáralos con sólo $80.000≈>	

How would you render the phrase *"confort y comodidad"* here? Discuss.

For the English of *"punto de venta,"* how is this defined in economics? Bring in a good definition. Think of several examples illustrating the concept. Find a collocation with the term used as an adjective. Is there an alternative term for the English you found? What is the difference between "POS" and "POP," if any, in economics?

What does "$" refer to in the text?

Go back to the following terms: *detalles, economía, sepáralos, centro, zonas verdes.* If you used the cognates for any of these, ask yourself if these are the most natural expressions in English. If not, challenge yourself to improve your renderings.

TRANSLATION TRAP

Word, Thing, Concept

Novice translators easily grasp that things, though they share a cognate or a mutually identified noun across languages (*perro*<>dog), may not "line up" conceptually; that is, they may not *really* describe the same reality. For example, a dog in North American culture is a pampered, quasi-member of the family; a *perro* in the Americas is far more likely to be either stray or not nearly so integrated into the family circle of affection and almost certainly does not sleep on, or in, the bed. In some Spanish-speaking countries, the *perro* is an *animal doméstico*, a classification that includes barnyard animals; only in select countries will *mascota* be used, and perhaps this is from North American influence. As for concepts, one must map them interculturally with great care. Marieke de Mooij (2005) offers this example:

> The word *freedom* has different connotations across cultures. The concept of freedom as described by U.S. students means "free enterprise." Dutch students tend to describe *freedom* as "freedom to express your feelings, to be yourself." In 1996, Russian students from western Siberia associated the word *freedom* primarily with "not being in prison" and secondarily with freedom from pollution and freedom of speech. To the Japanese, *freedom* means "to behave as you please, to transcend the group." It is experienced as "having individual ideas, escape from spiritual bondage," which is not the same as the Western individualistic notion of freedom that serves as a basis for asserting the precedence of the individual over the group, which is not seen as desirable in Japanese society. (90)

Activity: Translating Meaning

Read the following source text (ST) and a student's corresponding target text (TT). Then using whatever resources needed, consider errors (meaning errors, false cognates, word choice, sentence structure) and mark the TT accordingly, noting suggestions for improvement. Try to "deverbalize" (focus on the *idea* rather than *wording*). Regroup with the class and discuss. Comment on the following connotations: "shady," "discriminatory"; "deviations"; "living together." Produce a new version as a group on the chalkboard or overhead then read the two TTs aloud for comparison. Your version should be geared for an educated international readership of an online news service in the present year.

ST:

Un mundo asombrado y temeroso es el que se enfrenta hoy al falso dilema de orden indiscriminado, dictatorial, o terrorismo anárquico. El largo período de terror en

Latinoamérica, los secuestros de embajadores, las frecuentes desviaciones de naves aéreas y los hechos de los guerrilleros urbanos, sacuden al hombre y lo hacen pedir el retorno al orden, al respeto, a las normas tradicionales de convivencia nacional o internacional. (Adapted from *Siempre*, México, D.F.)

TT text for editing:

A shady, frightful world confronts itself in the false dilemma of discriminatory order, dictatorial, or terroristic anarchy. The large period of terror in Latin America, the sequestrations of ambassadors, the frequent deviations of airships and the facts of the urban guerrillas, shake the man and make it ask for the return to the order, the respect, the traditional norms of national or international living together. (Rivera et al. 1988, 303)

COMPONENTIAL ANALYSIS

Componential analysis is a method, *often unconscious in the experienced translator*, by which the process of transference of sememes (sense-components) to the target text takes place. Newmark's discussion (1981, 27–30) is illustrative. He describes this type of analysis as essentially a way for the translator to transfer meaning—translate—more effectively than can be accomplished with synonymy. Newmark considers the word "bawdy," for example, as comprising three essential emotive or factual components (shocking; related to the sex act; and humorous); secondary or descriptive features would be loudness and vulgarity (28). The translator is not obligated to work all components into a target text but will almost certainly be helped in eluding the one-to-one-correspondence trap to which novice translators are prone; further, the translator cannot go beyond the limits of a word's meanings, but rather uses the technique to mark boundaries (28–9). The procedure's main uses include distributing the source text components over a larger target text area (29), distinguishing between source text synonyms used together, and filling in gaps in the target text lexis (vocabulary). To give a simple example, componential analysis might be useful to translate the term "bakery" en>es if one compares the *confitería* (bakery for sweets), the *repostería* (bakery-delicatessen for sweets or deli meats), the *pastelería* (bakery for cakes), and the *panadería* (bakery for bread). So, *confitería*, for example, would be +sweets, −bread. Naturally, the translator looks at context for clues to which might work. Componential analysis may be useful in the process of *compensation by splitting*, which is used when a single word is translated by multiple words.

Minimal meaningful components (those that may help to distinguish the word from another) for each word or phrase are shown using the symbols (+) and (−) for the presence or absence of features.

Model 1: bachelor: −married
　　　　　+male
　　　　　+human

Model 2: *cursi*: +sentimental
　　　　　+corny
　　　　　+precious
　　　　　+tacky
　　　　　+affected
　　　　　+artificial or man-made
　　　　　+attempt at refinement and taste
　　　　　−refinement and taste

Model 3: voluntary manslaughter:

    +homicide

    −justified

    −premeditation

    (malice aforethought)

    +/−self-defense

    +"heat of passion"

Model 4: homewrecker:

    +female

    +perceived as predatory

     or blameworthy

    +extramarital

    +from outside the home

What happens to the usefulness of componential analysis when the context shifts? For example, when "bachelor," shown previously, is used to refer to an animal, do the components shift? Would componential analysis be more useful, then, to a lexicographer than a translator?

Task

Imagine you were translating Web site content for a travel insurance firm's travel health page. The copy reads as follows:

> *Chloroquine.* Travelers to Central America, north of the Panama Canal, can still use the old standby drug chloroquine. The drug must be started a week before the trip and taken weekly throughout the trip and for four weeks after return. (HTH Worldwide)

Try to tease out the strands of meaning in the phrase "the old standby" drug. Would one—or more than one—of those strands be used in your translation en>es? Does componentially analyzing these strands help you isolate, if need be, which strand to priortize? Discuss.

TRANSLATION TRAP

Pretend English

Inadequate translations often have a deviant quality: They use a language that seems legitimate until further inspection reveals otherwise.

Suppose that on a resort restaurant menu the phrase *ambiente moderno* is used to describe the restaurant. Now suppose that the translator calls this a "modern environment." We all think we understand "modern environment" and so we read this phrase without too much dissonance, if any. But suppose the translator revises this to "hip and trendy atmosphere" or "hip ambiance." Now you see the deficiency of the translator's original choices. In fact, now you may not even be inclined to call "modern environment" real English at all—but it sure is pretending to be, isn't it?

Three take-away lessons from this example: awareness, awareness, awareness.

Activity: Culturally Bound Terms (Nonequivalence at the Lexical Level)

Research the similarities and differences between the following pairs; some cases involve cognates that are false or semifalse for cultural reasons. In groups, discuss degrees of overlap, including register. You may find monolingual dictionaries quite useful for some items in this activity.

Model: *"motel"* and "motel."

Answer: A *motel* (Spanish) normally is for a short-term stay (i.e., for rendezvous), often with certain illicit connotations. In English, a "motel" is primarily a relatively respectable lodging for motorists or budget travelers. Overlap: Both are accommodations, the connotations making them quite different (vacationers do not stay in *moteles* in Spanish America). To achieve the effect of Spanish's *motel*, "motel" in English has to be modified—for example, "hourly motel."

1. *sobresaliente* and "A" (on a transcript)
2. *siesta* and "nap"
3. *buey* and "cuckold"
4. *notario* and "notary public"
5. *la Raza* and "the race"
6. *rancho* and "slum"
7. *rector* and "chancellor"
8. *S.A.* and "Inc."

9. *criollo* and "creole"
10. *modernismo* and "Modernism"
11. *charro* and "cowboy"
12. *rústico* and "redneck"
13. *quinceañera* and "teenager"
14. *churro* and "fritter"
15. *mestizo* and "mixed race"

Discussion

1. What strategy would you use to render the term "inner city" into Spanish? Consider the connotations in English, and show how poorer areas tend to develop in the Spanish-speaking world—not in the center of the city but in outlying areas; Mexico City is an example of this phenomenon. How many regional variants can you find in Spanish for the poorest quarters in a city? How about the richest? What is an *urbanización*? How would you render "suburban" (OJO: false cognate) into Spanish? Does the English term have class connotations? How could the English borrowing "barrio" (a semifalse cognate) be rendered (back) into Spanish? Finally, can you think of a context or contexts in which "barrio" could, or should, be rendered "borough"? As you work on these questions, keep connotations in mind.

2. Connect with your **Manual** Web site and use the link to explore real estate sites such as those in Mexico and others to find out how communities are denominated. Bring some examples to class and consider the parallels in English.
3. Try to map the differences and similarities in this set of words: *posada*, *pensión*, *hostal*, *mesón*, inn, bed and breakfast, boarding house, youth hostel, flophouse. Try to diagram the relationships visually. If you get stuck, try componential analysis.

TRANSLATION TEASER

Lexical Gaps

Is English "missing" any words or concepts? Quick: What's the opposite of "hungry"?

Did you say "full"? *Full* is a degree of satiety. How about "not hungry"? Perhaps in principle, but in practice, *not hungry* is a marked term—a phrase one uses to decline an offer of food, not as an independent assertion; so it's not the "opposite" of anything.

What conclusions can you begin to draw about languages from this example? What other examples in English or Spanish can you find that behave the same way?

LINGUISTICALLY BOUND LANGUAGE: SELF-REFERENTIAL PHRASES

Consider the following sentence pair:

The sentence below is a lousy translation into Spanish of this one.
La frase arriba es una mala traducción al inglés de ésta.

Although unlikely utterances, the pairing serves to illustrate the paradox of translating language whose very form is referenced at the semantic, or meaning, level. Anthony Pym (2004) offers the following exercise:

"Translate the following into Spanish:

The first word in this very sentence has three letters."

To help solve this dilemma, Pym reminds us of two translation functions:

"Translations can be either **documental** or **instrumentional** in function (emphasis mine; Nord 1997). They are documental when they help the reader understand the ST, which remains important and essential to the act of communication. On the other hand, translations are instrumental when they are focused only on creating a new text, the TT, which does not need the ST in order for the act of communication to be successful."

Now consider:

TT1: *La primera palabra de esta misma frase tiene tres letras.*

TT2: *La primera palabra de esta misma frase tiene dos letras.*

Compare TT1 and TT2. Which is instrumental? What limitations and strengths does each have? Now compare the author's third proposal:

TT3: *La primera palabra de la frase en inglés tiene tres letras.*

Pym notes that the reference to the ST becomes a key element in the TT, and that though "[w]e have lost the fact of self-referentiality, but we have gained a certain degree of honesty. We would call this an archetypical documental translation." Can you think of a context in which this function would not work? Can you think of yet another approach? Discuss.

Documental translations are appropriate, for example, for legal texts whose only binding version is the ST, and the reader is reminded that the foreign text is a part of the communication; instrumental translations attempt to sound natural, as if the reader were not reading a translation (Pym, op cit); in practice, both functions may be balanced in a single job.

Activities*

In pairs, read and discuss the following:

1. Translate the following text into English for inclusion in a textbook on historical theories of metaphors. You are not being paid very much for this job, and you have the whole book to do. State whether your translation is documental or instrumental.

   Los signos son traspuestos cuando los objetos mismos que nosotros designamos mediante sus términos propios son usados para designar otro objeto. Por ejemplo, decimos 'buey' y entendemos, mediante estas dos sílabas, el animal que se suele llamar con este nombre. (Saint Augustine 2000, 78)

2. In an English-language Western, the cavalry captain asks the captured Indian, "Do you speak English?" What will he say in the Spanish-language version of the film? Will the TT be documental or instrumental?

---

*Exercises 1–3 from Anthony Pym. *Translation and Text Transfer*. Frankfurt am Main: Peter Lang, 1992, 60–2.

3. In the film *Butch Cassidy and the Sundance Kid*, the two bank-robbing heroes leave the United States and go to Bolivia to rob more banks. The first thing they do there is learn Spanish. What will they do in the Spanish version of the film? Will the TT be documental or instrumental?

4. Now here is a case involving not a language but an orthographic feature not present in English—the "ñ":

   La Eñe En El Perú - El Triunfo De La Eñe
   > *En el idioma español, la eñe es muy importante y en todo computador debe ser una constante. [. . .] Para mi linda limeña no habría una piel de armiño. Tampoco habría cabañas para albergar a los niños. Sin eñe yo no te riño y aunque tampoco regaño, mira que no te engaño si te digo que te extraño.*
   >
   > *Sin sonido de zampoñas, sin beber un vino añejo, en una criolla peña ¿qué gracia tendrá el mañana? [. . .]*
   >
   > *Bueno, basta de regaños. Porque ya me vino el sueño y aunque pongo mucho empeño los ojos se me hacen extraños. Termino pidiendo a todos los que hablan el español, defiendan la EÑE. . . .**

   Discuss the translatability of the preceding text. Is a documental version possible? Would it *need* translating? Can you imagine an English text that would present a comparable problem in the other direction?

5. If you were researching supernatural creatures for a Spanish-language feature on a Web site you were writing, how would you deal with the following passage in your translation?

   > "Legends of bloodsucking creatures have been present in many cultures throughout history. One vampire-like creature that has been gaining a considerable amount of notoriety is the *chupacabra*. The literal translation for the Spanish word '*chupacabra*' is 'goat sucker'." (howstuffworks Web site)

6. Read the following passage, which appeared in an online forum on translation and was later anthologized in print. Suppose you were translating this piece es>en. What strategy would you use to approach the polysemy problem addressed?

   Free *es 'libre', no 'gratis'* (por María del Carmen Ugarte García 2002)
   > *El original en inglés de la licencia de software GPL (General Public License) comienza aclarando que en ese texto free no quiere decir 'gratis' sino 'libre'. Esa confusión se mantiene en español pese a disponer de dos palabras. Cuando hablamos de software libre, entonces, de qué hablamos?* (184)

   Does this text require "back-translation" as part of the translation? Discuss. Try a version to post in a multilingual forum of translation specialists. Optional: Each student posts his or her version in threaded format in a chat room or other e-learning online environment; students critique one another's versions.

   Describe the degree to which one must know about computers—what theorists call the *schemata*, or background knowledge one has in a particular domain—in order to successfully translate the passage.

---

*I am indebted to my former student Aimée Butler for bringing this text to my attention. The author is Hugo Pazos.

LINGUISTIC NOTE

OPERATION TRANSLATION

A current bit of similar jargon, perhaps unconsciously borrowed from the spy business, is that of **covert** versus **overt** translation (House 1977):

Covert translations are meant to *not* be recognized as translations (e.g., an ad).

Overt translations are meant to be recognized as translations (e.g., memoirs of Che Guevara).

Would it change the status of a covert translation if it were recognized as a translation in spite of its obvious covert strategy?

Do you think readers or viewers can sustain the illusion of an overt translation (e.g., pretending for the sake of convenience that el Che spoke English)? Are there dangers inherent to the voluntary amnesia of forgetting he spoke Spanish? What effect would a narrator of a Euripedes play have if he came out every half hour to announce, "Remember, ladies and gentlemen, they didn't really speak English like this in ancient Greece."?

Think up some text types or situations for which a covert or overt strategy would make the most substantial differences in the outcome of a translation.

Multilingual Texts

Multilingual texts constitute a unique problem. They remind us that our languages do not exist in isolation but in constant contact. The importance of a certain text being bilingual may lie in how the different languages are used within it. Is the non-English language merely "ornamental"? Or is it a marker of status or identity? What *function* does it perform within the text? This is the first line of questioning we must use when confronted with such a text.

In some cases, such as literature, multilingual texts announce their (or their protagonists') own internationalism. For example, James Joyce's *Finnegan's Wake* is full of multilingual, deliberately obscure puns. *Tres tristes tigres* by the Cuban writer Guillermo Cabrera Infante shows the heavy influence of U.S. popular culture and language and uses bilingual scenes strategically. Sometimes a source text will feature a language that is equally obscure to both source and target audiences; the translator may choose to bring it untranslated into the target text. Advertisements, in particular, do this for effect.

An intriguing case is found in the work of Ernest Hemingway, who often uses English *as if it were Spanish* in order to lend an immediacy and authenticity to the setting. In one story, "A Clean, Well-Lighted Place" (1933), this effect is achieved on two levels: the intrusion of Spanish words into the dialogue, and the use of false cognates *to give the impression we are reading Spanish*; for example, the narrator refers to the old drunk as a "good client" of the café, where we would expect the phrase "good customer." A famous example of the former occurs at the end of the story (notably, *nada* evokes both "nothing" and "nothingness," the philosophical concept often associated with Existentialism):

> *Give us this nada our daily nada and nada us our nada as we nada our nadas and nada us not into nada but deliver us from nada; pues nada.*

A reader (and translator) must recognize the intertext (the incorporated allusion) at work here—the Lord's Prayer. The text relies on the strangeness of the Spanish *nada* and on the characteristic Spanishness of *pues nada*, which is supremely evocative of alienation and despair. And, ironically, the full Spanishness of Spanish is evoked by mixing Spanish with English.

Sometimes language itself is the subject of a piece of writing. Self-referential writing can bedevil the translator when only one language is involved; imagine when there is wordplay *across* languages.

Discussion

Read the following comic strip and its translation into Spanish below it (they were not published adjacently, but separately, for separate audiences). What respective roles do English and Spanish play in the ST (source text)? In the TT (target text)? Can you devise another plausible strategy for translating the TT? Discuss in groups of three, then as a class.

Source: BALDO © 2004 Baldo Partnership. Dist. By Universal Press Syndicate. Reprinted with permission. All rights reserved.

CODE-SWITCHING

In "Address" by the Chicano poet Alurista, we find **code-switching** (*la alternancia*), a phenomenon especially typical of U.S. border communities in both speech and writing. Code-switching consists of the use of two codes (languages) in the same sentence or passage or one used in reply to the other. The practice generally follows traceable patterns; that is, certain switches regularly occur in certain linguistic environments. Importantly, code-switching, like all language practices, which are in varying degrees both inclusive and exclusive, assumes a bilingual audience. According to *The Cambridge Encyclopedia of Language* (1997, 365), code-switching is also used for reasons of group solidarity, where lexical gaps arise, and for emotional shifts and emphasis.

In the Chicano/a and U.S. Latino/a writing tradition, for example, code-switching often occurs at the lexical level, where *culture-bound language* specific to given Spanish-speaking communities are left in Spanish and embedded in the English text. This occurs with the "untranslatable" words linked to cultural identity (*jamona, jíbara,* and *dignidad*) in Esmeralda Santiago's novel, *When I Was Puerto Rican,* or in the title of José Antonio Villa-rreal's *Pocho.* One could argue that "untranslatables" often are left untranslated not so much where "equivalents" do not exist, but where an experience is *deeply lived through, or associated with, specific language*: Prayers, heartfelt emotions, titles and terms of endearment, slang, and exclamations often are not given in English in this writing tradition. In Santiago's novel, the chapter "Why Women Remain Jamona" (the title of which, moreover, uses a faux-translation of "quedar" as "remain" instead of the more idiomatic, and accurate, "wind up") metalinguistically "translates" the word by example, translating from the lexical plane to the discursive plane, where the connotations can more easily be absorbed and accounted for.

Tasks

1. Study the role of interlinguality—Spanish in an English-language U.S. Latino/a or Chicano/a writer's work, particularly the environments in which it occurs and to what effect. Possibilities include Rudolfo Anaya's *Bless Me, Ultima,* Piri Thomas' *Down These Mean Streets* (e.g., the chapter, "If You Ain't Got Heart, You Ain't got Nada"), or Junot Diaz' *Drown.* You may find chapter three of John S. Christie's *Latino Fiction and the Modernist Imagination: Literature of the Borderlands,* entitled "Latino Voices and 'English con Salsa'," to be of use.

2. In class, read the poem on your own, answer in groups of three, then discuss as a class.

    Address by Alurista
    address
    occupation
    age
    marital status
    —*perdone . . .*
    yo me llamo pedro
    telephone
    height
    hobbies
    previous employers
    —*perdone . . .*
    yo me llamo pedro
    pedro ortega
    zip code
    i.d. number
    classification
    rank
    —*perdone mi padre era*
    el senor ortega
    (a veces don jose)
    race

    (*Source:* Reprinted with permission of The Regents of the University of California from *Floricanto en Aztlán,* no. (1971), UCLA Chicano Studies Research Center. Not for further reproduction.)

Discussion

1. "Address" uses both English and Spanish. What role does each language play in the poem? What value systems are contained in and contrasted through them? Are the two voices communicating? If not, what effect does that create? How does the graphic presentation (the use of line breaks) contribute to the effect?
2. The Spanish is nonstandard. How does this contribute to the characterization of the Spanish voice?
3. Focus for a moment on the last word of the poem—the English word "race." Discuss its impact on the poem.
4. Consider the degree to which this poem is translatable. Who do you think its audience is? Does it "defy" translation? If so, in what way? Could other cultures or languages be substituted to similar effect?
5. Find Luis Sánchez's poem, "Sin pelos en la lengua," a counterattack on those who insist on linguistic and cultural assimilation in the United States. Compare it to "Address" from a translational perspective. What issues for translation does the text present?

LINGUISTIC NOTE

COGNATES, CODE-SWITCHING, AND CODE-MIXING

Are languages stored together in bilinguals' minds? The answer may be "partly": Field (2004, 34) notes that "[B]ilinguals' affective responses to words in Language A have been shown to be influenced by the existence of cognates in Language B which bear negative connotations. This suggests that the cross-linguistic links between words are primarily semantic; but contradictory evidence from priming experiments appears to support the idea that similar forms are stored together. In a French-medium task, French-English bilinguals recognize the word *four* (= 'oven') more rapidly if they have been recently exposed to the English word *five*."

   Performance in one language that is affected by knowledge of another is known, the author explains, as *code-mixing*. Here, the transfers happen not at boundaries, but tend to *collapse* boundaries—phonological, semantic, structural—and utterances reveal marked influence of the other language. You savvy?

TRANSLATION TEASER

Why is there a series of translations *in Spanish* with "Para Dummies®" in the title?

WORKSHOP TEXT #1: SOCIOLOGY/WORLD HEALTH

Before reading the source text, consider what you know about children's health issues. What do you think of when you read the words *"mortalidad infantil"* in the title? What factors do you expect to read about in the piece that follows? Using the *CIA World Factbook* (in print or online), find a list of countries ordered according to this statistic. Double-check the assertion given in the title. By comparison, where is the United States on the list? Now read the source text and, in groups, identify issues that will pose the greatest challenge in translation. Identify the domain, the level of language, and the target audience. Discuss the issues presented by the text and how you plan to go about solving each. You might try to identify *terms*, which are words used in a special way in a given field (more on this in Chapter 3). For example, *"mortalidad materna"* or *"indicadores"* may give you little margin for creative transfer if they are used in a specific way in this domain. A common trap is to mistake terms understood and expected by people in the field for ordinary language.

Brief: Translate the text that follows for a magazine on Spanish American social issues.

Guatemala: La mayor mortalidad infantil en Centroamérica
Por Celina Zubieta

GUATEMALA—Guatemala ocupa el primer lugar en América Central en mortalidad infantil, según el último informe del Fondo de las Naciones Unidas para la Infancia (UNICEF).

El documento de la agencia internacional establece que en promedio mueren en este país antes de los cinco años de edad 52 de cada mil niños nacidos, contra 16 de cada mil en Costa Rica, 34 en El Salvador, 44 en Honduras y 48 en Nicaragua.

En América Latina, Bolivia es la nación que presenta el peor índice (85 muertes de cada mil nacidos vivos), y en el mundo ese lugar lo ocupa Sierra Leona (316 por mil).

En lo que concierne a Guatemala, este indicador se suma a otros igualmente graves, como que es el país del istmo con mayor proporción de niños con bajo peso al nacer (15 por ciento del total) y mayor mortalidad materna.

La esperanza de vida al nacer es de 64 años, contra 78 en los países industrializados.

La tasa de mortalidad en los primeros cinco años de vida, en especial la infantil, es uno de los indicadores en salud más utilizados para identificar las condiciones de vida de una población.

El conflicto armado interno que vivió el país entre 1960 y 1996, que causó más de 200.000 víctimas, es una de las razones que explican el retraso de Guatemala en este tema.

Según el sociólogo Edelberto Torres-Rivas, 18 por ciento de las víctimas del conflicto armado interno son niños, que en su mayoría no recibieron la atención necesaria.

"Los niños se incorporaron a la guerra como soldados, hubo niños asesinados, pero lo más grave son los sobrevivientes de esa tragedia, hijos o familiares directos de las víctimas, huérfanos o parientes de desaparecidos," señaló.

Helen Mack, directora de la fundación que lleva el nombre de su hermana Myrna, una antropóloga asesinada por militares en 1990, afirmó que "las atrocidades cometidas durante la guerra aún las están cosechando los niños."

(*Source:* Reprinted by permission of Guillermo Rojas, Imagen Latinoamericana)

CHAPTER

3

Macrocontext: Skills, Tools, and Resources for "Connecting" Texts

TERMS, TERMINOLOGY, AND TERMINOLOGY MANAGEMENT

According to Translation, Training/education, and Testing (ttt.org)—CSL Framework, a **term** is "a designation of a defined concept in a special language by a linguistic expression" and "can consist of single words or be composed of multiword strings. The distinguishing characteristic of a term is that it is assigned to a single concept, as opposed to a phraseological unit, which combines more than one concept in a lexicalized fashion to express complex situations. *Quality assurance system* is a term, whereas *satisfy quality requirements* is a phraseological unit. . . ."

Following are some definitions:

terminology

1. The set of all the terms that are specific to a special subject field, a group of persons or a single individual.
2. The discipline whose object is the systematic study of the monolingual or multilingual designation of concepts pertaining to domains of human activity viewed in light of their social function as a response to the expressive needs of their users.

Note 1: Terminology studies is based on its own theoretical principles and consists primarily of the analysis of the concepts and concept structures used in a discipline, identifying the terms assigned to those concepts, recording terms on paper or in a database, managing terminology databases, and, when necessary, creating new terms.
Note 2: In terminology management, a distinction is made between ad hoc terminology management, which deals with a single term or limited number of terms, and systematic terminology management, which treats all the terms associated with a specific domain.

terminology management

Any deliberate manipulation of terminological information.
Note: Terminology management encompasses all activities involving terminology, e.g., term formation, language planning, term identification and extraction, definition writing, terminology research, terminology documentation, computer-assisted terminology management.

(*Source:* From "terminology", "terminology management". In Delisle, et al *Terminologie de la Traduction etc.*, 1999; p. 186. With kind permission by John Benjamins Publishing Company, Amsterdam/Philadelphia. www.benjamins.com)

OBJECT-CONCEPT-TERM

The "Object-Concept-Term" Triangle

> **Developer:** Approaches the triangle from the concept perspective and 'invents' the object that goes with it (software).
> **Children:** See an object and learn its name and function later, often by way of forming their own names first.
> **Adults** (esp. translators/localizers): Often see a term first and have to find out what object/concept is behind it.
>
> (*Source*: <http://www.notisnet.org/notis/archives/TermManagement.doc>, Accessed April 4, 2009)

Tasks

1. Your instructor will present to you, by turns, *objects*, *terms*, and *concepts* that you may or may not be familiar with (or which may be made up) from various domains. For each object, term, or concept, correlate the other two missing elements to complete the trio. (You may simply *draw* objects.)

   Model: atomizer (***term***)
   Student provides: "dispersal mechanism for perfume or medication" (***concept***)
              (*draws design on board*) (***object***)

2. In groups, find a single, coherent text that incorporates object, concept, and term. Color-code passages to demarcate each of the three as clearly as possible. What text type might work best for this?

TERMINOLOGY: THE MULTILINGUAL TERM BANK

The IATE (InterActive Terminology for Europe) is a term bank of over 5 million entries that is used by translators for the European Commission (EC) and others who work with their domains and official languages. The resource gives contexts for terms as well as references and notes.

Search the IATE lexicon (connect with your **Manual** Web site for a link) and provide a term in context for each given term. (Hint: Use "all fields" display.) There may be more than one possibility for each; for some, there is not. The context provided implies the term's context as well, not simply the text topic. You may need to double-check in monolingual dictionaries for some; if more than one term may be appropriate, rank in order.

en > es

Term = "interface." Text topic = welding. Es term = _____

    = "marketing." Text topic = e-commerce. Es term = _____

    = "joint." Text topic = human health. Es term = _____

    = "evolution." Text topic = Charles Darwin. Es term = _____

    = "management." Text topic = hurricane relief. Es term = _____

    = "cross-cultural." Text topic = international trade. Es term = _____

    = "ramp." Text topic = forestry. Es term = _____

    = "bay." Text topic = circuitry. Es term = _____

    = "set." Text topic = mining. Es term = _____

= "disc." Text topic = manufacture of dam values. Es term = _____

= "rotation." Text topic = soil replenishment. Es term = _____

= "regulator." Text topic = horology. Es term = _____

= "orient." Text topic = precious gems. Es term = _____

= "détente." Text topic = nuclear arms talks. Es term = _____

= "cam." Text topic = mechanical engineering. Es term = _____

es > en

Term = *alterado*. Text topic = viticulture and enology. En term = _____

= *elemento*. Text topic = statistics. En term = _____

= *giro*. Text topic = hydrography. En term = _____

= *viga*. Text topic = wine storage. En term = _____

= *paro*. Text topic = Wall Street. En term = _____

= *taco*. Text topic = lumberyards. En term = _____

= *polvo*. Text topic = celebrity rehab. En term = _____

= *cola*. Text topic = aerosol abuse. En term = _____

= *bala*. Text topic = papermaking. En term = _____

= *onda*. Text topic = glassblowing. En term = _____

= *medio*. Text topic = meatpacking. En term = _____

= *malla*. Text topic = deep-sea fishing. En term = _____

= *línea*. Text topic = Ebola virus. En term = _____

= *cuerpo*. Text topic = airplane engines. En term = _____

= *ala*. Text topic = steelworking. En term = _____

In which direction was it easier for you to work on these exercises?

Activity: Sport Terminology

Prepare the following text (read it through and gloss it) for 3 minutes. Without the aid of a dictionary, sight read the whole text, taking special care to render the terminology in bold as it is used in English by sportswriters, broadcasters, and fans.

29 Mayo 2005

Pedro domina a los Marlins

MLB.com—Aliviado de su dolor en la cadera, Pedro Martínez dominó a los Marlins de Florida. El dominicano lanzó pelota de cinco hits, durante ocho **entradas**, y **ponchó** a 10 **enemigos**, mientras que Cliff Floyd **conectó un doblete remolcador** para que los Mets de Nueva York vencieran el viernes por 1-0 a los Marlins de Florida.

"No es sólo por el clima, me siento saludable", dijo Martínez sobre las razones de su **buen desempeño**. "En realidad, lanzo siempre de la misma forma, dando todo lo que tengo. En este día sentí que tenía mucho poder, aunque no tanto control con **mis tres lanzamientos**".

Martínez (5-1) recibió una inyección de cortisona en su cadera dolorida, el 17 de mayo. **Su apertura** siguiente fue atrasada dos días.

Sin embargo, **el serpentinero** lució bajo una temperatura de 30 grados centígrados, en Florida.

Martínez ponchó a 10 oponentes o más por tercera ocasión en 10 aperturas durante esta temporada, y **no dio boletos**. Trabajó más de siete innings por segunda vez con Nueva York el 10 de abril, en Atlanta, lanzó un juego completo.

El dominicano tiene ahora 102 partidos con al menos 10 ponchetes. Se ubica cuarto en la historia de las grandes ligas, detrás de Nolan Ryan (215), Randy Johnson (204) y Roger Clemens (109).

"Por eso uno busca a alguien como Pedro: puede **anular** a una buena ofensiva", dijo Braden Looper, quien **resolvió a la perfección el noveno inning**, para su **undécimo salvamento**, completando la cuarta apertura de los Mets.

(*Source:* Reprinted by permission of Edwin Kako Vazquez, Escritor e historiador del béisbol. <http://www.1800beisbol.com/archives/beisbol-latino/>, Accessed June 8, 2005)

¿?

Did you know that whole sets of baseball cards have been issued in Spanish in the United States?

Activity: Terminology Gap

Three technology or business terms have been omitted from the following mission statement appearing on a tech company's Web site in Spanish.

First, consider what you know about mission statements. Find three or four examples on the Internet. What do they have in common? Who uses them, in what environment, and for what audience(s)? After inferring what they are and how they seek to accomplish certain business goals, draw up a list of guidelines for writing one. If you can, determine if they vary from culture to culture and language to language.

Go to PlazaConstructor.com's *catálogo de empresas* page and follow the menu. Find its mission statement. Use the following template to produce an English translation:

Our Mission:

We are a _____ company dedicated to the implementation of _____ with support from _____ technological resources, quality products, and highly qualified human resources.

Now edit, fixing any inaccuracies in the template as well. Come to a final version. Verify: Are any of your terms equally frequent or valid according to your research (including parallel texts, i.e., texts on the same topic used to harvest natural terms and phrases)? Prepare to discuss in class.

Finally, take your English term for "*[tecnología] de última generación*" and find at least two synonyms in Spanish for it. Can you come up with another acceptable English term? What is the Spanish for "mission statement"?

Write a mission statement of the ideal translation agency or bureau where you would like to work; translate it into Spanish.

COMPUTER-AIDED TRANSLATION (CAT)

Gain awareness of the translator's electronic toolbox as soon as possible and stay current with innovations. A good introduction at this level to CAT tools is Lynne Bowker's *Computer-Aided Translation Technology: A Practical Introduction* (2002). It covers the translator's need for technological literacy, data capture (scanning, optical character recognition [OCR]), corpora (which we will see in detail just ahead), terminology management systems, translation-memory systems, and emerging technologies. **Computer-assisted or -aided translation (CAT)** should be distinguished from **machine translation (MT)**, in the latter of which the computer, not the human translator, drafts the translation. (Amusingly, since the advent of MT, the term **human translation** has become necessary.) The term **translation environment (TEnT) tools** is becoming quite common now as well. In Appendix B (157–174) of Bowker's book, some key CAT tools are profiled along with questions a buyer might keep in mind for asking a vendor. Kenny (1999, 79) notes that "experience has shown that graduates who are conversant with CAT technology are at a real advantage when it comes to working in highly technologized translation environments such as the software industry and the organizations of the European Union" (Bowker 2002, 14). Translators, aided by CAT tools, now work along with companies to reduce time-to-market and facilitate "*simship*," or simultaneous shipment, of products worldwide (Bowker 2002, 13).

Dismissing technology is a luxury that translators cannot afford in the twenty-first century. We should, however, learn to use our tools critically and "surgically" so that we are efficiently served by them and are not simply using them for technology's sake.

Task

Familiarize yourself with Appendix B in Bowker (referenced earlier) and the online reviews of the tools. For each of the hypothetical tasks your instructor describes, assess which tool listed therein might be best suited.

TERMINOLOGY MANAGEMENT SYSTEMS (TMS)

Bowker (2002) notes that terminology management systems (TMS) can help with terminology tasks, including "storage, retrieval, and updating of term records. A TMS can help to ensure greater consistency in the use of terminology, which not only makes documentation easier to read and understand, but also prevents miscommunications. Effective terminology management can help to cut costs, improve linguistic quality, and reduce turnaround times for translation. . ." (77).

TMSs are searched with *wildcards* (e.g., the asterisk) or the more sophisticated *fuzzy matching* technique, which gives close results (a "hit list") for a search term, and *active terminology look-up*, which activates a comparison of the source text against the term base, and a relevant term record is displayed (79–81).

Task

1. Read Bowker's chapter (Chapter 4, p. 77) on terminology management. What do you think are the advantages of personal TMSs versus communal term banks (e.g., the

IATE)? What limitations? What innovations in storage and retrieval have been made in recent years?

2. What is term extraction? What approaches are there for term extraction? Do TMSs allow for shareability? How?

3. What is TM used for? What does *leveraging* text mean? How does TM *segmentation* work? What does *batch translation* mean?

TRANSLATION TIP

Study the comparative video reviews of translation environment tool vendors offered at the Translators Training Web site. Connect with your **Manual** Web site for a link.

LINGUISTIC NOTE

The translation source and target texts to be "chunked" or segmented for leveraging—reuse—in translation memory are called **legacy translation**. When a text such as a Web site is updated, TM can thus be used to identify changes more easily.

Discussion

1. Do you think MT and CAT pose a threat to translators' job security? From what you know about translation now, does it seem likely that the translator can be rendered obsolete? (Compare your answer to your reply to question 9 in "Thinking about Translation" in Chapter 1.) How do you think the translator's role will change as these tools evolve?

2. Earlier you were asked about repetitions in translation and how they should be charged. What role do repetition analysis modules now play in pricing translations (Bowker 2002, 121–2)? What is your personal feeling about being paid at full rates versus partial rates for fuzzy or exact matches? Do you think the proprietary controversy (who owns the database) has a clear-cut answer?

3. To what does the phrase *translator's workbench* refer?

4. Find an online demonstration or license one of the packages on offer in Bowker's Appendix B or a similar product. Take turns in groups trying out its features until you understand, not only conceptually but experientially—from hands-on trials—the rudiments of how these tools can help you.

5. Research the purpose of text alignment programs at what functions they can accomplish for the reuse of previous translations (translation segments).

6. Survey translation forums for discussions of *voice recognition software*. At this state of development, what do the current pros and cons of this tool for the translator seem to be?

7. How do you account for differences in terminology between different governmental bodies? For example, the Homeland Security Advisory System measures terrorist threat levels in a color-coded scale: severe (V), high (IV), elevated (III), guarded (II), and low (I). Find reliable versions in Spanish. Is there terminological consistency between Federal Emergency Management Agency (FEMA), Federal Communications

Commission (FCC), and other (including local) agencies? If not, think of ways to expedite standardization and discuss why it matters, particularly where texts are long or not contemporary with one another.

8. Find out about interagency initiatives among Web managers to build and manage multilingual Web sites; for example, the Federal Multilingual Websites Committee.

9. What advantages and disadvantages do you suppose real time translation for instant messaging chat and discussion forums has? What is a *translation bot*?

10. Connect with your **Manual** Web site and go to one of Google's translation FAQ pages. What limitations or potential problems do you see with Google's automatic translation? What kind of interactivity with users does their system provide, and what issues do you think that presents? What issues appear in Google Translate discussion group archives?

TRANSLATION TEASER

Connect with your **Manual** Web site and go to "Google in Your Language - translation style guide." Read the discussion on the "I'm Feeling Lucky" function. Work out a group translation en>es for the phrase, then follow up online and compare to any of the Spanish-language home pages (search Google+[country name in Spanish]). How does yours compare?

LINGUISTIC NOTE

Controlled Authoring

A term you ought to be familiar with is **controlled authoring**. This means constraining terminology, grammar, and syntax to prepare a text for machine translation, a process that may involve modularization, standardization, simplification, or reduction. The practice is more cost efficient and allows for text reuse (Helbich 2006, 3–4). What kinds of texts do you think are often re-used?

LOCALIZATION TOOLS AND SERVICES: ADS FROM "THE BUYER'S GUIDE," *MULTILINGUAL* MAGAZINE

Localization is the "hottest" area in the industry today. The following are ads for localization tools and services from *MultiLingual*, a monthly magazine that tracks trends in such areas as knowledge management, information retrieval, and product development.

1. Research and define "localization" (note the British spelling: "localisation") in your own words.

2. Take notes on what you find here regarding what localization offers the client. In other words, *what will localization help the client to do?* What can you infer about what clients value in terms of *how* these services are provided (i.e., what value-added qualities from the vendor are touted)?

In class, brainstorm as a group on the chalkboard (whiteboard, SmartBoard, or overhead) what is on offer and what clients can do with the vendors' help.

HINT   For a fuller understanding, see also the Web sites of the following companies: Trados®, Moravia Worldwide, TexTrans®, SDLX™, CPSL Worldwide, and adaQuest.

iDISC Information Technologies

Languages Spanish (all variants), Catalan, Basque, Galician *Description* iDISC, established in 1987, is a privately-held translation company based in Barcelona that focuses on localization into all variants of Spanish (European, Latin American, USA and Neutral) and the other languages spoken in Spain (Catalan, Basque and Galician). Services range from translation and localization to engineering, testing, DTP and consulting. Specialization fields are software localization, technical and telecom documentation, ERP, automotive and related marketing material. We have all commercially available tools and experience using many different proprietary customer platforms and solutions; internal workflow portal-based tools to reduce management costs and increase quality, consistency and on-time deliveries; and continuous support to the client PMs and process optimization to achieve the best project results and establish long-term honest partnerships.

iDISC Information Technologies Passeig del progrés 96, 08640 Olesa de Montserrat, Barcelona, Spain, 34-93-778-73-00, Fax: 34-93-778-35-80, E-mail: info@idisc.es, Web: www.idisc.es

(*Source*: Reprinted by permission of iDisc Information Technologies S.L.)

Lingo Systems, Translation & Localization

Languages 100+ *Description* Lingo Systems, powered by Language Line Services, provides customer-focused sole-source solutions for global companies in 170+ languages. We specialize in the translation and localization of technical documentation, software, multimedia applications, training materials, e-learning solutions and online applications. Other globalization services include quality assurance testing (hardware and software), integration of content management solutions, interpretation (170+ languages), cultural training and assessment, and internationalization consulting. Lingo Systems has never caused a late release. No other firm makes this claim. For a free copy of our award-winning book, *The Guide to Translation and Localization — Communicating with the Global Marketplace*, visit www.lingosys.com or call 800-878-8523.

Lingo Systems 15115 SW Sequoia Parkway, Suite 200, Portland, OR 97224, 503-419-4856, 800-878-8523, Fax: 503-419-4873, E-mail: info@lingosys.com, Web: www.lingosys.com See ad on page 7

(*Source*: Reprinted by permission of Lingo Systems, © 2008)

SDL International – E-nabling Global Business
Multiple Platforms

Languages All European, Scandinavian, Latin American and Asian *Description* SDL International is a leading provider of globalization solutions comprising localization, translation services and development of multilingual management applications. SDL combines state-of-the-art technology and a full range of in-house translation and engineering services to serve clients in a variety of industries, including e-commerce, enterprise resource planning and telecommunications. SDL is also a premier developer of language technology tools such as SDLWorkflow and SDLX Translation Suite. SDLWorkflow is the leading tool for enabling global business on-line, offering highly efficient multilingual content management of international Web sites, reducing work volumes and, therefore, your time-to-market. With offices worldwide, SDL is your complete globalization solution.

SDL International 5700 Granite Parkway, Suite 410, Plano, TX 75024, 877-735-5106, 214-387-8500, Fax: 214-387-9120, E-mail: info@sdl.com, Web: www.sdl.com See ads on pages 2-3, 68

(*Source*: Reprinted by permission of SDL International)

PTIGLOBAL
Windows, Macintosh, UNIX and WinCE

Languages All commercial languages for Europe, Asia and the Americas *Description* PTIGlobal is a quality localization company backed by twenty-five years of experience in the technical translation field. PTIGlobal provides turnkey localization services for software, Web-based applications, e-commerce sites, enterprise solutions and edutainment and games. All projects are customized to fit client needs; utilizing implements from our bottomless toolbox: end-to-end project management; internationalization consultation; glossary development; native-language technical translation; multilingual Web content management; translation memory expertise; localization engineering; linguistic, functionality and thrid-party testing; high-end desktop publishing; graphics; and complete video and audio services. PTIGlobal is committed to developing ongoing, long-term partnerships with our clients. This means a dedication to personal service, high-quality work and sensitivity to our clients' cost goals and timelines.

PTIGlobal 9900 SW Wilshire, Suite 280, Portland, OR 97225, 888-357-3125, Fax: 503-297-0655. E-mail: info@ptiglobal.com, Web: www.ptiglobal.com

(*Source*: Reprinted by permission of PTI Global)

CASE STUDY: TERMINOLOGY

Translators rely on much more than dictionaries, however extensive or up to date. By now you are aware of consultants (experts or practitioners in the field under investigation), special lexicons, shareable glossaries and hyperglossaries, multilingual corpora, discussion lists and newsgroups, and other points of access to "socialization," as some theorists call professional networking behavior in which translators engage to complete tasks. It may be useful to show you an example of the way a professional might go about solving a terminological gap; we are stressing *process* here, though you, the student, should focus too on ultimately finding a viable solution.

Suppose you are translating the next excerpt, which is from a coroner's report written in Mexico in 1991.* The register is high: doctor to doctor, with all the attendant technical vocabulary, because it will be read by doctors and lawyers during a criminal case. Pay close attention to textual clues that might help you find a valid translation for *arma blanca* (in bold):

Examen Externo

1. Una herida incisa de arma de fuego en la región torácica.
2. Dos heridas incisas de arma de fuego en la bóveda craneal.
3. Una herida punzante de **arma blanca** situada en la región abdominal.
4. Una herida de 30 cm. de longitud en la región cefálica de bordes irregulares, observando salida de material encefálico, sangrado abundante.
5. Contusión aguda en región cefálica caracterizado por edema y hematoma circunscrito.

The professional translator's mind likely is already working more or less as follows on this information: using logic and background knowledge (the so-called *schema*), he or she is comparing different types of wounds—clearly *incisa* and *punzante* refer to how the skin is broken (with what kind of instrument); considering roots (*cephal* = head) cognates for "encephalic" (brain matter? encephalic material/area?) and terms for *bóveda craneal* (craneal vault? cranium? calvarium? skull?), the issue of conversions (centimeters to inches?) if necessary; and debating "thoracic area" versus "chest area." The translator may make an almost-unconscious mental note to avoid the trap of *longitud* (not "longitude" but "length"). As for the *arma blanca*, this is, he or she reasons, a class of weapons, likely one that does not shoot or bludgeon, because the wound is *punzante*. Now is the time to find "the bigger picture"—for example, accessing Chapter 4 of *Forensic Science: An Introduction to Scientific and Investigative Techniques* (James and Nordby 2003), which classifies causes and manners of death; or, one can search .edu sites for lecture summaries on types of injuries in forensic science.

Now the translator has a better idea of violent deaths and their classifications. In the process, the vocabulary "rough edges" (a type of "blunt force" trauma) catches the translator's attention; he or she makes a note that *bordes irregulares* under item 4 in the source text may be the corresponding phrase. (This detail is inserted to show how translators often learn what they need serendipitously and unsequentially.) The translator spends a moment trying to correlate a seemingly similar term in Spanish—*cortopunzante*—with the term in question. Is the translator now any closer? Perhaps not much though the chart is filed away both in hard copy and electronically for future reference. No research is "wasted"!

---

*Reprinted in Holly Mikkelson, *The Interpreter's Edge* (Santa Barbara, CA: ACEBO, 1995), 3–55.

Quickly the translator makes an attempt to solve for x with new knowledge—could *armas blancas* refer to knives in general? This is immediately discarded as too narrow—other implements besides knives can puncture. Notice this very typical operation in the translator's mind: "Is x a subset of y (a wider term) or is y a subset of x (a narrower term)?" (The conceptual grids of hyperonymy and hyponymy later in this chapter will help you focus on this useful step.) So "bladed instruments"? "Penetrating implements"? These ruminations yielding little, the translator tries another print source (here, Orellana's *Glosario internacional del traductor*), which offers "cutting and thrusting weapons" and "cold steel." (Test your filtering skills: Why are these options hopelessly out of place here? Remember, dictionaries often only give *some potential meanings*.) Undaunted, the translator turns to LANTRA-L, in whose archives (February 10, 2000) the following conversation is found:

> "*>>Also, does anyone know how to translate "armas blancas"? I found "cold steel" but this sounds a little weird to my ears.*
> *[...]*
> *>As it did to me some years ago. The correct term seems to be "edged weapons".*

The conversation continues, and the suggestion is made that blunt instrument is used for nonpiercing implements; for piercing implements, the interlocutors felt it should be a "(sharp) edged weapon/instrument."

Much closer! Or not? Your assignment for class next session is to check up on the information discussed in the preceding transcript excerpt. Try different alternatives and recombinations to see if another term might not be even better. See if the term has come up or is included in a shareable glossary. Remember, we may not have the exact category in our legal system, in which case you have to compromise and follow precedent; that is, use a term that will be understood by your audience and that is appropriate for this text's translation brief (e.g., producing a coroner's report admissible in the U.S. system of jurisprudence). Are there any transculturations that were considered during your process? What do your consultants (perhaps professors of criminal justice) say? Prepare to discuss your search. Provide parallel texts.

TRANSLATION TIP

Terminology Management

Best practice calls for managing your terminology in a text up front, rather than during the translation, when your focus will be on sentence level and intersentential meaning, stylistics, coherence, and the other usual preoccupations.

ISO STANDARDS

ISO stands for International Organization for Standardization. ISO standards, which originally applied to the manufacturing industry, have to do with quality assurance and quality management principles, which from the client's point of view means a reasonable expectation of reliable process controls and compliance with both client and user benchmarks for translation services. Here are some examples of ISO standards negotiated in the 1990s:

ISO 10241:1992 (1992).

International terminology standards - Preparation and layout ISO 10241:1992.

International Organization for Standardization (ISO), Genéva.

ISO 1087:1990 (1990).

Terminology-Vocabulary ISO 1087:1990.

International Organization for Standardization (ISO), Genéva.

ISO 12200 (1998).

Computer applications in terminology - Machine-readable terminology interchange format (MARTIF)–Negotiated interchange ISO/DIS 12200.

International Organization for Standardization (ISO), Genéva.

ISO 12618:1994 (1994).

Computational aids in terminology–Creation and use of terminological databases and text corpora ISO/TR 12618:1994.

International Organization for Standardization (ISO), Genéva.

ISO 12620 (1998).

Computer applications in terminology–Data categories ISO/DIS 12620.

International Organization for Standardization (ISO), Genéva.

ISO 1951:1997 (1997).

Lexicographical symbols and typographical conventions for use in terminography ISO 1951:1997.

International Organization for Standardization (ISO), Genéva.

(*Source:* © ISO Central Secretariat (www.iso.org). Copyright remains with ISO.)

Research

1. Find out more about ISO standards (pronounced "isostandards")? (Connect with your **Manual** Web site and go to the International Organization for Standardization Web site.) Who recognizes these standards? Why are they important to quality? How are they determined? What does the adjectival phrase "ISO compatible" mean? Compare other standards (e.g., ASTM).
2. What is ISO 9001:2000 certification (or registration)? What is its relevance to translation? How does one attain certification? Who seeks this certification—individuals, organizations?
3. How may ISO standards be integrated into a translator's terminology research?

TRANSLATION TIPS

Frequently Asked Questions

"Should the same word be translated the same way every time?"

A short answer: if it's terminology, *yes*; if it's not, *it depends*. "Elegant variation" and other questions of style may condition consistency, as do shifts of context. For terms, the same word should be rendered consistently; CAT tools are increasingly used to store "translation memories"

(Continued)

that help ensure consistency and save labor. One industry specialist notes that text developers need to be consistent also: "Product development calls it a gadget, marketing describes it as a widget. Every company has its specialist concepts and terms, but not enough manage this corporate terminology centrally. As a result, authors waste time looking for the right word, and translators multiply the problem by translating terms in different ways. The quality of communications is significantly impacted by poor terminological control, as the inconsistencies that result can erode brand image and brand values and confuse customers." (Lawlor n.d.)

"What if my author made a mistake in terminology or of fact?"

There are options. Minimally, notify the client or author diplomatically. Some schools of thought argue that the translator's responsibility is to the text; however, this philosophy can work against communicability. Moreover, the use of "[sic]" ("thus" in Latin, used to note an author's error) can reflect poorly on the source text and source author.

"As a translator, can I coin words or phrases?"

If there is no equivalent, yes, as a last resort. If the source text uses neologisms, you have a wider berth, however, and in literary texts, accomplished coinages and "strange" turns of phrase can elevate a translation from serviceable wordsmithing to the realm of art. Some translators even strive for this "strangeness." Many, however, strive for the effect of rendering a text as if it were originally written in the target language.

"Do agencies ever give translators term bank, word lists, or 'in-house' terminology in advance of certain jobs, so the translators don't have to find out after the fact what is used?"

Yes. Ask.

COLLOCATIONS*

Also called recurrent combinations or fixed combinations, **collocations** are predictable co-occurrences of words in a given language. They are not rule bound but made conventional by usage. It is important for the translator to remember that *synonyms do not collocate identically*—for example, "happy medium" is not substitutable by "glad medium." And, naturally, collocations do not line up unproblematically across languages.

Grammatical Collocations

Phrases accepted as natural by general speakers of the language. Note that the following phrases marked with an asterisk are considered substandard.

Types:

Noun + preposition (e.g., influence on; vs. *influence at)

Noun + to + infinitive (e.g., an attempt to; vs. *an attempt for)

Nouns + that clauses (e.g., We reached an agreement that would be binding.)

Preposition + noun (e.g., in dismay; by land or by sea; at loggerheads; on drugs)

Predicate adjectives + to + infinitive (e.g., It was necessary to buy this car.)

Adjective + that clause (e.g., She was afraid that everyone knew her secret.)

various verb patterns

Source: BBI Dictionary of English Word Combinations. This book updates the older *BBI Combinatory Dictionary of English* (Amsterdam; Philadelphia: John Benjamins, 1986). Rodale's *Word Finder* is one of the oldest combinatory dictionaries; it is more complete than the BBI but older and harder to find. –Author's note.

Lexical Collocations

Phrases featuring the co-occurrence of elements not including prepositions, infinitives, or clauses.

> **Types:**
>
> Verb of creation + noun/pronoun (e.g., make an impression; reach a verdict)
>
> Verb of eradication + noun (e.g., reject an appeal; wreak havoc; annul a marriage; rescind an offer)
>
> Adjective + noun (e.g., mighty river; vs. *sturdy river; veiled threat; vs. *secret threat)
>
> Noun + verb (e.g., blood circulates; bombs go off; the cookie crumbles; day breaks)
>
> Units associated with a noun (e.g., herd of buffalo; pack of wolves; deck of cards)
>
> Adverb + adjective (e.g., highly suspect; strictly confidential; widely quoted)
>
> Verb + adverb (e.g., argue heatedly; humbly accept; bitterly deny)

NEGATIVE PROSODY, COLLOCATIONS, AND CORPORA

Collocations are identified and analyzed these days with the use of *corpora* (the plural of the word "corpus," the Latin for "body"). **Corpora** are electronic bodies of linguistic data—texts—that linguists extract (isolate from their larger texts) and concordance (align by keyword) to generate natural language samples for term, phrase, or syntax modeling. Corpora can help translators empirically verify their intuitions about sense, connotation, and near-synonymy; show patterns of actual frequencies or potential language use; reveal the lexical density of a text (particularly in translation research); identify semantic prosodies (connotations) and semantic preferences (the "clustering" of words around certain poles of meaning); and assist in overcoming imperfect overlap in collocational ranges across languages. Hatim and Munday (2004) map corpora in translation use as an interface with the language engineering discipline. Customized corpora may be generated with leaseable software, whereas "found" corpora—some in the multimillions of words—are available on Web-based concordancing sites.

    Comparable corpora are two monolingual originals in the language pair; **parallel corpora** are originals and their translations. **Concordancers** allow for "querying" or "interrogating" (searching) corpora to find patterns of phrasing, terminology, and cultural differences. Connect with your **Manual** Web site to find a link and have a look at the Collins Cobuild Corpus Concordance tutorial. Corpora such as this one even allow searches for syntactic collocations, known as **colligations**.

    Many words overwhelmingly collocate with negative or positive experiences. For example: If you saw the verb "wreak," you would naturally collocate it with something destructive. But some apparently innocuous words behave the same way. Take "cause," for instance—most nouns associated with it are negative (death, accidents, etc.). The term "negative prosody" is used to describe the gravitation of a word beyond fixed collocates toward whole attitudes and semantic classes.* How the negative prosody of words remaps across languages remains to be fully studied.

> [Corpus-aided discovery learning] has an important consciousness-raising function, as learners are sensitized to the existence of such phenomena as

---

*Mike Rundell, "If Only They'd Asked a Linguist," *Humanising Language Teaching* 4, no. 4 (July 2002). The example given is from this source.

collocational restrictions and semantic prosodies . . . and become increasingly skilled at 'seeing through language' (Carter 1993), at recognizing the intentions and strategies behind a text by setting it against the backdrop of the culture of which it is a product. (Bernardini, *Translation in Undergraduate Degree Programmes*, 2004)

The methodology involved in making corpora and extracting terminology should be part of the teaching curriculum—not an optional extra—particularly given the pressure on translators to use computer-assisted tools. (Maia 2003)

Using Corpora in the Translation Process

Here's a concrete example of how corpora can be used profitably in the translation process. Suppose the phrase *"resabio gótico"* [lit. "Gothic aftertaste," describing a carryover or remnant defect in artistic perspective] comes up in a workshop text on architecture. Modulating with other metaphors ("hangover"?) having failed, one may try the modifier "lingering" with "Gothicism" to shift the suggestion of *negativity* to the target language (TL) adjective. We can then test that instinct in the Cobuild demo by querying with "lingering" in the concordance sampler part. Connect with your **Manual** Web site for a link. This gives us the following "concs":

[Terminology: **KWIC**: keyword-in-context (in this case, "lingering"); **Co-text**: words *around* the KWIC, in **fields** (lines) of variable, predetermined length; **collocate**: a word that occurs 4 words [= the "**span**"] to the left or right of keyword or node]

Concordance A: "lingering":

by an international group of doctors on the **lingering** effects of radiation from nuclear weapons

of thing is usually polished off with a long, **lingering** kiss." She felt soft and warm in his arms

1630 in 1979. Be that as it may, and as this **lingering** interest in Latin America can be described

will say, his voice still carrying the **lingering** traces of a Norfolk accent, 'although I'd

remain hidden. One image plagued her mind, **lingering** in its shadows, refusing to step into the

inflexible personality, for example, or the **lingering** effects of childhood abuse or trauma

the meeting,' Marlette said, breaking the **lingering** silence. 'It would certainly explain why he

all that mattered to her. Quickly pushing any **lingering** doubts from her mind, she reached for a

disease, whatever it is, will be sufficiently **lingering** to enable me to complete my book [p] In a

works onto the table on time the prospect of **lingering** in the kitchen in 1996 no longer appeals,

Ernest Hemingway and tseliot insufficiently **lingering** side-glances, I should say; after all, if

party's political fortunes." He said that any **lingering** Bank concerns on inflation that may be

suspect the decision will kill off **lingering** hopes that a new multi-million-pound opera

of ripe, juicy damson fruit, with a long, **lingering** taste. Waitrose Irish Whiskey [p] Waitrose

when the first pitch was delayed because of a **lingering** players' strike that reduced fixture lists

falls asleep. [p] And if there are still any **lingering** doubts he will tell them to dwell on this

happier days. [p] Ma Bates has a deep and **lingering** desire for a home of her own and so she

been calls from couples who remember that **lingering** kiss at Arnos Grove, or want a memento of

with a passionate kiss. [p] But Melanie's **lingering** glance as she disappeared through passport

of year, and there's plenty of wildlife still **lingering** in the valleys before moving to the high

to Tirpitzian principles. Resolution of these **lingering** difficulties, however, would have to await

If the horrors of modern combat permitted any **lingering** romance about the art of war, it could be

up and gave him a warm kiss on the mouth, a **lingering** peck, slow and careful, her leg brushing

adventure, and it quickly dispelled any **lingering** doubts Gerard may have had about Truffaut's

(*Source:* Material from the Bank of English® reproduced with the kind permission of HarperCollins Publishers Ltd. Bank of English® is a registered trademarks of HarperCollins Publishers Ltd.)

Interpreting Concordance A: A practiced eye can determine in under 10 seconds that "lingering" collocates in *negative, positive, and neutral* environments, with a predominance of erotic contexts. Making the same determination would take at least three to five times longer in Google. So our solution is not the best, and we propose another.

Connotations: Is "ambition" as negative as *la ambición*? Corpora can help sort out the potentially differing connotations of cognates. One can also test collocations for negative prosody via the scientific method. Someone in class might defend collocating **"impending wedding"** in a given environment. To test for the perceived negativity ("negative prosody")—desired or not—of "impending" here, we would query Collins Wordbanks Online English Corpus (56 million words) in the section "Collocation Sampler" (T-Scores). Connect with your **Manual** Web site for a link. The results give us:

[Terminology: **Joint frequency**: number of times in the corpora the words appear within the span; **a T-score** assigns weight to the evidence of nonrandom association between these two words—a higher score shows a more certain relationship]

TABLE 1: "impending"

Collocate	Corpus	Freq Joint	Freq Significance
of	1100578	121	7.348786
an	136157	38	5.358373
the	2313407	126	3.703965
about	106379	16	3.029479
resignation	1142	9	2.986108
death	9137	8	2.710540
rumours	636	7	2.636979
loss	4025	7	2.590234
crisis	4121	7	2.588910
his	184325	17	2.491674
doom	210	6	2.446361
arrival	1442	6	2.428007
sign	4143	6	2.387767
mrs	9793	6	2.303592
news	12021	6	2.270399
rumors	165	5	2.233375
storm	1476	5	2.211979
sense	9766	5	2.076685
or	156128	13	2.025328
disaster	1536	4	1.971973

(Continued)

TABLE 1: (continued)

Collocate	Corpus	Freq Joint	Freq Significance
proved	2422	4	1.955807
thatcher	3216	4	1.941319
marriage	3468	4	1.936721
announced	4298	4	1.921577
attack	6058	4	1.889463
visit	6716	4	1.877457
her	111700	10	1.873250
deal	8791	4	1.839595
move	9419	4	1.828136
when	102483	9	1.753364
avert	146	3	1.728975
disasters	281	3	1.726130
shortages	335	3	1.724993
separation	633	3	1.718714
divorce	1453	3	1.701437
any	50225	6	1.701228
somewhat	1757	3	1.695032
fears	1979	3	1.690355

(*Source:* Material from the Bank of English® reproduced with the kind permission of HarperCollins Publishers Ltd. Bank of English® is a registered trademarks of HarperCollins Publishers Ltd.)

Interpreting Table 1: Let us now ask about **clustering**: How do the majority of high-hit collocates tend to cluster? (*Negatively, positively, neutrally?*) In this case, **resignation, rumours, death, loss, doom, storm, disaster** all *cluster negatively* and are more frequent than "marriage." Conclusion: *An undercurrent of negativity to the tested collocation can be inferred. [The collocation is "correct," but the likelihood is high that a native speaker will ask, "'Impending' wedding? That sounds disastrous."]* Advantages of corpora for this type of task over *BBI* and the Internet: words sorted by frequency; ease of comparability; higher relevance of data.

Corpora Exercises

1. Try an online search of your own: for the keyword "so-called," determine prosody.
2. a. Connect with your **Manual** Web site for a link; select all text and copy (up to 4,000 words): Charter of the United Nations.
   b. Now concordance it.

   c. Discuss output with your partner. What preliminary determinations can you make about the text?
3. Connect with your **Manual** Web site to explore these links and discuss what usefulness they may have for translation:
   a. *Sketch engine site; synonym collocational comparison (lemma 1, lemma 2) (registration required).*
   Note the multiple-lexeme comparison feature of the sketch engine.

b. Just the Word site (Search, for example, the word "death.")
c. Parallel corpora (translation corpora)/subcorpora: corpora as bilingual super dictionaries; for example, OPUS>Europarl (proceedings—download Spanish/English).
d. TranSearch (bitext aligned/password protected).
e. Real Academia Española: Banco de datos (CORDE) [en línea].
f. *Intratexts, digital libraries, and hypertextualized works;* for example, Intratext

Word lists and **word frequency lists** are also a good tool. They are useful for:

Forming "schema" of text content (for prereading)
Gaining awareness of types/tokens (ratio of different words to total words)
Determining usage by experts
Knowing conventions of a given domain (redundancy tolerance)
Surveying lexical density (richness)
Dictionary making

4. Connect with your **Manual** Web site to find a link to create concordances out of the Web itself or to generate wordlists.

Activity: Editing with Corpora

Edit the following flawed, hypothetical target text (TT) passage from a general interest news magazine (also hypothetical) using the corpora you have been shown. Use the most fitting, unmarked (familiar) collocations in each instance. Document and prepare to defend your findings (8- to 10-minute activity; groups of two):

"The deteriorated environment in the U.S. today was an unpredicted by-product of capitalism; technological advancements may be a strongly affirmative endorsement for the open market, but they can play havoc to Mother Earth."

Did you know . . . you already use corpora? Google™ is a corpus (in a manner of speaking) of a few dozen trillion words.

Collocation Activities

1. Produce all the collocations you can for the following words (try not to use idioms, which often are not included as collocations; clichés are fine). Run "frequency checks" online or use the *BBI* (or Rodale's *Word Finder*).
   Model: love (unrequited love, true love, puppy love, everlasting love, crazy love, undying love, forbidden love, love potion, love nest, love hangover, love note)

1. death	2. hand	3. matter	4. play (v.)
5. echar	6. cuento	7. mal/-o(s)/-a(s)	

2. Match each adjective with a noun with which it most typically collocates. Each should be used once.

1. evil	**a.** pig
2. confirmed	**b.** lunatic
3. guilty	**c.** liberal
4. cruel	**d.** zombie
5. knee-jerk	**e.** warlord
6. ambulance-chasing	**f.** bacteria
7. flesh-eating	**g.** lawyer
8. undead	**h.** idiot
9. incurable	**i.** robot
10. killer	**j.** bachelor
11. blithering	**k.** romantic
12. bleeding-heart	**l.** element
13. soulless	**m.** professor
14. absent-minded	**n.** reactionary
15. old	**o.** monster
16. raving	**p.** taskmaster
17. capitalist	**q.** party
18. unsavory	**r.** liar

3. Read the product label that follows. The legal language lends itself to familiar collocations in English. First, consider the product: a soft drink made in Mexico—"Jarritos"—whose very name evokes a cultural context—serving beverages from an earthenware jug. Notice the bilingual label ("Tamarind/Tamarindo")—why do you think it is produced that way? Who is/are the audience/s? Notice the bold lettering on the back panel: "For complete official rules in English . . .", the only English used on the back. Is the Spanish source text targeted for the Latin American or Spanish market or for the U.S. Latino market? Give evidence to support your answer.

What kind of game is a *sorteo* here? (contest? giveaway? promotion? sweepstakes? drawing? raffle? etc.) Does the "*Destapa tu suerte*" feature give you a clue? What kind of tops does this product use (the text says "*corcholatas*")—are they pull-tabs, twist-offs? Can you think of a name for "*Destapa tu suerte*" (careful with the collocation)? What month is 31/5/01? What is a "*sobre tipo número 10*"? If you don't know, what is your hunch? Where can you look to follow up on this?

Now try to think of these "fine print" phrases we commonly use in English then read the "Notes" that follow:

No se requiere compra   *Premios que no se reclamen*
premios instantáneos   *Juego disponible sólo para residentes*
un sobre previamente estampillado   *agencias de publicidad*
deberá ser sellado   *El sorteo se anula*
límite de una solicitud por sobre   *o donde la ley lo prohiba*

NOTES Notice the word "*solicitud*"—did you avoid the trap of "application"? "*Publicidad*" is semifalse here. Go back to the phrase "*previamente estampillado*": did you think to omit "*previamente*"?—there is a way to imply "previously stamped" without saying it. There is also a common abbreviation for the phrase in English—did you think of it? In the phrase "*deberá ser sellado*," the word "*sellado*" is used in a way probably unfamiliar to you, but context should give you the idea. (Hint: It does not refer so much to an action by the sender as to an action by the office sending it.)

Source: Label image provided with the approval and cooperation of Tipp Enterprises, L.P. dba Novamex and Jarritos, Inc.

4. Examine this sentence for collocations, marked and unmarked. Identify all that you can. Test word strings of different lengths.

> Eager souls, mystics and revolutionaries, may propose to refashion the world in accordance with their dreams; but evil remains, and so long as it lurks in the secret places of the heart, utopia is only the shadow of a dream.
> (Lionel Trilling 1950, 5)

Task

Now compare the findings to a similar search on the Cobuild corpus. Discuss. Tentative conclusions: Even fairly high-frequency collocates can sound marked (infrequent, literary); recombinations of collocations in actual usage can "bury" them beyond immediate recognition. Individual languages may be said to differ along collocational lines—no translation may realistically be attained that could replicate the frequencies of these strings in just the same way (*lugares secretos* has 47,800 hits, but *lugares secretos del corazón* only 18), nor would the degree of marked to unmarked remain in equilibrium. Corollary for the translator: Check and recheck collocations as a routine part of your self-editing, particularly in domains with which you are less familiar.

TRANSLATION TRAP

Marked and Unmarked Collocations

Take care that you don't reject a collocation as marked (an extension of conventional usage) or as a miscollocation simply because it is unfamiliar to you. Research thoroughly to determine whether a phrase is in currency.

Try an experiment with the following collocations from various domains; circle those you guess are marked or nonexistent:

(Continued)

nondenominational church	directly earthed	halcyon days
embarrassment of riches	saw arbor	box-office poison
unmitigated gall	planetary gears	complete and udder
flash point	modem interface	due and payable
tax-loss carryback	to fire weld	well and truly
open repo	diamond bit	agitate the bottle
subvention grant	to incur liability	indemnify and hold guiltless
preparedness plan	cash holdings	light, sweet crude
war neurosis	risk tolerance	liens, claims, charges,
blood-aqueous barrier	hamhock legislation	and encumbrances
occasional verse	market fluctuations	Brahmin cow
country doctor	loan translation	suicide by cop
unshriven sin	dry farming	shucking onward
unholy thirst	foregone occlusion	whited sepulcher
full court press	front-end cost	victimless leather
plumb bob	to discharge an obligation	soylent green
revenue stream	death tax	madcap hijinks
fair dinkum	comfort food	many-splendored thing
flagrant misuse	motion to vacate	subvert the dominant paradigm

TRANSLATION TEASER

Collocational Clash: The Unrelenting Soup Prize for Worst Collocation

Come up with a short list of the most outrageously bad collocations you can. Share the worst with the class.

LINGUISTIC NOTE

TAPs

Think-Aloud Protocols (TAPs) are studies in which a translator, whether expert or novice, verbalizes and records his or her decision making during a translation task as it happens. Researchers believe that the informants' thought processes can be captured in this way, providing insight into the "black box" of translation methods.

LINGUISTIC NOTE

THE CASE OF –ISMO

We have just seen some instances of words ending in –ismo contextualized in the last activity. Now let's consider this class of words separately. The Spanish suffix –ismo is used differently, and more broadly, than the English –ism. Note the following examples:

influyentismo	*nerviosismo*	*liderismo*
fisiculturismo	*apatismo*	*golpismo*

(Continued)

olimpismo	*popularismo*	*entreguismo*
ciclismo	*cultismo*	*facilismo*
hipismo	*noventaiochismo*	*pactismo*
iatismo	*abandonismo*	*torredemarfilismo*
machismo	*islamismo*	*americanismo*
marianismo	*resistencialismo*	*violentismo*
leísmo	*arcaismo*	*amiguismo*
loísmo	*oficinismo*	*integrismo*
cristianismo	*perdonismo*	*zapatismo*
barbarismo	*abstencionismo*	*intermediarismo*
cafeinismo	*tabaquismo*	*enchufismo*
virtuosismo	*idiotismo*	*ignorantismo*

1. What classes of meaning are covered by *–ismo* words vs. –ism words? Is there a class that correlates perfectly es<>en? Is there a single semantic prosody to all *–ismo* words? Do any depend on knowledge of political or cultural realities? (Consider also *arielismo, gorilismo, foquismo.*) Can *–ismo* words be pluralized?
2. Clearly, the morpheme *–ismo* will signify differently based on text type and communicative situation. Give examples of strategies you would use for some of the preceding specific cases, positing contexts for each. In what cases, if any, would you need to explicate?
3. Find more examples of *–ismo* words and discuss how they might be translated in different linguistic environments.
4. Give an example of how contexts might lead to the same *–ismo* word to be translated in different ways.
5. A recent English-language book by the University of Texas Press is titled *Cinemachismo*, a neologism. Which do you think is more amenable to coinages with –ism / *-ismo*, English or Spanish? Discuss. Are there equivalents for ageism, lookism, and so on in Spanish? If not, are they theoretically possible, or is there precedent? Find the limits of neologism in English by testing some of your own invention.
6. Determine three plausible translations for the word *familismo*, distinguished by three distinct contexts (text types or audiences).

SYNONYMY, HYPERONYMY (SUPERORDINATION), AND HYPONYMY (SUBORDINATION)

'*Un*important, of course, I meant,' the King hastily said, and went on to himself in an undertone, 'important—unimportant— unimportant—important—' as if he were trying which word sounded best.

Alice in Wonderland, XII

Technically, **synonyms** are only approximations, pretenses of sameness (as, indeed, some argue about translation itself). Similar words, or words in the same field (subject), may be distinguished on the basis of register (degree of formality), connotations, frequency (whether the term is presently used, or to what degree), and many other factors. One of these important factors we focus on now is the *narrowness* versus *broadness* of a word or phrase. You may also find it helpful to think of hyponyms as *subsets* of hypernyms, or hypernyms as *supersets* of hyponyms.

In upcoming activities (see Chapter 10) you will learn about *semantic fields*, the organizing categories of experience. First we can look at a feature of semantic fields that shows how each field is organized from the general to the specific (or the *broad* to the *narrow*, as we just mentioned). Baker (1992, 20) is worth quoting here at length:

> The general word is usually referred to as **superordinate** and the specific word as **hyponym**. In the field of *vehicles*, *vehicle* is a superordinate and *bus, car, truck, coach*, etc., are all hyponyms of *vehicle*. It stands to reason that any propositional meaning carried by a superordinate or general word is, by necessity, part of the meaning of each of its hyponyms, but not vice versa. If something is a bus, then it must be a vehicle, but not the other way round. We can sometimes manipulate this feature of semantic fields when we are faced with semantic gaps in the target language. Translators often deal with semantic gaps by modifying a superordinate word or by means of circumlocutions based on modifying superordinates.

Hervey, Higgins, and Haywood (1995, 84–91) have a useful discussion of hyperonymy and hyponymy, which they rightly note are cross-cultural discrepancies, cases where synonymy is not full, or in other words, where overlap is not complete. By now you realize that languages "map out" the world along different lines, each with different emphases, peculiarities, and blind spots (Baker [1992] notes the notorious example of the word *privacy*, which is a cultural construct; when issues of international law and private property are involved, for example, making subtle distinctions and surmounting nonequivalence can be paramount for the success of a translation.)

TRANSLATION TRAP

Overlap

Considering semantic relations carefully can help avoid undesirable shifts of emphasis in a translation. Suppose, for example, you are translating >es a line on a housing survey. You are looking at your first draft, which uses *familias necesitadas* for "low-income families." To verify your choice, do a taxonomy check: Are all needy families low-income families? Or: Are all low-income families needy families? If you can generate exceptions—"no" answers—in this check, your overlap may not be as complete as you imagined. Try for something closer.

Hyperonymy/Hyponymy Task

Read the source (English) and target (Spanish) that follow. Comparing the narrowness and broadness of terms, draw up a three-column chart with the headings "English," "Spanish," and "hyperonym/hyponym." In the third column, note whether the Spanish TT is one or the other. Include at least four or five terms. Focus on "vertical" relationships (hyperonymy-hyponymy) rather than "horizontal" ones (words with a relationship of contiguity, cause-effect, etc.). First consider the translator's vertical strategies employed, then evaluate the success of his or her choices.

SIGNS AND SYMPTOMS OF COMPULSIVE GAMBLING

- Gambling makes home life unhappy.
- Feeling remorse after gambling.
- Desiring to win back losses.
- Desiring to win again and again.
- Gambling to escape worry or trouble.
- Changing sleeping or eating habits due to gambling.
- Celebrating good fortune by gambling.
- Losing work time due to gambling.
- Gambling to obtain money for debts.
- Borrowing to finance gambling.
- Considering or committing an illegal act to finance gambling.
- Considering self-destruction as a result of gambling.

SIGNOS Y SÍNTOMAS DEL JUEGO COMPULSIVO

- Jugar hace que la vida familiar sea infeliz.
- Sentir remordimientos después de jugar.
- Desear recuperar lo que se ha perdido.
- Desear ganar una y otra vez.
- Jugar para olvidar los problemas y preocupaciones.
- Cambiar los hábitos de sueño y alimentactión debido al juego.
- Celebrar la buena fortuna jugando.
- Perder tiempo de trabajo debido al juego.
- Jugar para obtener dinero para pagar deudas.
- Pedir préstamos para financiar el juego.
- Considerar cometer o cometer un delito para financiar el juego.
- Considerar la autodestrucción como resultado del juego.

(*Source:* "Know When to Stop Before You Start" *Harrah's Entertainment and Responsible Gaming, informational brochure*, 2000)

WORDNETS

A related online resource you may find useful is a **wordnet**. Here are some definitions:

- [noun] A wordnet is a network which models the relationships between words, for example, synonyms, antonyms, hyponyms, and so on. Such networks can be invaluable in applications like information retrieval, translator workbenches, and intelligent office automation facilities for authoring. (*Source*: <http://portal.bibliotekivest.no/terminology.htm>)
- A machine-readable lexical database organized by meanings; developed at Princeton University. (*Source*: <http://www.cogsci.princeton.edu/cgi-bin/webwn2.1>)
- WordNet is a semantic lexicon for the English language. It groups English words into sets of synonyms called synsets, provides short definitions, and records the various semantic relations between these synonym sets. The purpose is twofold: to produce a combination of dictionary and thesaurus that is more intuitively usable, and to support automatic text analysis and artificial intelligence applications. (*Source*: <http://en.wikipedia.org/wiki/WordNet>)

Searches on Princeton's WordNet will yield senses and glosses, followed by **troponyms** ("ways of doing x," or narrower versions of the search term) and **hypernyms** ("x is one way of doing y"), or a wider hierarchy of relations. Try it out, and speculate on the resource's usefulness for translators.

TRANSLATION TRAP

Thesauri

Overuse of thesauri, both print and electronic, is a tempting trap for the novice writer and translator, but all too often this tool leads to improper word choice. If thesauri are used, an unfamiliar word should always be cross-checked with great care to ensure accuracy. Be aware that Spanish-language thesauri are available—they are called *diccionarios de sinónimos y antónimos* (or *y contrarios*), or *diccionarios de ideas afines*.

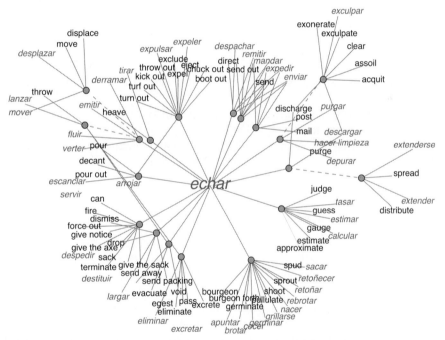

Bilingual visual thesaurus for keyword "echar," created using Thinkmap®,
(*Source*: Reprinted by permission of Thinkmap, <http://www.visualthesaurus.com>, accessed March 25, 2009)

Parallel Texts

Parallel texts (PTs)—texts in the same subject field and ideally written by native speakers—are boons to the translator, and constitute one of the main resources for creating authentic target texts. If one is working into English, one looks for texts written in English on the same subject (and perhaps with the same audience). Existing translations can be parallel texts, particularly when they can be correlated to an available source text (see "Rosetta stones" [Chapter 5]). Many texts written by nonnative speakers, however, can be poor sources for parallel texts in that language interference can create the very problem one seeks to avoid by seeking parallel texts—the problem of unnatural or nonspecialist language. *Always evaluate the legitimacy of your documentation, particularly parallel texts found online.*

The source text with which you are going to use parallel texts is on the topic of *winemaking*; it is from a Larousse encyclopedia. Your instructor will provide it.

Activity

Think of everything you know about winemaking. As a group, make a list of words in English that you suspect may come up. Make a separate list of the types of wine you can think of.

Read through the ST, an encyclopedia entry on *vino*. When do you think this text was written? How do you know? What kind of text is it (expressive, informative, vocative)? How technical is it? What issues do you see immediately? "Gloss" the text (pull out terms and annotate possible meanings). Now read PT1 and PT2, provided next. What terms are covered? Compare to your original guesses. Make a brief glossary of terms that the parallel texts have (provisionally!) solved.

As a group, think of other places you could consult for researching this text. Who do you think the ideal translator of this text would be? What Spanish-speaking countries likely produce documents about wine? What kind of documents?

Tasks

1. Make a bilingual glossary of 20 to 25 terms for this text. Document sources for terms found.
2. In teams of three or four, translate the whole text, double-checking one another's work. Variation: one group works with parallel texts, the other with only glossaries. Compare.

Parallel Text 1 (PT1)

Wine-making in brief is a series of simple operations, the first of which is crushing or smashing the fruit to liberate the sugar in the juice for fermentation, which is the second step and occurs naturally when yeast cells come into contact with sugar solutions. The new wine must then be subjected to various treatments to ensure clarification and stabilization and various other cellar operations which are collectively called élevage before the final step, bottling. . . .

Before fermentation, some amelioration of the grape juice may be needed. Since more than half the sugar in grape juice is converted to end products other than alcohol (mostly carbon dioxide), a sugar concentration of about 20 per cent by weight is needed in the crushed grapes (see must weight) to produce a sound wine of around 11 per cent (see alcoholic strength for the practical range of alcohol levels in wine). In many cooler wine regions fermentable sugars may be added to the basic fruit juice to increase the eventual alcoholic strength (see chaptalization). . . .

The new wine is usually separated from its lees once fermentation is complete (except in the case of some white wines deliberately matured with lees contact). The normal technique is to let all the debris settle on the bottom of the container for a few days before racking, drawing off the wine from the top. This wine, opaque with its load of suspended yeast cells and fine debris, is further clarified, usually by filtration or centrifugation. This clarification process is often encouraged by adding a fining agent which attracts suspended particles towards it and then helps them fall to the bottom of the container.

. . . Other optional steps include maceration of skins and pulp or wine which may take place before, during, and/or after fermentation, assisted in the case of red wines by remontage.

(*Source: The Oxford Companion to Wine*, 1069–70)

Parallel Text 2 (PT2)

Principles of vinification

Addition of alcohol

Fortification raises the alcohol content to a level toxic to yeast.

Racking

Draining the clear wine off its lees, or sediment, into another vat or cask is known as 'racking' because of the different levels, or racks, on which the wine is run from one container to another. In modern vinification, this operation is usually conducted several times throughout the maturation period in vat or cask.

Cold Stabilization

When wines are subjected to low temperatures, a crystalline deposit of tartrates can form a deposit in the bottle. Should the wine be dropped to a very low temperature for a few days prior to bottling, this process can be precipitated, rendering the wine safe from the threat of a tartrate deposit in the bottle.

Vin de goutte and *vin de presse*

Whatever the style of wine, the moment the skins are separated from the juice the wine is divided into two: free-run, or *vin de goutte*, and press wine, or *vin de presse*. The free-run juice is, as its name implies, freely run out of the vat when the tap is opened. What remains, that is to say the manta of grapeskins, pips and other solids, is put into a press that extracts a very dark-coloured and extremely tannic juice called the press wine. The free-run wine and the press wine are pumped into separate containers, either vats or casks depending on the style of the wine to be produced. These wines then undergo their malolactic conversion separately and are then racked several times, fined, racked again, blended together, then fined and racked once more before being bottled.

(*Source: Sotheby's World Wine Encyclopedia,* 18–21)

TRANSLATION TRAP

Extraneous Information

Be sure not to work extraneous information from a parallel text into your translation in order to "show off" or justify your research, or to "embroider" the source with newfound knowledge. Successful translation is built on two different kinds of discipline: *thoroughness* on the one hand, and *restraint* on the other.

TRANSLATION TEASER

Translation or Source Text?

Develop discernment about whether a text is a translation or whether it was originally authored in the language in which you are reading it.

Connect with your **Manual** Web site and open the address for the page entitled "Pre-lanzamiento de software de Microsoft: condiciones de licencia."

How quickly can you determine if you are looking at a translation from English or a text written originally in Spanish? Accumulate evidence to support your argument.

LINGUISTIC NOTE

POORLY WRITTEN SOURCE TEXTS

Some source texts are very badly written. Speculate as to some of the reasons for this. Here's a reason to get you started: The "source text" your client gives you may itself be a translation or even a back-translation!

TRANSLATION TRAPS

Quotes and Intertexts

 Suppose you were translating es>en and came upon a quote like this one that appeared in a major media outlet:

> "We have tried to pay this overdue social debt with a program of housing without parallel in Ecuadorian history, which certain corrupt members of the press—in function of their political interests—now want to discredit, pointing out the inevitable houses that—out of 80,000—are going to have defects," he said. But he said such complaints were outweighed by the "tens of thousands of happy families with their own worthy little houses ... and all the people who can testify to the success of the program."

(Ecuadorian President Rafael Correa)

Too many novice translators simply would translate the quotation unreflectively, as if it were the original source text, thus creating a *back-translation* (an instance of a translation of a translation into the original source language). This is something you would be wise to avoid, because the original quote most likely will not be recognized in your translation, and more importantly, you will be *misquoting*.

Find the actual Spanish quote online. In pairs, discuss the English translation, focusing especially on its ideological distortion and miscollocations.

A second, related phenomenon is spotting **intertexts**. An intertext is a reference, anywhere between veiled (parodied, for example) and obvious, to an existing text, whether an idiom, a distinctive turn of phrase, a title, a famous quote, or an allusion to a familiar cultural icon. For example, if someone describes a politician's latest brainchild as so much "tilting at windmills" ("*acometer molinos de viento*"), the intertext is the mad Don Quixote, whose exploits in the seventeenth-century novels have made "quixotic" behavior proverbial. Intertextual translation, then, involves recognizing the reference and determining how it is recognized in the target language (if indeed it is). Sometimes this involves consulting canonized (time-honored) translations that exist in the target, which can have the same status—or higher—as the source. In English-speaking traditions, many people are familiar, for example, with the phrase "through a glass darkly," which is a translation from the Corinthians 13:12 passage about imperfect human knowledge. When the original meaning of an allusion becomes obscure, mistranslations can occur, and retranslation can restore the meaning (indeed, the New International Version [NIV] translation reads: "Now we see but a poor reflection as in a mirror"). The complication, however, is that the intertext "through a glass darkly" has already passed into the vernacular, even if most people have but a "poor reflection" of what it means anymore!

Another example of the translator's response to intertextual allusions: Leandro Wolfson (2005, 30) notes how a *Time* magazine article used the following phrase: "the brave new mobility of our world." Wolfson correctly notes the best solution for a similar audience: "*la nueva movilidad de nuestro 'mundo feliz'*". . ., understanding that *Un mundo feliz* is the established translation of the title of Aldous Huxley's dystopian novel, *Brave New World* (1932).

As a class, discuss what you would do with this hypothetical headline (c. 2003) into Spanish: "Pundits hope Iraq doesn't become Bush's white whale." What contextual determinations would you have to make in order to effectively translate this line?

Task

Translators online often help other translators who are unknown to them simply out of a sense of community. Imagine that while reading threads one day on the Lantra-l list, you come across the following post. You've been anxious to participate, to "break the ice," and you have learned enough that you can help out this poster, who you realize is a novice translator. Answer the following query as helpfully as you can; if all the information you need to reply is not given, assume different scenarios and answer completely, or refer the person to where they can find the needed information.

```
Date: Wed, 10 May 2006 23:57:20 +1000

From: Ima Linguist <imalinguist@NOVICENET.COM.AU>

Subject: Re: TERM: mattress sizes

Hello: I'm doing a translation of a bill of lading English to Span-
ish and want to know the best way to say "single," "twin," "king,"
"full," and "queen." I think I've heard of "matrimonial" but that
sounds sort of like something you'd find in a honeymoon suite,
but it may be right. My contact said something about MERCOSUR but
didn't really say what country this is for. Thanks.
```

TRANSLATION TIP

Inttranews

International news affecting language service providers is good to read every day. Connect with your **Manual** Web site to find links to stay up to date on all the latest developments on awards, business, conferences, jobs, publications, technology, and more.

Activity: Scavenger Hunt for Translator Internet Resources

(Format based on Richard Samson, Chapter 5, *Training for the New Millennium*)
Cite fully documented resources and send to your professor's email:

1. What translations by Helen Lane were published 1990 to the present?
2. What newsgroups for es<>en technology translators exist?
3. Which is more frequent in British written discourse, "The point I want to emphasize" or "The point that I want to emphasize"?
4. What legal protections should a translator insist upon in a contract?
5. What editions of *Our Bodies, Ourselves* exist in Spanish?
6. What recourse does a translator have in the case of client nonpayment?
7. What translations of science textbooks en>es exist?
8. What qualified translators work es>en in the biomedical field and can do desktop publishing and Web design?
9. What journals in the social sciences accept translations?
10. Is the Hispanic Reading Room at the Library of Congress a patron of translations in any way?

HINTS Library of Congress search, Index Translationum, Books in Print, Spanish Books in Print, ALTA homepage, WorldCat, ProZ, corpora. (Note: Online bookseller catalogues may not be complete.)

If time is limited, you may do this exercise in teams, and then pool all the information upon completion so each student has it for reference.

TRANSLATION TIP

Use Print Resources

Don't rely exclusively on Web-based sources for your translation research, whether background reading, parallel texts, or terminology. First, it's wishful thinking to assume that all resources are posted online—they simply are not; not even close! *Millions* of books and periodical articles do not have copyright clearance to be scanned for free consumption, and many other resources that *have* been, have not been updated regularly online or are plagued with inaccuracies (probably the Net's biggest scourge, for all its wonders). Second, peer review (the process by which a jury of academics critique and evaluate a work before publication is authorized) is usually in place for article and book publication, ensuring at least a certain measure of standards for most print materials. Online, virtually anyone anywhere can post anything any time, and it takes skill and time to recognize and separate the wheat from the chaff. Learn to use one resource to verify another and to read critically—print resources too.

Research

The role of translation technology in content delivery has extended to *distance learning environments*. What is being done in this area? Where? What seem to be the advantages and disadvantages of this delivery format? Are there particular skills you think would be ill served by online instruction? Pull up some well-known offerings online and survey them as a class.

WORKSHOP TEXT #2: RADIO PROMOTION ARTICLE

In pairs, translate the ST that follows for a radio journal's international newsletter, which provides radio industry professionals with the latest information on radio technology. Your team should complete the assignment and edit your work in 1 week's time. You will be editing one another's work. You may have to compromise at times if there are disagreements about solutions. Be sure that each member is accountable for a fair share of the workload. Your instructor may ask you to save all drafts, parallel texts, a continuous transcript of your group's email discussions, and/or inserted comment boxes on one another's work to turn in.

At all stages of the process, watch especially for proper *terminology* and *collocations*. Read your TT out loud for naturalness. Look up "Radio World International" and have a clear idea of your audience.

Rally de AM responde a expectativas

By Gabriel Sosa Plata

Mexico City Martha Dávila se animó a participar. Encendió su receptor a partir de las 11:00 horas, siguió las instrucciones del locutor y durante dos horas y 20 minutos sintonizó 30 estaciones de AM ubicadas en esta enorme metrópoli.

En su recorrido, Martha fue respondiendo en una hoja de papel las preguntas sobre la programación que en cada una de las radiodifusoras hicieron los conductores en turno.

Martha envió su cuestionario con las respuestas correctas a uno de los 13 buzones colocados en diferentes puntos de la ciudad. Después de varios días de espera, Martha se convirtió en la flamante ganadora de un automóvil último modelo y también obtuvo un conocimiento más amplio sobre la radio AM en México.

Hay de todo

"Todas tienen muy buena programación y hay mucho de todo", dijo Martha al recibir las llaves de su auto. "Estoy feliz de esta experiencia. Fue muy grata".

Martha fue una de las miles de personas que participaron en el Rally AM 1998 organizado por la Asociación de Radiodifusores del Valle de México (ARVM) el 15 de agosto.

El rally se efectuó con el fin de dar a conocer lo que se ofrece en la banda de amplitud modulada y elevar su número radioescuchas, sobre todo entre los jóvenes.

En total llegaron 11.562 cartas con las ilusiones de muchos pero sólo dos se hicieron realidad con una rifa supervisada por un interventor de la Secretaría de Gobernación. El otro ganador del automóvil fue Orlando Camarillo.

Mayor audiencia

Esta es la segunda ocasión que la ARVM lleva a cabo un rally con resultados muy positivos, según sus organizadores.

"El año pasado recibimos poco más de 9.500 cartas y en esta ocasión incrementamos de forma importante la participación", dijo Adrián Vargas Guajardo, presidente de la ARVM. "Esto es bueno porque respondió casi el 2 por ciento de la población a nuestra promoción, pero no nos conformamos".

. . .

El propósito de los radiodifusores de la capital es incrementar el 25 por ciento del auditorio de la AM apoyados en rallies y en otro tipo de promociones en un plazo de cinco años.

Esto significaría pasar del 25 por ciento del auditorio que actualmente capta la radio de AM a un 30 ó 31 por ciento del total de los radioescuchas, según A.C. Nielsen.

Sin embargo el reto es complicado, según Vargas.

"Es muy difícil cambiar los hábitos de exposición a la radio de un día para otro", dijo Vargas, quien también es presidente de MVS Radio. "Pero por lo menos se está conociendo la banda y a través de campañas más agresivas trataremos de alcanzar nuestro objetivo".

Entre los planes de la ARVM se encuentra la realización no sólo de uno, sino de dos rallies al año junto con diversas promociones. Entre esas promociones se incluyen anuncios en la propia radio, visitas a universidades y controles remotos.

También se busca una mayor participación de los jóvenes —más habituados a la FM— en las estaciones de AM a través de concursos, juegos y visitas a sus instalaciones.

"La idea central es que las nuevas generaciones de radioescuchas conozcan la AM", dijo Vargas. "Y cuando lo hagan se llevarán una grata sorpresa ya que son muchas las alternativas que ofrece la AM. Desde radionovelas hasta programas deportivos y hablados. Y además, es gratis".

(Sosa Plata n.d.)

(*Source:* Text courtesy of Radio World/Radio World International)

CHAPTER

4

Purpose in Translation: Audience, Text Typologies, Register, Regionalisms

SEMANTIC AND COMMUNICATIVE TRANSLATION

Communicative translation "attempts to produce on its readers an effect as close as possible to that obtained on the readers of the original. **Semantic translation** attempts to render, as closely as the semantic and syntactic structures of the second language allow, the exact contextual meaning of the original" (Newmark 1981, 39, emphasis mine).

It should be noted that semantic translation does not necessarily mean word-for-word translationese; on the contrary, it can be a valid approach for certain text types, according to Newmark.

Discuss the notion of *producing an effect on readers*. How is this accomplished? Can you give an example? Discuss limitations of each approach. Which do you think is more widely used, and for what text types?

> ### TRANSLATION TIP
>
> The translator must earn the reader's trust. A quality translation inspires confidence in the messenger and in the message.

SKOPOS

Skopos theory posits a functional, rather than merely linguistic, approach to translation. Vermeer (1978) proposed that the initiator (the client) determines prospectively what the function, or *skopos* (Greek, "purpose") of a target text is to be, not the text, the author, or even its recipient. Katharina Reiss contributed to this idea to create a general translation theory whereby a text is seen as an *offer of information* from a producer to a recipient. Where the skopos of receiver culture and the source culture differ, adequacy (appropriateness) of the source text to the skopos will be the standard, not to any perceived kind of equivalence to the source; this concept, although not freeing the translator from constraints, redirects the antiquated notion of faithfulness to functionality. Reiss and Vermeer (1984), following Bülher (1934), indicate the following text types in terms of their function:

Informative texts (corresponding to the *descriptive* function of language)
Expressive texts (corresponding to the *expressive* function of language)
Operative texts (corresponding to the *appellative* function of language)
(Baker and Malmkjær 1998, 235–8)

THE TRANSLATION BRIEF

The **translation brief** or **translation assignment** or **commission** is defined as the instructions to the translator about what a translation is to be used for and how; it may include special considerations or constraints that will determine the translator's microstrategies and macrostrategies. It is

> either given to the translator by the initiator/commissioner or established in discussion between the translator and initiator/commissioner. The translation brief will guide translators with regard to the information they choose from the initial offer of information (ST) and the way they package this information in the TT. . . . If the translation brief states that the function or purpose must be changed or maintained in the translation, the translator will have to do so since the purpose overrides all other translational considerations. A translation will therefore no longer be judged in terms of equivalence principles . . . but in terms of principles of its **adequacy** with regard to the translation brief. (Nord 1997, 35, emphasis mine)

Stated more schematically and formally:

Information Contained in a Translation Brief

Intended function	» What for?
Audience for	» Whom?
Time of reception	» When?
Place of reception	» Where?
Medium of transmission	» How?
Motive for production	» Why?

(*Source*: <http://www.hablamosjuntos.org/sm/translation_basics.asp>, accessed April 10, 2009)

Sample Briefs (Translation Assignments)

The following are some sample briefs quoted from a functionalist English-German translation textbook (Schäfner and Wiesemann 2001); only the briefs are printed here, and they are each for different jobs. Note that Sample 1 indicates that the translation solicited was to be reused; for some translators, this fact has implications for the translation rate charged (on the argument that the work in effect is not for one-time use but for "serial" use and should be remunerated accordingly). Note also the brevity of Sample 2.

Sample Brief 1
This text was a real translation assignment from the Ethnic Relations Department from the West Midlands Fire Service. The original assignment was rather general and vague, though. It only said:

> With the possibility of a greater number of foreign visitors and workers coming into the West Midlands from Europe in the future, it would be of great benefit if we have details of how the emergency services can be contacted and the telephone number to use, available in as many European languages as

possible. After clarification talks, the assignment was specified as follows: production of a German text to be published in the form of a small information leaflet to be distributed among native-speakers German living and working in the West Midlands, or on a longer-term visit in the area.

The original time of TT production was 1993, but it was intended to use the text for some more years to come. (83)

Sample Brief 2
A German version of this text is to be published in the weekly magazine *Der Spiegel* in January 1994, in the regular section 'Prisma-Wissenschaft', i.e. the section reporting on new scientific findings and developments. (122)

Sample Brief 3
The German weekly *Die Zeit* wants to report on the current (i.e., February 1996) political situation in the UK after the IRA had declared an end to the cease-fire. In order to have a politically well balanced account, they decide to include statements from various politicians. The text by Gerry Adams [from *The Guardian*, 12 February 1996] was chosen among others to be translated for subsequent publication in *Die Zeit*. The publication is intended for the end of February 1996. *Die Zeit*'s motivation for dealing with this topic was that with the UK being a member of the European Union, every development concerning Northern Ireland is of relevance and news-worthiness for Germany as well. The German text is to be submitted to the editors of *Die Zeit*. (146)

Sample Brief 4
The German government would like to have translations of all addresses spoken at the Commemoration ceremony on the occasion of the 50th Anniversary of the Warsaw Uprising, Warsaw, on 1 August 1994. These addresses are meant to be studied and analysed by government advisors. (168)

Sample Brief 5
The Berlin publishing company Siedler Verlag is interested in finding out how its publications are reviewed in other countries. In spring 1996, the Siedler Verlag asks you to prepare a German version of the review of the book *Götterdämmerung* that appeared in *The Economist* (3 February 1996), for internal use of the publishing company. (191)

Sample Brief 6
Birmingham Marketing Partnership wants to produce a trilingual illustrated brochure (English, French, and German) to promote Birmingham. For this purpose, the English text has to be translated. In the brochure, the three language versions will be printed side by side, interspersed by photos and other illustrations. The brochure is meant to be freely available for distribution in travel agencies, information offices, at the airport, etc., within Birmingham, i.e., it is not primarily intended to send the brochure abroad. (207)

(*Source:* Reprinted by permission of Multilingual Matters Ltd.)

Activities

1. Write a translation brief for a well-known document. It may be serious or playful, but try for *plausible* circumstances. Remember the features of *skopos* as you write your brief.
2. Think of a text and two separate, vastly different briefs. Explain which version would pose greater challenges to the translator and why.

3. Could a translation brief precede the existence of a source text? Discuss.
4. The Lonely Planet series of travel guides are translated into dozens of languages. Discuss how the brief might change for these books and what content revision the non-English editions would entail. Examine one for ideas.
5. Identify a brief for the target text your instructor will provide. Can you hypothesize that the source text brief was different from the target brief?
6. Find a Web site online the content of which would have to undergo a shift in communicative strategy in translation; write a brief for it to reflect that need.

7. Learn to quickly assess the primary audience for a given site. Connect with your **Manual** Web site and use the link to find the Chaa Creek Lodge. To whom is this page targeted? The services offered are in Belize. Does the site appear in any other language but English? Why or why not?

Seeing the Job from the Buyer's—and End User's—Point of View

The American Translators Association (ATA) accreditation exam began specifying translation briefs in 2003. The ATA organization has produced a short buyer's guide to translation called "Translation: Getting It Right." More and more clients are learning that clear notes on what a translation will be used for is cost-effective and headache preventive. In its brochure, the section "Tell the translator what it's for" is worth quoting:

> A speech is not a web site. A sales brochure is not a catalog entry.
> A graph heading is not a directional sign. An article in The National
> Enquirer is not a prospectus for an Initial Public Offering. (Durban 2003)

The translator can increase the brief's effectiveness by *clarifying* any missing or partial information, *communicating* any concerns, and *corroborating* when discrepancies arise. As the brochure emphasizes, the key is to create "maximum impact for that particular audience and vector."

Task

Connect with your **Manual** Web site and use it to find the link to the Institute of Translation and Interpreting, then read the British version of the ATA brochure.

Now answer these questions:

1. a. What differences do you think the American version of this publication has or should have from the British version?
   b. Translations of this text from English exist. What issues do you think would have to be considered for an into-Spanish version? Describe what the brief might include.
2. Name examples of types of misunderstandings that can break down the buyer–seller relationship.
3. List and prioritize the preventive measures that a translator can put in place with a client to ensure both quality and client satisfaction.

4. Connect with your **Manual** Web site to find the link to the ATA site and read the brief brochure, "Translation: Buying a Non-Commodity." With a partner, write a brief paragraph of five to seven lines summarizing why translation is not a commodity.

PRÉCIS WRITING

The précis is a type of writing that condenses the ideas and styles of longer works. Précis are used in international organizations and in academic circles (e.g., book reviewing) to save time and space when quoting lengthy passages is impractical. The translator-in-training can greatly benefit from the comprehension and assimilation that this type of writing demands—it is far more taxing than mere note-taking or critiquing, which are less rigorous and less comprehensive skills, because they need not follow entire trains of thought and they involve judgment of a more subjective nature. A précis is not an interpretation but a reconstruction in one-third scale of the original. The précis writer learns to give weight to what is important and to sift out what are anecdotal or incidental—even supporting or peripheral facts, illustrations, or arguments. (Poor translations often elevate incidentals into the focus, a distraction; the importance of précis writing for translator training, thus, is paramount.) Following are some ground rules (with the proviso that précis can vary in type):

- Do not quote or use the writer's own words, except unavoidable key words. The précis requires that the writer use his or her own words.
- Use all the elements that are important to the author's argument.
- Use the elements in the order they are presented.
- Make your précis one third the length of the original (i.e., reduce it by two-thirds).
- Ensure that relative emphases are the same as the original.
- Rewrite very carefully for fluidity.

Task: Try a Précis

Read the following passage and attempt a précis. Note that the précis follows the development of the original closely; by contrast, a summary may reorder elements.

HINTS   Underline key ideas. Determine which details are tangential, or redundant, to the writer's thesis and bracket them. Study the logic of the passage. Define in your mind who your audience will be: Perhaps the précis will be used by an acquisitions editor, a reviewer, an academic, a librarian or cataloger, or a forum moderator.

To share your précis, do a pair-share with a classmate; then volunteers can read their versions to the class for group comparison.

In the early 90's a visiting Eastern journalist, after a week's close reading of coast newspapers, remarked to Arthur McEwen: "Why are you all roaring and roaring all the time, against the Southern Pacific? It is only one railroad. Can't you find anything else to complain of?"

The answer might have been that California's citizens feared the corporation because in one way or another they were all under its domination and because two decades of effort to break its control had accomplished nothing. The Big Four have succeeded in the early 70's in their effort to control the movement of freight to and from California and within the borders of the state, established their rate-schedules on the basis of "all the traffic will bear." And they succeeded in maintaining that policy for more than thirty years. It was perhaps the nation's choicest example of a complete and sustained monopoly, an almost ideal demonstration of the power of a corporation to control for its own profit the economic resources of a region comprising one sixth of the area of the nation. That practically the entire population of the Coast realized what power the Big Four held over them and for years fought stubbornly to break it, adds to the magnitude of the achievement. Although the citizens had on their side every important newspaper of the state save those frankly in the pay of the Southern Pacific, efforts to remedy the situation were uniformly unsuccessful because of the railroad's controls of the legislature, of state regulatory bodies, of city and count governments, and in many cases, of the courts.

The result was that from the middle 70's to 1910 the major share of the profit of virtually every business and industry on the coast was diverted from its normal channel into the hands of the railroad and its controlling group. The merchant who brought stock from the East paid freight bills so high that to sell his goods at all he had to cut his profit almost to the vanishing point. The degree of prosperity of every business or industry was directly dependent upon the officials at Fourth and Townsend Streets who fixed the railroad's freight rates. The latter performed their numerous and delicate duties with skill. They and their agents kept watch on the businesses of the railroad's customers: in San Francisco they even claimed—and were given—the right to make periodical inspections of shippers' books. If merchants were found to be growing prosperous, rates were raised: if too many went bankrupt, rates were lowered. The manufacturer was allowed to earn enough to keep his plant in operation; freight rates on the farmer's products were nicely calculated to enable him to clear enough to plant and harvest his next year's crop and to support himself, not too extravagantly, in the meantime. (Lewis 1938)

Connect with your **Manual** Web site to compare your précis with the one given.

TRANSLATION TIP

The United Nations Competitive Examinations

Source: Logo reprinted by permission of the United Nations

The United Nations (UN) holds open exams to create rosters for any future vacancies for English-language editors and translator/précis-writers. Successful applicants may be posted in New York, Geneva, Vienna, Nairobi, Addis Ababa, Bangkok, or Santiago de Chile and must make a 5-year commitment. Your English and Spanish—two of the official languages of the United Nations—need to be outstanding, but you must also have excellent knowledge of French. Written exams for editors (5½ hours) consist of editing two short texts in English and a test on style and usage, a summary of a Spanish text of your choosing, and editing of an English text to make it parallel to a text edited in French; written tests for translators and précis writers (6½ hours) include a translation es>en; a fr>en text (or you may choose an Arabic, Chinese, or Russian ST); a summary >en of a French speech; and a >en translation of a specialized text (economic, legal, or scientific/technical) from Spanish or a general text in a third official UN language.

SUMMARY (GIST) TRANSLATION

Summary translation requires superior analytical skills. A summary translation is called for when:

- the client wants to save time and money
- the volume of potential translation is too large
- the text in question is for *information-only* purposes (i.e., not for external consumption or publication)
- a text's details are not all relevant to one's needs (e.g., of conference proceedings, long reports, an initial interview, etc.) or when a broad overview of a text is what is needed

According to Gregory Shreve, summary translation is especially prevalent in government, where it is contrasted with *verbatim translation*. (For more on this, see Shreve 2006, 87–109.)

Task

Compare and contrast the following: **selective translation**, **abstract translation**, and **keyword translation**. What does each involve, in what environment, why would they be used, and by whom? What is an *executive summary*, and how does it differ from an abstract?

TRANSLATION TRAP

Information-only translations and **translations for publication** are not the two poles of the shoddy-to-excellent continuum. They refer to *purpose*—internal versus external use. The key difference usually lies in presentation; both may be highly accurate.

 Sometimes translations are for reference and are not meant to stand in for an official document. For example, the forms library housed at the United States Citizenship and Immigration Services (USCIS, formerly INS) has forms that must be filled out in English, though translations are in some cases provided to assist applicants. (Connect with your **Manual** Web site to find the link to the USCIS site and check the immigration forms.)

It is true that some use "for reference purposes only" as a legal disclaimer, which is a way to not be held liable for any inaccuracies or unprofessional work. A hired translator, however, should never take these labels ("information only" or "for reference") as a mandate to deliver a slipshod product. If professional pride isn't enough of a motivator, there's always the possibility of lawsuits; as Edwards (1995, 11) reminds us, virtually "any document can be litigated. So too, any translation of any document. . . ."

SIGHT TRANSLATION

Sight translation, *la traducción a la vista* or "sight" (also a verb), has been theorized only rarely. It is a skill most commonly used in interpreting—particularly where a written document is entered into evidence or to be filled out or at multilingual business meetings. It is widely used as part of translation and interpreting exams. The skill requires techniques that can be used to good advantage in prepping a text. Note: These tips are for *sight translation*, not *written translation*:

1. When sight reading, *read ahead*. Keep your attention focused on recastings that will require you to make substantial shifts in syntax—these are the main stumbling blocks in sight translation, not individual words and phrases.

2. *Superordinate* when a term doesn't occur to you—move up the hierarchy (e.g., don't grapple to find the term "handgun"; use "gun").
3. Keep a steady pace and a pleasant reading voice; don't translate by fits and starts or with swings in your modulation.
4. Sight read on your own, prepping first for 3 to 5 minutes. Texts for sight translation should be approximately 50% to 75% of the difficulty of texts commonly assigned for written translation; give yourself a "pass" on the less obvious terminology—the sight translator is concerned more with *structures* and learning to think resourcefully. Have a "spotter" listen for meaning, without the source text. Use semi-technical, basic legal, journalistic, and general texts. One caution on sight translation: Once a part of your routine, it can be a difficult impulse to suppress when you want to read *without* translating.

CASE STUDY: TRANSLATION AND IDEOLOGY IN COLUMBUS DAY AND DÍA DE LA RAZA

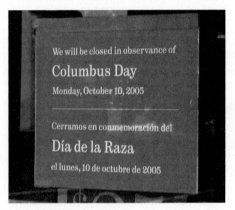

Source: © Jeff Gates

What are the ideological differences between the two juxtaposed texts in the sign? How are cultural values conveyed in the name in the holiday(s)? Insight: Most of those celebrating Columbus Day have little idea what Día de la Raza stands for; those celebrating Día de la Raza, by contrast, have a very clear idea of what Columbus Day is.

Role-Play: "Fishbowl"

A translator and a project initiator, the latter of whom charges angrily that the translation is inaccurate; the translator defends the translation. The class can watch and take sides.

CULTURAL NOTE

Receiver Specificity and the Body Politic

Ed Morales (2002), in his article "The Fine Art of Translation: Overcoming the Pitfalls of Bringing Books from English into Spanish," notes:

> Juana Ponce de Leon's Siete Cuentos Press . . . is breaking new ground in translating books for U.S. Spanish-language readers. Ponce de Leon's task in translating the feminist classic *Our Bodies Ourselves* posed an unusual challenge.

(Continued)

The difference in sensibility between North American feminism and Latin American feminism was one of the main themes in Siete Cuentos's strategy for translating the book. Latin American feminists, according to Ponce de Leon, are less willing to exclude men in their worldview. 'That book was translated by about 12 different women's groups,' says Ponce de Leon. 'The way the information needed to be provided was different for a Latina. We added issues about spirituality and home environment, and did not use words like 'patriarch.'

Find out more about this book and its complicated and revealing history in translation around the world.

TRANSLATION TEASER

Imagine that you've gone to a tropical forest to visit a Spanish-speaking culture that has had very little contact with the outside world. They speak an indigenous tongue among themselves. Suppose, if you like, that you traveled back in time to get there.

Your goal is to test for yourself a famous hypothesis by the philosopher Willard Quine that a proposition such as "*Neutrinos lack mass*" is untranslatable to preindustrial societies. What strategies would you try in order to stand the best chances for success? How would you know if you've been successful?

HINT 1 Read Roman Jakobson's (2004) article "On Linguistic Aspects of Translation" for an idea.

HINT 2 Warm up by explaining the Internet to them, which may suggest a strategy to you.

What do the presence of a *literate* culture and an *oral*, or preliterate, culture have to do with this problem? In which direction do you think would be harder for ideal communicators to translate concepts, *into* this people's culture or *from* their culture? (Assume the existence of these ideal communicators—speakers making the full and best use of the languages' resources at all times.)

LINGUISTIC NOTE

BRAILLE TRANSLATION

Braille, the system of embossed dots on the printed page for the blind and partially sighted, is actually a complex mathematical code, not a language. Software exists to translate into Braille, but the output must be human edited. Maps and other illustrations can be rendered with tactile graphics. Braille has been adapted to many of the world's languages.

REGISTER

Genre, as Munday (2001, 90–1) defines it, is "the conventional text type that is associated with a specific communicative function," and it determines the **three variables of** *register*: field, tenor, and mode. The following summary may help you remember them:

> **field: the "what"** (not the subject of the text, which is wider, but the *function*; e.g., a sales pitch, a legal disclaimer)

tenor: the "to whom" and "from whom" (the degree of formality reflected in the "power" relations of addresser and addressee of a message; e.g., a surgeon to other surgeons or a doctor to a patient)

M. Joos (1962) described five styles: **frozen**, **formal**, **consultative**, **casual**, and **intimate**; in the three-part division described previously, essentially these are *tenors*, levels of language formality, from highest and least flexible to lowest and most flexible.

mode (medium): the "how" (e.g., written vs. oral forms of communication)

The "OED Model" of register (Gramley & Pätzold 2004, 2) incorporates two of the three aforementioned categories:

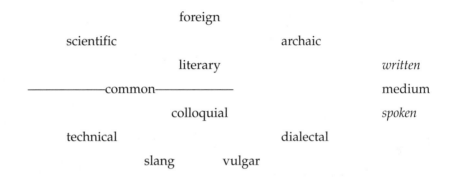

Functional tenor adds a dimension to the OED model; it is a term put forward by Gregory and Carroll (1978, 53, in Hatim and Mason 1997, 26) to describe what the speaker/writer is *attempting to do*—for example, to persuade, to exhort, to condemn, to satirize, or to inform. The OED model does not account for this fundamental, *pragmatic* element of language. Gramley and Pätzold (2004, 3) summarize the speech act functions as follows:

Type	Subtypes	Examples
Representatives/ Assertives	statements and assertions	*(I maintain that) he was there!*
Directives	requests and questions	*(I request you to) please leave me alone*
Commissives	promises, threats, and offers	*I'll be on time (I promise I will)*
Expressives	thanking, apologizing, and congratulating	*Gee, thanks! I'm sorry, I apologize*
Declaratives (a.k.a. performatives)	the marriage, baptism, and sentencing formulas	*By the authority vested in me I declare you husband and wife*

Activity

1. Now give an example of a speech act *in Spanish* from each of the preceding categories.
2. Rewrite the following utterances with the new variable(s) given:
   a. "Good faith efforts have been made to secure all necessary permissions." >> (casual)
   b. "Don't just chuck out leftover hard parts in the trash—runs lots of water and let it go down the drain. This stuff'll kill you and give you cancer—put gloves on before you pick it up. Don't touch it to your eyes and nose." >> (written mode; formal register)
   c. "We will not be undersold" >> (casual tenor; oral mode)

d. "Quality patchbays and jackfields mean the best broadcast connectivity for you, our valued customer" >> (tenor = specialist to layman [hint: define terms])

e. "Here we show that a recent mass extinction associated with pathogen outbreaks is tied to global warming. Seventeen years ago, in the mountains of Costa Rica, the Monteverde harlequin frog (*Atelopus* sp.) vanished along with the golden toad (*Bufo periglenes*). . . . We propose that temperatures at many highland localities are shifting towards the growth optimum of *Batrachochytrium*, thus encouraging outbreaks [of a pathogenic chytrid fungus]. With climate change promoting infectious disease and eroding biodiversity, the urgency of reducing greenhouse-gas concentrations is now undeniable." >> (commissive function) (Pounds et al. 2006, 161)

3. Connect with your **Manual** Web site to find the link to Orquídeas del Bosque. Rewrite the following text that appears there. Orquídeas del Bosque is an e-tailer based in Costa Rica catering to the local and international orchid market. Make the pragmatic function *exhortative* (take your cue from the information given about unregulated practices in the industry). The beginning and ending of the text from the site is as follows:

Text begins: "Orquídeas del Bosque es una pequeña empresa orientada al mercado externo e interno de especies nacionales de orquídeas, sembradas a partir de semillas por la técnica 'in vitro'. [. . .]"

Text ends: "Orquídeas del Bosque, al reproducirlas en laboratorio, ayuda a aliviar la presión que los coleccionistas ejercen sobre el medio natural."

Now go to the English version of this page and edit.

4. Your instructor will pass out copies of the following text. Identify the elements that show it to be a speech. Give a 75-word abstract of it, replacing the *speaker/listener* relationship with a *writer/reader* one, as if the text were appearing in a political science journal or an international policy bulletin. When you are finished, describe the strategies you used to transform the text's oral elements. Discuss the following: Were you able to maintain the text function? Is an abstract of a persuasive text also intended to be persuasive?

Text for this task (your instructor may wish to choose another one) is: "An Unequal System of Trade: A Better World Is Possible," address by Ali Rodriguez Araque, Minister of Foreign Affairs, Venezuela, delivered to the Ministerial Conference, Sixth Session in Hong Kong on December 15, 2005.

5. Hatim and Munday (2004) argue that the long-held view of a single text adhering to a single register is a myth and that, in fact, issues of power, intention, intertextuality, and what we might call the "remove" at which the information is given (firsthand, secondhand, etc.) all affect the utterance and call for the translator's attentiveness. Find a text with multiple registers in a relatively short space. Mark the shifts on the text and summarize what each shift is attempting to accomplish. This task may be especially fruitful if you seek out purportedly objective (factual) material and try to uncover underlying rhetorical goals.

CASE STUDY: REGISTER

Identify the register occurring in the text that follows ("*Un encuentro en la calle*"). Imagine that you are hired by a cognitive linguist on a university grant to study regional Spanish variation. You are charged with creating an English script for U.S. consumption—an educational video that parallels the Spanish; each script will be acted by separate actors. Decide in your groups what regional variety of speech you will use for your English. Gloss the text for 15 minutes. Groups should then volunteer to sight read a performance of their text for the class. For variation, groups may be assigned or adopt alternate scenarios (e.g., make the speakers 1960s surfers or hippies, 1990s ravers, or urban millennials, or give them regional identifications; social class can also be manipulated: turn them into two old country club habitués). As an alternative, you could film your scenes and post online.

Un encuentro en la calle

Pepe: ¡Eh! ¡macho!

Paco: ¡Joder! No te había visto.

Pepe: ¿Qué hay? ¿Cómo te va?

Paco: Psa, tirando . . . ¿y tú?

Pepe: Yo, me voy tirao tirao.

Paco: Joder, ya será menos.

Pepe: Quita, tío, quita, que estoy de una mala leche.

Paco: Bueno, a ver qué coño te pasa ahora.

Pepe: Que me se ha escacharrao el coche.

Paco: No, ¿otra vez?

Pepe: Otra vez, joder, otra vez.

Paco: Mucha pasta.

Pepe: Coño, no sé . . . jo, pero como sea mucha lo tiene claro porque hasta que yo no cobre el mecánico no ve un duro.

Paco: Va, tío, olvídate. Esta noche me voy al cine con unas tías. ¿Te vienes?

Pepe: Hum, no sé. Tengo faena.

Paco: Pero que coño vas a tener tú faena. Pero, macho, de que vas. Si es esta noche.

Pepe: Es que . . . no sé, joder, no sé.

Paco: Pero coño, tío, si es un rato. No me seas cabrón.

Pepe: Jo, tío, que plomo eres, pero ¿no te he dicho que no lo sé?

Paco: ¿Que tienes plan?

Pepe: Te pego un telefonazo.

Paco: Bueno, bien . . . Pero . . . jo, es que esta noche no ceno en casa. Mira, yo te llamo y te digo lo que hay.

Pepe: Hecho.

Paco: Sobre las nueve.

Pepe: Muy bien, tío, nos vemos.

(*Source*: Batchelor, R.E. and C.J. Pountain. 2005. *Using Spanish. A Guide to Contemporary Usage*, 2nd Edition. Cambridge University Press.)

To what extent do you think registers are shifted up or down in translation? Why?

Source: © James Mauseth

Task: Language Variation—Localizing Out of U.S. English

Localize the following Web site copy for a European, English-speaking market. Translate en>es for Spain. Make any necessary conversions. Take note of your principal sources during the documentation phase.

> We sell young misses' shoes sizes 5–9. From dress shoes to amphibious shoes to sneakers and flip flops, and in 45 sassy colors. Whether you're dressing to impress on your first day of high school, or are off to the food court or out at the movies, we have shoes starting around $6. Same day shipping.

Activity: Register—Baroque Journalism

Read the following authentic account of an accident in a Guatemalan neighborhood recounted in a local newspaper, *El Imparcial* (July 13, 1963). In pairs, make a list of details that would *not* be included in a U.S. newspaper. Rewrite the story in the style acceptable in U.S. journalism, only including the details that a U.S. reader would expect in a local newspaper. The excerpt is author D. Canfield's translation, given with semiliteral transparency.

Humble Vendor of Ice Cream

Dies Plastered by a Truck

The Pilot Rolled Him on Trying to Pass Another Vehicle

Beneath the wheels of a heavy truck perished yesterday Mr. Mario Salomé García, a humble vendor of ice cream, who every day was located in front of the building of the Central School of Commercial Sciences, in order to distribute his product among the student body of that plant.

It was 17:05 hours when the truck, license plate C-40753, driven by Mr. Francisco Javier Soto Chiu, was passing along Tenth Avenue, in front of the School of Commerce, but in passing another vehicle it ran over Mr. García, who was getting ready to return to the building of Sharp Ice Cream.

Upon the impact of the violent blow, the ice cream cart turned over on the sidewalk, while its unfortunate conductor was struck by the rear wheels of the truck, which passed over his entire body.

The death of Mr. Garcia, 52 years of age, was instantaneous, since his cranium remained completely broken, as well as various fractures in the legs and possibly in the ribs.

The body remained before public view for nearly an hour, as a consequence of the absence of the coroner, who was late in arriving to issue the report according to law.

Many curious ones grouped around the cadaver, which produced the bottling of traffic in that sector.

The pilot, Soto Chiu, was conducted to the first precinct of the National Police, from where he will be consigned to the tribunals of justice.

(*Source*: *East Meets West, South of the Border: Essays on Spanish American Life and Attitudes* by D. Lincoln Canfield © 1962 by Southern Illinois University Press; reproduced by permission of the publisher.)

1. List details that are inappropriate in U.S. mainstream journalism.
2. Rewrite the newspaper account as it might appear in contemporary U.S. journalism.

Discussion

1. The word "baroque" in the title of this exercise refers to Latin American tendency toward high-flown oratorical style where Anglo cultures prefer unadorned and unmetaphorical language. In what other domains have you seen or heard of these tendencies? Are they only manifested in writing?
2. What sociological and psychological differences can you construe between the ideal readers of a text like the preceding one and your rewritten version? Do ideal readers of each have the same view of subjectivity and objectivity? Of privacy issues?
3. Would all Spanish speakers outside the United States know what is meant by "right to privacy"? Can such an article even appear, do you think, in societies where libel laws exist? Collect and share extreme examples of baroque prose in Spanish and Americanize them in straightforward English.

Tasks: National and Transnational News Magazines

Research and discuss the differences in two editions (English and Spanish) of the same hard-copy news magazine. They may be published nationally for Anglophones and Hispanophones, respectively, or you may compare an international edition to the national one. Possibilities include, but are not limited to, both current events sources and special interest publications such as *Discover en español*, *Selecciones Reader's Digest*, *Time en español*, or *Popular Mechanics en español*. What allowances for audience have been made? How much content is duplicated, if any? Is content parallel month to month in the English and Spanish editions or is there a time lag? Are any demonstrably *transnational* in focus? What happens to titles like *Scientific American* in Spanish? What is the marketing strategy behind the formula "(English title) + 'en español'"? Do the same for news magazine Web sites that have versions in English and Spanish (e.g., *National Geographic en español*). What general interest Spanish-language weekly publications are translated?

As a bonus, see if you can find a written editorial policy of any of these publications specifically addressing or defining their readership. Find out, too, if translation is done in-house by production staff, and if the translators' names appear with each feature article.

Your instructor may assign an article for review from a bibliography on news translation.

Tasks: Spanish-Language Media

1. Find a translated news item and do a close reading of the source and target texts. What editorial changes occur that alter the presentation of information?

2. Find an obituary of the same well-known individual in English and Spanish news sources. Can you find evidence that translation played a role in the content exchange? How do matters of audience affect the two different texts?

3. Detail the role that newswire services play in the directionality of worldwide information flow. Are there services that seem to promote translations *out* of English, or do many seem to do the contrary?

4. Univisión is received in many U.S. households with cable access. Connect with your **Manual** Web site and use it to find the link to Univisión. Go to its home page and note what materials are produced in bilingual format. Is its programming available with English closed-captioning? Where is its primary market?

Source: Michael Newman/PhotoEdit Inc.

5. a. Examine some of the Spanish-language newspapers in the United States with the highest circulations such as *El Diario-La Prensa* (New York), *El Nuevo Herald* (Miami), *La Opinión*, (Los Angeles), and *Hoy* and *La Raza* (Chicago). Is their content translated? Are their target markets restricted to the immigrant group that predominate locally (e.g., Cubans in Miami, Mexicans in Los Angeles, etc.) or do they aim wider?

   b. Early in many Spanish-language newspaper operations, their direct-marketing strategy has included mass mailings to people with Hispanic surnames. What do you think of this plan? How would you improve it to make the best use of marketing dollars to reach Hispanics?

6. Compare the marketing strategies behind the ads in a particular niche, for example, prenatal magazines in English and Spanish (for the latter, see *Espera* [Expecting] or *Primeros doce meses*).

7. Read and discuss "Adapting Time Magazine for Latin America" by Robert C. Sprung and Alberto Vourvoulias-Bush, *Translating into Success*, 13–27.

8. What targeted specialty magazines produced in Spanish in the United States can you find? For example, *El nuevo constructor* is for Hispanic contractors.

9. In what arenas and for whom are interviews usually translated?

10. Study shifts in the translations of newspaper headlines.

> **TRANSLATION TIP**
>
> **News**
>
> Follow the news around the world daily in English and Spanish from a gateway page such as CNN or the BBC. Listen to streaming radio and read the text, particularly when the same story is covered in English and Spanish.
>
> On the international front, you may find that comparing the en<>es content of the UNESCO *Courier* will give you translation insights.

TONE

"Tone" is a word used to measure *mood*. For example, note how the entire tone of this business phrase changes with the shift of a single closely related word:

> *Thank you for your business!*>>>
> *Thank you for your money!*

(A stickler may argue that a customer's patronage and his or her money are two different things; a cynic may reply that they are not.)

Hone in on the differences in tone in the two sentences. Describe each of them. A nuance emerges: Tone has to do with *how the writer (or translator) implicitly or explicitly regards the reader*. (By the way, do you know how Spanish usually renders the first phrase?) The relevance of tone for the translator almost goes without saying: Mistakes in tone are perceived emotionally and can lead to a visceral rejection of a text.

Take an example from your everyday activities: Have you ever sent an email the tone of which was misconstrued as hostile or short? Are you *sure*? Have you ever taken offense at someone's message based only on tone? Here's an email a professor sent to a student about computer problems that the latter was having while submitting a paper:

> I am not having any such problems with other students' work. Call the support line. As far as I can determine, you and I see and get the same thing as far as attachments and your work goes.
>
> (Young 2002)

The student on the receiving end was mortified; the professor was equally mortified to discover that the student objected to the coldness of tone. Which of them is "right"? Is there a "right" interpretation of meaning without participants and a communicative context? Do we even have the whole context (e.g., Does the professor use a salutation? Is this the tenth email in an hour? Is it the professor's native language? Did the student ask "Are you having any such problems with other students' work?")? What might lead a student to infer that the professor is being impatient? What would lead a professor to assume that this email is inoffensive? Task: Edit it to soften the tone or make unmistakably not hostile.

Tasks

1. Take a very short text and write it in two different tones. Let the class guess as to what tone you were trying for with each. Alternatively, put a series of texts on the

board and see if the entire class achieves a unanimous, independent assessment of what tone is used.

2. Collect ads in English and Spanish that use different tones. Do any of them surprise you? Discuss: Can a person sell a product or service with any of the more aggressive tones? If so, how?

Discussion

1. What expressive limits does email have relative to face-to-face dialogue? What expressive limits does email have relative to other written forms of communication (particularly in matters of tone)?
2. Try the difficult task of defining tone. Is the word *tone* a metaphor in this context?
3. What factors affect tone? What general tone qualities can you identify? Do certain tones have specific purposes or intentions?

CASE STUDY: "THE CORNER OFFICE IN BANGALORE"

 Connect with your **Manual** Web site and use it to find the following *New York Times* op-ed piece entitled "The Corner Office in Bangalore." Describe its tone as thoroughly as possible. Discuss specific ways that this tone could be preserved in translation.

Follow-Up

 Connect with your **Manual** Web site to find the Business Letter Corpus site. In groups, search for tone markers such as "feel free," "looking forward to," and others. Analyze the output. Describe the environments and ways in which each is used.

TRANSLATION TRAP

Irony

How is irony conveyed? How do you recognize irony? What is the very important difference between the words and concepts of *facetious* and *sarcastic*? Give an example of each that distinguishes their use.

 Connect with your **Manual** Web site and use the link to read about the nuances of irony as a pragmatic rather than a semantic problem in an article in the journal *Meta*, which includes examples in English and Spanish.

TRANSLATING SURVEYS: CULTURAL APPROPRIATENESS

One of the most often translated texts is the survey. However, few clients appreciate the degree to which surveys have high cultural content, and Latinos in particular often do not respond with *confianza* to the surveys' standardized—and yet highly personal—questions. Designing the instrument with **cultural appropriateness** is perhaps most paramount with this text type. Remember, too, that the surveyees' written replies are often assigned for translation.

Activities

1. Go online in pairs and brainstorm a list of types of surveys used in different fields (not only government but also private industry).
2. Bring a few survey Rosetta stones (en<>es) to the desktop. Discuss the strategies you see in the translations and how successful you deem them to be and why. Can you infer different audiences?
3. What procedures can you discover that are unique to the process of cross-cultural adaptation or of the quality control of surveys?
4. What major shifts can occur in an interlingual translation (e.g., en>es) of a survey? Describe some of the typical shifts for a health survey, for example. Can you find an example or description of an entire approach changing, for example, from the written medium (Anglos) to door-to-door contact (Latinos)?

Research

1. Read in translation journals this important aspect of the profession. Report back on what studies are finding about cultural differences in the use of these instruments and the role of translators and client education in survey development. (This would even make an appropriate end-of-semester project.)
2. What evidence of translation activity can you find related to Gallup polls, computer-assisted personal interviewing (CAPI), computer-assisted telephone interviewing (CATI), and other kinds of face-to-face and telephone surveys and scripts? Are these questionnaires always professionally translated? What evidence leads you to think they are or are not? Explain how a translated survey or poll is pretested. Finally, describe the technology used to conduct and analyze these instruments.

Role-Play

Give a brief to translation vendors for the translation of a health information data-gathering instrument or health campaign project. Prescribe formats, audience, and any and all information about the target audience that the translators will need. You may even include details on how the terminology will be standardized.

CASE STUDY: BRIEF SURVEY OF COMMUTER HABITS

First in pairs, then as a class, solve some of the terminological difficulties presented in the following brief survey (Ventura County Air Pollution Control District's Transportation Outreach Program). Sight translate en>es. Find the Rosetta stone for it online and critique, or find parallel texts and glossaries to follow up the choices of the class. As always, be aware of the likely users of such a survey.

> ### TRANSLATION TIP
>
> Learn Quark Express, Adobe Pagemaker, or Framemaker. These are useful tools for formatting brochures.

Ventura County Air Pollution Control District
Transportation Outreach Program

Company Name Here
Commute Survey

Name: _____

1. What is the driving distance from your home to work? _____ miles (one way)

2. Do you normally work at least 36 hours per week? ◯ Yes ◯ No

3a. Do you work a compressed schedule (9 or fewer work days in 2 weeks)? ◯ Yes ◯ No
   if No, **Skip to Q4**

3b. If you answered "yes" above, what type of schedule do you work? ◯ 9/80 ◯ 4/10 ◯ 3/36

4. Mark <u>only</u> one ◯ in each column to indicate your commute method for that day.
   (Note: When more than one commute method is used, mark the method used for the longest distance).

COMMUTE METHODS	Mon. Apr 29	Tues. Apr 30	Wed. May 1	Thurs. May 2	Fri. May 3
Drive Alone	◯	◯	◯	◯	◯
2-person Car/vanpool	◯	◯	◯	◯	◯
3-person Car/vanpool	◯	◯	◯	◯	◯
4-person Car/vanpool	◯	◯	◯	◯	◯
5-person Car/vanpool	◯	◯	◯	◯	◯
6-person Car/vanpool	◯	◯	◯	◯	◯
7+ person Vanpool	◯	◯	◯	◯	◯
Bus	◯	◯	◯	◯	◯
Bicycle	◯	◯	◯	◯	◯
Walk/Skate	◯	◯	◯	◯	◯
Telecommute (worked at home all day)	◯	◯	◯	◯	◯
Compressed schedule day off	◯	◯	◯	◯	◯
Reported to another location	◯	◯	◯	◯	◯
Didn't work (off, sick, vacation, etc.)	◯	◯	◯	◯	◯

Thank You!

**Please return this form to Human Resources Department
by Friday May 3, 2002**

Source: Ventura County Air Pollution Control District, Ventura, California. <www.vcapcd.org>

LINGUISTIC NOTE

FILE FORMATS

According to Jost Zetzsche (2006), there are *five file formats that the translator typically handles:*

1. office files (word processing, spreadsheet, presentation); **2. tagged files** (HTML, XML, SGML); **3. Desktop Publishing Files** (InDesign, Quark, Framemaker, etc.); **4. database content**; and **5. software development formats**.

TRANSLATION TEASER

Often a translator will reason "The writer *meant* 'x' but *wrote* 'y.'" Can you adhere to "what the author meant" or can you only adhere to what the author *actually wrote*?

SLANG: REGIONAL VARIATIONS

Slang varies from country to country, city to city, and even neighborhood to neighborhood. In Madrid, a type of slang is known as *cheli*; Buenos Aires's slang, *lunfardo*, developed among Italian immigrants and working-class neighborhoods and passed into mainstream use. *El País* (1997) posts a multilingual lexicon of slang for Madrid, Bogotá, Buenos Aires, Caracas, México, D.F., and Santiago de Chile.

Connect with your **Manual** Web site and use it to find the chart at the *El País* Web page.

Tasks

1. From the Spanish, try to "triangulate" the current English slang in your region for each term.
2. For the second task, invent your own game based on the *El País* chart. You may want to incorporate role-play or use dice or other props. One game can be chosen and field tested by the class. Ideally it should involve translation, including the use of wider, actual contexts for the slang words.

Activity: Yearbook Picture Service Ad Copy

1. How would you describe the register of the source text that follows? What is the relationship between the register and the target audience?
2. What is the effect of sentence length in the source text? Try this: Read the ad copy, adding "and" and commas to produce longer sentences that avoid all repetition. What is lost?
3. Now produce a version of the first part of this ad for a different Spanish-speaking country; that is, assume that the products are for export. Take these three steps to accomplish it:
   a. Check where yearbook portraits exist and how they are sold. What similar ads can you find? You may want to take the extra step of finding lexicons of current slang or extract it from chat sites where the language you need is used.
   b. Find a Spanish-speaking informant from the country you chose and ask for feedback about your version. Make any edits you find to be improvements. Back in class, compare different versions. Did you make any cultural substitutions?
   c. Translate the whole text for a U.S. Latino/a audience.

4. Now let's add a constraint: Suppose the client contacts you in the eleventh hour, insisting on a synonym for one of the terms you used (let your partner, role-playing as the client, choose a term for you to swap out; he or she can flag it on your completed translation). What changes to rhythm and/or rhyme will you have to make? Make them. How much did the client parameter derail your schedule or translation strategy? Do the layout (*maquetación*) for the Spanish translation; import graphics or design your own with the new audience in mind.

ENGLISH	SPANISH
Capture the look.	
You're the show. So bring it. Let them know. The you they knew. Bring it out. Get your smile on. Get your style on.	
It's easy with our Portrait Preview. During proofing, just choose the proofs you like on our password-protected site. For your best look, try our patented touch-up technology.	
You had a blast. Now make it last. Un4gettable photos. Strike a pose.™	

Activity: Regionalisms and National Variation

1. Supply the missing ingredient for a cookbook submission to a Puerto Rican online community; you are self-translating (en>es) your own recipe from a nonexistent original you often cook from memory.

---

20 onzas de _____ enlatadas y escurridas

2 cucharadas de Sofrito

2 cucharadas de cáscara de limón raspada o $\frac{1}{4}$ taza de jugo de limón

$\frac{1}{3}$ taza de pimientos rojos enteros (opcional)

$\frac{1}{3}$ taza de aceitunas verdes picadas (opcional)

(recipe for black bean salad)

---

2. Translate this line of patient instructions from an eye care center in Miami, Florida, for Cuban expatriates in the area: "The glasses should not be worn with contact lenses."

3. A colleague of yours, an apprenticing translator, has to write and translate 60-second on-air "spots" for his internship at the Spanish-language TV station on the Monterey Peninsula. The script he is working on calls for an average contemporary Mexican laborer in Mexico City saying "Pardon me?" to a coworker in an everyday context (the laborer is hard of hearing). The translator calls you to see if you can help.

4. In a passage of dialogue from a stage play, a Spanish editor has objected to your translation of *huachito* as a term of endearment, arguing that it connotes being born out of wedlock. A second editor, the director, argues that it is meaningless in Spain. The term occurs between two lovers in a contemporary play premiering in Barcelona. Research the origin and usage of this term and argue your case or concede to one of the editors. You want to know if it can be used endearingly, or if it has resonance in Spain.

5. Your project manager (PM) has left an urgent message on your answering machine about a confused and somewhat upset semi-bilingual client who did her own back-translation of a job and came up with "lie" (!) in back-translating "bleach" from your Spanish. The text is a safety warning you rendered en>es; they specifically want the word "that would be understood by Nuyoricans and Dominicans." The text is part of the fine print on a bottle and warns against ingestion; the product is intended for household use in cleaning clothes. You don't know what "lie" could possibly refer to; you don't remember specifically or have your text in front of you. After some research, you suppress your frustration at the back-translation and make your best guess at the source of this confusion and how you could fix this situation for the PM.

6. You are translating a cover letter to accompany an international waybill. The client's ST is essentially an offer to expand the scope of business with a prominent security company in Colombia that provides screening of containerized cargo shipments of furniture. You need to address the letter to "Enrique María Escobar, CEO" and cannot find him online, so you must use the Colombian equivalent of "CEO" as a best guess at his actual title.

7. Cancún has been hit with a hurricane, and part of the relief efforts entails sending 2,000 frozen turkeys there. The crates have to be clearly labeled "turkey" in Mexican Spanish for quick offloading in Mexico. The job is urgent.

8. Your client is a sign maker who in turn is working for a huge tire dealership based in the "Rubber City," Akron, Ohio. The dealership wants roadside billboards reading "Tires changed here" with the company logo as a part of a branding effort on the Caribbean coast of Venezuela. Render the signs appropriately for the audience.

9. Intimates, Inc., the leading manufacturer of undergarments, has a new Argentinean office. You are the head of the PR Division and are writing up an interactive consumer advertising campaign to drive the new line of seamless lingerie. You decide on a banner ad that challenges women "You're wearing the wrong bra" (the "hook" of which is the double meaning of "wrong"—it apparently refers to size but also is baiting the customer toward the brand). You become stuck on the term that the average Argentinean consumer would use for "bra." Solve and verify.

10. You are the PM on a big job—producing an in-flight video for several Spanish-speaking affiliate airlines of the worldwide parent company, Flapping Emu Airlines. Panaire is a new subsidiary that flies the Canal Zone. As the deadline approaches, you notice that the translation team from Spain has used *azafata* for "crew member" in all 36 instances it occurs in the video script. You realize that Panama may not use the same term, and you want the most localized version of every term and visual. Check on it.

TRANSLATION TEASER

Recipes

Because we don't eat lexical equivalents, but foods, how does a recipe translator handle regional foods that don't exist in the target culture?

Recognizing Dialectical Variation

Where would you most likely be if you read or heard each of the following phrases?

1. *Pibe, vos sos loco. Dejá el auto en la playa de estacionamiento.*
2. *—Vieras las chancletas que vi en el chinamo.*
   —¿Porta a mi?
3. *El carnet de conducir no se consigue aquí sino de 2 a 3 los lunes.*
4. *¿Qué onda, güero?*
5. *¡Ay, Dios! Nos va a tocar el tapón saliendo de Luquillo.*

TRANSLATION TIP

Differences among Regional Varieties of Spanish

Patrice Martin (in Yunker, *Beyond Borders*) provides a list of terms used for five different constituencies: English, Argentinean Spanish, Colombian Spanish, Mexican Spanish, and universal Spanish. The English "batch" is listed as *lote*, *tanda*, *control*, and *batch* in the respective Spanishes; "assembly" as *equipo*, *ensamblaje*, *montaje*, and again *montaje*; and "goods" as *mercadería*, *mercancía*, *artículo*, and *producto*. The lesson is to be aware that not only slang but even the most common specialized vocabulary can undergo regional variation.

For what kinds of texts would these variants have special relevance and be attended to especially closely?

¿?

Translators often are commissioned to produce a text in "neutral Spanish." Realistically, do you think this is possible? What do you think clients mean by this term?

TRANSLATION TRAP

Biases and the Quality of Writing

Examine and reexamine your biases about Spanish from different regions and countries. Often what we deem to be inferior writing on close inspection is simply unfamiliar to us. Worse, we frequently repeat platitudes about which nations communicate "better" than others. This kind of thinking clouds the translator's ability to read sympathetically. Remember too that most of the writing that has ever been done was not intended for translators or for translation; your job involves *receptivity to the language as it is used in the source and sensitivity to how it might be used in the target*. Textbook Spanish (unless you're translating a textbook!) doesn't occur in nature.

It is the mark of the amateur, moreover, to complain unduly about or make excuses due to the quality of writing in a given source text. (One recourse is to get involved "upstream" to improve the authoring of a source text.) Challenge yourself to focus on *what* and *how* a text is communicating, and resist the urge to get frustrated as you disentangle others' ideas. Understanding comes quicker when you set aside judgment.

 Which is better in a given situation: the "correct" Spanish word, or the word that the end user will understand? Would you use a word (e.g., *camión*) even knowing that your reader will expect another (e.g., *troca*)?

SPANGLISH

Define the following terms, giving common features and some examples of each, and quoting your sources: Spanglish; Cyberspanglish; pochismo. Who uses these language variations and why?

Before the discussion to follow about attitudes toward these realities, consider that those on the prescriptivist side of the divide lament, and even try to prevent, the rise of Spanglish, whereas descriptivists tend to see it—and all languages—as phenomena constantly in flux.

Discussion

What are your feelings about Spanglish's legitimacy? Is nonstandard language the same as substandard language? Do you agree that it is a new language in the making? Does it make sense to you to uphold the "purity" of a language? What is Spanglish's relationship to translation? Does Spanglish use translational transfer strategies?

Task

Research the recent reevaluations of Spanglish's status. Bring in a dictionary of Spanglish, and critique the latest studies and predictions on its growth in the United States.

In-Class Activity

In pairs with each partner working independently, rewrite in standard Spanish or English the Spanglish narrative that follows. Then regroup with the other to compare versions. (Note that you are performing a translation of sorts on the text, not a "correction".) Here is the text:

"Talk con un pana on my first pasos in La Yuma"

Bro:

Fue one día like today, hace años, when I first llegué a La Yuma. It wasn't el hielo sino Miami, antes called "The capital of the Cuban exilio" pretty parecida a Cubita la bella, hot and humid, con el español and Spanglish que se escuchaba all around, sobre todo en la Sauesera.

Al día siguiente I went to la Migra to meter papeles y apply por un estato legal. In the meantime, ya empezaba to work doing patios, o sea, cutting grass en las yardas de Miami. Un amigo was already working de junkero y un relative de friends in Cuba bregaba en una pompa. Pa' tener a good job I had to moverme pero didn't have plata for a buen carro, so le compré un tranporteichon a una yoni. It lasted about un año, yompeándolo algunas veces, of course.

I shared a duplex con my familia but other amigos I knew rentaron un efiche. They had to pagar casi the same and had solo one cuarto! Days después I got mi tarjeta con el número del Social and a few semanas later pude landear un better job.

Tenía que trabajar no less than 12 hours por día, but I felt bien, 'coz tenía libertad pa'cer whatever yo quisiera. Empecé a uerkaut y me puse bastante cortao, though not muy grande. Un pana dominicano sí que was really cortao, but él hacía uerkaut more hours por día que yo. También pinché como badiman y otros jobs part time.

Eventually pude landear una pincha pretty good in security, then como translator e intérprete, en lo medical y luego in the legal terreno. I incluso worked en un funeral home y as a teacher! Tuve friends que used to work as pomperos, ruferos, yunkeros, grueros, en tormotos, de dílers, serving mesas, carpeteros, en los desks de los hoteles, como reps, troqueros, vendiendo áiscrim y balloons, but always estudiando y mechándose pa'salir ahead. Nada de janguear con la wrong ganga.

Cuando aquello era fashionable estar faxeando, bipeando y calling de dondequiera. Poco a poco la technology digital fue taking over y los celulares arrived. In one of the pinchas yo tenía (o, perhaps more clarito, tuve) que carry two bípers: uno de voice y el other de numbers. Era bien cool! A few años later, finally me moví pa'l hielo 'coz el dinero was much better. It is cold, pero me visto de oso!

Well, tengo que quitear this paper to ponerme a work de verdad. Espero that tú truly enjoy todo este mejunje de three lenguas: inglés, Spanish and Spanglish.

Take it easy, cógelo suave y no dejes de chill out y relax. Dropéame unas lines!

Hey bro, remember not to janguear con gangas ni los wrong guys: that leads to nothing bueno!

Tu bróder, pana y buen pal.

(*Source:* Eduardo González, <http://accurapid.com/journal/38spanglish.htm>, © Copyright Translation Journal and the Author 2006. Reprinted with permission.)

TRANSLATION TEASER

El hangyeo es culísimo

A well-known sign hangs in the Greyhound bus station in Springfield, Massachusetts. It announces: *Prohibido el hangyeo. Violadores serán juzgados.*

TRANSLATION TIP

Expect English among the Spanish

As an interpreter or translator, particularly one who works in the United States, you may be caught flat-footed when a Spanish speaker uses an English word or phrase, particularly because Spanish phonetics may camouflage that the word is not Spanish.

Israel Reyes reports that "the Miami-based magazine, *generation ñ*, has a somewhat regular column titled 'Cubanamericanisms,' by Bill Cruz, which includes such gems as *Bibaporrú* for Vick's Vapor Rub and *Tensén* for a Woolworth's or other five-and-ten stores."

Not sure what the plaintiff's going on about when in his sworn statement he refers to a *hüinchil*? That would be a "windshield." *Güelfare*? "Welfare." An acquaintance in Pamplona once wrote this author to come visit for the "Festival de Guemin Güey." You guessed it—the Hemingway Festival.

TRANSLATION TIPS

Document Delivery

Avoid sending corrupt files!

Use a professional subject heading and tone. Don't send a note saying, "Here's my translation :), Joe." Reference the job by its title, job number, and/or date. Remind your PM or client of previous conversations ("Per your request, I am sending the files in two different formats for the Bay Area mass transit questionnaire job [6/04/08]"). Remember that the one on the receiving end of your mail has many documents to keep straight. Be personable without being overly familiar or a drain on others' time.

Name your files consistent with agency policy, including your last name as part of the file name if so requested. Sending out files named "translation.doc" is interpreted as self-centeredness, because you may be the only one who knows *what* translation; *see things from the receiver's point of view*.

Version control: Label the number of your edit so multiple drafts aren't mistaken for one another on either end. It's a good idea to date each draft as well, even as part of the file name.

Don't send unfinished work or work with terms missing, claiming you "couldn't find them." This is akin to a mechanic giving you back your car with only three tires on it.

For follow-up, be available or reachable after delivery to troubleshoot or resend if needed. Use one medium to follow up another: Call to confirm a fax; email to confirm an agreement over the phone, and so forth. Give your point person a "heads-up" that a package or file has been, or will be, sent. Don't assume.

Don't wait until the eleventh hour to send out clarifications, SOSs, requests for extensions, or other kinds of troubleshooting or unwelcome surprises. Send questions in "digest" form (in fewer emails rather than many in succession), number the questions if you can, send well in advance, and proofread for clarity.

(Continued)

Don't ruin hours, days, or weeks of work with slipshod, last-minute insertions that add errors or typos. Delete track change scaffolding. Make no pen marks on hard copies. Make sure attachments match disk content exactly.

Make absolutely certain that nothing has been left out, because omissions can be difficult to catch and irksome to the client to find after the fact.

Use document deliveries as opportunities to express your willingness to continue your working relationship or to expand ("Please keep me in mind should any local escort interpreting opportunities arise.")

All of the above goes for work for your translation teacher as well! Be conscious of his or her specific instructions for delivering assignments. Start good habits now. Your mantra is: *Please the client*.

THE CLIENT PORTAL

"Crunched" time frames for delivery and retrieval has made the client portal an up-and-coming standard service for tracking a project or otherwise providing access for real-time collaboration with translation teams. For example:

> **Elanex Products and Services—Client Portal**
>
> The Elanex Client Portal provides clients with an easy online way to manage their translation projects. It includes the following features:
>
> - Summary and details of all translation projects and their real-time status
> - Invoice history
> - Client-specific glossaries and styleguides
> - Ability to upload new translation projects at any time, and receive instant feedback that the work has begun
> - Ability to retrieve translated documents online
> - Multiple logins for different individual users
> - Administrative summary of projects submitted by different users
> - Budget constraints and project pre-authorization, enabling administrators to place restrictions on submissions by individual users
>
> The Elanex Client Portal is available to any Elanex client. For more information on the features of the Client Portal, or for a demonstration, please **contact** us!"
>
> (*Source*: Elanex, Inc. Web site, <http://www.elanex.com:80/EN/client_portal.aspx>, accessed August 10, 2008)

 Another kind of portal has emerged in the industry: the **language portal**. Connect with your **Manual** Web site to find the Microsoft Web page. Search the site and describe the goals of such a resource.

TRANSLATION TIP

Determining the Reliability of a Web Site

Reliable Web sites are:

- "from educational, not-for-profit, or government organizations"
- "from expert authors" (Follow up on their names in other reliable sources)
- "from reliable print sources"

(Continued)

- "well supported with evidence and presented in a balanced, unbiased fashion"
- "current or recently updated"

  Dubious sites are:

- "from commercial organizations" (.com or .biz)
- "from anonymous authors or authors without identifiable credentials" (including "chat rooms, personal web pages, blogs, bulletin boards, and similar networks . . . when they don't give credentials or other qualifying information")
- "secondhand excerpts and quotations" (particularly where biased editing has distorted the source material)
- "unsupported or biased"
- "old or not recently updated"

(Troyka and Hesse 2005, 190)

TRANSLATION TRAP

Are the posts in the WordReference.com forums consistently reliable? Who is posting there? Is this a site for professionals?

"ROSETTA STONES"

"Rosetta stones" are sites with texts presented in more than one language. They are easily found—search online by common keywords in both languages together, for example, "instructions for" + "*instrucciones para*" for a broad search for instruction templates, or, for example, suppose you want a site where "*lomo*" + "*loin*", and "bone-in" + "*con hueso*" appear, which yields a Rosetta site on cuts of meat: Scroll down the directory page to "1999 US Meat Export Federation" and see the .pdf beginning usmef.org. This method may yield glossaries as well. It is a good idea to save and label the resources you find for easy access later. Rosetta stones in print exist as well; sometimes texts and their translations are printed side by side or consecutively (installation instructions, safety warnings, instructions for use) or in alternating lines with different fonts (commonly, for applications and registration materials, and much less commonly, for poetry). Frequently Rosetta stones are multilingual. (Hot tip!: Include "pdf" in your search parameters.)

Instances of a subcategory of the Rosetta stone—the "self-glossed text"—can be singularly useful. Because its sources are in English, it uses "doublets" (parenthetical English for each Spanish term used).

A Rosetta stone can be used to harvest terms for a new translation, and strategies can be learned from how other languages dealt with a given problem. A package insert for cigars by the Cuban firm Habanos, S.A., for example, reads in part as follows in its three languages. What can you surmise about the terms "Habanos/Havanas"?

> *Estos Habanos han sido elaborados con hojas del mejor tabaco del mundo.*
> These Havanas have been made with the finest tobacco in the world.
> Diese Havanas sind unter Verwendung der weltnbesten Tabklätter hergestellt worden.

Note that the Spanish and English instructions recommend that the product be stored in a "humidor"; the German has "Klimarschrank (Humidor)". What does the presence of two terms in the German suggest?

The original Rosetta stone was found in 1799 by Napoleon's troops. It featured three aligned texts in Greek and Egyptian and written in hieroglyphic, demotic, and Greek scripts, each for a different intended audience. The stone was the key to breaking the long-mysterious "code" of the ancient hieroglyphics.

Source: Terry Smith/Creative Eye/MIRA.com

Activity: Rosetta Stone Scavenger Hunt

Challenge your classmates to a Rosetta stone scavenger hunt. Agree on a text type that all have to find in physical form (an example of the same text and its already existent translation). Start easy (product labels, catalogues and pamphlets, newsletters, clothing tags, a bookmark, a map, CD track listings, labels, a bilingual edition of a book) and work your way harder (Spanish and English versions of a movie poster, an FBI most wanted poster, a video press release, a billboard, a children's restaurant placemat, a calendar, . . . currency?). Or try a winner-take-all round for the hardest-to-find text type.

More on Finding Rosetta Stones and Glossaries

Half an hour now with the following sites can save you many hours of fruitless trolling in the long term. Connect with your **Manual** Web site and use it to find the link to pick up tips such as switching the language code in the Web address to find translated pages.

Also on your **Manual** Web site, find the link to the site where you'll discover ways to search for a term in a page in the target language. (Note: Author Tanya Harvey Ciampi uses the term "parallel text" here to mean a Rosetta stone.)

Finally, Calishain and Dornfest's *Google Hacks* (2003), a publication frequently made available online as an e-book, lets you in on advanced search syntax and programmers' secrets to maximizing your research.

LINGUISTIC NOTE

TRANSLATION BLOGS

A growing trend is the translator's weblog, or "blog," an online journal. Some are written by translation insiders, and others by novices just finding their way in the profession. As Adriana Francisco notes, they can be excellent as a marketing tool as well as a way to share and compare experiences, and reading and writing them can keep you current in tracking industry trends and developments. Connect with your **Manual** Web site to find links to the translation blogosphere. What others can you find?

TRANSLATION TIP

Field Research

Translators will visit factories, workshops, or job sites to touch, taste, smell, hear, see, ask, learn, and experience—whatever helps them capture in words the process or product they are after.

TRANSLATION TRAP

Literalism

One of the most common traps the novice falls into is the practice of word-for-word translation. The warning signs and symptoms are easy to spot: If you aren't comprehending a source text, the result will be a "horizontal glossary" of logjammed words. *Meaning* must come across in translation, not words.

Learn this parable by heart:

The fish trap exists because of the fish; once you've gotten the fish, you can forget the trap. The rabbit snare exists because of the rabbit; once you've gotten the rabbit, you can forget the snare. Words exist because of meaning; once you've gotten the meaning, you can forget the words. Where can I find a man who has forgotten words so I can have a word with him?

(Chuang-Tzu 1996)

In translation, before expressing comes a forgetting. Over two thousand years after Chuang-Tzu, translation scholars would call this "forgetting" stage of the translation process **deverbalization**.

Here's a good example involving literalism: Cartagena (2005, 192) relates that if one translates "safe sex" literally—*sexo seguro*—the result is quite the opposite—"guaranteed sex," or a "sure thing"! (Note: This hasn't prevented the widespread use of the term, which would be far better rendered as *sexo sin riesgos*.)

Paradox: the "faithfulness" of literalism usually produces unfaithfulness.

TRANSLATION TIP

Use electronic databases (e.g., library catalogs) and bibliographic databases, which often can allow searches of thousands of journal articles by keyword.

TRANSLATIONESE

Do translators all share a common mother tongue? At our worst, perhaps we do: translationese. This is never a complementary word. Translationese refers to a translation that is stilted or jarringly stuck in *interlanguage*, a limbo where the translation apes the source language's syntax while doing violence to the target's. If the diction or syntax obstructs meaning, translationese is often to blame. When the translation *process* has involved insufficient decoding and reencoding, the translation *product* is beset by interference. Critic Alan Duff called translationese "the third language." *You cannot translate what you do not understand*—our recurring theme—and translationese bears this truism out.

Translations are often called translationese when *patterns* of poor choices become apparent. Baker (see next) posits *translation universals* that characterize translated texts regardless of languages involved.

A classic example from Spanish to English would be the excessive use of the impersonal phrase ("It is probable that . . . ," "It is significant that . . .") instead of a more natural phrasing (" . . .probably . . . ," "significantly"). From English to Spanish, the stigma of translationese attaches to the abuse of –*mente* when used with adjectives, instead of the translator creating adverbs *de forma más castiza*, with "con + adj." (e.g., quickly > *con rapidez*). Rather than owing to specifics, though, translationese is usually a *general* malaise—treatable with wholesale checks against the source text, and then revision performed after setting the source text aside.

TRANSLATION UNIVERSALS

The notion of translationese is widely accepted, and so, too, the idea that specific languages present high incidences of certain constructs used to translate the source language in question (descriptive translation tools such as corpora studies can now allow for powerful such analyses of translated texts). The idea of **translation universals**, however, is still being debated. One prominent proponent is Mona Baker (Baker, Francis and Tognini-Bonelli 1993), who, following and expanding on other scholars' work, theorized a number of translated texts' general features; Laviosa (2002) enumerates them:

- **Explicitation** (cohesive shifts, additions, and increased redundancy)
- **Disambiguation and simplification**
- **Textual conventionality**
- **Avoidance of source text repetitions**
- **Tendency to overrepresent features** of the target language
- **Specific distribution of lexical items** in translated texts *vis-à-vis* source texts

All of this, in sum, would indicate that the translator "plays it safe," collapses the rich interpretive veins of a text, paints with a narrower palette, and does all this with a certain statistical *predictability*.

The implications of these observations –one almost wants to call them "charges"!—are serious: What do *you* think? Why do these phenomena occur in translations, assuming you agree they do? Is there something unconscious in the translator that chooses impoverishment, or is entropy inherent in any act of interpretation or representation? Do these findings, or hypotheses, suggest that the translator *holds back*, refusing to use fuller resources of the language because of a myopic faithfulness to transmitting the *message* to the neglect of the author's *voice*? Can you spot any of these tendencies in your work thus far? In translations you've read? How could you track these features in your work if you decided to try? What else can a novice translator do to help counteract these universals?

TRANSLATION TRAP

World Knowledge

To paraphrase Tolstoy's line about unhappy families, every poor translation is poor in its own way. Yet most poor translations have this in common: They have little traction, that is, they aren't successful in describing any coherent reality as we know it or imagine it. As Umberto Eco argues, world knowledge must anchor a translated text: "In order to understand a text, or at least in order to decide how it should be translated, translators have to figure out the possible world pictured by that text" (20). This is a very different and far more complicated operation than simply transferring words.

STRATEGY

Translators use strategies, though as González-Davies observes (2005, 74), theorists have not reached a consensus on what a strategy is. She helpfully offers a pedagogical definition of strategy as "a procedure which has been chosen consciously to solve a translation problem which does not allow an automatic transference (Lörscher 1991, 76) and which can be present either in a text segment (micro level) or in the text as a whole (macro level) (Scott-Tennent, González-Davies, and Rodriguez Torras 2000, 108)," whence **microstrategy** and **macrostrategy**. Multiple versions of a single text—either compared in a classroom workshop or revealed through analyzing *learner corpora*—make strategies more visible.

In light of the preceding definition, could one argue that a translator *must* have a strategy for virtually any text, even by default?

TRANSLATION TECHNIQUES

Translation techniques, known also as procedures or strategies, are choices that translators can use to achieve similar effects. They are not prescriptive for the contexts given next; each textual circumstance is different and will call for a solution determined by more than apparent linguistic "equivalence." This partial list of procedures can, however, offer a repertoire of some of the possible choices in many situations. Be aware that entire texts should be taken into account in the measure possible to validate the use of these strategies at the phrase level. Techniques may be, and are, used in combination.

Chesterman (1996) distinguishes three broad types:

Syntactic—e.g., *shifting of word class, changing cohesion*

Semantic—e.g., *hypernyms, hyponyms, shifting level of abstraction*

Pragmatic—e.g., *naturalizing, adding/omitting*

Implicitation (Condensation, Compression)

Implicitation can be described as leaving out information that the target text reader would not need.

For example, from a photo caption from Spain translated for the BBC online:

ST: *Tony Blair, Primer Ministro de Gran Bretaña, hizo hincapié en que lo primordial de su intervención es mantener la paz.*

>>**TT:** "[Prime Minister] Blair stressed that the peace-keeping part of his role is fundamental."

NOTE He may be called "Tony Blair" in the first instance in English, without identification of his office for readers in the UK; the BBC seems to also use "Mr. Blair" with some regularity.

Explicitation

Pragmatic explicitation is the strategy by which the translator interpolates an explanation of a lexeme bound to the source culture. It is less "invasive" than a translator's footnote but more documental than other more naturalizing choices (for example, dropping the foreign borrowing and using only the description of its sense). Pragmatic explicitation involves the loan word plus a brief definition following it, usually as a restricted clause. The following are three examples (emphasis added) not from translations but actually from source texts that illustrate pragmatic explicitation as a source-text writing strategy; however, the effect is the same, and you will clearly see this procedure's mechanics and usefulness for translation. The supplemented description usually only partially suffices to exhaust all that is implied by the borrowed term, but the reader is given comprehensive enough information for the purposes of the text.

Model 1: "What we have here is the old *bracero* **program, a guest worker program**, and it primarily benefits one group and one group only—big business." (Molly Ivins 2007)

Model 2: "According to Vallejo, it's those *nortes*, **the November and December cold fronts that blow in from the Gulf**, that shock the orchid plants into increasing production of the many flavoring agents that give Mexican vanilla its distinctively potent flavor." (Suzanne Murphy-Larronde 2005, 39)

Model 3: "[José Guadalupe] Posada's *calaveras*, **or costumed skeleton figures**, were perhaps his best-known figures." *St. James Guide to Hispanic Artists*, p. 477

Javier Franco Aixelá (62) distinguishes *extratextual glosses* (e.g., a footnote: "Arnold Rothstein*, *Célebre gángster de los años 1920. (N. del T.)*") and *intratextual glosses*, which are interpolated explicitations—St. Mark > Hotel St. Mark (52–78). Incidentally, use "—Trans." whenever you add a translator's footnote; otherwise, the reader may be confused as to its source.

WHAT TO USE AFTER EXPLICITATING.   After using an explicitation, translators (and authors) commonly use only the foreign term—italicized—thereafter. An example from a text written in English and with parenthetical explicitation rather than a dependent clause follows:

> Around 1920 there were more than fifty *mutuales* (working class and artisan self-help societies) throughout [El Salvador]. [. . .] It was not until the 1920s that a process of ideological and social differentiation of the associations occurred, with some *mutuales* becoming unions that radicalized ideologically under the influence of anarchist and socialist ideas. . . . (Acuña Ortega 2004, 40)

Particularization and Generalization

Do you remember our discussion of hyponymy and hyperonymy (see Chapter 3)? The processes of applying one or the other are known as *particularization* and *generalization*, respectively. These are sometimes necessary; when they cause preventable distortion, they are ill advised. As an example of generalization, if the term *homicidio calificado* arises in the text, under the Mexican penal code this designation denotes that the aggressor held a physical advantage over the victim; a translation of "murder" or "homicide" would be a generalizing translation, or *generalization* (Mikkelson 1995). Translating a sacred text's *divinidades* as "God" would be a prime example of particularization. The optional versus mandatory nature of these processes, as well as their ideological ramifications involved, their role in semantic loss/gain, and their capacity for cross-cultural (mis)representation make them an inevitable focus in discussions of translation method.

Modulation

Modulation is a recasting by changing the point of view, metaphor, or image of a text segment.

Model 1: ST: *Se necesitan muchos pantalones para enfrentar a un ejecutivo importante.* (police interrogation transcript)
>>**TT:** "It takes some serious guts to take on a bigwig."

NOTE   This translation uses two modulations. Discuss "bigwig"—does it *particularize* too much? "Head honcho," "rainmaker," "top exec"?

Model 2: ST: *Si bien Julio Iglesias no cumplió con la promesa de llamar a su primer hijo "Chile", nunca ha dejado de reconocer que Viña del Mar **fue su trampolín a la fama** mundial.*

Here's a possible translation that uses a modulation of the image:
>>**TT:** "Although Julio Iglesias never kept his promise to name his first son "Chile," he has never failed to acknowledge that Viña del Mar **catapulted him to world fame**."

NOTE   Notice too that *trampolín* shifts to a verb—"catapulted"—in the TT; this is a recategorization, which we will overview later.

Discuss: What about if "springboard to stardom" were used? Is this a modulation of *trampolín a la fama*?

Model 3: closet racist>>*racista encubierto*

NOTE   The metaphoric part of "closet" shifts to a more explicit phrasing in Spanish.

Model 4: *Los jugadores están con ganas de repetir* (headline)
>>"Players anxious for a rematch"

NOTE   Here is an example of why procedures cannot be applied blindly: When one goes back to a buffet, one might use the same verb, *repetir*, in Spanish; hence, "to go for seconds." Context!

Recategorization

Recategorization, formerly called transposition, involves changing the word class in transfer.

Model 1: ST: *El autor subraya **el carácter patético y emotivo** de los grandes murales realistas.*
>>**TT:** "The author underscores **the pathos and emotion** of the great Realist murals." ("Pathos" and "emotion" are different parts of speech, used here to avoid a wordy, clumsy construction in English.)

Model 2: ST: *Te llaman!*
>>**TT1:** You've got a call!
>>**TT2:** Call!
>>**TT3:** Call for you!
Note that TT2 implicitates as well.

Model 3: ST: "An Army of one" (bumper sticker)
>>**TT:** "*Yo soy el Army*"

NOTE   One of the banes of the translator, novice or experienced, is the overuse of nominals in English, which quickly produces translationese. Note TT1 (flawed) and the improved TT2.

Model
ST: *Hay que efectuar la evaluación y seguimiento de los pacientes de cáncer.*
TT1: The carrying out of the evaluation and following up on patients with cancer must occur.
TT2 (denominalization): Screening and follow-up on cancer patients must be implemented.

NOTE In TT1, the accumulation of nouns is cumbersome. TT2 is succinct and easily understood. In general, excessive use of the noun pattern "the x of the y" is characteristic of obtuse, bureaucratic writing, and suggests insufficient attention to the verbalization part of translation transfer; in other words, the translator is stuck in interlanguage mode.

TRANSLATION TIP

Gerundial Constructions

Gerundial constructions create a temporal dimension that often requires some real resourcefulness in English. Here are some examples:

Como venía diciendo	=>	As I've been saying all along
Fue creciendo la planta	=>	The plant grew and grew
Anda recogiendo latas	=>	He goes around picking up cans/He has been going around picking up cans
¡Voy comprendiendo la materia!	=>	The lesson is sinking in/I'm getting it, slowly
Me voy quedando atrás	=>	I'm falling behind

Here's a strategy for dealing with this construction in poetry:

Iba cantando por el camino	=>	Singing, singing, on his way he went

---

NOTE **Recategorization** should not be confused with **recasting** (*reestructuración*), which mainly refers to the syntactic reorganization of a sentence into a more language-appropriate order of words or ideas, usually focusing on idiomatic flow or naturalness and the structuring of *theme* (the organizational axis) and *rheme* (what follows from the theme).

Moreover, don't confuse others' use of the words **addition** (the unwanted introduction of tangential material) and **amplification** (the use of more words in the TT where the target language lacks the recourses to express the idea as succinctly).

Some theorists use one of these terms for the *other* concept. Be sure you understand which meaning is intended: Sometimes a need exists for such supplements; other times, they can make translations opaque or simply wrong.

Cultural Substitution (Adaptation, Transculturation)

This is the use in translation of a local variant of something with high cultural specificity; it is an invariably domesticating (familiarizing) choice. For example, suppose a menu translator uses "Spanish appetizers" for "tapas" instead of "tapas" (which would be a valid choice for certain clientele).

Task

Read the opening to the chapter "Hips" in Sandra Cisneros' *The House on Mango Street* (1985). Think about how you would approach the italicized part of the passage—the bit beginning "*I like coffee, I like tea.*" Research and offer at least two solutions for two different audiences.

Read the rest of the chapter in Cisneros and offer cultural substitutions for all the passages in italics. Then find out about some of the translation history of this work into Spanish.

Compensation

Compensation occurs where there is a loss and indirect making up for that loss with other means. In practice, compensation may occur elsewhere in a text.

> **Model 1: ST:** *selvas impresionantes **ríos caudalosos** y reliquias históricas*
> >>**TT:** spectacular rain forests, large teeming rivers and vestiges of the past

> **NOTE**   An example of *compensation by splitting*: The word *caudaloso* has two features the translator wants to preserve, and so two adjectives are used; this is especially effective in poetry, in which, for example, the word *blanco* might embrace "white" and "blank," and thus both meanings can be recovered by *alternating* the English.

TRANSLATION TEASER

Try this line from a legal transcript (spoken by a complainant to her lawyer over a pending case):
Si el juez es blanco, no va a haber justicia. Si la jueza es negra, sí va a haber.
What techniques would you use to translate this line without information loss?

Activity: "Scramble"—Recategorizations and Modulations

Your instructor will give you slips of paper with either a Spanish or English phrase on it. Go around to classmates until you find the corresponding expression in the opposite language of the pair. Compare the underlined portions and be able to explain what lexical category (part of speech) is recategorized or modulated in your pair. Each student should be given the same number of slips. The first round will feature transpositions; the second, modulations. Complete the matching "scramble" in 3 to 4 minutes, then the class will do a read back of selected pairs with explanations for each.

. . . .

Activity: Identification

Identify what technique is used in the following text segments; if there is more than one, identify them:

1. **ST:** *El movimiento social reivindicaba muchos beneficios concretos, entre ellos "pan, techo y abrigo".* (from a history book)
    >>**TT:** The social movement demanded many real benefits such as "food, clothing, and shelter."
2. **ST:** *Le dieron una sentencia de cadena perpetua.* (news item)
    >>**TT:** "He was given a life sentence."
3. **ST:** *Despreocúpate de tu equipaje, pues aparecerá "como por arte de magia" en tu camarote.* (theme cruise Web site)
    >>**TT:** "Leave your luggage to us. It will appear magically in your cabin."
4. **ST:**

    El Presidente ha reiterado que aceptará la resolución del CNE. La oposición, en cambio, ha llevado a cabo en las últimas semanas una campaña denigratoria contra este organismo, donde tienen lugar preponderante miembros de la propia oposición. . . .

(Source: Bilbao, Luis. "Apoyo internacional para Ernesto Villegas". aporrea.org. <www.aporrea.org/actualidad/a6839.html>, Accessed May 20, 2009)

>>**TT:** "The President confirmed that he will accept the CNE's (National Electoral Council's) resolution. However, in recent weeks the opposition party has carried out a smear campaign against this organization, where opposition members dominate." (Discuss: *"la propia oposición"* is not accounted for in this passage—Do you think you can adjust this translation to include it?)

5. **ST:** (On Nabisco's Premium Saltine Crackers, a bilingual box features this language to promote the product's low fat): "Sensible Snacking"
   >>**TT:** *La opción sensible*
6. **ST:** *Me da verguenza ajena.*
   >>**TT:** I'm embarrassed for him.
7. **ST:** Who are you wearing? (at a televised movie premiere)
   >>**TT:** *¿Quién fue el diseñador que le hizo este traje?*
8. **ST:** *Historia universal* (book title)
   >>**TT:** *World History*
9. **ST:** (from Practice Questions for U.S. Citizenship Exam, early 2000s:
   Who makes the laws in the United States?
   Congress
   >>**TT:** *¿ Quién crea las leyes federales en los Estados Unidos?*
   El Congreso
10. **ST:** Patient comatose. (note on an inpatient's chart)
   >>**TT:** *Paciente comatosa.*

Bonus Question: What combination of strategies appears in this pairing (from a TV news caption)?
ST: *Candidata a la presidencia Hillary Clinton*
   >>**TT:** Presidential hopeful Hillary Clinton

Calques, Loans, Borrowings, and Neologisms

calque: 1. a loan translation resulting from bilingual interference in which the structure of the source language word or phrase is kept, but its morphemes (the smallest meaningful part of a word) are replaced by those of the target language; e.g., *cerveza de raíz* (for "root beer"); *perrito caliente* (for "hot dog"); *rascacielos* (for "skyscraper"); *interviú* (for "interview"); 2. in translation, a procedure whereby the translator transfers the elements of the source text literally. Also *v.* to calque

loan translation: the process by which a compound word results from a literal translation of each of the morphological elements of the source; e.g. *superman* (from the German *"Übermensch"*); *cowboy* (from *vaquero*)

loanblend (hybrid): a compound word or phrase including elements of two languages; e.g. *Disneylandia; macho man; internauta; generation ñ*

loanshift: extension or change in the meaning of a word through the influence of a foreign word; e.g. *emilio* (a play on the name "Emilio"), now a name for an email [also *correo electrónico*].

borrowing: word on "permanent loan" to a language and that usually adopts that language's phonetics, but sometimes is altered, e.g. *grifo*>reefer; *charqui*>jerky; *placer*>placer; *juzgado*>hoosegow; *rodeo*>rodeo; *lazo*>lasso; *caballerangero*>wrangler; *sabe*>savvy (see, for example, the intriguing *Cowboy Talk: A Dictionary of Spanish Terms from the American West* by R. Smead [2004])

neologism: 1. a word or term newly created or borrowed; 2. a word or term from another language whose meaning is new, e.g. paparazzi; narcotraffic (the latter is also a loanblend or conceivably a calque)

LINGUISTIC NOTE

Nontranslation is:

1. not translating (as a practice, belief, or instance), usually represented as "ø" in translation theory; **2.** the borrowing of words or whole passages straight into the target text.

CASE STUDY: PHOTOCOPIER WARNING TRANSLATION STRATEGIES

Compare the following target text (Spanish) to the English source. They are part of a multilingual warning sticker on an actual business photocopier.

ST: Be sure to keep the glass clean to prevent unwanted marks or lines on the copies.

TT: *En caso de que aparezca una línea negra en la copia, limpiar el cristal del lector con cuidado de no dañarlo.*

How would you describe the shifts in the target above? What techniques (strategies) does the translator employ? Does the translation suffer on account of them? What happens to the idea of "unwanted"?

CASE STUDY: MANUAL CAPTION TRANSLATION STRATEGIES

In a user manual for a printer, the following captions appear in their respective language sections:

ST: If you cannot resolve the problem, see the support flyer that came with the printer, or visit http://www.hp.com. In the **Select a country/region** field at the top, select your country/region and click ➡. Click the **Support** block.

TT: *Si no puede resolver el problema, consulte el folleto de asistencia al cliente que acompaña a la impresora, o visite http://www.hp.com. En el campo* **Select a country/region (Seleccione un país/región)** *situado en la parte superior de la página, seleccione su país/región y haga clic en* ➡. *Haga clic en el bloque soporte.*

1. In the preceding manual captions, the Spanish translation includes English words. Explain why. (They are excerpted from different language sections of the same hardcopy user manual.)
2. Consider the term *soporte* (bottom line of the target, above right). Is this a standard translation for "Support" (bottom line of the source, above left) in this sense, or is it a borrowing or *calque*? If it is a borrowing, it has the burden of interference, at least as a verb—to *soportar* a customer is hardly supportive!

Research

Come to a consensus or discusssion on the issue—perhaps evidence will show you that it has become *lexicalized* (accepted as natural in a language). If you are a native Spanish speaker, what's your take on it? Do you viscerally accept or reject the use of *soporte* here, independent of usage norms? Consider the issue of prescriptive versus descriptive terminology use.

A second, equally important, and related issue here is the rendering of "support flyer" (second line of the source). Is the *folleto de asistencia al cliente* related to *soporte*? Is this aspect made *explicit*, or *coherent*, in translation? If not, should it be, or are these unrelated meanings of the same term? Or do you not have enough information to determine? Discuss.

Activity: Translation Procedures for "*Duelos y quebrantos*" in *Don Quijote*

"Let any one draw [my picture], if he pleases," said Don Quixote, "but let him not abuse the original." —Miguel de Cervantes *Don Quixote*, Motteaux/Ozell translation

Yantar aquí es un encanto, si tomas "duelos y quebrantos"—popular proverb

1. Read the following well-known opening to Miguel de Cervantes' *Don Quijote*. Afterward, note the various procedures that translators over the last four centuries have used to translate the term "*duelos y quebrantos*" (in bold):

    En un lugar de la Mancha, de cuyo nombre no quiero acordarme, no ha mucho tiempo que vivía un hidalgo de los de lanza en astillero, adarga antigua, rocín flaco y galgo corredor. Una olla de algo más vaca que carnero, salpicón las más noches, **duelos y quebrantos** los sábados, lantejas los viernes, algún palomino de añadidura los domingos, consumían las tres partes de su hacienda. El resto della concluían sayo de velarte, calzas de velludo para las fiestas, con sus pantuflos de lo mesmo, y los días de entresemana se honraba con su vellorí de lo más fino. Tenía en su casa una ama que pasaba de los cuarenta, y una sobrina que no llegaba a los veinte, y un mozo de campo y plaza, que así ensillaba el rocín como tomaba la podadera. Frisaba la edad de nuestro hidalgo con los cincuenta años; era de complexión recia, seco de carnes, enjuto de rostro, gran madrugador y amigo de la caza. Quieren decir que tenía el sobrenombre de Quijada, o Quesada, que en esto hay alguna diferencia en los autores que deste caso escriben; aunque, por conjeturas verosímiles, se deja entender que se llamaba Quejana. Pero esto importa poco a nuestro cuento; basta que en la narración dél no se salga un punto de la verdad.

2. Now compare these versions of *duelos y quebrantos*. Name the techniques used.

    Shelton (1612/1620)—**"collops and eggs"**
    Phillips (1687)—**"parch'd Peafe"**
    Motteaux (1700–3): **"griefs and groans"**
    Ozell's revision of Motteaux (1719): **"Eggs and Bacon"** (plus footnote)
    Jarvis (a.k.a., Jervas, 1742): **"pains and breakings"**
    Jarvis, rev. and corr. (1848): **"sheep's chitterlings"** (plus footnote)
    Jarvis/Riley (ed. 1992): **"omelet"** (plus footnote)
    Smollett (1755): **"gripes and grumblings"** (plus footnote)

> Ormsby (1885): **"scraps"**
> Clark, ed. (Motteaux/Jarvis trans.; c. 1900–10): **"griefs and groans"**
> Putnam (1945): **"scraps"** (plus footnote)
> J. M. Cohen (1950): **"boiled bones"**
> Starkie (1954): **"'tripe and trouble'"**
> Jones/Douglas (1885/c. 1981; revision of Ormsby): **"bacon and eggs"**
> Raffel (1995): **"leftover scraps"**
> Rutherford (2000): **"lardy eggs"**
> Grossman (2003): **"eggs and abstinence"** (plus footnote)

3. Note this footnote to *duelos y quebrantos* in John Ozell's 1719 revised Motteaux (into English):

   Strictly, Sorrow for his Sops, on Saturdays, Duelos y Quebrantos; In English, Gruntings and Groanings. He that can tell what Sort of Edible the Author means by those Words, *Erit mihi magnus Apollo*. Caesar Oudin, the famous French Traveller, Negotiator, Translator and Dictionary-maker, will have it to be Eggs and Bacon, as above. Our Translator and Dictionary-maker, Stevens, has it, Eggs and Collops (I suppose he means Scotch-Collops) but that's too good a Dish to mortify withal. Signor Sobrino's Spanish Dictionary says, Duelos y Quebrantos is Pease-Soup. Mr. Jarvis translates it an Amlet (Aumulette in French) which Boyer says is a Pancake made of Eggs, tho' I always understood Aumulette to be Bacon-Froise (or rather Bacon-fryze, from its being fry'd from frit in French). Some will have it to mean Brains fry'd with Eggs, which, we Are told by Mr. Jarvis, the Church allows in poor Countries in Defect of Fish. Other have guest it to mean some windy kind of Diet, as Peas, Herbs, &c. which are apt to occasion Cholicks, as if one should say Greens and Gripes on Saturdays. To conclude, the 'forecited Author of the new Translation (if a Translator may be call'd an Author) absolutely says, Duelos y Quebrantos is a Cant-Phrase for some Fasting-Day Dish in use in la Mancha. After all these learned Disquisitions, Who knows but the Author means a Dish of Nichils!

4. Discuss which translations you find most effective and your reasons for thinking they are effective. Defend your ideas with solid research.

Research

Research the term even more thoroughly, and decide how you would deal with it in your own translation. Provide documentation. You may wish to lend credence to your arguments by first determining how the controversial term was considered by the writer's own contemporaries.

CASE STUDY: WARNING SIGN

People have died for lack of translations and interpretations from both natural disasters (police instructions to evacuate) and everyday natural phenomena (unsafe conditions).

What strategies did the en>es translator try with this warning sign? Consider how the term "rip current" was negotiated. Why do you suppose? Without showing Spanish-speaking informants the visual, ask them what *Escápese de la resaca* might mean. (Did anyone guess a hangover remedy?)

Source: Reprinted courtesy of the National Weather Service

THE "TELEPHONE" EXPERIMENT: WHAT GOOD ARE TRANSLATIONS OF TRANSLATIONS?

Translations of translations usually are substandard practice, though they occur in cases where infrequent languages combinations need what is called a *relay language*; for example, for Serbian to German, a text might be rendered out of Serbian into French, and then from French into German. (Interpreting has a similar system, called by the French term, *pivot*, an arrangement by which simultaneous interpreting booths are connected to form a relay "middleman" between uncommon language combinations.) Rather than studying the theories behind why translations of translations are not ideal practice, let's try something more immediate: a brief exercise so you can prove it to yourself using English and Spanish.

Task

Your instructor will give you and each of your classmates a very short and relatively simple text for translation, in either English or Spanish, and a corresponding brief. At the 5-minute mark, the ST is folded over, and each student's TT becomes the new ST for the student to his or her *right*. For the second round, all the new STs are translated, then, in the opposite direction (en>es or es>en). At the 5-minute mark, this second round of translations is covered and the process continues. Do at least 5 rounds (25 minutes). Volunteers then can read out the original ST and the resulting text at the bottom of the page or the text in the same language that is furthest down the page. Compare. (This is a variation of González-Davies' "accordion translations" [2004, 179–80].)

Sample texts:

Los choferes (que estén especialmente entrenados) de vehículos comerciales que estén construidos para dar mantenimiento a pozos petrolíferos, no deberán incluir el tiempo que esperen en los sitios de gas natural o pozos petrolíferos como tiempo en servicio. Todo ese tiempo será considerado completamente y exactamente en los expedientes que se mantendrá el autotransportista.

(*Source:* <http://www.fmcsa.dot.gov/spanish/pdfs/tm_hos_sp_ppt_index.htm>, accessed April 11, 2009)

Certain terms and conditions governing the money transfer service you have selected are set forth on the back of this form. By signing this form, you are agreeing to those terms and conditions. In addition to the transfer fee, Western Union also makes money when it changes your dollars into Mexican pesos. (Western Union money transfer form)

Debriefing: Based on your experience with this exercise, what conclusions would you draw about translations of translations? The effect in a classroom setting is exaggerated for effect. What disadvantages and constraints are present in the experiment that might not be present in "real life"?

WORKSHOP #3: TWO BRIEFS AND TWO TRANSLATIONS

For this workshop you will be choosing your own short source text (250 words) and translating it for two different audiences for a total of 500 words. You should write a clear, detailed brief for each. Each audience should be well defined; choose a text that would lend itself well to this task. Append to your translation a paragraph analysis in which you describe, and give examples of, the strategies you used to distinguish the two audiences and/or purposes.

Your work will be evaluated based on the quality and adequacy of your translations, but also on how well your text choice relates to the task and the insight you provide into the translation process in your appended narrative. You should not write briefs that call for very minimal differences in your target texts.

5

Translating Figurative Speech

What do you think the challenges are in translating figurative language?

OJO: Don't make the mistake of thinking that figures of speech only occur in poetry and other expressive texts. In fact, you would be hard pressed to find a text type that *doesn't* make use of the wide repertoire of figurative speech. The question for you throughout this chapter and beyond is: How does figurative language—a product of its culture—tranform between cultures and yet still "do" what it's doing? This kind of language puts the most linguistic and cultural demands on the sender and receiver of a message. And yet it is our everyday—very human—way of communicating abstractions. Let's look at some issues and examples.

IDIOMS

Form groups of three students each. Each group will be given a set of shuffled cards with idioms in the source language (Spanish) and target language (English). The target language cards will have twice the number of source language cards, because half of them will be *false leads*—nonequivalent idioms. For example, for *meter la pata* you might find both "trip up (someone's plans)" and "stick one's foot in one's mouth." Remember that each target language phrase offers a *possible* translation, not a definitive one. The object of the game is to match the idioms in each set of cards faster and more accurately than the opposing teams. All teams complete the pairings, calling out in order as they finish; the team that finished fastest must then read out each pair before the group. At the first mistaken pairing, that team loses its turn and the next team to finish takes over, and so forth until all the pairings are read through without mistake (variation on González-Davies 2004, 162–3). Your instructor will give you the shuffled cards with the SL prompts as follows; they should be read back with their matching English phrase in this order:

1. *tener el pico de oro*
2. *dar el visto bueno*
3. *se armó la gorda*
4. *Me pone los pelos de punta*
5. *un día sí, un día no*
6. *refrénate*
7. *estar hecho polvo*
8. *echar la bronca a uno*
9. *¡qué vaina!*
10. *Eso es pan comido.*
11. *hacer su agosto*
12. *estar a la edad del pavo*
13. *porfa*
14. *estar hecho una ruina*
15. *donde el diablo dejó el poncho*
16. *pleitista*
17. *papar moscas*
18. *sangripesado/a*
19. *decir algo de dientes para afuera*
20. *hora pico*

21. *suerte perra*
22. *tener hormigueo*
23. *como si tuviera monos en la cara*

24. *en la onda*
25. *tener palanca*

CASE STUDY: IDIOMS

Here's an example of the relevance of idioms to translation and localization. Consider this line that was at one time on Kodak's Web site: "Now that's a horse of a different color." On the original page, the zebra changed colors as the user rolled over the camera colors in turn. Kodak, knowing the phrase wouldn't translate into other languages, used the design globally but removed the phrase outside the United States.

In pairs, see for yourself how difficult it would have been to translate the phrase into a relevant Spanish, remembering to harmonize with the graphics, upon which much of the impact depends. Kodak knew what many companies learn the hard way—when to translate, and when not to.

Source: Image used courtesy of Eastman Kodak Company

INSULTS

Italo Calvino, in *Il cavaliere inesistente* (*The Non-Existent Knight*) . . . underscored, in epic terms, the importance to be given an accurate translation of insults [during battle]. [. . .] Calvino postulates a roving corps of interpreters [of insults]: 'These interpreters, by tacit agreement on both sides, were not to be killed.'
(Alexander Rainof 2001, 53)

Source: BEETLE BAILEY © King Features Syndicate

In pairs, discuss the headwords that follow in terms of their cultural and linguistic issues in translation. Considering the definitions, decide on your choices and share them with the group. *Avoid bilingual dictionaries*, though you may use a Spanish-Spanish dictionary or a thesaurus to brainstorm. Remember componential analysis and splitting as strategies. Where necessary, give different contexts, including historical ones, where one equivalent may be preferred over another, or to account for different meanings given in the definitions. Give an alternate register where possible.

Which do you think are the most culture bound? Test your choices by finding authentic source texts that use the word in the way you imagined it used.

NOTE   Many of the insults are exclusive to Spain.

Cachondo. Sujeto rijoso, capaz de excitarse con el solo pensamiento y recuerdo de asuntos y situaciones lascivas que él recrea en su imaginación. . . . También se dice de quien es en exceso burlón y divertido, haciendo chistes a cualquier cosa, y tomándose la vida a chirigota.
(Celdrán 1995, 48)

Cagado, cagón. Metafórica y despectivamente se dice del individuo cobarde, carente de espíritu y de presencia de ánimo, que ante cualquier pequeña dificultad o mínimo peligro huye o vuelve la espalda.
(Celdrán 1995, 50)

Chulo. Mezcla de rufián, pícaro, valentón de taberna y bocazas. También se dijo del individuo que se conduce a sí mismo con gracia, desvergüenza y desparpajo barriobajero, distinguiéndose por la afectación y guapeza de su indumentaria o atuendo.
(Celdrán 1995, 74)

Engendro. Tiene connotaciones físicas y morales: monstruo, deforme, criatura mal formada. Muchacho perverso, en cuyo caso se hacía preceder el calificativo del adverbio 'mal'.
(Celdrán 1995, 96)

Gabacho. Despectivo por 'francés'.
(Celdrán 1995, 117)

Huevón. Individuo tranquilo, perezoso y torpe, cuya cachaza y escasa energía exaspera a quienes lo rodean; bobalicón; sujeto de reacciones muy lentas, que por nada se inmuta.
(Celdrán 1995, 144–5)

Malaleche. Persona de permanente mal humor; sujeto mal intencionado y avieso; individuo de mala índole, que siempre anda buscando las vueltas a las personas o las cosas.[. . .] Tener mala leche es como tener . . . condición torcida, raíz borde desde el principio, adquirida con la leche que mamaron.
(Celdrán 1995, 180–1)

Marrullero. Adulador que echa mano de todo tipos de halagos, fingimientos y zalemas para liar, embaucar y enredar con astucia a la gente;

liante de buenas palabras, que pone su pico de oro al servicio de tramas inconfesables.

(Celdrán 1995, 201)

Repipi. Se dice de quien es afectado en sus modales y pedante en el hablar; persona que se conduce de manera manifiestamente ridícula, sin apercibirse de ello.

(Celdrán 1995, 284)

Tiquismiquis. Persona atildada, que gusta de ofrecer aspecto cuidado, y da importancia excesiva a tonterías y a cosas que no la tienen. [Da a entender] los escrúpulos y los remilgos, los cuidados y prevenciones de quienes ponen gran atención en sí mismos y en la imagen que proyectan.

(Celdrán 1995, 307)

Tiralevitas. Lacayo. Sujeto siempre dispuesto a dar coba a quien considera superior a él, en la esperanza de lograr un beneficio o trato de favor, sin importarle el daño que pueda acarrear a terceros, generalmente sus compañeros de trabajo o colegas.

(Celdrán 1995, 308)

Torpe, torpón. Es palabra que afecta a diversos ámbitos: el de la inteligencia, el de la habilidad y el de la catadura moral de las personas....Y en cuanto al orden moral, donde se torna más grave y ofensivo, alude a la persona ignominiosa, de costumbres y conducta muy relajadas, siendo sujeto capaz de cometer cualquier bellaquería y bajeza. [. . .] En cuanto a la voz 'torpón', es uso familiar menos grave que torpe, ya que excluye la torpeza moral.

(Celdrán 1995, 317)

Vacilón. Bromista pesado y guasón; sujeto que disfruta tomando el pelo a los demás; persona a la que le va el vacile: acción y efecto de cachondearse del prójimo. También se emplea en el sentido de individuo a quien le gusta chulearse, hacer ostentación vana de su palmito y figura.

(Celdrán 1995, 331)

TRANSLATION TIP

Al pan, pan, y al buey, buey

Translators can't afford to be squeamish. If an insult or a curse word is strong, it cannot be softened in translation to suit a translator's sensitivities. This is no idle topic: Heated arguments have broken out in open court over how insulting the word *pendejo* should be rendered, for example. Translators are honor bound not to censure, particularly in legal contexts. Historically, however, expurgations and bowdlerizations of translations were common: *The Arabian Nights* in the Victorian era was accommodated to tastes at the time.

Hispanic cultures will have far more culture-bound insults related to cuckoldry (a wife or girlfriend's unfaithfulness)—usually expressed by a horned animal: *buey* or *cabrón* (note that in English, oxen are associated with being dumb), which relates to the expression *ponerle los cuernos a alguien* (not to stick it to someone, as it seems to mean, but to "give them horns"—to rob someone's manhood, and metaphorically, even his humanity, by running around behind his back). English, by contrast, true to its Puritanical roots, tends toward the scatological: impugning someone's *cleanliness*, whether literal, moral, or biological.

Tasks

1. Identify some regional profanity. What challenges to translation would it present in a legal transcript in the United States, for example?
2. Identify some profanity that references some aspect of Catholicism. How does the Catholic framework impart meaning to the swear words? Would it have to be compensated for in English? Give an example, and provide a text type and communicative context.

TRANSLATING GESTURES: THE *MANO CORNUTO*

What does the "hooked horns" gesture (with index and pinky finger extended) mean in different cultures and subcultures? Is it obscene, insulting? Do you know of other symbols that have multiple meanings from country to country? Do you know of gestures that don't translate interculturally at all?

Source: J. Scott Applewhite/AP Wide World Photos

TRANSLATION TEASER

'Frankly, Scarlett, me importa un . . .?'

The American Film Institute chose "Frankly, my dear, I don't give a damn" from "Gone with the Wind" as the greatest cinematic putdown. But how to capture the tone in Spanish? One critic muses: " *'Francamente, querida, me importa un bledo', en la traducción suave, o 'un carajo', en la dura.*" The problem lies in that it's an *expresión justo a mitad de camino entre el bledo y el carajo*. Ending the film with a swear was a big deal at the time, and its use arguably made Rhett Butler's abandonment of Scarlett far more devastating. The censors scrambling for alternatives, David O. Selznik finally had to pay $5,000 to use "damn"! (Soto 2005).

Can Rhett Butler's "Frankly, my dear, I don't give a damn" be rendered into a Spanish appropriate for the period and Spanish-speaking audience of 1939, or is it doomed to lie *a mitad de camino entre el bledo y el carajo*?

Activity: Proverbs and Sayings

1. Fill in the grid with a corresponding proverb (more than one may apply). If necessary, negotiate a suitable target text proverb with an informant, describing the meaning of the phrase and discussing how the idea is usually rendered in proverbial speech. For example, if the ST phrase is *A falta de pan, buenas son tortas*, you might discuss the idea of how one settles for something less when choices are limited: "Beggars can't be choosers," for example, may be suggested, weighed, and accepted or discarded. Be prepared to discuss to what degree you find overlap in your solutions, or shifts of emphasis. You may also consider using traditional *refraneros* (proverb books) if available, or consult the *Prentice-Hall Encyclopedia of World Proverbs* (1986).

Spanish	English
Confidencia quita reverencia.	
El dinero gobierna el mundo.	
	Practice makes perfect.
El comer y el rascar, todo es empezar.	
Cuando el río suena, agua lleva.	
	Where there's a will, there's a way.
	What's done is done.
Borrón y cuenta nueva.	
El que no quiere aventurar, no puede gran hecho acabar.	
A cada puerco su sábado.	
Cuando el diablo no tiene qué hacer, con el rabo mata moscas.	
Gusta lo ajeno, más por ajeno que por bueno.	

2. Explain the meaning of each proverb in your own words.
   a. *Más sabe el loco en su casa que el cuerdo en la ajena.*
   b. *El que no llora no mama.*
   c. *Pescar con mazo no es renta cierta.*
   d. Many are called, but few are chosen.
   e. Penny wise, pound foolish.

3. Match each proverb and saying en<>es to its best counterpart. Each is to be used only once.

   f 1. *La madera que nace para cuñas no admite pulimiento*
   a 2. *No digas nunca de esta agua no beberé.*
   g 3. *Hablando de Roma, el burro se asoma.*
   c 4. *Aunque la mona se vista de seda, mona se queda.*
   d 5. *Desnudar un santo para vestir otro.*
   e 6. *Quien fue a Sevilla perdió su silla.*
   b 7. *El mundo es golfo redondo; quien no sabe nadar se va al fondo.*
   h 8. *A buen entendedor pocas palabras.*

   a. Never say never.
   b. The world is a ladder for some to go up and some down.
   c. Clothes don't make the man.
   d. Robbing Peter to pay Paul.
   e. If you leave your place, you lose it.
   f. You can't make a silk purse out of a sow's ear.
   g. Speak of the Devil.
   h. A word to the wise (is sufficient).

4. The following idioms, sayings, and figurative expressions were translated too rigorously word for word. Revise them into a more flexible English. Try for semantic transmission and, if possible, figurative language. Where necessary, ask an informant to identify situations in which each might be appropriate, though each should give you enough of a clue to revise for meaning.

a. *No había visto una cosa así ni en pintura.* → I had never seen such a thing even in a painting. →

b. *Ella anda más perdida que una cucaracha en baile de gallinas.* → She looks as lost as a cockroach at a hen dance. →

c. *Cría cuervos y te sacarán los ojos.* → Raise crows and they'll pluck your eyes out.→

d. *Hay que coger la sartén por el mango.* → You've got to take the frypan by the handle.

TRANSLATION TEASER

A recent online personal finance tutorial had the following bit of advice:

Págate a ti primero
Ojos que no ven, corazón que no siente. No extrañarás dinero que estás ahorrando si lo depositas directamente en tu plan 401(K) o en otra cuenta de jubilación. (Pardo 2008)

Assuming a similar context, how would you render the proverb, *"Ojos que no ven, corazón que no siente"* for a North American audience?

Did you know that a number of our most common idiomatic expressions and proverbs in English are translations from *Don Quixote*? It's true: "the haves and the have-nots," "the pot calling the kettle black," "mind your own business," "the sky's the limit," "all that glitters is not gold," and "hunger is the best sauce," the latter of which has both a literal phrasing in Cervantes—*La mejor salsa del mundo es el hambre*—and a figurative one: *A buen hambre no hay pan duro*.

CASE STUDY: FIGURATIVE LANGUAGE

Connect with your **Manual** Web site to find the link to H&R Block's Spanish page and check how it features culturally customized content for the Latino customer, as do its television ad campaigns. In the video script that follows, the copy clearly has been crafted for those for whom the signifier of the rooster and the equation of frequency (by extension, speed) with the rooster crowing all have resonance. The Spanish expression *antes que cante un gallo* proverbially means "in an instant." The spot currently appears on Spanish-language television in the United States. Producers have included an English translation, though the actors only speak the Spanish.

VIDEO		AUDIO
1	OPEN ON A DESERT WITH ROBERTO AND HORACIO DRIVING A SIDECAR MOTORCYCLE	HORACIO	Hola, somos Horacio *Hello, we are Horacio*
2	THEY GET OFF THE SIDECAR AND WALK THROUGH A BARN WHERE THEY PICK UP A ROOSTER	ROBERTO	Y Roberto *And Roberto*
3	THEY WALK INTO AN H&R BLOCK OFFICE WHERE WE FIND AN EMPLOYEE WORKING WITH A CUSTOMER	HORACIO	de H&R Block y vamos a demostrarte que con un Préstamo de Reembolso Anticipado *from H&R Block and we'll demonstrate to you that with an Instant Money Refund*
		ROBERTO	Dinero al Instante *Anticipation Loan*
		HORACIO	podrías recibir dinero antes que cante un gallo. *you could get money before a rooster can sing.*
4	ROBERTO PLACES A ROOSTER ON TOP OF THE EMPLOYEE'S DESK		
5	ROOSTER STARTS PREPPING ITS VOICE WHILE CUSTOMER AND EMPLOYEE WORK THE W2 FORM	SFX: ROOSTER CLEARING THROAT	
6	CUSTOMER STANDS UP AND LEAVES WITH AN ENVELOPE ON HIS HANDS.		
7	ROOSTER STARTS SINGING	SFX: ROOSTER SINGING	Volar contigo mi amor *Fly with you my love.*
8	HORACIO AND ROBERTO LOOK AT CAMERA	SFX: ROOSTER SINGING HORACIO & ROBERTO	¡Comprobado! Recibió su dinero antes que cantara un gallo. *Proven! She got money before the rooster could sing.*
9	WE SEE HORACIO AND ROBERTO PLAYING WITH ROOSTER.	AVO	En H&R Block, podrías recibir dinero rápido. ¿Por qué? Porque estamos contigo. *At H&R Block, you could get money fast. Why? Because we are with you.*
10	SUPER: 1-800-HRBLOCK Hrblock.com/espanol		
11	LOGO: H&R BLOCK. TAGLINE: ESTAMOS CONTIGO.		

HR BLOCK
30-Second Film
"ROOSTER"
FAST MONEY OPTIONS

(*Source:* Reprinted by permission of H&R Block)

METONYMY

Metonymy is a rhetorical device by which a word is substituted by something associated with it in order to transfer sense (Fass 1997, 32). The device is used for relations of contiguity (adjacent things or concepts), possession, degree, proximity, or causality. Synecdoche—relations of part for the whole or whole for the part—is sometimes included (metonymically!) in metonymy and sometimes used interchangeably with the term. The difference between metaphor and metonymy is that metaphor is based on similarity and comparison across two unlike domains; metonymy is based on connectedness, with one entity *standing in* for another (47). Some argument remains about whether metonymy is a kind of metaphor.

The special, frequently overlooked relevance of metonymy for the translator's toolbox lies in that it affords a sense of flexibility, much like how we saw with recasting, recategorization, and modulation. Moreover, it should be noted that many modulations are metonymic shifts. Often, one must use some kind of communicative strategy because metonymies, predictably, differ from language to language and cannot be rendered literally. Sometimes an intermediate step of a literal paraphrase or explicitation is necessary to render an acceptable target language phrase from a source text metonymy. Efforts are underway to develop machine translation programs that can read—translate—metonymy.

The following are a few examples of metonymy and their corresponding types (after Fass 1997, 461–9):

"50 *head*" (of cattle)	part for whole
"*America* beat *France*"	whole for part
"a *Casanova*"	antonomasia (name that embodies a characteristic)
"A watched *pot* never boils"	container for contents
"He totaled his *Ford*"	producer for product
"Remember the *Alamo*"	place for the event

Translators should attune their sensibilities to connotations when attempting a change of metonym—is a "Casanova" exactly a "Don Juan" in Spanish?

Interlinguistic Examples

Phrase level: *la planicie desértica y* **marina** ≈> desert and **coastal** plains [Strictly considered, this is also a modulation in that it is a change in the point of view—from ocean to land.]

Sentence level (1): **Moja** *la pluma en el tintero.* ≈> He **dips** his pen [quill] in the inkwell. [This not only creates a natural collocation in English, but the metonymy emphasizes the action rather than the result in English, a *modulation of cause and effect,* if you will.]

Sentence level (2): *El restaurante ofrece una variedad de platos de nuestra* **cocina** *internacional.* ≈> The restaurant offers an assortment of entrees from our international **menu**. [The menu is a representation of what is prepared in the kitchen, hence there is no translation loss—on the contrary, arguably the English may be clearer.]

Frequently, a metonym will need to be shifted (modulated) to another metonym in the TT; for example (en>es):

The speaker has **the floor**. ≈> *El presidente tiene* **la palabra**.

The objection that translators do not think in terms of metonymies to solve problems is simply *unfounded*, particularly in the more expressive domains. Whether or not translators consciously call metonymies by that name, they are constantly "doing metonymy":

—diagnosing their own solutions based on relationships of contiguity, which may be different from those of their own language;

—brainstorming possible solutions based on the alternate "points of view" metonymy analysis affords;

—assessing the appropriateness of others' translations based on relative frequency comparisons (statistically or intuitively) that provide evidence of inadequate transfer or translation success.

It is also one more resource in the novice translator's repertoire—thinking metonymically when you translate can dramatically help you avoid literalism and translate with a "wider palette." Awareness of metonymy allows the learner to self-check with confidence in the knowledge that overlap between languages can occur obliquely, not only transparently. As we suggested, too, metonymy is closely related to modulation, a key translation technique. Major translation scholars currently are investigating further the links between metonymy and translation.

METAPHOR

Translation and metaphor share the meaning of *carrying across*. Spanish has a word—*verter* (to pour, to overturn, to shed [tears])—that itself is used metaphorically to mean "to translate." Metaphors are tropes (figures of speech) that directly or indirectly highlight a relationship of comparison, analogy, similarity, or identity. Essentially the metaphor consists of representing one thing in terms of another, or the transference of the properties of one domain to another, frequently from concrete to concrete or abstract to concrete. Metaphor, according to Roman Jakobson (2004), is more properly the domain of poetry; metonymy, that of prose. They are phenomena that arise only in discourse and so as Paul Ricœur wrote memorably, "[t]he dictionary contains no metaphors" (2003, 97). It should be remembered that metaphors are violations of a sort in that they force a *defamiliarization* in the way something is perceived, though many metaphors over time become "stock" or "cliché." Some words are recognizably born as metaphors (e.g., "hippopotamus" means "river horse"), though some theorists contend that at bottom, all language is metaphorical. A metaphor may even "die," becoming fossilized (overly stale or familiar to the point of everydayness, when we no longer think of it as a metaphor). Examples of dead metaphors include: to arrive (to come to shore); a blockbuster (a bomb in a military sense, now having the meaning of a big hit); lunatic (a person crazed by the influence of the full moon); decimate (to kill every tenth soldier drawn by lots as a punishment). On the other extreme are wild metaphoric leaps that can make the reputations of their authors by renovating language and virtually creating a new thought. John Donne's (1633) "The Flea," for example, features a flea whose bite unites the blood of the two lovers into a sacramental force: "This flea is you and I, and this/Our marriage bed, and marriage temple is." Debate has emerged as to whether translating live metaphors poses more of a challenge than dead metaphors, in part because each culture's stock of associations will be different—a cliché in one culture may be a revelation in translation; similarly, a "fresh" metaphor may be too strained after transfer. Be sure to consider the receiving culture's degree of familiarity with the semantic field before undertaking the translation of a metaphor, particularly when religion, politics, and popular icons are involved: *Nuestro éxito ha sido un regalo de Reyes* (in a newspaper interview with a rock band member) would certainly be better rendered "Our success has been a blessing/godsend/pennies from heaven" than "Our success has been like a present on the Epiphany" (or even ". . . on Christmas," which is somehow both corny and flat in English). Another example is: the (perhaps now sexist) endearment *mi costilla* (my "old lady"/better half) would be lost in English were a similar allusive metaphor attempted—the reference to Adam's rib is oblique at best. (Arguably, Spanish-speaking cultures on the whole have stronger, more active connections with their cultural stock of proverbs, Biblical knowledge, history, and mythology.)

Some Strategies for Translating Metaphor (En>Es)

literal   skeletons in her closet ≈> *esqueletos en el armario*
          [*can* be safe, if the metaphor is uncomplicated; frequently nonsensical]

figurative   skeletons in her closet ≈> *cadáver en el armario*
          [to be preferred when possible]

explicated   skeletons in her closet ≈> *secreto vergonzoso de la familia*
          [communicative but loses stylistic dimension]

In some cases, a *simile*, explicated or not, can do the work of a metaphor (*Está hecho un toro* ≈> He's as strong as an ox [note the change of trope and animal]). The best alternative is usually one relevant metaphor for another (*andar de capa caída* < > to go downhill), but a translator is sometimes constrained by the existence, register, and currency of prospective equivalents (witness the quaint impression given by the English in this pair: *No vale un higo.* ≈> It's not worth a tinker's damn.). Perhaps the *least* effective strategy for translating metaphor then, and regrettably one that is all too common, is to either ignore it or neutralize it with a stale expression found readily at hand in the target text. Whether this is the result of translators' low recognition of fresh language, laziness, time constraints, lack of verbal acumen, or temerity is a matter of speculation. It is in the genius of each language, however, to use metaphors in a way peculiar to its users' thinking, and often where one language commonly uses a metaphor, another will explicate:

una ***magnífica*** *cantidad* ≈> a **princely** sum

brilla *por su ausencia*   ≈> **it is conspicuous** by its absence

This can be explained partly by the fact that different languages have different levels of tolerance for metaphoric language (French, for example, uses metaphor even in highly technical texts), and also that languages develop differently—metaphors "die" at different rates and that "live" and "dead" are a matter of perception. It is likely in the preceding example that the speaker of the ST sample would barely perceive *brillar* as a metaphor in the idiom given.

It may be of use to understand the two parts of a metaphor: **tenor** (source domain) and **vehicle** (target domain). For example, in the sentence, "The oak is the patriarch of the forest," "patriarch" is the vehicle whose conceptual grid is mapped onto the tenor, "the oak." The tree, then, takes on *selected* qualities of a grand old man: stateliness, age, wisdom, a certain "presence." Rarely do a tenor and vehicle imply complete identity: Someone "martyred to a cause" then need not actually die—the idea is he or she suffers greatly for a belief.

> ### TRANSLATION TIP
>
> **Translating Metaphors**
>
> Translate a fresh metaphor with an equally fresh metaphor. If the source text metaphor is weak, try a literal version; the result may be a quirky new one in the target text (if it is too opaque or transla toresque, refrain).
>
> Watch for places where metaphors between languages line up, or transfer, at oblique angles. Nigel Lewis (1994) on this score: "When [metaphors between languages] do concur [. . .], when they are not idiosyncratic or random fancies, but apparently 'universal', [. . .] there may be a cognitive significance in the fact of their concurrence" (9–10).

SPORTS METAPHORS

Our culture, consciously or unconsciously, views sports as war, and this is reflected in our sports lexicon: *scrimmage, sudden death, kill shot, blitz*. Sports are so all-pervasive that language used to talk about baseball, football, hockey, basketball, boxing, and other popular American sports makes its way into politics, business, and other arenas (a sports metaphor itself). In some sense, as some commentators have noted, this usage is insidious in that it encourages hazy thinking and mere spectatorship while it superimposes a certain set of expectations—that business *is* football (or war, or what have you) and behaves by its rules, or conversely, and to worse effect, that war is a mere game (military leaders and strategists use sports metaphors continually). On the other hand, as the book *Cultural Metaphors* (2001) argues, sports may owe their appeal to their incarnation of an ideal—and familiar—business model of teamwork. Regardless, sports metaphors are inherently exclusivist—many people inside and outside the United States do not follow sports, nor should it be assumed they do (or should).

The translator and interpreter alike do well to "denude" the sports metaphor, or change it to another, more universal one. Failing this, the translator risks great communication loss. Occasionally one may find a suitable soccer metaphor (for example), or a transferable war metaphor, but it is a good instinct to render sports metaphors as unambiguously as possible, in part because they often occur in key negotiations. Business personnel are often reminded to avoid them to begin with whenever dealing with an international public or speakers of English with limited proficiency (LEP), or relaying a message that will be translated or interpreted. When tempted to translate a sports metaphor literally out of English, put yourself on the receiving end for a moment: How would you cope with a reference to bullfighting's *doble paso* in a news brief on political events if you were translating for a newswire? Or a sumo wrestling maneuver? Or terminology from cricket (you may get "sticky wicket" all right, but how would you do with a "googly")*? Transparent sports metaphors in translation can be—and frequently are—"left at the starting gate."

---

*Try your luck with this one: "Cardinal Rufini [the conservative archbishop of Palermo] played his usual role of opening batsman and, with the keen eye and built-in caution of a born opening bat, he dealt firmly with any swing that he detected in theological terminology and biblical quotation" (Hurley 2005). Now consider this gem from a British Cabinet member's resignation speech: "It is rather like sending your opening batsmen to the crease, only for them to find, as the first balls are being bowled, that their bats have been broken before the game by the team captain" (Howe 1994).

In a recent survey of 1,000 translators, "googly" in fact recently made a list of one of the top-ten hardest words to translate: 1. Plenipotentiary; 2. Gobbledegook; 3. Serendipity; 4. Poppycock; 5. Googly; 6. Spam; 7. Whimsy; 8. Bumf; 9. Chuffed; 10. Kitsch. It refers to a special type of breaking ball (curve ball) (Today Translations 2004).

Tasks

1. Here are some common sports metaphors used in mainstream media, politics, and the corporate world. Find texts in different genres online that use one or more, and with a partner, discuss how they might be handled into Spanish for the contexts in which they appear.

   stalemate, level playing field, the front runner, knockout, pitch (e.g., a product or idea), on the ropes, homestretch, key players, to throw in the towel, sudden death, team-building, team player, sidelined, win-win, slam dunk, to field (a question), to tackle a problem, game plan, to go to bat for, to play hardball, dead heat, let down her guard, to ace a test, down for the count, to throw a curve

   To what extent was your instinct to neutralize the metaphor in translation?.
2. One student gives a speech by a world leader who speaks in sports metaphors; another student consecutively "interprets" (scripts may be used) into English.
3. Find a coaching manual or rule book in Spanish or English for a given sport and translate passages into the opposite language of the pair. What cultural differences, even in sporting terminology, appear? Do rules of play, terms, illustrations, and strategies change that much between language communities?

TRANSLATION TEASER

The Hard-Boiled School of Detective Fiction

The so-called pulp fiction magazines and cheap paperbacks of the 1920s and 1930s yielded a uniquely American amalgam of grit and wit that heralded the golden age of detective fiction. Read the beginning of the following novel, 1934's *Trouble Is My Business* by Raymond Chandler, and discuss in groups your (macro and micro) strategies for handling the wordplay translation issues that the paragraphs in bold (added) would present working en>es. What situational variables (e.g., with respect to audience or other functional factors) would affect these strategies? Pay particular attention to *rhythms*, which are vital to wordplay. The first person narrator is the detective Philip Marlowe.

Anna Halsey was about two hundred and forty pounds of middle-aged putty-faced woman in a black tailor-made suit. Her eyes were whiny black shoe buttons, her cheeks were as soft as suet and about the same color. She was sitting behind a black glass desk that looked like Napoleon's tomb and she was smoking a cigarette in a black holder that was not quite as long as a rolled umbrella. She said: "I need a man."

I watched her shake ash from the shiny top of the desk where flakes of it curled and crawled in the draft from an open window.

"I need a man good-looking enough to pick up a dame who has a sense of class, but he's got to be tough enough to swap punches with a power shovel. I need a guy who can act like a bar lizard and backchat like Fred Allen, only better, and get hit on the head with a beer truck and think some cutie in the leg-line topped him with a breadstick."

"It's a cinch," I said. "You need the New York Yankees, Robert Donat, and the Yacht Club Boys."

"You might do," Anna said, "cleaned up a little. Twenty bucks a day and ex's. I haven't brokered a job in years, but this one is out of my line. I'm in the smooth-angles of the detecting business and I make money without getting my can knocked off. Let's see how Gladys likes you."

Then come up with a suitable title in Spanish; *Trouble Is My Business* comes a few lines later in the text: "You might get into trouble, of course," Anna said. [. . .] "Trouble is my business," I said.

TRANSLATING HUMOR

> Because if you are translating jokes, for example, if you get anything wrong,
> nothing works. You have to get it absolutely right. Then you realize that all
> translating is really that way.
> (W. S. Merwin)

Jokes and riddles are beloved by children, but translating them is certainly not child's play. Essentially one must try by trial and error to reproduce *how a joke produces its effect*. Note that the effect of the joke—its payoff—is more important than strict "meaning." Meaning is a pretext for the laugh.

Let's take a look at a few classes of humor and have a try at some exercises.

Activity: Riddles

For the following riddle, fill in the blank, *substituting a different setup* that would work with the same punch line (*remate*):

1. *¿Qué pide un vampiro cuando entra en un bar?* >> <u>*Un vaso sanguíneo.*</u> (A blood vessel.)

> **HINT**   Think of the multiple meanings of "vessel" in English and exploit that ambiguity in your question.

Now try translating some on your own or with a partner:

2. *¿Qué es una losa?*
   Una flol muy helmosa.

3. *Graffiti:*
   Si existe un más allá, habrá un menos acá.

4. *¿De qué murió el señor que inventó la cama de piedra?*
   De un almohadazo.

> **HINT**   Review augmentatives to consider how to handle "-azo."

(*Source:* Chistes.com © 1995–2007)

Activity: Puns and Wordplay

Some jokes depend entirely on phonetics and require some serious rethinking if they are to be translated. Using a pun, try a translation with substitutions:

1. *¿Cuál es el objeto más gracioso que existe?*
   La escoba.
   ¿Por qué?
   Porque siempre va riendo...

2. La profesora en el colegio dice:
   A ver, tú Antonio, dime 3 partes del cuerpo humano que empiecen por la letra c,
   y él responde:
   Cabeza, corazón y cuello.

La profesora dice:
Muy bien, Antonio.
Luego dice:
Tú Joselito, dime 3 partes del cuerpo humano que empiecen por la letra p, y el niño dice:
Pues, pierna, páncreas y pulmón.
Entonces la profesora dice:
Veamos tú Juanito, dime 3 partes del cuerpo humano que empiecen por la letra z
y dice el niño:
¿Por la letra z? Ahora mismo se lo digo: Las zejas, los zojos y las zuñas.

 The following is a serious challenge. Brainstorm, chronicling your strategy:

3. *Si estuvieras en medio del mar ahogándote, ¿qué harías?*
   Lloraría para desahogarme.

(*Source:* Chistes.com © 1995–2007)

CULTURAL NOTE

The Humor of Cantinflas (Mexico, 1911–1993)

Mario Moreno Reyes grew from humble origins as a boxer and stage actor to become one of the best-loved Mexican film icons of the twentieth century. His rapid-fire verbal and visual humor put him in a class with such greats as the Marx Brothers and Charlie Chaplin, though in English he is virtually unknown (his forays in Hollywood films were bombs, and his classic films have been subtitled but not terribly artfully).

A world-famous mural by Diego Rivera on the Teatro Insurgentes on the main thoroughfare of Mexico City features Cantinflas taking from the rich and redistributing to the poor. One of Cantinflas' most enduring legacies—in addition to his championing of the poor—is the verb *cantinflear*, to go on and on saying nothing despite seeming to say something; the noun is *cantinflada*. The Real Academia de la Lengua has even given the word its own entry: "**cantinflear. 1.** intr. *Cuba y Méx.* Hablar de forma disparatada e incongruente y sin decir nada." Cantinflas made a high art of depicting picaresque anti-heroes with the gift of long-drawn, *cantinflesque* gab. (The adjective *cantinflesco* also exists.)

1. Watch Cantinflas shorts (*cortometrajes*) or any of the feature-length movies he made from 1936 to 1981. Choose a scene and write *cantinflesque* dialogue for it in English for a screen adaptation; use the Spanish as a starting point and "transcreate." Remember that 1 minute of screen time is equivalent to one page of a screenplay. Perform for the class from scripts or "off book."

2. Watch a sequence from *El analfabeto* (e.g., the court scene) first without subtitles and then with only subtitles. Discuss the different effects produced. Transcribe a section and do your own version.
   Though subtitling is beyond the scope of this book, its basic principle, like that of comedy itself, is compression—which can be assisted by the domain-appropriate translation technique of *condensation*.

CULTURAL NOTE

El "Choteo" Cubano

"*Choteo*" is a uniquely Cuban type of humor, part of the island nation's cultural identity and practically a philosophy. Dictionaries, naturally, do not do the term justice, defining it as the practice or attitude of taking everything *a relajo*—as a joke. But there are nuances of defiance and irreverence

(Continued)

toward authority in the word. Raquel Aguilú de Murphy (1989, 5) defines "*choteo*" as "*el concepto del humor que mejor caracteriza al pueblo cubano. El choteo cubano es una actitud del pueblo frente a la autoridad establecida; es una forma de no tomar nada en serio. Por medio del choteo, el cubano se burla de la autoridad, de lo más sagrado, y todo aquello que conlleve intrínsecamente un sentido de autoridad.*" Jorge Mañach's classic study of the phenomenon, *Indagación del choteo* (1940), explores many of its manifestations and its underlying motivations, noting that it frequently reveals a state of impatience with, or resentment toward, limits, order, dignity, hierarchy, and prestige. Translator Carol Maier notes that it is also an exclusionary practice of male privilege in Cuba: "*Choteo* is a difficult word to translate out of context and it's very important in Cuban culture; it's a particular way of teasing or ridiculing people 'affectionately,' and it's always impressed me as something very male. I talked to some Cuban women to see whether this kind of linguistic, conceptual play was possible for women and they did not believe it was" (Godayol Nogué 1998). (For further discussion of the phenomenon, see Pérez Firmat 1986.) This brings another aspect—dialectics, "confrontation," performance—to the term. Verbal sparring seems to be common to most discussions of the word, and some observers have seen similarities with "*signifying*" (what some in the African American community have called the empowering use of highly creative wordplay, insult, indirection, and subversive jokes at the expense of the "masters").

Whatever the definition, something serious lurks behind the playful inventiveness of *choteo*.

TRANSLATING COMICS

The essence of dialogue, particularly for humorous effect, is naturalness and concision.

Task

1. Your instructor will pass out Spanish-language comics with multiple-choice options for the *remate* (punch line). Choose the letter of the phrase that best fits as a translation for the final frame in each comic. You may choose the last letter and instead write in your own dialogue. Practice the line out loud to ensure comic effect. For this type of text, can you use poetic license and create a better punch line while still staying "faithful" to the idea to be expressed?
2. Choose a *Mafalda* comic strip from an online site; translate, making source and target into a Power Point slide. Present to the class the strategic challenges you faced; solicit feedback and revise accordingly..

TRANSLATION TEASER

Greguerías

The playful invention of Ramón Gómez de la Serna (Spain; 1888–1963), the *greguería* is one of the oddest, most charming genres: a humorous, brief, metaphoric aphorism-poem that gives a momentary flash of insight as it reimagines relationships between things. How do they come across in English? Connect with your **Manual** Web site and use it to find the link and try some for yourself.

PIROPOS: THE UNTRANSLATABLE?

Piropos are short flirtatious remarks usually made in the street, part of the long tradition of verbal gallantry in the Hispanic world. Used to compliment or catch the attention of passing women, they range from *groseros* (crude) to highly lyrical and clever.

Read the following and consider if there are cultural equivalents in English-speaking cultures for any of the phrases. What do we call this class of utterance, if anything? Does political correctness account for cultural differences here? If so how? What transculturations (adaptations to the target culture) would you make in certain contexts? Why? If translated more or less literally, are they effective? If not, why not? Invent some *piropos* in English that imitate the phrasing of Spanish ones (you may even want to reverse gender roles for some!). Avoid giving deliberate offense.

- *¡Qué curvas y yo sin frenos!*
- *Si Cristóbal Colón te viese diría, ¡Santa María, vaya Pinta que tiene la Niña!*
- *Desearía ser una lágrima tuya ... Para nacer en tus ojos, vivir en tus mejillas y morir en tu boca.*
- *Fui hasta el mar para hablar con los peces pero no encontré el piropo que te mereces.*
- *¿Dónde venden los números para ganarse este premio?*
- *Deberías caminar a la sombra, porque el sol derrite los bombones.*
- *¡Niña, si San Lázaro te ve, suelta la muleta y se manda a correr!*
- *Estás como la historia de Cuba: vieja pero interesante.*
- *"Las tres mariposas, la del medio es una rosa"*
- *¿Qué haces aquí tan temprano? ¿No sabes que las estrellas siempre salen por la noche?*
- *Si amas a Dios que murió por tanta gente, ¿por qué no me amas a mí que muero por ti solamente?*
- *¡Ahora resulta que los ángeles andan!*
- *Mírame un poco que me estoy muriendo de frío.*
- *Si la belleza es pecado, tú nunca serás perdonada.*
- *Bendita sea la yerba que se tragó la borrega de donde sacaron la lana para hacerle la sotana al cura que te bautizó.*
- *—Se te cayó ... (—¿Qué?)*
  —Un pétalo.

TRANSLATION TEASER

Once while consecutively interpreting a noted Central American activist's two-hour speech, an interpreter (this author) was caught slightly off guard by the speaker's controversial criticism of the Peace Corps. In the activist's opinion, the organization has done little good for her country, and those who have participated in the program have not done much strenuous work. "El Cuerpo de Paz?" she scoffed. "El Cuerpo de *Paseo*, mejor." Assuming you have unlimited time (or at least more than this poor interpreter), devise a solution that communicates her meaning and, if you can, preserves some kind of wordplay (and remember: You don't have to agree with her assessment!).

TRANSLATION TEASER

La Bamba

The lyrics to the song "La Bamba" have puzzled Anglophones for decades. Find the Spanish online. Then read the following letter and the reply then see if you can discover the play on words to which the column's authors are referring. Verify their reading of *gracia* and the meaning of *la bamba*.

(Continued)

"Dear Straight Dope:

I've always liked Richie Valens' classic, "La Bamba." The problem is, my Spanish isn't quite up to speed, and I can't understand what he's singing about. Could you help me out on this? An English translation would be helpful, also. —Arnold Wright Blan

SDSTAFF Songbird replies:

No problema, Arnold. "La Bamba," a Mexican folk song from the state of Veracruz (on the Gulf coast), is a favorite of mariachi groups everywhere (long before Richie Valens covered it). Here is an English translation:

To dance La Bamba. To dance La Bamba one needs a bit of grace/wit.

A bit of grace/wit and another little thing — get going, get going! (literally 'get up and get up')

Ay! Get going, get going. I'll be for you, I'll be for you, I'll be for you.

I'm not a sailor. I'm not a sailor, I'm a captain, I'm a captain, I'm a captain.

The song contains several plays on words. For starters, what exactly does "La Bamba" mean? Consider: "Bambolear" means swinging or swaying, and a "bambollero/bambollera" is someone who likes to boast (e.g., "I'm not a sailor, I'm a captain!"). So "La Bamba" is probably best understood as a strutting, swaying dance.

Another tricky expression is "una poca de gracia," translated here as "a bit of grace/wit." It's a pun on the several meanings of "gracia." The dog-eared Spanish/English dictionary I used in high school lists these: "grace, gracefulness, benefaction, graciousness, pardon, mercy, remission of a debt, witticism, wit, joke, joker, jest . . ." You need a bit of grace to dance "La Bamba," and the singer is slyly suggesting you need a bit of wit as well.

(SDSTAFF Songbird [Tammy Brecht Dunbar]
Straight Dope Science Advisory Board 2007)

(*Source:* The Straight Dope, www.straightdope.com. Copyright 2007 Creative Loafing Media, Inc. Reprinted with permission.)

CASE STUDY: FIGURATIVE LANGUAGE IN PRAGMATIC DOMAINS AND ACADEMIC ABSTRACTS

Identify the figurative language in these source and target abstracts, particularly metaphors and metonymies. Connect with your **Manual** Web site to find the link to them.

In pairs, defend your choices (what to you is a metaphor may be a dead metaphor to your partner). Then do the same for the target text, noting what operations have been performed on the figurative language you identified.

Follow-Up

1. How difficult was it to determine if a metaphor is live or dead? Is "semi-dead" a useful category? Metalinguistic awareness of such matters may help you learn to spot instances in which a language may not admit a certain metaphor and thus require a modulation or neutralization.

2. Edit the target abstract. Focus especially on the figurative language, but also remove any clutter or pseudo-English (to what does "each corporate performance" refer?).
3. Find out more about e-business and its relationship to the translation industry today.

Abroche o Pague
T E X A S

The well-known "click it or ticket" campaign in Spanish format in the United States. Translators convey the message over the style when wordplay proves resistant. Ideally translations of this sort are both informative and persuasive.

Source: Courtesy of the Texas Department of Transportation

TRANSLATING GREETING CARDS

One feature unique to greeting cards is that a text translation usually will appear in small print on the back of the card. Though many broad-appeal greeting cards are produced bilingually nowadays, others are targeted to a niche market—for example, cards from *padrinos* or that celebrate Three Kings Day, the *quinceañera*, the saint's day, or Cinco de Mayo.

Activity

1. Find other examples of greeting cards targeted to a niche market. What other language-related goods and services may be related to a *quinceañera* (*mis quince años* or *mis quince*) party?
2. What general issues do you think translating greeting cards and similar products presents? In which direction do you think cards are generally translated?
3. Find a case in which the graphics would have to be changed to accommodate a transculturation, in other words, visuals that would contradict the text in translation.
4. In one case, the line "*En tu ausencia, mi vida no tiene razón*" appears on a "missing you" card in Spanish. Could this be translated "In your absence, I have no reason to live"? What issues of register and tone would this present for a greeting card? How could you remedy this?
5. Find a card with rhyming text in English or Spanish and try a rhymed version in the opposite language of the pair.

   HINT   Do a literal version for your first draft and word associate your way to natural rhymes.

6. Translate these messages for bilingual e-cards to be sent in the United States:
   a. *Recibe el más sentido de los augurios de que este tu día sea memorable ¡y de que la vida te colme de bendiciones en el futuro!*
   b. *Hago llegar mis deseos de bien para tu persona y los tuyos. Próspero año y felicidad.*

Research

1. Find some samples from Hallmark's Spanish-language "Sinceramente" or "Radiante" series, or American Greetings' "La Flor" line. Discuss their cultural and linguistic features. Does Hallmark make *Spanglish* greeting cards? If so, for whom?
2. a. What about e-cards? Are they translated?
   b. What about invitations?
   c. How about baby shower favors? (Are baby showers a tradition exclusive to Anglos?)
   d. What is the difference in use between *felicidades* and *felicitaciones*?

. . . .

WORKSHOP #4: "LAS MENINAS"

For workshop #4, you will be translating an entry in a museum guidebook that introduces one of the world's great paintings, "La familia de Felipe IV," popularly known as "Las Meninas."

Read the passage for translation and go through the following steps to produce your workshop text before you begin your translation proper.

1. Go online and read all you can, in both English and Spanish, about the painting. Study it closely in the best possible reproductions. Consider its perspective, proportions, use of light, composition. Find out more than you need immediately for the text; for example, more about the life of Velázquez, the name of the figure on the stairs, and so forth.

   HINT   If you are getting a lot of "noise" in your Web search, try searching the painting title and the dimensions "318 × 276" to find similar entries and ones that refer to the specific work in question. Also be sure to try a variant spelling on "Velázquez."

2. Compile for your own use a bilingual miniglossary of terms that come up frequently—technique, historical terms, names. Mark up your text.
3. Troubleshoot: Go back to terms that have eluded you. Document your parallel texts; print them out. Double-check their reliability.
4. Consider the register of the source text: Who is the intended reader, and what level of education, and knowledge of art, do you think is presumed?
5. Translate from "Es ésta . . ." to "(1181)." The four-digit numbers are catalogue numbers.
6. Proofread carefully, paying particular attention to this chapter's focus: figurative language. Watch for false cognates (there is one potentially problematic one). Research further into the historical linguistics involved: for example, *meninas*. Think critically about word choice—if you have used a word like "babysitter" or "nanny" in your draft, be sure these words or concepts existed at the time of this painting. Be sure you have such aspects as roles and clothing indicated appropriately (important details).
7. Read your text out loud. Have you written a line including a phrase like "capturing the air"? Be self-critical: Does that make as much sense as you would like? *Revise*.
8. As a final phase, read your text while comparing to the painting that it describes. They should match!

Source: *Las Meninas*, The Family of Philip IV 1656. Artist: Velázquez, Diego, 1599-1660, Spanish. Museo del Prado, Madrid/Dagli Orti/ The Art Archive

Escuela Española:

Pintura del Barroco

«**La Familia de Felipe IV**» o «**Las Meninas**»* (1174) [es] la obra príncipe del Museo del Prado y de la pintura española, y una de las cotas más altas de la pintura universal. Incluido el propio pintor en la composición, se nos ofrece retratando a los reyes Felipe IV y Mariana de Austria, cuyas efigies se reflejan en el espejo del fondo. La escena, que se desarrolla en el propio taller de Velázquez, la componen un grupo de figuras en torno a la infanta niña Margarita, en ese momento heredera de la corona por desaparición del príncipe Baltasar Carlos. Meninas y meninos la rodean, atienden y acompañan; se daba este nombre a los acompañantes y cuidadores de los niños reales. Las dos jóvenes damas (Agustina Sarmiento e Isabel de Solís), y los dos enanos (Maribarbola y Nicolasillo), eran controlados por la dama con tocas monjiles (Marcela de Ulloa, guardamujer) y el caballero guardadamas, responsable de todo el grupo. Una última figura se recorta en las gradas de la escalera del fondo. Aparte de la belleza de esta composición, su logro más extraordinario es la captación del aire, de la atmósfera que se interpone entre los cuerpos de los personajes, y que Velázquez logra pintar desdibujando los perfiles y matizando los colores de las figuras colocadas más lejos, para que aparezcan a los ojos del espectador tal y como podrían ofrecerle en la realidad.

Este retrato colectivo es el retrato por excelencia, pero otros muchos hizo Velázquez de su rey (en diferentes momentos de su vida), y de otros miembros de la familia real. Así los presenta como cazadores: **Felipe IV** (1184), su hermano **Fernando** (1186), y su hijo **Baltasar Carlos** (1189); como consumados jinetes: **Felipe III** y su esposa (1176 y 1177), **Felipe IV** y la suya primera (1178 y 1179), el mismo **Baltasar Carlos** (1180), y también el tan próximo primer ministro del rey, **Conde-Duque de Olivares** (1181).

(*Source:* Reproduced by permission of Museo Nacional del Prado)

Translating the Visual

In "The Quadrature of the Hermeneutic Circle: The Picture as 'Text,'" semiotician Göran Sonesson proposes the idea of an "interpictorial translation"; that is, one picture translating another. Look at Wilkin's "Las meninas (After Velázquez)," 1987, which renders Velázquez' painting into modern idioms. Do you accept the proposal that this is a translation? Can you think of other examples?

Source: Joel-Peter Witkin, *Las Meninas* (Self Portrait), 1987, toned gelatin silver photograph, 14-1/2 × 14-3/4 inches. Collection of the New Mexico Museum of Art. Museum purchase with funds from Barbara Erdman, 1988

CHAPTER

6

Commercial and Financial Translation

Commercial and financial translation covers the gamut of economic life from hospitality to manufacturing to marketing. To name only a few examples, a translator in this arena may work on insurance or banking documents; financial information such as balance sheets, annual reports, or cash-flow statements; or on marketing materials such as international multimedia campaigns or product catalogues.

Activity: Marketing and Advertising

First, let's get more familiar with the Latino populations in the United States. What is their approximate purchasing power? What are their numbers, broken down by country of origin or descent, in the United States? In addition, how has marketing to these populations grown and changed? (Hint: Consult the U.S. Census Bureau, HispanTelligence, Pew Hispanic Center, and Media Economics Group.) Discuss.

Advertising warm-up: Bring in two ads—an ad in English and another in Spanish—for the *identical product* but for different audiences (different not only in language, but in identity, values, and psychology). Discuss the differences. Find the identical product in two variants of Spanish.

TRANSLATING IN THE "THIRD GENERATION"

In the Boston Consulting Group's study, "Advancing to the Next Level of Latino Marketing: Strike First, Strike Twice," the traditional task of the translator is shown to lie in the "first generation" of marketing: translating and sponsoring national events. In the second generation, acculturation and home country differences are understood and marketing to Latinos takes place. However, it is only in the third generation that microsegmenting of the market occurs and community presence is increased. The growing sophistication and fragmentation of the market—including different levels of acculturation—have spurred greater efforts to resonate with Latino audiences by tapping into cultural choices and behaviors. For example, Häagen-Dazs has extended its line by introducing Dulce de Leche ice cream (Lowry, Ulanov, and Wenrich 2003, 7), whereas others "leverage the travel trail" by "reinforcing brand preferences in the home country as well as the new one" (8). Given this scenario, the translator of marketing campaigns—and their translation initiators—now have to be thinking *far* beyond first-generation approaches and learn to *reconceptualize*. Increasingly, the translator must serve as cultural broker and linguist in one. Net effect: It will become much more rare in our industry to be asked to simply "translate what's on the paper" for a Latino audience, as we saw in Kiraly's claims (see Chapter 1, "What Is Expected of Today's Translator?").

Marketing firms must often rethink visuals as well, including colors and motifs, because of their associations. In *Designing Across Cultures*, Lipton (2002, 27) relates that

> Newman-Carrasco inherited a 1950s-type Hispanic campaign for (now defunct) Home Savings of America that only changed the language from [that of] the general market. The English headline was "banking the way it used to be, except for the computers and stuff." The Norman Rockwell imagery wasn't going to work for the Hispanic immigrant. . . . Many Latinos immigrated in the 1970s, so they couldn't relate to the U.S. 1950s experience. For others, who had arrived by then, the image wasn't irrelevant so much as negative: the 1950s weren't a good time for non-Anglos.

Doyle, Fryer, and Cere (2006, 254) offer an example of this type of cross-cultural market segmentation. An ad for the Got Milk? campaign won an award from *Ad Age* magazine for its innovation:

> El comercial se basa en la leyenda hispana de "La Llorona" y representa una importante expresión de estrategia de la Junta de Procesadores de Leche de California para dirigirse a los jóvenes biculturales y bilingües. El comercial en español fue desarrollado por estudiantes hispanos de Los Ángeles y se transmitió en las redes televisivas de habla inglesa y española de California [. . .] En la película es plena noche y la Llorona se desplaza a través de una casa de familia buscando, por supuesto, un poco de leche. Al abrir la nevera, La Llorona se sorprende y dice "Leche", deja de llorar (por primera vez en siglos) y levanta el cartón de leche con alegría. Pero resulta que el cartón está vacío y en un dramático impulso de desesperación, cierra la puerta de un golpe y vuelve a llorar y a lamentarse. El comercial termina con su ahora famosa pregunta . . . GOT MILK? (Hispania News)

La Llorona, of course, is the culturally significant legend of a phantom woman who is said to have drowned her children when alive and who roams the earth looking for replacements.

Task

In groups, culturally transplant a Hispanic legend, myth, event, or historical figure into a familiar Anglo ad campaign. Block out the scenes, visuals, and essential dialogue. (Task is based on Doyle et al. 2006, 254.) Can it work bilingually or must all of your ad be in English? (Realize that in some major markets, all-Spanish-language spots have run on mainstream television during prime time.) Share your ad with the class, defining your target audience as exactly as you can.

Follow-Up

1. Find out about Goya, one of the leading Latino-owned companies in the United States, and what language(s) are involved in its marketing strategy. In what language are its products labeled? What about its Web site? Does Goya translate its materials (i.e., press releases, in-store promotions, advertising slogans)?
2. Research other prominent Latino-owned corporations that may cater to a Spanish-speaking clientele and the role translation plays in their operations.
3. Search "Proctor & Gamble" + "Spanish-language." In what consumer outreach initiatives in Spanish has this top advertiser to Latinos been involved?
4. What state and federal packaging regulations require companies to translate?

TRANSLATING PRINT AD SLOGANS

Bilingual aisles—Customers shop in the Tianguis market in Montebello, California, where the clerks and signs are bilingual to serve the growing Hispanic population.

Source: Lennox McLendon/AP World Wide Photos

To succeed, advertisements must be pitch perfect in tone and fit comfortably in the target group ethos. When the Milk Processor Education Program wanted to translate its ubiquitous "Got Milk?" into Spanish—the literal translation of which would be wildly inappropriate in Spanish—one eventual result was "Más Leche, Más Logro," which specifically targeted Hispanic mothers (Whitman 2003).

Task

Let's see how translation is approached in this genre. With a partner, Google the word **"transcreation."** Come up with a consensus definition. What is generally meant by "creativity" in those definitions that use the word?

Translate for a national U.S. audience, making whatever cultural and linguistic changes necessary. Alternately, you may create a different profile of your target readers for each.

1. *Con el frigorífico Edesa, horas y horas de grata convivencia.*
2. *Campanas Mepansa, la máxima aspiración para su cocina.*
3. *Precisión inalterable.* (Seiko)
4. *La tónica Schweppes sabe magnífica sola.*
5. *El arroz Flora es más resistente.*
6. *Flan Dhul, igual que el de la abuelita.*
7. *El padrino de los vinos, Vinos Casa.*
8. *Gran Duque de Alba, el brandy de los brandies.*
9. *Nescafé Oro, el café liofilizado.*
10. *Peugeot, la calidad que no se discute.*
11. *Esta es su casa. El Corte Inglés.*
12. *Quincena del hogar en Almacenes Vázquez. Hay preciosidades para su ajuar.*
13. *Ahora libérate, vive y deja vivir a tus prendas de punto.* (Woolite)
14. *Listerine: Estrena tu boca.*
15. *Citroën brilla menos que un diamante, pero corre más que una visión.*
16. *Desodorante Rexona. Ni le abandona ni se abandona.*
17. *Wrangler no cede si tú no cedes.*
18. *Hay personas que tienen razones de peso para preferir endulzar con Natreen.*
19. *Sin olor. Sin color. Sin riesgo. Sin duda, Ladyshave.*
20. *Seat: un pequeño gran coche.*
21. *Ford Fiesta, fuerte. Felices fiestas, Ford Fiesta.*
22. *Mangado y Ochoa expone para que usted no se exponga.*
23. *TVes mejor con Adelfia.* *
24. *Cajas de Ahorro Confederadas. El interés más desinteresado.*
25. *Su colonia de siempre . . . Más joven, más al día. Más actual.*
26. *Pepsi Cola en latas: esta lata trae mucha cola.*
27. (Try this one >es): *"Coke. The Real Thing."* *

(Cuadrado 1984; plus some sighted in Puerto Rico by K. Washbourne denoted by an *)

¿?

Did you know that the soft drink Inca Kola outperforms Coca-Cola and Pepsi in Peru due to its nationalist appeal—at one point billing itself as "de sabor nacional"? Another memorable slogan was: "Inca Kola, sólo hay una y no se parece a ninguna". Coke finally joined forces with its long-time competitor in 1999.

TRANSLATION TEASER

Ad slogans sometimes are recognizable in translation. For a time, a popular product had a Web address, now defunct, that included "sigueysigue." Can you guess from the name what brand this site was selling?

Activity: Language and Ad Campaigns

Think of foreign words used in U.S. advertising (print and electronic media). What effect is achieved through their use? What Spanish is used? Why? Is it used in a way consistent with Spanish-speaking populations' cultural values, or is it used for the receiver culture's own ends? Does it assume or depend on a lack of familiarity with Spanish? Discuss.

As Korzenny and Korzenny (2005) observe, Hispanics tend to prefer bilingual materials because their households may be made up of a mix of English-dominant, bilingual, and Spanish-dominant individuals; because marketers try to sell to households, not individuals, a diverse household requires a diverse approach (92). The Spanish speakers in the house may look to the English to learn the language, the English speakers learn Spanish, and the bilinguals will compare, often mistrustful of the translation (92). Revealingly, the authors, Hispanic marketing experts, shun "correctness" in favor of cultural adaptedness:

> . . . there is an elitism implied in most professional translations. The notion of correctness creates noise between the marketer and the consumer. *Only a consumer-oriented translator/interpreter could aspire to do justice to the marketing objective of the marketer.* Most consumers, including Hispanic consumers, have relatively low levels of education. (Korzenny and Korzenny 2005, 89, emphasis added)

Source: Chuan Khoo/Getty Images, Inc - Artville LLC

Activity: Ad Analysis

Your instructor will provide a Spanish-language print ad for you to analyze carefully. Indicate as precisely as you can who the target demographic is and where this ad would or should appear. What linguistic and cultural cues help you identify its audience? Has the copy writer used any "crossover" strategies? What subliminal or subtle signifiers create associations for the viewer/reader?

Now imagine a whole new target Spanish-speaking audience, one in an untapped market. Rewrite the ad and rethink the visual. Mention where the ad will appear.

Some ad campaigns are adapted specifically for the Hispanic market.
Source: Bill Aron/PhotoEdit Inc

TRANSLATION TRAPS

Businesses looking to cut their bottom line by hiring hapless translators—and not using focus groups and informants—often pay dearly in the end. Some mistranslations of note include the following:

- One food company advertised its giant burrito as a *burrada* (a "big blunder" or "stupid thing to do").
- When Eastern Airlines translated its slogan "We Earn Our Wings Daily," the resulting Spanish suggested the airline's passengers wouldn't get out alive.
- One international corporation had its annual report translated into Spanish; in the line "Our vast enterprise achieved record sales . . .," the word "vast" came out *basto* (for *vasto*). The result: "Our crude and uncultured company . . ."
- The Spanish-language thesaurus in the Mexican version of Microsoft's Word 6.0 suggested the word for "man-eating savages" in place of "Indians."
- When an American toothpaste manufacturer promised that its customers would be more *interesantes* by using its products, they overlooked the fact that this is a euphemism for *pregnant* (*en estado interesante*).
- U.S. tobacco companies in Latin America advertised their "low-tar" cigarettes as low in *brea*. The problem? *Brea* is the kind of tar used for paving roads! (Ricks 1983, 77, 79, 84, 85, 87).

¿?

Did you know there is a corporation called Grupo Bimbo whose product, Pan Bimbo bread, is a mainstay throughout Latin America? The ubiquitous Bimbo truck is very much a part of the south-of-the-border landscape; in *el norte* too, Bimbo Bakeries USA is one of the largest names in the bakery industry.

CULTURAL IGNORANCE IS BAD FOR BUSINESS

Linguistic ignorance can hurt companies, but what are the costs of *cultural* ignorance on American export markets? A recent report relates that

> when Microsoft Corporation developed a time zone map for its Windows 95 operating system, it inadvertently showed the region of Kashmir lying outside

the boundaries of India. India banned the software, and Microsoft was forced to recall 200,000 copies of the offending product. . . . In addition to the adverse economic consequences of such mistakes to individual companies, they foster negative attitudes toward America, as the mistakes are rarely viewed as accidents by the offending countries, but instead are considered negligent indifference or intentional slights attributed to all U.S. companies. (Research and Policy Committee of the Committee for Economic Development 2006, 6–7)

TRANSLATION TEASER

Hard Sells

What's in a name? Let's test drive a few. The Mazda Laputa will get you remembered, surely. But maybe the car to bring out your personality would be the Ford Fiera (if "mean old shrew" is the impression you're going for). Does your driving make your passengers carsick? Then the Fiat Marea may be your car. Ah, yes! Why not try the ultimate in class—the Nissan Moco?

(These are all real car names.)

Activity: Infer Translation's Role

Research and define the role that translation plays in each of the following text types. Who are the primary participants (commissioner and addressee or user)?

1. Real estate
2. Human resources
3. Investor relations
4. Foreign exchange
5. International banking

Groups report to the class on a respective domain assigned from those listed.

Research

1. Brainstorm commercial and financial document types that are translated.
2. In groups, list what issues and difficulties may be especially germane to commercial and financial translation.
3. What features or details characterize the Web sites of commercial and financial translators (or specialist agencies)? How can you determine the relative quality of services offered at one site or another? Give a specific example.

CASE STUDY: ONLINE INTERACTIVE MENUS

For this task you're going to do a translation en>es of the Coin Counting Demonstration of an automated coin conversion system, Coinstar®. The demonstration in six screenshots appears sequentially on their customer Web site, where its services are described.

Brief: Coinstar® offers automated services in many retail stores and features kiosks with a bilingual menu. Write in Spanish for users in the United States, without a marked preference for one dialect over another. Consideration: The Spanish terms for this Web site should coincide with the machine's actual Spanish interface (with which you may not be familiar). In the editing phase this can be remedied, because the corresponding Spanish-language site uses terms consistent with the machines'. If you wish to know more about the product or company, connect with your **Manual** Web site to find the link to Coinstar®, where you can also find the actual demo. *Do not go to the Spanish page* yet.

Translate the demo with a partner. This part of the task should take no longer than 15 to 20 minutes.

When you have finished, compare to the Spanish-language site. List that site's solutions that you would use to improve your own version. Next, compare the site's English and Spanish FAQs for customers and investors.

Multilingual ATM screen. What special banking services do you think Hispanophone populations tend to use?

Source: Citibank International

TRANSLATION TEASER

Customer vs. Client

Working only from Web page content written by service providers (no glossary posts or dictionaries), write a working definition that distinguishes "client" and "customer." Are these words used haphazardly or inconsistently in business? If possible, determine the Spanish that could be used for each.

TRANSLATION TEASER

Mr. User

Consider the word *"usuario."* Is this word entirely covered in English by the cognate? If not, find examples in Spanish that would produce as many different plausible possibilities in English, in similar textual circumstances, as exist. Don't forget the common phrase *"Señor usuario."*

TRANSLATION AND MARKETING: *"LIBROS EN ESPAÑOL"*

Go to Amazon.com's *"Libros en español"* category. Sort the results by "Bestselling." Take note of trends among the top 100 bestselling books. How many are translations? What genres and subgenres are represented? Compare English titles for some. Can you find examples of different graphic presentation or other readily apparent localized content or visuals? How are different Spanish-language Bibles marketed differentially? Are there translations from other languages besides English? Are any customers' reviews low due to (perceived) poor translations?

Connect with your **Manual** Web site to find the link to Publishers Weekly or MyLibros.com for other viable titles.

Activity

Imagine that you are a book acquisitions editor at a major publishing house. Look at the bestselling books on the English-language list. Basing your decision on trends that you spotted on the Spanish list, in pairs, perform the following:

- Decide on three books that you would like to approve for translation into Spanish, assuming the rights are available.
- Justify your decisions to the class by identifying your genre and market segment as best you can.
- Determine that the books you selected have not been translated.
- Show that similar books have been translated successfully.
- Discuss the difficulties that may be encountered in translating your selections.
- Describe the qualities or credentials that your ideal translator for each book should have.

INTERNET MARKETING (FACTS AND TERMS)

This section includes information by Siegel (2006).

- The international Internet population, rather than being defined by national borders, is usually defined in terms of **online language communities**, groups who share a language regardless of from where they are communicating electronically (139).
- Offline, 5.6% of the world's population speak Spanish as their primary language (140).
- Online, 37.9% of the online populations use European non-English languages as their primary languages. English comes in at 35.8% (140).
- More than 64% of Internet users worldwide do not speak English (148).
- "For large businesses targeting multiple international markets, it can take US$15 to $30 million or more to create, launch, and maintain a single web-selling site" (143).
- "[V]isitors stay twice as long on sites written in their native language and adapted to their culture" (148).

"Translation takes place on many levels. It can be as superficial as translating one page for offshore visitors or as deep as offering a fully translated mirror site localized to each served market. To be effective, translation should include content text as well as frequently asked questions (FAQs), feedback forms, product specifications, privacy statements, security warnings, shopping cart instructions, contact information, and the like. It also requires registering with popular local search engines in target markets and using local-language keyword descriptors for metatags. In most cases, easily misunderstood colloquialisms, slang, buzzwords, and idioms must be avoided unless they have been adopted locally." (149)

International approaches, broadly, are three:

A **localized Internet marketing strategy.** This strategy *culturizes*, or "adapts marketing offers to accommodate local preferences and customs in each served international market. It includes creating web pages and emails, sponsoring links and promotions in local languages, and adapting them to local cultural preferences. This is a customized approach consistent with believing buyer groups are heterogeneous with many different needs, wants and preferences. A localized strategy can be used for one or many markets" (145).

A **glocal strategy.** This is an approach (global + local = "glocal") that "localizes and makes site, email, and promotion adaptations to appeal to local markets, but standardizes where feasible." The noun is *glocalization* (145).

A **global strategy.** Global marketing is "offering an undifferentiated marketing mix to homogeneous markets worldwide"; in other words, a culture-neutral approach. The theory is that tastes will converge if the same products are on offer everywhere, eliminating the complications of adapting for each local market (145).

Tasks

1. Can you find clear examples of a localized, a glocal, and a global strategy? Bring strong examples to share with the class. Critique the examples you found. Find out more about glocal strategies. Contrast the role of the translator in each of the three strategies.
2. Determine what Fortune 500 companies have done with multilingual Web sites to date: how thorough, what percentages, what strategies, trends, and so forth, and if there are "holdouts" that use only a monolingual strategy.

3. What about Spanish-language companies translating their materials out of Spanish for shareholders and other interested parties? Connect with your **Manual** Web site to find the link to *Latin Trade* magazine. Download "Las 500 mayores empresas (pdf)" and survey 8 to 10 of them for *type* and *volume* of translated documents or texts.

Activity: Educational Marketing E-mail Translation Task

Imagine that you are working in a public relations capacity in a study abroad office and are called on to do a translation.

1. a. Circle the cognates from the list that follows that might be valid in a translation for an email mass marketing of a Spanish program abroad (see the following) that will also be excerpted in a study abroad consortium's electronic newsletter. The translation would be directed at university-level Spanish teachers and advisors and (presumably monolingual) administrators and staff. Discuss those that you deem not quite true cognates and why they are not (they may not even be legitimate words in English).

   1. novelty   impart   formation
   2. patrimony privileged   immersion
   3. massified subventions inscribed

   b. Find three collocations online (in a reference corpus) using "novelty" as an adjective ("novelty" + [noun]). What does this structure suggest about the semantic prosody of "novelty"? Can the same be said about the word as a noun? If you decide against using the word in a translation, what strategy might work in English for the passage beginning "*La novedad este año es que . . .*"?

2. Discuss the proper names in the ST and how you would render each for the audience and medium (email) mentioned. Where would you look to verify if "patrimony of humanity" is a set phrase used *in the discourse*? Note in what type of discourse it can be found.

3. a. Summarize the email's basic content in English in one sentence.
   b. Write an appropriate subject line in Spanish for this mailing.

From   subdireueda@usal.es
Sent   Monday, May 8, 2006 2:02 pm
To
Cc
Bcc
Subject

Estimados/as Señores y Señoras:
Un año más, el Campus de Ávila de la Universidad de Salamanca, en España, ofrece sus Cursos de Lengua y Cultura Españolas y el Curso Superior de Didáctica del Español como Lengua Extranjera (con Practicum en escuelas locales). La novedad este año es que, además, comenzamos a impartir el Curso de Español Policial y Legal, en colaboración con el Centro de Formación del Cuerpo Nacional de Policía de España, que está situado en Ávila.

La bella ciudad medieval de Ávila, primera española en ser declarada Patrimonio de la Humanidad, es una población de 58.000 habitantes ubicada a sólo una hora de Madrid, y constituye un lugar privilegiado para la inmersión en la lengua y cultura españolas, en el marco de la prestigiosa tradición académica de la Universidad de Salamanca.

Los Cursos del Campus de Ávila de la Universidad de Salamanca se imparten en un área no masificada de estudiantes extranjeros. Los precios son también más bajos, ya que el Ayuntamiento de Ávila subvenciona los Cursos. Podemos recibir estudiantes inscritos individualmente o grupos organizados desde 7 alumnos, adaptando a sus necesidades los contenidos, calendario y duración del curso. Si el grupo viene con su profesor, ofrecemos a éste condiciones muy ventajosas de alojamiento.

Toda la información puede obtenerse de nuestra página web, www .usal.es/turismo

Quedo a su disposición si necesitan más información, o si desean recibir los programas en archivo pdf o los catálogos por correo postal. Saludos cordiales,

Profª Dra. Sonsoles Sánchez-Reyes
Coordinadora Cursos de Español
Escuela Universitaria de Educación y Turismo
Universidad de Salamanca - Campus de Ávila
Calle Madrigal, 3
05003 Ávila (España)
Telf: (34) 920 353 600, Fax (34) 920 353 601
E-mail: avila@cursos.usal.es; subdireueda@usal.es
(*Source:* © Cursos Internacionales Universidad de Salamanca, Campus Ávila)

Research

Find English<>Spanish memoranda of understanding or student exchange agreements on the Web, or ask your school's international programs office, and compare. Is the language more concrete, as one would expect in, for example, an action plan, or does it tend toward

abstractions (harmony, cooperation, goodwill, and understanding)? (Realize that a standard modulation is from abstraction to concretion, particularly because English often has less tolerance than does Spanish for abstraction; however, one must be careful here not to make rhetorical language into binding clauses.)

CULTURAL VALUES AND THEIR IMPACT ON WEB SITES

This section includes information by Singh and Pereira (2005, 54–55), Hofstede (1980), and Hall (1976).

> All business is global, yet all markets are local.
> Robert Rosen, *Global Literacies*

The following five values have been shown empirically to represent a society's "perceptual, symbolic, and behavioral elements" (Singh and Pereira 2005, 55), and thus are indicators of how a culture, or an online community, might receive a given Web site or advertisement.

Individualism-collectivism: the extent to which the goals of the individual versus those of the group take precedence

Power distance: belief in a vertical structure of power with higher authority at the top (high-power distance) versus the belief in more egalitarian, distributed power (low-power distance)

Uncertainty avoidance: whether a culture values order, predictability, and security or whether it has a higher tolerance for ambiguity, risk, and adventure

Masculinity-femininity: the placement of value on achievement and status symbols (masculine) or on nurturing relationships (feminine)

High-low context: cultures with close ties and a communally shared, implicit knowledge base (high context) versus societies that communicate rationally, logically, and explicitly (low context)

The United States, for example, scores *low* on the power distance value relative to countries such as Ecuador, Guatemala, Panama, and Venezuela; *high* on the individualism-collectivism value relative to Chile, Colombia, Costa Rica, and Spain; roughly *equivalent* to Mexico on the masculinity-femininity index; and *low* on uncertainty avoidance compared to Uruguay, Argentina, and El Salvador (Singh and Pereira 2005, Appendix 3.1, 63–4; Hofstede 2001).

Discussion

Brainstorm the features included, excluded, emphasized, or de-emphasized in Web site design if the preceding values are taken into account.

1. In pairs, find local Web sites that show contrasting ends of the scale for each value. Write down the features of each that justify your choices.
2. Identify Web sites in the translation industry from different Spanish-speaking countries and/or cultures and demonstrate how their sites reflect the values under discussion (variation on Singh and Pereira 2005, 89).
3. Find a global gateway, landing page, or "splash" page that offers alternate language options either in the language in question or through the use of icons (e.g., flags).

LOCALIZATION AND GLOBAL BUSINESS

A good layperson's introduction to localization and global business can be found in a *Time* magazine article from 2001. Connect with your **Manual** Web site to find the link to the magazine.

In "Does Your Website Speak Spanish?" John Yunker (2004) notes that some firms are taking the lead in not simply translating a few random pages, but, as in the case of Southwest Airlines, engaging the Spanish-speaking customer right from the online reservation system and through culturally appropriate, localized features such as featuring the date as month/day (the opposite of the English format).

Tasks

Connect with your **Manual** Web site to find the links to the following:

1. An overview of the issues of addressing Spanish pages, navigation, and promotion;
2. Southwest Airline's *Vámonos* homepage for Spanish speakers and compare to the English layout and content; and,
3. Yunker's column, which gives a link to an extensive list of companies that have produced their Web sites in Spanish for U.S. Hispanics.

For multiple viewpoints, and a somewhat more advanced series of discussions on localization issues, see Sprung (2000).

Follow-Up

Connect with your **Manual** Web site to find the link to WalgreensEspanol.com and explore the site. (Notice that there is no "ñ" in the URL address. Do you see a potential problem in that?) Now compare and contrast other pharmacies and their Spanish-language features.

Localized Spanish-language Web sites may involve visually representing the ethnic diversity of the various Spanish-speaking communities in addition to reflecting—and respecting—their cultural preferences, customs, and belief systems. The Walgreens site in Spanish features images of Hispanic people (or at the very least, they are of ambiguous ethnicity); this detail goes a long way toward creating the all-important *confianza*.

Research

List ways in which Web sites must be culturally customized for optimum effect. Consult Nitish Singh and Arun Pereira, *The Culturally Customized Web Site: Customizing Web Sites for the Global Marketplace* (2005).

1. What cultural adaptations or other imperatives discussed seem particularly relevant for Spanish-speaking populations?
2. Can you find evidence of an ad from a Spanish-speaking country that has localized for another Spanish-speaking country—in other words, multiple, different ads for different segments of the Spanish-speaking market? How about an ad with marked regional U.S. Spanish variants? Bring in examples for discussion.

3. Sensitize to regional Spanish usage by holding a "quiz bowl" of Web site texts and ads to see who can correctly guess the most regions of origin or target markets. The contest may be held with face-to-face competitors representing teams or in multimedia format with students writing out answers.

4. a. Case Study 1: Research the Olympics and Special Olympics sites and identify any special considerations or hurdles they encountered in translating/localizing materials related to their organizations, including their marketing and press relations.

   b. Case Study 2: What tax preparation software exists in Spanish? What professional tax preparation services will print a copy of your return for you in Spanish? What tax preparation sites have been translated? To what extent? How "neutral" is their Spanish?

   c. Case Study 3: Find the Web page for the Bureau of Motor Vehicles (Department of Motor Vehicles) for your state. Make a brief description of materials and services offered in Spanish and a needs analysis of what remains to be done. Imagine that you are a freelancer in search of new clientele. In a brief email to the head of operations of the appropriate department, offer a summary of why the partially translated or partially localized site needs your services.

NOTE Don't actually send the email.

TRANSLATION TRAP

One of the caveats of creating materials in other languages is that it creates the assumption that customer service personnel are available in that language. It may be of little use for a company to translate into a language in which it cannot service its customers. A recent radio PSA addressed this issue: "*Los operadores telefónicos de Eyecare America® no hablan español. Favor de tener alguien que habla inglés llame por su parte a la línea telefónica de remedios de EyeCare America®*".

Task: Shipping Company Advertisement Translation

Translate the following transportation broker's ad for an international audience. The ad will be featured on its Web site, linked via targeted Ads by Google in the Google AdSense program, featured in the firm's investor relations publications, and reused in campaigns yet to be determined. The client lets you know that if she is pleased with the work, you will have the opportunity to translate their annual report and work with them closely to improve workflow.

Suppose you began working with this company's multilingual content management team on the specific tasks of keeping all the Spanish and English content matching and avoiding duplication. Make a recommendation about including something that logistics and freighting companies tend to include in their advertisements in the United States that clients might expect (i.e., local content) and that in this case would improve the ad. Using your creative writing and research skills, author the features directly in English. Make your addition and run it by a classmate to check for appropriateness.

Acarreo y Transporte Martes Jiménez

CALLE PASCUA 4BIS 16 BAYAMÓN, PR

00616

"Por todas las vías, hasta la Vía Láctea"

Nos especializamos en frutas y flores tropicales, ultramarinos, juegos de sala de mimbre y derivados de caña

- por vía marítima, en buques de arqueo bruto de 1,000 y sitios de atraque directo
- por tierra, en camiones de poca tara
- por vía aérea, en cualquier horario, incluyendo movimientos de cargas de cabotaje

Cotizamos el envío. Costo, seguro y flete incluídos. Franco destino disponible a petición.

Translate your additions to Spanish for inclusion in the original ad.

TRANSLATION TEASER

Incoterms

What are Incoterms? What relevance do they have for translation? When translated into Spanish, are their *meanings* translated or the acronyms themselves? What kinds of documents do they appear on? Is their Spanish version standardized?

Find the Incoterms. What distinguishes groups C, D, E, and F?

 Connect with your **Manual** Web site and interrogate a specialized corpus, the Business Letter Corpus, in order to see how the incoterms are used (e.g., query: <CIF>: Cost Insurance Freight; <FOB>, Free On Board).

Terms and their commonly co-occuring words in specialized discourse are called **phraseologisms**. Note these patterns in the corpus output:

[pattern = incoterm + destination city [or +destination country]

[pattern = incoterm + price [or +percentage or +cost] (+denomination) + figure]

[pattern = incoterm + destination + sum]

Find examples of each.

Does business correspondence exhaust the possible constructions? (e.g., Are incoterms also used on international waybills? Are incoterms always translated?)

Activity: Import-Export Classified Ad

1. Imagine that a classified ad for an import-export specialist (your instructor will choose one) needs to be translated for a Spanish-language job listing site. Its primary readers will be educated Spanish-speaking U.S. nationals who are most familiar with the transportation terms commonly found in trade documents relating to the North American Free Trade Agreement (NAFTA).

2. As a follow-up, do a "read around" with at least three classmates giving you feedback on your version. They may append comments or questions, or you may each keep your comments and regroup to bring up issues you saw in others' work, defending or amending your own as the discussion unfolds. Turn in a final version with your class draft stapled to it.

KNOWLEDGE ORGANIZATION ACTIVITY: INTERNATIONAL TRADE DOCUMENTS

According to E. Hinkelman (2002), buyers and sellers need international trade documents for "bookkeeping, accounting, taxation, export and import formalities, as well as making payment using letters of credit and other documentary payment methods" (Hinkelman 1994, 345). These documents fall under the document category headings listed next, limitless examples of which are translated all over the world every day.

Task

Now we will do a background knowledge task that also will increase your knowledge of text types as you research their conventions and uses and become aware of their Spanish names, which are not always obvious.

1. Fill in the missing information for the summary that follows.
2. Find the names of three examples or subtypes of each type of document and briefly list the main features of each.
3. Give the Spanish term for the document type. For example, consider the *letter of credit* and what category it would fall in, what it is used for, and its name(s) in Spanish.
4. For "Import Documents," which vary from country to country, find a type that applies to the Spanish-speaking countries of your interest.
5. Can you find evidence of imperfect overlap English>Spanish in any of the category types? Explain.

Categories and descriptions are modified from Hinkelman 1994, 345.

Transaction Document(s)

- Key transaction document = _____.
- Used for accounting and bookkeeping purposes.
- Required for import-export and payment procedures.

Export Documents

- Required by the customs or export authority.

Transport Documents

- Key transport document = _____.
- Issued by a "shipping line, air cargo carrier, trucking company or freight forwarder that detail the terms of transport for cargo."

Inspection Documents

- Issued by third-party inspection firms "at the request of the buyer to certify the quality and quantities of a shipment."
- Required for import-export.

Insurance Documents

- Demonstrate insurance coverage of a shipment.
- Form of a policy or a certificate.

Banking/Payment Documents

- Banking and payment documents include _____.

Import Documents

- Minimal requirement = _____ and
  _____

- Sensitive merchandise (e.g., animals, weapons, drugs) or imports under special programs (e.g., NAFTA) may require more forms.
- Required by customs.

Scenario

Suppose you are heading an international business consulting firm. What kinds of texts would you need translated routinely? What kinds of interpreting services would you need?

TRANSLATION TIP

Organizational Glossaries

 National and international organizations' glossaries can be gold mines and are commonly used by translators outside the organizations themselves. Examples include the United Nations Multilingual Terminology Database and the International Monetary Fund (IMF) multilingual glossary. Connect with your **Manual** Web site to find the links to these two sites.

TRANSLATION TEASER

At a branch office of Missouri Capital Finance, a sign was spotted reading:

NO RENTE MAS
COMPRE SU CASA SIN
ENGANCHE SE HABLA
ESPANOL LOS LUNES

Logically, what do you guess *sin enganche* refers to in the sign's message?

a. No hidden fees
b. Collateral not necessary
c. Zero down
d. Hassle-free
e. Electric installation not included
f. Without interest
g. "Cash up front" (CUF)

h. No homeowner's exemption
i. Adjustable-rate mortgage
j. Childless couples only
k. Security deposit waived
l. Coapplicant/guarantor not required
m. Stop throwing your money away by renting

ASPECTS OF TRANSLATING FORMAL CORRESPONDENCE: THE BUSINESS LETTER

The examples in this section are based on Valero-Garcés (1995, 172–185).

Note that the English and Spanish salutations and closings are very different in formal correspondence. One main difference is that in English, the writer gets right to the point of the letter, whereas in Spanish, formalities are attended to first; otherwise the letter can sound demanding or harsh. The translator uses frequent *condensation* and even *omission* to bridge the considerable gap between these two text conventions.

Some common phrases:

Por la presente me es grato informarle … (O) *Me complazco en informarle …*	This is to inform you . . . (Notice the **omission**).
En contestación a su amable carta …	In reply to your kind letter . . .
En respuesta a su atenta carta …	
Me es grato adjuntarle …	I am happy to send herewith . . .
Me es grato acusar recibo de …	I acknowledge receipt of . . .
Le agradezco enormemente su carta de fecha 20 de junio de 1994.	Thank you for your letter dated June 20, 1994.
En espera de recibir noticias suyas / Pendientes de sus noticias	I look forward to hearing from you

Closings:

Le saluda atentamente	Yours faithfully/Yours sincerely
Se despide muy atentamente	
Quedo de Usted, su obediente servidor	I am at your service (not: I am your humble servant)
Agradeciendo de antemano este servicio	Thanking you in advance

Task

Translate this brief letter into Spanish. The head of personnel of an international conglomerate has received a cover letter from an applicant and must keep a record of all correspondence in English and Spanish for a grant she has received.

Málaga, 20 de junio de 2010

Estimados señores:

Me dirijo a Vds. con motivo del anuncio publicado en el diario "El País" de fecha 19 de junio del presente, en el que requerían una persona para desempeñar el puesto de Auxiliar Administrativo.

Para su conocimiento y consideración, adjunto mi "curriculum vitae" así como los documentos acreditativos de cuanto se expone en el mismo.

Pendientes de sus noticias aprovecho con agrado la ocasión que se me presenta para saludarles muy atentamente.

Ma. Cristina López y Guzmán

Follow-Up

1. Study the business correspondence templates that appear in many bilingual dictionaries (e.g., the HarperCollins) and make a summary of the differences in *formatting conventions* between English and Spanish letters.
2. Using business correspondence, make a mini-glossary of Spanish language verbiage (closings, formulas, and all frozen register phrases) that would be streamlined in English.

CULTURAL NOTE

Archaic Forms (Abbreviations)

The use of abbreviations, a casual if not sloppy practice in English, is highly codified in Spanish business correspondence. Until very recently, it was possible to find the formulas "QBSP" ("*que besa sus pies*") and "QBSM" ("*que besa sus manos*") in the closings of business letters in Spanish. Now that's customer service!

Among the abbreviations that have survived are:

s. s. s. = *su seguro servidor* (≈> *sincerely*)

atto. = atento (≈> *respectful*); for example, *Quedo suyo atto. y s.s.* (*atento y seguro servidor*)

afmo. = *afectísimo* (≈> affectionate)

D. m. = *Dios mediante* (≈> God willing)

Countless ones are used for business terms, including:

p. p. = *porte pagado* (freight/carriage/postage paid)

m. n. = *moneda nacional* (national currency)

c/, cta. = *cuenta* (account)

CULTURAL NOTE

Titles in Business Correspondence

A cultural difference that translators need to negotiate is that of titles. Rubén Candia (2001) notes that in the matter of professional titles, English and Spanish forms of address differ greatly. In English, he states, only "Doctor" and "Professor" are in widespread use, whereas in Spanish, *Licenciado* is a form of address used with university graduates, particularly *Licenciado en Derecho* (lawyer). "Other professional titles not recognized in English are Ingeniero (Engineer), Arquitecto (Architect), Maestro (Distinguished Teacher, but not a professor or doctor) and Contador Público (CPA)." Another trap is that *ingeniero* may refer not to an engineer but to a degree holder in business administration. Thus, if a business letter is signed "Ing. José Infeliciano," a rendering of "Eng. José Infeliciano" in English translation would be inscrutable. "Mr." is the solution there, or as often happens, no title is used at all, simply his position name alongside the proper name (e.g., José Infeliciano, Managing Editor). Another option for a lawyer is to use "Esq." for "Esquire" after the name (Candia 2001).

Activity: What Can We Know about an Absent Source Text?

How well can you, looking only at a translation, intuit what its source text *must have been*? This task will give you some sense of the extent to which the logic of a text allows you to make predictive assumptions (in this case, "retrodictions"). Premises to think about during and after this task are: Must a translation be accurate in order to reconstruct a likely source text? Can one read a translation and make accurate judgments about its source? In addition and perhaps most intriguing: *Can a student of translation read translations, absent the works' sources, and learn translation techniques and strategies*? (Note: We are not back-translating for this task but examining what is knowable about a previous text judging only by a secondary text.)

Read the target text, "*Sectores de la industria . . .*" and answer the True/False questions that follow. Do not use dictionaries or other secondary sources. Correct those that are false.

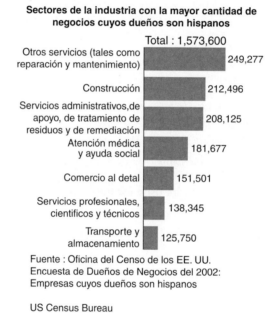

Sectores de la industria con la mayor cantidad de negocios cuyos dueños son hispanos

Total : 1,573,600

Otros servicios (tales como reparación y mantenimiento)	249,277
Construcción	212,496
Servicios administrativos,de apoyo, de tratamiento de residuos y de remediación	208,125
Atención médica y ayuda social	181,677
Comercio al detal	151,501
Servicios profesionales, cientificos y técnicos	138,345
Transporte y almacenamiento	125,750

Fuente : Oficina del Censo de los EE. UU.
Encuesta de Dueños de Negocios del 2002:
Empresas cuyos dueños son hispanos

US Census Bureau

Source: <http://www.salonhogar.net/Nueva_York/Hechos.htm>, Accessed December 17, 2007

Answer "True" or "False" based on your instincts about this text and its likely source text:

1. The English probably reads "Spanish heritage speakers" where the target uses *hispanos*. _____
2. A strong indication that this is a translation, if a reader has no other contextual clues, is that the variant proper names "Oficina del Censo de los EE.UU." and "US Census Bureau" appear in the same text credits. _____
3. In the title, the phrase "*mayor cantidad*" probably is a translation of "highest quantity" of Hispanic business owners. _____
4. *Reparación* is a false cognate of "reparation." _____
5. *Reparación*, because it is paired with *mantenimiento*—which is blue-collar work— logically would also refer to blue-collar occupations, which are usually in the statistical majority of any population sample of workers. _____
6. *Tratamiento de residuos* is probably a translation of "waste management." _____

7. *Remediación* in this context likely refers to "medicine." _____
8. *Remediación* in this context likely refers to "remedial education." _____
9. "Medical attention" and "social help" are *both* set phrases in English for commonly rendered services. _____
10. "Medical attention" and "social assistance" are *both* set phrases in English for commonly rendered services. _____
11. *Al detal* is a misprint for *al detalle*—the text appears to have been cut off. _____
12. *Al detal* must refer to either "wholesale" or "retail" because something to do with sales almost certainly would appear in the top professions. _____
13. *Almacenamiento* is paired with *transporte* so it must refer to housing the product shipped, or "Storage." _____
14. *Almacenamiento* is the counterpart of the English "stockpiling," or because the text refers to food transport, "hoarding," because the common collocation is that one *hoards food.* _____
15. The title is sexist, because *"Hispanos"* only covers *"Hispanas"* implicitly; the English would be more apt to be inclusive here for this text type: *"Latinos and Latinas."* _____

Find the source text for this target text, and discuss your answers to the True/False questions.

Follow-Up

1. Identify several online Hispanic-oriented "yellow pages" for which this information might be useful to publish in order to inform advertisers.
2. Enumerate what materials the U.S. Census Bureau uses regularly in Spanish. How is it used (what media) with whom? Collect samples of U.S. Spanish from bureau translations that explicitly show awareness of audience for these materials. Can you find modifications of cultural content English>Spanish?
3. The U.S. government is the largest patron of translations in the United States. Does the bureau have staff translator positions, or is this work freelanced?
4. What are "blue-collar" and "white-collar" occupations? In what ways do sociologists working in Spanish usually render these terms (assuming the distinction exists outside English)?

LINGUISTIC NOTE

RECKONINGS OF TIME

In Spanish, you will often see *quince días* in contexts in which English uses "two weeks"; similarly, *ocho días* is used for "a week" or "one week." This is because Spanish speakers include today when they count days into the future. There may be times when *quince días* literally means 15 days; be aware of both possibilities.

Also, Spanish sometimes prefer military time in everyday usage; in these instances, domesticate to the 12-hour a.m./p.m. system.

A point about seasons: The seasons in some tropical Spanish-speaking regions of the world—as elsewhere—are not divided so commonly as spring/summer/winter/fall but as *estación seca* (*época seca*) and *estación de lluvias* (*época de lluvias* or *época lluviosa*)—wet season (rainy season) and dry season.

Contract Activity: The Insurance Policy

Suppose an auto accident has occurred in California involving a couple from Baja, California. Their policy (see the template that follows) has to be translated because the courts want the form in English. From what you know about the language of this industry, take

---

Póliza de seguro de automóviles Aseguradora Cuauhtémoc S.A.
— Gerencia Regional —
Pasaje Alamos y Jalapa No. 1008-A
Centro Cívico Comercial
Tel. 57-15-24
Mexicali, B.C.

POLIZA No. _____

La compañía mencionada, que en lo adelante se llamará "La Compañía", asegura dentro de los límites de la República Mexicana, a favor del
Asegurado: _____

Dirección: _____

_____

llamado en adelante "El Asegurado", de conformidad con las condiciones de esta póliza, y durante el plazo establecido, contra aquellos riesgos de la especificación de riesgos que más adelante aparece que sufra o cause el vehículo descrito a continuación
Marca: _____   Modelo: _____

Año: _____   Motor No. : _____

La cantidad máxima a que asciende la cobertura que se otorga mediante esta póliza, queda determinada en la especificación de riesgos siguiente :

Riesgo	Límite de responsabilidad
Vehículo asegurado	
Choque	$ _____
Fuego, robo	$ _____
Responsabilidad civil	
Daños a propiedad de terceros	$ _____
Lesiones o muerte de terceros	
Cada persona	$ _____
Cada accidente	$ _____
Gastos médicos	
Ocupantes del vehículo	
Cada persona	$ _____
Cada accidente	$ _____

Deducibles
Choques, vuelcos, rotura de cristales, 2% de la suma asegurada o $500, la mayor de las dos cantidades. Fuego, robo, alborotos populares, temblor, erupción volcánica, explosiones y derrumbes, 5% de la suma asegurada o $1.000, la mayor de las dos cantidades.

Plazo establecido para el seguro

Tiempo: _____

De: _____ / _____ / _____   Hora: _____ _____ a.m.
       día   mes   año

A: _____ / _____ / _____
Costo de la póliza

Prima: _____   Impuesto: _____   Total: _____

Conformes:

_____   _____
Agente del asegurador   Asegurado

Source: Jarvis et al., *Spanish for Business and Finance,* Sixth Edition. Copyright © 2000 by Houghton Mifflin Company. Reprinted with permission.

your best guess at the following terms and phrases, then research the phrases with parallel texts and correct your work.

Asegurado	*Daños a propiedad de terceros*
de conformidad con las condiciones de esta póliza	*Alborotos populares*
Marca	*Plazo establecido para el seguro*
Motor No.	*Prima*
Límite de responsabilidad	*Conformes*
Choque	*Agente del asegurador*

TRANSLATING TRADE FAIR CALENDARS

When translating for tourism and international business fairs especially, it is good to keep in mind that you are often translating for nonnative speakers of English, albeit highly educated ones. English, as you know, is a lingua franca in international leisure and business travel. International conference organizers cannot logistically produce materials in 40 languages, so English is often the common denominator.

Brief: Translate the following texts, which are part of IFEMA's 2005 trade fair calendar, in this case appearing in Iberia airline's in-flight magazine, *Ronda Iberia* (January 2005). The clientele tend to be from around the world and represent businesses in countless industries. The first text is part of the overleaf, on the back of the page with the calendar dates. It is multicolored and features photographs of Madrid's convention centers. Because the attendees to this event are expected to be predominantly from European countries, use *British* spelling conventions. Use the IFEMA Web site to extract photographs and then format your text as a detachable magazine insert that doubles as a bilingual informational brochure. Enter the Spanish—format your English in italics after the block of text for the first source text and under each event for the second. The second text (below the first one) features excerpts from the calendar of fairs organized (or perhaps in this case, *organised*) by IFEMA. The source texts follow. The Web site will provide many of your solutions for the calendar section. Connect to the **Manual** website to find the source text in electronic format.

IFEMA, Feria de Madrid es uno de los primeros organizadores europeos de ferias, actividad que lidera en España gracias a la solidez de sus convocatorias y a su fortalecido posicionamiento internacional.

Sus recintos feriales, ampliados y mejorados en los últimos años, conforman un elemento diferencial de primer orden, junto a su equipo humano y un modelo de gestión caracterizado por la eficacia y capacidad para ofrecer un servicio de calidad en el ámbito de ferias y convenciones.

> Bienvenido a las grandes citas del mundo de los negocios

Feria de Madrid se integra en la zona más vanguardista de la ciudad, exponente del nuevo Madrid de los negocios. Muy próxima al Aeropuerto Internacional de Barajas, y rodeada de las vías rápidas de acceso a Madrid y a la red de carreteras. El cómodo acceso en transporte público, a través de la red de autobuses y Metro, le permite un traslado privilegiado al aeropuerto y al centro de la ciudad.

El atractivo de las convocatorias y espacios de reunión de IFEMA se beneficia de las propias características de la Región de Madrid, cuyo dinamismo e infraestructuras de todo orden, junto a la calidad de su oferta cultural y de ocio, propician un entorno idóneo para esta actividad.

Ferias organizadas por IFEMA

enero

13 | 17	**Semana Internacional del Regalo, Joyería y Bisutería Intergift** Salón Internacional de la Joyería, Platería, Relojería e Industrias Afines

febrero

10 | 13	**Casa Pasarela** Pasarela de la Moda del Hábitat
11 | 14	**Intermoda** Salón Internacional de la Moda Pronta **Iberpiel Peleterí** Salón Internacional de Peletería y Confección en Piel

marzo

9 | 13	**Aula** Salón Internacional del Estudiante y de la Oferta Educativa

abril

1 | 3	**Sipiel** **Semana Internacional del Calzado y la Marroquinería** **Fitness** Salón de la Industria del Gimnasio e Instalaciones Deportivas

mayo

12 | 14	**Expofranquicia** Salón de la Franquicia
26 | 29	**Multiproducto Selección**

junio

10 | 19	**Salón del Vehículo de Ocasión**

octubre

4 | 7	**TRAFIC** Salón Internacional de la Seguridad Vial y el Equipamiento para Carreteras
18 | 22	**SICI** Salón de la Cocina Integral
19 | 22	**Horeq** Salón del Equipamiento para Hostelería

Ferias no organizadas por IFEMA

3 | 6	**Venatoria & Subaru** Cita con la Caza Organiza: Expovenatoria, S.L.
12 | 20	**ExpoOcio** Feria del Tiempo Libre
19 | 21	**Eurovending** Feria Europea del Vending

(*Source:* Texts used by kind permission of IFEMA, Feria de Madrid)

Word count: 336

LINGUISTIC NOTE

COMPUTER-ASSISTED, MULTILINGUAL BUSINESS MEETINGS

Using Group Decision Support System (GDSS) software, participants in a real-time business meeting can each use their respective mother tongues. The computer sorts the anonymously typed ideas, the discussants vote on ideas to be addressed, and the system keeps a record of the meeting. As it is refined, this mode may prove more useful than using business interpreters.

Team Task: Author and Create a Business Plan and Glossary

The purpose of this task is *fivefold*:

- To expose you to business plan formats and writing strategies
- To consider a product or service in terms of production and marketing
- To weigh competing uses of e-translation and integrate it to best effect in a sales strategy
- To author text with an eye to the resulting text's translation and globalization
- To help you develop writing skills in Spanish for a highly pragmatic text type

You will be working in teams of three. As always, it is up to each group to ensure that the workload is distributed fairly; each group may wish to assign a project manager.

In sum, this task involves conceiving and writing a brief **business plan** for a translation- and/or localization-related product or service. Your group may choose what form that will take. Be innovative but practical. The second part of this task will involve creating an es>en glossary of your plan for another translation team, though you would do well to work on the glossary as you draft the Spanish, not afterward. The instructions (in Spanish) follow.

Van a inventar una pequeña empresa que lanzar, sea a nivel nacional o internacional, de cualquier producto y/o servicio relacionado con la traducción. El modelo para su proyecto está aquí (U.S. Small Business Administration): http://www.sba.gov/espanol/Biblioteca_en_Linea/plandenegocios.html

Recuerden que un plan de negocios establece un enfoque para la empresa, una serie de metas, estrategias y orientaciones. Incluyan lo siguiente:

- Introducción
- Descripción del negocio
- Productos y servicios

- Ventas y mercadeo
- Requisitos de operación
- Administración financiera

El plan de negocios: Van a organizarlo según el modelo, en un plan de 2-3 páginas escritas a máquina. El sitio Web anteriormente citado tiene modelos de planes comerciales para darles ideas. Su trabajo será calificado según: lo factible *(feasible),* lo coherente y lo original de su plan; lo ingenioso de sus ideas; su investigación; la calidad de su redacción y la organización de la misma. Pueden usar el formato 1.1, 1.2, tipo "bosquejo" si quieren. Basen su información en sus investigaciones de negocios parecidos, y en su sentido común. Su meta es un plan general y manejable. Ojo: No se trata de un anuncio —no llenen el plan con mera "propaganda" (i.e., con muchos adjetivos e hipérbole); es *un plan para crear un negocio rentable a través de inversionistas o préstamos, no para atraer al público que va a usar el producto o servicio.* La traducción: *La traducción o localización tiene que figurar como parte integrante de su plan.* El glosario: Incluyan un glosario bilingüe en Excel con las fuentes. Optativo: Definan los términos en la lengua término.

Consulten con el sitio Web de **Manual** para encontrar más recursos útiles.

TRANSLATION TEASER

A job on proZ.com gave a sample text featuring the term "Boleta de Garantía de Seriedad de la Propuesta." The text type is an RFQ.

Connect with your **Manual** Web site to find a link to ProZ.com and see if you can make sense of the sample source text for this assignment.

Activity: Business Ethics

What do you know about business ethics? Who advocates them? Are they part of a business education in the United States? In Spanish-speaking countries? (Search school catalogues and course syllabi.) What about government ethics? What documents can you find online, in parallel English and Spanish, that empirically compare governments' levels of corruption? (Hint: Include "Transparency International" in your search.)

The text that follows is from the Cleveland Better Business Bureau's (BBB) Web site; it is the BBB's mission statement and service pledge. Before reading it, determine the extent to which BBBs around the country have translated their materials into Spanish. Then gloss the text below for discussion in class; you may use any resources. Your instructor may wish to produce a group translation, with each class member contributing a section and feedback on others' contributions.

The Better Business Bureau is a public service organization that advocates ethical, responsible conduct in the marketplace. Through the support of business members sharing its goals and standards, the BBB offers programs which promote informed buying and giving decisions, truthful advertising and selling practices, and the resolution of marketplace disputes.

The Better Business Bureau Customer Service Pledge

As employees of the Better Business Bureau, it is up to us to strive for and maintain the highest possible standards of customer service. We know that we can best challenge area firms to excel in customer relations by leadership through example. We have therefore established a customer service pledge as a constant reminder of our commitment to member firms and the entire business-consumer community. Everyone who asks for our help is entitled to respect, sincerity and the benefit of our experience—our best. To give less breaches our responsibility to ourselves and the BBB tradition.

In fulfillment of this commitment, we promise to:

- Advocate fairness and responsible behavior in the marketplace;
- Foster informed decision-making through objective, accurate and useful information presented in a professional manner;
- Assist those who seek to resolve disputes and treat them with respect;
- Work to bridge gaps between consumers and businesses, and reflect impartial and reasonable positions to both;
- Commit to excellence in the marketplace, not only in products and services, but most importantly, in people.

(*Source:* Logo and Text Reprinted by permission of the Better Business Bureau)

Find out the role of the Chamber of Commerce both on the local and national levels. What involvement with translation do chambers of commerce have?

Activity: Accounting

Read the text *Balance General Consolidado* that follows. Is this a profit and loss (P&L) statement, an income statement, a balance sheet . . . ? After you have determined what kind of text it is, come up with reasons for and a context in which such a document would be translated. Then translate for that context. While researching for this brief task, take note of whether amounts in national currencies are typically converted for this text type.

Balance General Consolidado
(millones de dólares estadounidenses)
Ejercicio Actual

Activos		Pasivos y patrimonio	
Caja y bancos	138.230	Créditos bancarios	23.035
Préstamos comerciales	250.000	Proveedores	34.076
Colocaciones contingentes	.0	Inversión de los accionistas:	
Muebles y Enseres	31.770	Capital social	65.219
Cartera vencida	31.034	Utilidades acumuladas	0
Pagos anticipados y circulantes	25.000	Cesantías consolidadas	122.547
Amortización (menos)	−5.252	Acumulación para indemnizaciones laborales,	
		neta de anticipos al personal	142.000
Total activos		Utilidades por distribuir	106.686.65
		Total pasivos y patrimonio	
470.552			470.552

Lic. P. Nipinscher
Sub Jefa de Contabilidad

Activity: Mining Parallel Texts

Suppose the stock market simulator and tutorial at Investopedia.com were to be translated, either as a parallel site or to be used as part of an economics education resource bank for teachers in Spanish American schools. Who do you think needs this page in English? Who do you think needs this page in Spanish? Is it a similar demographic?

1. Read "Stock Basics: How to Read a Stock Table/Quote" on pages 189-190. What culturally specific features appear that might have to be altered in Spanish? What would you do about the financial sites listed at the end of the tutorial? Look at their dictionary: Would a comparable one have to be compiled?

2. Make a basic glossary that would be useful for translating this text and similar ones at the Investopedia page. Document and verify your sources. You can leverage existing glossaries, but do not include too few or two many terms or terms irrelevant to the parameters of tasks related to the stock market (i.e., make it narrower than an "investment glossary," though you may mine investment glossaries for your terms). Remember, you can use monolingual glossaries and match equivalents.

3. Translate the column heads 1 to 12 and the phrase "Quotes on the Internet." Provide parallel texts. Don't forget the NYSE's links to world exchanges, which appear in their respective national languages.

LINGUISTIC NOTE

A MINIMAL EN<>ES GLOSSARY OF STOCK MARKET TERMS

Here are some essential terms to get you started:

la Bolsa	Stock Exchange
la bolsa	stock market
a bolsa de valores	securities exchange
la bolsa de mercancías	commodities exchange
el mercado de divisas	currency exchange
bursátil (adj.)	stock exchange related
el símbolo bursátil	stock ticker
el/la bolsista, corredor/a de bolsa	(stock)broker
el vaivén	ups and downs; vicissitudes
la contratación bursátil	stock trading; market transactions
el retoque	correction; adjustment
la tendencia alcista	upward trend; bull market
la tendencia bajista	downward trend; bear market

TRANSLATION TEASER

What is the "crawl" of stock readings across the TV screen called in Spanish?

Follow-Up

1. A volunteer should explain in his or her own words, in Spanish, how to read a stock table, using only the terms acquired from this task and a parallel table found in Spanish. The class can compare against the information given in the English.

2. As a follow-up task, one half of the class can mock up a brochure on a given topic related to personal finance (e.g., financial services offered by a mutual fund company). The other half of the class translates it when the first group delivers the files. The first group then critiques the translation. Variation: Class members can either switch roles or both halves can author and translate a text for the other half (first third of the allotted time for the task: authoring; second third: translating; last third: follow-up). The second third can be assigned as group homework. The Investopedia tutorial follows, verbatim; find an investor's newspaper or financial section of a daily to follow the explanations.

Stock Basics: How to Read a Stock/Table/Quote

Columns 1 & 2: 52-Week High and Low—These are the highest and lowest prices at which a stock has traded over the previous 52 weeks (one year). This typically does not include the previous day's trading.

Column 3: Company Name & Type of Stock—This column lists the name of the company. If there are no special symbols or letters following the name, it is common stock. Different symbols imply different classes of shares. For example, "pf" means the shares are preferred stock.

Column 4: Ticker Symbol—This is the unique alphabetic name which identifies the stock. If you watch financial TV, you have seen the ticker tape move across the screen, quoting the latest prices alongside the symbol. If you are looking for stock quotes online, you always search for a company by the ticker symbol.

Column 5: Dividend Per Share—This indicates the annual dividend payment per share. If this space is blank, the company does not currently pay out dividends.

Column 6: Dividend Yield—This states the percentage return on the dividend, calculated as annual dividends per share divided by price per share.

Column 7: Price/Earnings Ratio—This is calculated by dividing the current stock price by earnings per share from the last four quarters. For more detail on how to interpret this, see our P/E Ratio tutorial.

Column 8: Trading Volume—This figure shows the total number of shares traded for the day, listed in hundreds. To get the actual number traded, add "00" to the end of the number listed.

Column 9 & 10: Day High & Low—This indicates the price range at which the stock has traded at throughout the day. In other words, these are the maximum and the minimum prices that people have paid for the stock.

Column 11: Close—The close is the last trading price recorded when the market closed on the day. If the closing price is up or down more than 5% than the previous day's close, the entire listing for that stock is bold-faced. Keep in mind, you are not guaranteed to get this price if you buy the stock the next day because the price is constantly changing (even after the exchange is closed for the day). The close is merely an indicator of past performance and except in extreme circumstances serves as a ballpark of what you should expect to pay.

Column 12: Net Change—This is the dollar value change in the stock price from the previous day's closing price. When you hear about a stock being "up for the day," it means the net change was positive.

(*Source:* Reprinted courtesy of Investopedia. Investopedia.com)

Activity: "Silent Translation"

Read *The Wall Street Journal* daily, online or in hard copy. Practice quickly sight translating to yourself (i.e., neither oral nor written) the news capsules under *"Otras noticias importantes"* (examples from June 6, 2008, follow); suppose a North American audience. If you are stumped by a term or phrase, circle and do follow-up research. Verify any domain-specific terminology that is new to you. Connect with your **Manual** Web site to find the link to the *Wall Street Journal* site and others, via the Latin American Network Information Center.

> Nubes negras sobre las fusiones: El colapso de dos grandes acuerdos en los últi-mos días muestra que el mercado global de fusiones y adquisiciones tiene un panorama sombrío. El efectivo manda.

> Bonanza subsidiada: Con los precios de los granos por los cielos, los agricul-tores estadounidenses están viviendo una bonanza.

WORKSHOP EN>ES: THE INTERNAL REVENUE SERVICE'S 2001 1040EZ INSTRUCTIONS

This task is offered as an alternative should your instructor wish to work en>es this week.

The following source text appears in the instructions to the Internal Revenue Service's (IRS) 2001 1040EZ instruction booklet. It appears in order to show the average tax-payer the percentages allotted to different categories of federal spending. Brief: Translate for a U.S. Latino national audience, as if you were continuing with all of the instruction book publication.

You may also wish to find and download the U.S. government's Spanish-English tax glossary (Publication 850) for future reference.

Major Categories of Federal Income and Outlays for Fiscal Year 2000

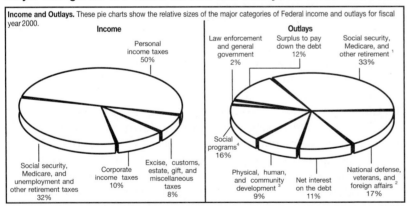

Income and Outlays. These pie charts show the relative sizes of the major categories of Federal income and outlays for fiscal year 2000.

Income
- Personal income taxes 50%
- Social security, Medicare, and unemployment and other retirement taxes 32%
- Corporate income taxes 10%
- Excise, customs, estate, gift, and miscellaneous taxes 8%

Outlays
- Law enforcement and general government 2%
- Surplus to pay down the debt 12%
- Social security, Medicare, and other retirement [1] 33%
- Social programs [4] 16%
- Physical, human, and community development [3] 9%
- Net interest on the debt 11%
- National defense, veterans, and foreign affairs [2] 17%

Note. The percentages on this page exclude undistributed offsetting receipts, which were $43 billion in fiscal year 2000. In the budget, these receipts are offset against spending in figuring the outlay totals shown above. These receipts are for the U.S. Government's share of its employee retirement programs, rents and royalties on the Outer Continental Shelf, and proceeds from the sale of assets.

On or before the first Monday in February of each year, the President is required to submit to the Congress a budget proposal for the fiscal year that begins the following October. The budget sets forth the President's proposed receipts, spending, and the surplus or deficit for the Federal Government. The plan includes recommendations for new legislation as well as recommendations to change, eliminate, and add programs. After receiving the President's proposal, the Congress reviews it and makes changes. It first passes a budget resolution setting its own targets for receipts, outlays, and surplus or deficit. Next, individual spending and revenue bills that are consistent with the goals of the budget resolution are enacted.

In fiscal year 2000 (which began on October 1, 1999, and ended on September 30, 2000), Federal income was $2,025 billion and outlays were $1,789 billion, leaving a surplus of $236 billion.

Footnotes for Certain Federal Outlays

1. Social security, Medicare, and other retirement: These programs provide income support for the retired and disabled and medical care for the elderly.

2. National defense, veterans, and foreign affairs: About 14% of outlays were to equip, modernize, and pay our armed forces and to fund other national defense activities; about 2% were for veterans benefits and services; and about 1% were for international activities, including military and economic assistance to foreign countries and the main-tenance of U.S. embassies abroad.

3. Physical, human, and community development: These outlays were for agricul-ture; natural resources; environment; transportation; aid for elementary and secondary education and direct assistance to college students; job training; deposit insurance, commerce and housing credit; and community development; and space, energy, and general science programs.

4. Social programs: About 11% of total outlays were for Medicaid, food stamps, temporary assistance for needy families, supplemental security income, and related programs; and 5% for health research and public health programs, unemployment com-pensation, assisted housing, and social services.

Source: Publication 20011040EZ, Internal Revenue Service, United States Department of the Treasury

WORKSHOP #5: STRATEGIC PLAN FOR TEAM TRANSLATION EN>ES

This task will involve translating a strategic plan en>es. First, have a clear idea what strategic plans are and the role translation can play in implementing them. Connect with your **Manual** Web site to find a link to the National Library of Medicine site. On this Web site is an example that uses Spanish as part of its outreach to Spanish speakers.

From this and other sites, including definitions found on the Web, compile a list of features common to the strategic plan. Who are the strategic plan's intended readers? Are any *actions* expected of them?

The text you will be working on is the Great Smoky Mountains National Park's strategic plan for 2005 through 2008. Connect with your **Manual** Web site to find the link to the National Park Service site. The background of this document's production is discussed on pages 2 and 3 of the Web site. How do the reasons for this text's existence square with the definitions you have found for strategic plans in general?

Read through the text to page 7. You will work on the following passage in teams of three. One person will be the terminologist, another will be the proofreader, and the other will be the translator. The terminologist will be responsible for finding and verifying those terms determined by the group in advance; the translator will translate and enter the text (word processing); the proofreader will be responsible for the grammaticality and adequacy of the Spanish, verifying with consultants, print or online resources; the latter collaborator may wish to keep a log. The work should be divided equally, and all should be equally responsible for the final product. Your brief is very simple: Produce a Spanish-language version of the text for the public, both print (for those who request it) and online. Translate into a Spanish diatype and dialect appropriate for the most obvious potential readers. The source text is as follows:

> Strategic Plan (Excerpts)
> October 1, 2005 – September 30, 2008
> Great Smoky Mountains
> National Park
> National Park Service
> U.S. Department of the Interior
> Great Smoky Mountains National Park
> Tennessee and North Carolina
>
> **Introduction**
>
> Great Smoky Mountains National Park was established by Congress on June 15, 1934, and has become the most visited of all national parks. Situated within a day's drive of over half of the population of the United States, the park provides for public benefit from and enjoyment of its resources by over 9 million visitors each year in such a way as to leave them basically unaltered by modern human influences. The Park's 800 square miles are almost equally divided between eastern Tennessee and western North Carolina.
>
> Great Smoky Mountains National Park is world renowned for the diversity of its plant and animal resources, the beauty of its ancient mountains, the quality of its remnants of American early settlement culture, and the extent and integrity of the wilderness sanctuary within its boundaries. The Park preserves 160 historic buildings and structures and maintains over 800 miles of trails including a section of the Appalachian Trail with elevations ranging from 800 feet to 6,642 feet at Clingman's Dome. Residing in the Southern

Appalachian Mountains, the Park is one of the most biologically diverse regions in the world and contains the richest flora and fauna of any temperate area of comparable size anywhere on earth. This is evident in the Park's status as the core unit of one of America's few International Biosphere Reserves and its designation as a World Heritage Site in 1983.

Foremost of all the challenges facing Great Smoky Mountains National Park are the impacts to the natural environment. Air pollution is dramatically shrinking scenic views, damaging plants, and degrading high elevation streams and soils. Human health is at risk from ozone pollution. Non-native insects and invasive species threaten forest health. On an operational level, the Park is dealing with the cumulative effect of years of absorbing fixed cost increases and across the board reductions without a significant base budget increase. In recent years, the Park has seen extraordinary success in revenue enhancement through partnerships and support from gateway and adjacent communities. Annual contributions now exceed $3 million in funds and volunteer services. Partnerships support numerous programs in science, education, and resource management; however, major shortfalls still exist. Budget shortfalls and reductions in staff have forced the park to consider which of its core functions are the most necessary. As the Park has increased its reliance on non-base, non-recurring funding to pay for its daily operations, Park management has been forced to cut back and rely heavily on project funding to maintain their basic level of function.

The Park has several long-term investments currently underway such as the building of a Science Center, conversion of the Park's radio system, and three Environmental Impact Statements that will amend the Park's General Management Plan.

Mission of National Park Service at Great Smoky Mountains National Park

The mission of the National Park Service at Great Smoky Mountains National Park is rooted in and grows from the Park's legislative mandate found in the Act of Congress dated May 22, 1926, which states that Great Smoky Mountains National Park is "for the benefit and enjoyment of the people." The Park's purpose is "to preserve exceptionally diverse resources and to provide for public benefit from and enjoyment of those resources in ways which will leave them basically unaltered by human influences." Our mission statement is a synthesis of this mandated purpose and the Park's primary significance as itemized below. The mission of the National Park Service is to preserve the exceptionally diverse resources of Great Smoky Mountains National Park and "to provide for the enjoyment of these resources in such manner as will leave them unimpaired for the enjoyment of future generations."

Legislative Intent

The enabling legislation for the Park states "The tract of land in the Great Smoky Mountains in the States of North Carolina and Tennessee being approximately seven hundred and four thousand acres, recommended by the Secretary of the Interior in his report of April 14, 1926, which area ... shall be known as the Great Smoky Mountains National Park: Provided, that the United States shall not purchase by appropriation of public moneys any land within the aforesaid areas, but that such lands shall be secured by the United States only by public or private donation. . . ."

(*Source:* Reprinted by permission of the Great Smoky Mountain National Park)

Word count: 741

Activity: Self-Assessment of Recurrent Errors/Competence

 Connect with your **Manual** Web site to find the self-assessment instrument. Fill it in based on your work in translation to date.

CHAPTER

7

Legal and Political Translation

EXPLORING TRANSLATORS' OWN ATTITUDES ABOUT BILINGUAL MATERIALS

Before you read the opinion piece that follows, consider these questions: How do you feel about the need for bilingual voting materials? Which should take precedence when a citizenry is casting votes—a common language or adequate comprehension of the issues and candidates? Can you not be a U.S. citizen if you are more comfortable voting in a language other than English?

Read George Will's column that follows, which appeared at the end of May 2006 at the very beginning of the national dialogue over whether English should be the official language and just as debate in the legislature over new immigration reform was heating up.

Have a frank discussion about Will's column. Supposing you agree with Will in whole or in part, does that make your work in translation problematic? Does Will's view of the United States coincide with yours? Do you find it realistic? Does accepting Will's argument entail accepting certain premises wholesale (e.g., "Declaring English the national language is a mere gesture.")? Examine one of Will's key conclusions—that those who receive assistance understanding the political discussion are de-motivated to learn English. Look at several related issues and how they relate to voter proficiency, including literacy and access to education. Taken to its logical conclusion, his argument would suggest that translators are complicit in perpetuating poor English skills, an implication worthy of our attention here.

Bilingual ballots won't serve new citizens

By George F. Will, Syndicated Columnist

Washington—"Of course not." That was Attorney General Alberto Gonzales' answer Sunday on ABC's "This Week" when asked if he would favor prohibiting bilingual ballots.

"Of course not"? Did he mean, "This is not something about which decent people differ"?

To understand why millions of conservatives do not trust Washington to think clearly or act reasonably about immigration, consider bilingual ballots. Those conservatives, already worried that both the rule of law and national identity are becoming attenuated because of illegal immigration, now have another worry: The federal government's chief law enforcement official might need a refresher course on federal law pertaining to legal immigrants.

In 1906, Congress passed and President Theodore Roosevelt signed legislation requiring people seeking to become naturalized citizens to demonstrate oral English literacy. In 1950, the requirement was strengthened to require people to "demonstrate an understanding of the English language, including an ability to read, write and speak words in ordinary usage in the English language."

If someone needs a ballot in a language other than English, that need proves the person obtained citizenship only because the law was not enforced when he or she sought citizenship. One reason for ending ballots in languages other than English is that continuing them makes a mockery of the rule of law, including even the prospective McCain-Kennedy law that pro-immigration groups favor.

It contains several requirements that those aspiring to citizenship demonstrate "a knowledge of the English language" or "English fluency" in order "to promote the patriotic integration of prospective citizens into the American way of life" and into "American common values and traditions." How can legislators support both language like that and ballots in multiple languages?

Fifty-six House Republicans have sent a letter asking that Section 203 of the Voting Rights Act be allowed to expire. When the VRA was enacted in 1965, it said nothing about bilingual ballots. Section 203, requiring bilingual ballots in jurisdictions with certain demographic characteristics, was added in the 1975 extension of the VRA. The letter was sent to Rep. James Sensenbrenner of Wisconsin, chairman of the House Judiciary Committee. He favors extending Section 203 and the rest of the VRA *until* 2032 because it helps facilitate "the participation of language minority citizens in the political process."

But what public good is advanced by encouraging people who, by saying they require bilingual assistance, are saying they cannot understand the nation's political conversation? By receiving such assistance, they are receiving a disincentive to become proficient in English.

It takes political bravery to propose pruning the VRA, given the predictable charges of racism nowadays. Senate Minority Leader Harry Reid, for example, has a liberal's reflex for discerning racism *everywhere* and for shouting "racist" as a substitute for argument. During Senate debate on a measure to declare English the national language, he said: "While the intent may not be there, I really believe this amendment is racist."

Questions crowd upon one another. Was his opaque idea of *unintentional* racism merely a bow to Senate rules against personal slurs? What "race" does Reid think is being victimized? Are Spanish speakers members of a single race? Evidently Reid thinks something like that because his next sentence was: "I think it is directed basically to people who speak Spanish." Indeed, it is, but what has that to do with racism?

Declaring English the national language is a mere gesture. But by ending bilingual ballots, U.S. law would perform its expressive function of buttressing, by codifying and vivifying, certain national assumptions and aspirations. Among those is this: The idea of citizenship becomes absurd when sundered from the ability to understand the nation's civic conversation.

What makes Americans generally welcoming of immigrants, and what makes immigrants generally assimilable, is: This is a creedal nation, one dedicated to certain propositions, not one whose origins and identity are bound up with ethnicity. But if you are to be welcomed to the enjoyment of U.S. liberty, then the United States has a few expectations of you. One is that you can read the founding documents and laws, and can comprehend the political discourse that precedes the casting of ballots.

Unreasonable? Of course not.

(*Source:* "A Vote for English" by George Will © 2006, The Washington Post Writers Group. Reprinted with Permission.)

Model: Bilingual Voting Instructions and Sample Ballot

Consider the voting materials on page 197 from local elections held in April 2006 in Culver City, California. What advantages or disadvantages do you see in formatting voting materials this way?

Follow-Up

1. Can you find allegations of voting irregularities in U.S. elections due to a language barrier?
2. Some politicians have been accused of holding one position on their English-language Web site and another on the Spanish version (for example, on the issue of immigration). Check out your own state's politicians' pages. Are their sites in Spanish? Do you see a shift in stance between their pages?

Hispanics registering to vote, Chicago, Illinois

Source: Marc Pokempner/Getty Images Inc. - Stone Allstock

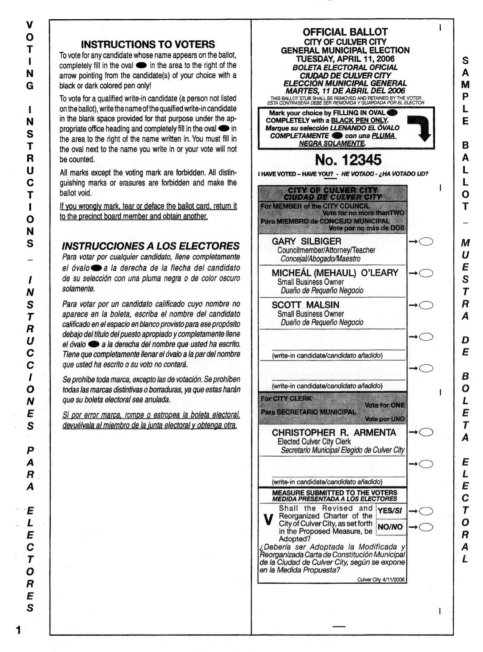

Source: Created by Martin & Chapman Co. for the City of Culver City. Reprinted with permission.

OFFICIAL TRANSLATION

According to Mayoral Asensio's (2003) *Translating Official Documents* (which informs this section), **official translations** are translations performed by an official translation service or *traductor público/traductor jurado* (in the United States, and for this context, ≈ ATA-certified translator) of economic or legal documents (e.g., certification of birth or death, transcripts, wills). They are received primarily by an administrative or judicial body, and meet *"the requirements to serve as legally valid instruments in a target country"* (1). An official translation by law is prescribed as "true and faithful" (a vague phrase!—a shrewd lawyer versed in the most basic translation theory could challenge a translation as false and faithless to suit his or her needs). An application for study in the United States, for instance, typically will require certified translations of all supporting materials. Like most treaties and peace agreements, these are translations on an international playing field.

Usually the translator or agency will affix their oath (certification, hence "certified translation"), seal, and signature, authenticating the translation. On occasion, notarization by a notary public—who must take the translator's word for the document's accuracy and authenticity—accompanies official translations. Laws and protocol differ widely from country to country, as do translator qualifying procedures and credentials.

> **¿?**
>
> The author notes that the translator's loyalty is not to the *client* but to the *recipient* of an official translation. Why do you think this might be so?

Where elsewhere professionals use the word "text," the word "document" is used in reference to an official translation. A document "reflects facts about the legal subject or subjects" (9)—the interested parties. A translation (which inevitably is an interpretation in the wider sense of the word—a way of understanding) can benefit one or the other of the contending parties in a dispute or contract.

Here is the curious part of official translation: *any* text type can be the source of an official translation because a legal act, such as a subpoena or trial, may involve the document in question. The most common documents are (28):

Births, marriages, and deaths	Wills
Divorce	Adoption
Academic	Rogatory letters
Agreements and guarantees	Sentences and resolutions
Powers of attorney	Identification

Official translations should always be performed on the original, *not a copy* (72), a reminder that forgery can and does occur, for which reality the official translator must be a *jurilinguistic expert* (37) to mediate cultural and linguistic ambiguities and incongruities. In many instances, the source and target texts must accompany one another where feasible and allowed.

In general, the official translator reflects the original document's information as it appears: "text (be it handwritten or typewritten), drawings, signatures (legible or illegible), letterheads, stamps and seals, erasures and alterations, interruptions in the original, etc." (71). The official translator frequently uses brackets to reflect this information: for example, "[There is a red ink seal which reads 'X']" or "[illegible signature]."

Activity

Translate your own birth certificate into Spanish (or into English if it's in Spanish). Make it an official translation, and have it comply with a specified Spanish-language country's requirements. Include a small summary of what changes in format were called for, and what certifying formula is prescribed.

This activity was adapted from Mayoral Asensio (2003, 87).

NOTE If they are cooperative, you may wish to ask them for a template or example of a translated transcript—with identifying information blacked out—from a Spanish country.

¿? Do you think self-translated official documents would be valid in the United States? Have a class representative call your school admissions office and ask them if academic materials can be self-translated.

On the topic of transcripts, which occupy a considerable amount of translator hours every day around the world, beware of *interpreting* the facts, which the authorities on the receiving end are paid to do; if the student scores "16" out of 20 in a course, you should *not* convert to a B+ (or what have you). You should, according to Mayoral Asensio (2003), use a validating system such as offering the pass grade for the institution as a point of reference, or the equivalent percentage of a score in brackets. Inequivalencies may be handled, for example, with a source + target solution, in this case maintaining the degree name in English:

ST (Eng.)		TT (Span.)
Bachelor of Arts in Psychology	>>	Bachelor of Arts in Psychology [+ explicated description of degree program]

Discussion

1. Which do you think are more useful for official translation, authentic texts (actual texts and actual translations) or blank templates found in books or electronic libraries of legal or economic forms? Discuss.
2. What, then, is an "unofficial translation"? Why are they used?

CULTURAL NOTE

Certification

Sworn translations bear a certification quite similar to the following used by sworn interpreters (Anexo 1, Orden de 8 de febrero de 1996, Spain):

Certificación

Don/Doña... (nombre y apellidos), intérprete jurado de.....................(idioma), certifica que la que antecede es traducción fiel y completa al...................(lengua de destino) de un documento redactado en........................... (lengua de origen).
En................. (lugar), a................. (fecha)
Sello (Conforme al artículo 7.6)

Find a standard translation es>en for this text or the corresponding English.

 Connect with your **Manual** Web site to find standard wording for translation certification.

BIRTH CERTIFICATES

The birth certificate (*acta de nacimiento* or *partida de nacimiento*) is one of the most commonly translated documents. Birth certificate translations are used for immigration, academic transfers, marriage licenses, and other legal matters.

The following is a composite of authentic South American and Spanish birth certificates and their most common features; the facts are fictitious, though the information is of the sort required for this text type (place of birth, parent's names, mention of witnesses, etc.).

No. 061411

Se inscribe el NACIMIENTO de una *niña* ocurrido a las *tres y veinte* horas del día *dos* de *marzo* de mil novecientos *ochenta* en la *Alcaldía de Salsipuedes.*

NOMBRE *Maricarmen*
Primer apellido *Guzmán*
Segundo apellido *Villanueva*
HIJO *la legítima* del presentante *Daniel Guzmán Ochoa*, de *veinte y cuatro años*, natural de *Villa Edén*, domiciliado en *Madrid, Gran Vía 22bis*, profesión *técnico servicio*, y de *María Constancia Villanueva*, de *treinta y un años*, natural de *Guanajuato, México*, domiciliada en *el del cónjuge*, profesión de *normalista*.

Se practica la inscripción en virtud de *l acta inscrita al número sesenta y uno mil trescientos dos en el registro civil local de la misma fecha*

Fueron testigos presenciales: Don *José Rafael Quebrado*, profesión *sobador*, y Doña *Gladys Cotilla Metiche*, profesión *estilista/manicurista*.

Leído el asiento se sella con el del Consulado y lo firma el Señor Cónsul con los testigos.

y el Secretario, que CERTIFICA.

EL QUE SUBSCRIBE CERTIFICA QUE LA PRESENTE ES COPIA FIEL DE LA PARTIDA ORIGINAL QUE SE ENCUENTRA INSCRITA EN EL LIBRO RESPECTIVO QUE SE CONSERVA EN EL ARCHIVO DE ARCHIFONDO

SAN DEMIO......**13 MAR 1980**..........

MA. LOURDES CRUCIRAYA
CONSTANCIAS-AGENCIA SAN DEMIO
REGISTRO NACIONAL DE IDENTIFICACION
Y ESTADO CIVIL

Source: Created by K. Washbourne

Tasks

1. First, discuss global strategies for translating the text. How do you account for signatures or illegible writing? How closely should you render formatting?
2. Identify boilerplate language. Important: In what neighboring text types are the same set phrases used?

3. Find parallel texts.
4. Now compare U.S. birth certificate applications that are available online in Spanish. Contrast information requested on templates with the model that follows.

Follow-Up

Get a fix on the going rates for birth certificates—find high and low quotes, and determine a rough average. Bear in mind that translators usually have a minimum—the lowest amount they will accept for a job.

CULTURAL NOTE

Translation and Adoption

Under the Child Citizenship Act of 2000, translations of non-English birth certificates or adoption decrees are necessary for children of American citizens (biological or adopted) to obtain a passport to enter the United States as lawful permanent residents.

PATENTS

Patent translation is well beyond the scope of an introductory textbook, but we would be remiss to not mention its importance and outline a few related issues.

Tasks

1. Go to the Oficina Española de Patentes y Marcas Web site. Find a similar authority in English. Compare how patents are listed and accessed. Read a few patents on the Spanish site. Determine the difficulty level; assess the approximate percentage of boilerplate.
2. List the sections of a patent application (*solicitud de patente*) and a brief description of the function of each. What is the most important part? What is the most often translated part?
3. Why are patents and patent applications translated? What fields are most often represented in our language pair? Would you characterize patent translation as hybrid?
4. What gets patented—ideas, improvements, devices, methods? Can *chemicals* be patented? List the patentability criteria in the United States; compare to a Spanish-speaking country. See, for example, the "Guía de Patentes y Modelos de Utilidad" by the Instituto Mexicano de Propiedad Industrial.
5. What is the role of a patent attorney? Do they play a role in the translation of patents? If so, what?
6. Visit the Web sites of patent translators. How exclusively do they appear to work in this area of the industry? What resources do they list, what tips do they give? What else can you learn about patent translation from these sites? Do any of them mention a liability insurance of any kind? How considerable *is* the patent translator's liability?
7. Find out about the Patent Cooperation Treaty and the basic filing procedures and priorities for filing patents in the United States and abroad.

U.S. VISAS

Legal information for those wishing to emigrate—such as 'Obtaining a U.S. Visa' (see next)—does not always exist in translation. Note how the information density is low.

Obtaining a U.S. Visa

For years the United States of America has required that many people wishing to travel to the United States to study, visit, or conduct business first obtain a visa. Recently, the United States, like many other countries, has updated visa policies to increase security for citizens and visitors. Yet, much remains unchanged.

Today, as in the past, most travelers to the United States must obtain a visa. The process still includes application forms and interviews as well as the collection and cross-checking of names in a highly sophisticated interagency database. As a visa applicant today, it is important that you recognize that these name-checking and registration processes are a necessary and crucial element that protects our citizens and our visitors, so please allow for extra time in your planning. Because of this process, many visas take at least several weeks, but some can take longer. Although individual experience may differ, here are the basic steps you should follow and what you can expect throughout the process.

1. If you have access to the Internet, visit the visas section on the U.S. Department of State Web site. This Web site has been created to help you find the information about current visa policy and procedures quickly and easily, based on your own situation and circumstance. Whether you are a student, a tourist, or a business traveler, this Web site can serve as a useful first stop on your journey.

   There are many different types of visas, and this site can help you determine which kind you need and how to obtain it. If you do not have access to the Internet, contact the nearest U.S. Embassy or Consulate for further information.

2. Make an appointment to visit the U.S. Embassy or Consulate. Visa application procedures vary somewhat among embassies and consulates, depending on local needs. In most countries, you will need to make an appointment. This can be done by telephone, mail, over the Internet, or in person, depending on circumstances in your country. Wait times for appointments may be longer than in the past. Schedule your appointment as soon as you know you need to travel to the United States.

   Be sure to ask what fees are required and how they can be paid. Application fees are nonrefundable and must be paid before your appointment.

   (*Source:* <www.eb2009.org/pages/documents/ObtainingaUSVisa.pdf>, Accessed June 25, 2009)

ACADEMIC TERMINOLOGY

Academic affairs

coursework, studies—*carrera*
academic year—*curso escolar*
major—*especialización*
minor—*segunda especialización*
courses—*asignaturas*
to fail—*suspender* (Esp); *ser reprobado*
academic probation—*período de prueba académico; probatoria académica*
college—college ≈ *Universidad*

Transcript notations

internship—*internado; pasantía*
registration—*matrícula*
transfer—*traslado de matrícula*
audit (v.)—*estar de oyente*
academic record, transcript—*expediente académico*
high honors—*con honores*
Cum.; G.P.A.—*calificación media*
elective—*asignatura de libre elección*

(Continued)

congregation; commencement—*ceremonia*

dissertation, thesis—*tesina*; tesis*

class of *x* year—*promoción de (año)*

examination period—*convocatoria*

certificate—*certificado*

class ranking—*clasificación; lugar en su generación*

Academic degrees

B.A. (Bachelor's) (≈) *bachillerato; licenciatura*

M.A. (Master's)—*maestría; título master*

Ph.D (Doctorate)—*doctorado*

AA (Associate of Arts)— *titulación universitaria de 2 años*

Academic offices

registrar—*secretaría*

school (of Nursing, e.g.)—*Facultad (de Enfermería)*

Academic ranks , titles, and other classifications

professorship, chair—*cátedra (puesto de un profesor)*

tenure**—*la permanencia*

sabbatical—*sabática; año de permiso*

professor emeritus—*profesor emérito*

full professor—*catedrático*

associate professor—*profesor asociado*

tenured professor—*profesor efectivo*

tenure-track professor—*profesor interino*

visiting professor—*profesor temporal, profesor visitante*

lecturer, adjunct professor—*profesor adjunto*

nonacademic staff—*personal no docente*

faculty***; professorate—*profesorado*

president ≈ *rector*

chancellor ≈ *rector*

dean—*decano (of a school); vicerrector*

department chair—*jefe del departamento*

---

*A *tesina* can also be a senior (undergraduate) project.

**Many students are largely unaware of the tenure system in higher education. An institution grants tenure to professors who have proven their commitment to teaching and scholarship in its various forms and have made a demonstrable contribution to the field. Tenure review is a comprehensive evaluation, both internal and external, of a candidate's dossier, as well as a *projection* of that individual's likely output and "value" in the future; the pretenure period during which the professor works toward tenure—often with the rank of assistant professor—usually lasts five years or more. Once granted tenure, a professor is not exactly "unfireable," as the popular imagination would have it, but he or she *is* granted protections—guarantees of academic freedoms (*libertad de cátedra*) to espouse views that may be unpopular and of immunity to arbitrary firings or demotion. Promotion to higher rank often happens in tandem with the tenuring process. Most schools in the Spanish-speaking world do not work on the tenure system.

***Be aware that in some English-speaking countries, "staff" includes faculty.

Activities: Academic Jargon

Connect with your **Manual** Web site to find the link to the University of Navarra's academic lexicon page.

1. Make a bilingual glossary for a subdomain out of the existing term base. Focus your term selection on a given text type (e.g., a transcript, academic outreach, recruitment materials, or an online university catalogue). Produce 25 to 30 terms.

2. Make a chart using Excel of any *differences* you find between the European (Castilian) Spanish academic terms and the Spanish American. For the latter, find sites and document your sources for terms. You should produce 15 to 20; use a column for country code for where the terms are used if regionalisms; otherwise use "Span. Amer."

3. Now look up *titilación* and *titulación* in the *Real Academia de la Lengua* dictionary. Note the definitions you find. Search for each word separately in a search engine. Document examples of what you find in academic sources. How can you explain the counterintuitive findings (i.e., the seeming interchangeability of the two terms in actual use)?

4. As a group, gloss and translate page 2 of the Universidad de Alicante transcript that follows on page 205. Page 1 of the transcript is presented for reference. See if you can come to a consensus on the most difficult terms and passages (e.g., the meaning and English of "*el no presentado no consume convocatoria*").

5. Discover some issues (pragmatic, cultural, or legal) in diploma translation.

Código	Asignatura	Cred	Dur	Tip	Año	Cur	Conv	Cons	Calificación
2254	TEORIA Y PRACTICA DE LA TRADUCCION	6	AN	T	98-99	1	J	1	APROBADO
2255	LINGUISTICA APLICADA A LA TRADUCCION	6	AN	T	98-99	1	J	1	SOBRESALIENTE
2256	DOCUMENTACION APLICADA A LA TRADUCCION	4	1Q	T	98-99	1	J	1	MATR. HONOR
2257	LENGUA B (I):INGLES	8	AN	T	98-99	1	J	1	NOTABLE
2258	LENGUA C (I):FRANCES	8	AN	T	98-99	1	J	1	APROBADO
2263	LENGUA MATERNA A1 (I):CATALAN	8	AN	T	98-99	1	J	1	SOBRESALIENTE
2264	LENGUA MATERNA A2 (I):ESPA?OL	8	AN	B	98-99	1	J	1	NOTABLE
2266	TRADUCCION GENERAL ESP./INGLÉS, INGLÉS/ESP	10	AN	B	98-99	1	J	1	APROBADO
2267	PRACTICAS DE LA LENGUA B(I): INGLES	4	AN	B	98-99	1	J	1	SOBRESALIENTE
2268	PRACTICAS DE LA LENGUA C (I):FRANCES	4	AN	B	98-99	1	J	1	NOTABLE
2272	TRADUCCIÓN GENERAL CATALAN-ESPAÑOL (I)	8	AN	O	98-99	1	J	1	MATR. HONOR
2277	LENGUA B (II): INGLES	7	AN	T	99-00	2	J	1	NOTABLE
2278	LENGUA C (II): FRANCES	7	AN	T	99-00	2	J	1	NOTABLE
2283	LENGUA MATERNA A1(II): CATALAN	8	AN	B	99-00	2	J	1	SOBRESALIENTE
2284	LENGUA MATERNA A2(II): ESPA#OL	8	AN	B	99-00	2	J	1	MATR. HONOR
2286	INTRODUC. TRADUCCION LITERARIA ESP/INGLÉS- INGLÉS/ESP	8	AN	B	99-00	2	J	1	APROBADO
2287	ANALISIS DE CONTRASTES DE LENGUAS INGLÉS-ESPAÑOL	4	1Q	B	99-00	2	J	1	NOTABLE
2288	INTRODUCCION AL DERECHO	6	AN	B	99-00	2	J	1	MATR. HONOR
2289	INTRODUCCION A LA ECONOMIA	6	AN	B	99-00	2	J	1	APROBADO
2290	PRACTICAS DE LA LENGUA B(II): INGLES	5	AN	B	99-00	2	J	1	NOTABLE
2291	PRACTICAS DE LA LENGUA C(II): FRANCES	5	AN	B	99-00	2	J	1	SOBRESALIENTE
2295	CULTURA Y SOCIEDAD DE PAISES LENGUA INGLESA	4	AN	B	99-00	2	J	1	NOTABLE
2296	TRADUCCION GENERAL CATALAN-ESPA#OL(II)	8	2Q	O	99-00	2	J	1	MATR. HONOR
2301	TÉCNICAS DE INTERPRETACION CONSECUTIVA (INGLÉS-ESPAÑO	8	AN	T	00-01	3	J	1	SOBRESALIENTE
2302	TRADUCCION LITERARIA ESPAÑOL/INGLÉS-INGLÉS/ESPAÑOL	6	AN	T	00-01	3	S	2	NOTABLE
2303	INT.TRAD.JURIDICO ADMINISTRATIVA ESP/ING-ING/ESP	6	AN	T	00-01	3	J	1	MATR. HONOR
2304	TERMINOLOGIA (I)	4	1Q	T	00-01	3	J	1	NOTABLE
2305	INFORMATICA APLICADA A LA TRADUCCION	4	1Q	T	00-01	3	J	1	APROBADO
2306	TRAD.GRAL.FRANCÉS-ESPAÑOL/ESPAÑOL-FRANCÉS (I)	4	AN	T	00-01	3	J	1	SOBRESALIENTE
2310	IN.TRAD.ECONOM.FINANC.COMERCIAL ESP/ING-ING/ESP	4	AN	T	00-01	3	J	1	SOBRESALIENTE
2311	ANALISIS Y REDAC. DE TEXTOS (I)-CATALAN	6	AN	B	00-01	3	J	1	NOTABLE
2313	LENGUA C (III): FRANCES	8	AN	B	00-01	3	J	1	SOBRESALIENTE
2427	INTROD. A LA TRADUCCION ORAL Y EL INGLES (ESPAÑOL-ING	6	AN	O	00-01	3	J	1	SOBRESALIENTE
2428	TRADUCCION TEXTOS INFORMATICOS INGLESES	6	AN	O	00-01	3	J	1	MATR. HONOR
2429	TRADUCCION TEXTOS MEDICOS INGLESES	6	AN	O	00-01	3	J	1	NOTABLE
7640	INTRODUCCIÓN A LA LITERATURA ROMÁNICA I	4,5	1Q	L	00-01	3	J	1	SOBRESALIENTE
8607	SEMÁNTICA Y LEXICOLOGIA CATALANAS	6	2Q	L	00-01	3	J	1	SOBRESALIENTE
2334	TÉCNICAS DE INTERPRETACION SIMULTANEA (INGLÉS-ESPAÑOL	8	AN	T	01-02	4	J	1	APROBADO
2335	TRAD. JURIDICO ADMINITRATIVA ESP-ING/ING-ESP	4	1Q	T	01-02	4	F	1	APROBADO
2336	TERMINOLOGIA (II) (INGLÉS)	4	1Q	T	01-02	4	F	1	MATR. HONOR
2337	TRAD.GENERAL FRANCÉS-ESPAÑOL/ESPAÑOL-FRANCÉS (II)	4	2Q	T	01-02	4	J	1	NOTABLE
2341	TRAD. ECONOM. COMER. Y FINANC. ESPAÑOL-INGLÉS/INGLÉS-	6	1Q	B	01-02	4	F	1	SOBRESALIENTE
2342	ANALISIS Y REDAC. DE TEXTOS(II)-CATALAN	4	1Q	B	01-02	4	F	1	NOTABLE
2344	LENGUA C (IV) : FRANCES	8	AN	B	01-02	4	J	1	SOBRESALIENTE
8240	TRADUCCIÓN JURÍDICA (ESPAÑOL-INGLÉS)	6	2Q	O	01-02	1	J	1	NOTABLE
8650	DIDÁCTICA DE LA LENGUA Y LA LITERATURA I (VALENCIANO)	6	2Q	L	01-02	1	J	1	MATR. HONOR
8677	LENGUAJE DE ESPECIALIDAD DE LAS CIENCIAS EXPERIMENTAL	6	1Q	O	01-02	1	F	1	MATR. HONOR
	Reconocimiento de Créditos:								
2000684	TRADUCCIÓ NO LITERÀRIA(INVERSA) I INTRODUCCIÓ A LA TR	6		L	01-02		D	0	APTO
2000686	TRADUCCIÓ LITERÀRIA (directa i inversa) I TRADUCCIÓ	4		L	01-02		D	0	APTO
20010774	APLICACIONS PRÀCTIQUES DE LA FILOLOGIA I LA TRADUCCIÓ	3		L	01-02		J	0	APTO
20020064	III CONGRÉS ESCOLA VALENCIANA. L'ESCOLA VALENCIANA I	1		L	01-02		J	0	APTO

FEB 0 9 2004

252234   2 / 2

Universitat d'Alacant
Universidad de Alicante

UNIVERSIDAD DE ALICANTE
CERTIFICADO ACADÉMICO DE
ASIGNATURAS SUPERADAS

DATOS DEL ALUMNO/A:

Nombre y apellidos:
D.N.I. :

Tipología de las asignaturas: T=TRONCAL; B=OBLIGATORIA; O=OPTATIVA; L=LIBRE ELECCIÓN;
C=COMPLEMENTOS DE FORMACIÓN; P=PROYECTO FIN DE CARRERA; X=TESINA.

Convocatoria: el valor mostrado en la columna "conv" hace referencia al mes en que se
obtiene la calificación o se convalida o adapta la asignatura.

Nota media de asignaturas superadas, ponderada según el Real Decreto 1267/1994: 2,54
1=APROBADO; 2=NOTABLE; 3=SOBRESALIENTE; 4=MATRÍCULA DE HONOR

De acuerdo con la norma de permanencia de la Universidad de Alicante, aprobada por
acuerdo del Consejo Social de 14.02.1989, el NO PRESENTADO no consume convocatoria.

LOGROS DEL ALUMNO/A

Convocatoria Logro Académico obtenido por el Alumno/a.

J /2001-02 LICENCIADO/ A EN TRADUCCIÓN E INTERPRETACIÓN.
J /2001-02 LENGUA B: INGLÉS. LENGUA C: FRANCÉS.
J /2001-02 ESPECIALIDAD: TRADUCTOR/A ESPAÑOL-CATALÁN

OBSERVACIONES DEL EXPEDIENTE.

EL ALUMNO HA SUPERADO LOS 32 CRÉDITOS VINCULADOS AL ÁREA DE FILOLOGÍA CATALANA QUE PERMITEN OBTENER EL CERTIFICADO
DE CAPACITACIÓN LINGÜÍSTICA, REGULADOS POR ACUERDO DEL DPTO. DE FILOLOGÍA CATALANA, APROBADO POR LA JUNTA DE
GOBIERNO DE ESTA UNIVERSIDAD EL 22 DE OCTUBRE DE 1998, TENIENDO COMO BASE LEGAL LA ORDEN DE 24 DE MAYO DE 1995 DE LA
CONSELLERÍA DE EDUCACIÓN Y CIENCIA.
HA SUPERADO UN TOTAL DE 64,5 CRÉDITOS DEL ÁREA DE FILOLOGÍA CATALANA.

HA ABONADO LOS DERECHOS PARA LA EXPEDICIÓN DEL TÍTULO CON FECHA 18.09.2002 POR IMPORTE DE 101,40 E

Y para que así conste y a petición del interesado/a, se emite esta certificación con el visto bueno del Ilmo/Ilma.
Decano/a-Director/a y el sello de esta Universidad, a 2 de febrero de 2004 .

Vº.Bº. DEC./DIR.

EL/LA SECRETARIO/A

EL/LA RESPONSABLE
ADMINISTRATIVO

Salvador Palazón Ferrando

Teresa Gámez Reus

Rafaela Grau López

Source: Reprinted by permission of Silvia Borrás

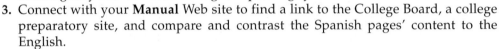

Follow-Up

1. Add to your bilingual academic glossary over the semester. How complete (or completely *focused*) can you make it? How *user friendly* (e.g., how searchable) can you make it? With each update, continue to note the sources with some kind of notation you can readily understand. Verify terms in other reliable sources. At the end of the term, merge your terms with your classmates' and vice versa.
2. Go to the Eurydice link on the page listed earlier and open the page related to European Community academic vocabulary. Take notes on *patterns* of difference between American and English usage. Are there concepts or categorizations used in the European system that have no correlation in the United States? Translate 10 terms intralingually between the two English-speaking systems.

3. Connect with your **Manual** Web site to find a link to the College Board, a college preparatory site, and compare and contrast the Spanish pages' content to the English.

Academic Major Catalogue Descriptions: *El Traductorado Público*

Read the career description and answer the questions that follow.

- El **Traductor Público** es un profesional universitario, de acuerdo con el artículo 28 de la ley 12.997 del 28.11.61. Ejerce una profesión liberal, siendo depositario de la fe pública, y su actividad es de naturaleza eminentemente intelectual.
- El ejercicio de su profesión abarca un vastísimo espectro en el campo del conocimiento—lo que supone una constante puesta al día en la medida en que se amplía incesantemente el ámbito de la ciencia y la técnica—, exigiéndosele una total pericia idiomática, por cuanto el dominio de los idiomas en que actúa es "conditio sine qua non" para el desempeño de su profesión.
- Las leyes uruguayas determinan la actuación perceptiva del Traductor Público para el diligenciamiento de documentación que proviene del extranjero o que se remite del exterior, de los que son ejemplos los exhortos, poderes, sentencias, testimonios, certificaciones, documentos personales, comerciales, financieros y técnicos en general.

Título Expedido: Traductor Público (Plan de estudios 1988)

Duración: 4 años

Requisitos Para Inscripción:

A esta carrera se ingresa mediante una Prueba de Admisión en Idioma Español y en Idioma Extranjero (escritas). Aprobadas éstas, es obligatorio rendir examen oral de la lengua extranjera elegida (Alemán, Francés, Inglés, Italiano, Portugués).

Documentación necesaria para el ingreso a facultad:

- Certificado de aprobación del Bachillerato cualquier orientación (Fórmula 69)
- 2 fotos tipo carné
- Credencial Cívica (si la tuviere)

- Cédula de Identidad
- Partida de nacimiento

Los cursos son de carácter reglamentado (asistencia obligatoria)

(*Source*: Universidad de la República, Facultad de Derecho, Departamento de Bedelía, Uruguay, Carreras Cortas: "Traductorado Público")

Discussion

1. What do we call a "traductor público" in U.S. English? Do we have the same course of study or profession? What points of the ATA Code of Professional Conduct and Business Practices (see Chapter 1) coincide with those of this text? What points are included here but not explicitly stated in the ATA?
2. Guess the meaning of the word "*liberal*" in line 2. The phrase "*pericia idiomática*" recalls a set phrase in the language industry: *perito traductor*. What does this phrase mean?
3. In the line below where the above-mentioned phrase appears, a Latin expression is used. How would you deal with it in English? Do we use it in legal or formal writing in English?
4. Make a bilingual mini-term bank of 10 ST terms and 10 TT terms for a translator to use in translating this text.
5. Translate the following phrases as part of an international student's dossier for admittance to a U.S. graduate program:
   a. *Las leyes uruguayas determinan la actuación perceptiva del Traductor Público para el diligenciamiento de documentación que proviene del extranjero o que se remite del exterior*
   b. *Los cursos son de carácter reglamentado (asistencia obligatoria)*
   c. *Ejerce una profesión liberal, siendo depositario de la fe pública*
   d. *Aprobadas éstas*
   e. *Si la tuviere* [note: future subjunctive]

TRANSLATION TEASER

The future subjunctive in Spanish, like the crocodile, has lasted unchanged for an eternity. What is its role in present-day legal texts? What are some of the most common set phrases involving the future subjunctive mood?

TRANSLATION AND SCHOOL ADMINISTRATION

CULTURAL NOTE

Education Code Section 48985: Parental Notification Requirement

"When 15 percent or more of the pupils enrolled in a public school that provides instruction in kindergarten or any of grades 1 through 12 speak a single primary language other than English, as determined from the census data submitted to the Department of Education pursuant to Section

(Continued)

52164 in the preceding year, all notices, reports, statements, or records sent to the parent or guardian of any such pupil by the school or school district shall, in addition to being written in English, be written in such primary language, and may be responded to either in English or the primary language."

Source: California Department of Education

What role could translation and interpretation (T&I) play in grammar school classrooms, administration, and outreach (including parents and prospective students)? Imagine that you are a school superintendent's T&I Committee tasked with allocating considerable funds for helping bridge language gaps in a bilingual school district. Give a bullet-point action plan for what could be implemented to ensure a system of successful two-way communication between all concerned in the children's education. What specifically would need translating? Interpreting? Would you have staff linguists? Hold translators on a retainer (paid a guaranteed minimum even if workload ebbs and flows)? What system would you put in place to initiate, execute, deliver, distribute, and evaluate translations? (Needs assessment of some sort? Who would initiate translations? What technologies would be involved, etc.?) What is a "dual language" school? What particular translation challenges are involved in running one? What about *in* the classroom itself—would you start children on translation?

HINT   Look online at different state boards of education for ideas.

Translation studies and language-acquisition theory are not always in accord, for example, on the issue of whether translation activities—usually reduced to a mechanical substituting of "equivalents"—should be used in language learning. (Many translator trainers are against this practice.) What do you think?

What can you find out about what theorists feel should be the earliest point that translation should be introduced into one's education? What work can you find on children translators? (See, for example, the work that the journal *Two Lines* is doing with children translators in school programs in California.)

CASE STUDY: DOMESTIC VIOLENCE PROTECTION ORDER

A legal education, or at least a way to educate oneself about legal options available, has been democratized through Web access.

Connect with your **Manual** Web site to find the link to the City of Vancouver, Washington, Web site and then follow the links "services and public safety," "police department," "crime prevention and awareness," and "domestic violence" page to page. Next, go to the box feature on "How to Obtain a Domestic Violence Protection Order in Clark County." Listen to and watch the English clip (6 minutes 44 seconds). Then play the Spanish and take notes about solutions and strategies, bearing in mind the English as you do so. This task will force you to keep a storehouse of the English at the ready, and keep you listening comparatively—"stereophonically"—in both languages, making comparisons from an internalized text to the translation. Next, listen to the Spanish with captions ("*con títulos*"). Start the procedure again if you have missed points you would like to discuss; remember you are discussing strategies. Regroup. What solutions defied your expectations? What legal terms were you not aware of? Mention any changes you would make in the Spanish audio or titles as they appear. One group can focus on making a term list of en<>es domestic violence terms for the benefit of the group. (Note: The Windows Media Player works best with a broadband Internet connection.)

When you are finished discussing the translation, compare the English and Spanish videos on the same topic at the Virtual Self-Help Law Center (connect with your **Manual** Web site to find the link to the Superior Court of California, County of Contra Costa Web site and follow the Domestic Violence [petitioner] links). Compare this video to the one you saw earlier from the point of view of a translator. Which would present more challenges, and what kind? Discuss. What differences in terminology do you notice? What about audience? Organization of the material? How about the production itself—is the Spanish an overdub of the English, or is it produced separately? Does that change the content of the presentation? If so how? Why do you think this topic was formatted as it was in both videos?

Tasks

1. Search Amber Alert electronic bulletin boards for translations. Are these generated by humans or machines? How can you tell?
2. a. What Spanish-language print materials are available for victims assistance, education, and abuse prevention? When translations are submitted, what kind of form do translators fill out certifying their work? (Hint: See restraining orders.) You may wish to see the Family Abuse Prevention Act and form libraries related to it.
   b. What other formats and media do bilingual domestic violence education or emergency resources take?
3. What T&I services do prisons provide? Does state or national law provide specifically for these services? Are they provided equally in all cases? Explain.
4. a. Research the culturally bound term "crime of passion." Is this a legally sanctioned category? What variations can you find country to country?
   b. Do the same for the relatively new term "hate crime." (Hint: Search "hate crime" + *delito*.)

Research Task: Legal Query

Answer the following newsgroup query as helpfully as you can; if all the information you need to reply is not given, assume different scenarios and answer completely, or refer them to where they can find the needed information.

```
Date: Wed, 10 May 2006 23:59:12

From: Mr. Wade V. Roe <legaleagle@novicenet.com.au>

Subject: Re: Query: Miranda rights en>es

Does anyone on the list know what translation of the
Miranda Rights I need to use for a police training manual
in Colorado? It's a section on common Spanish phrases they
will need, and the client wants to make laminated carrying
cards for the patrol officers with the Rights printed in
both languages. What translations are good, since I don't
know. Muy amable. Mr. Wade V. Roe P.S. Does "mirandize"
have its own verb in Spanish?

>Miranda Rights (Miranda v. Arizona, 384 U.S. 436 (1966)
```

```
Warning Of Rights
```

1. You have the right to remain silent and refuse to answer questions. Do you understand?
2. Anything you do say may be used against you in a court of law. Do you understand?
3. You have the right to consult an attorney before speaking to the police and to have an attorney present during questioning now or in the future. Do you understand?
4. If you cannot afford an attorney, one will be appointed for you before any questioning if you wish. Do you understand?
5. If you decide to answer questions now without an attorney present you will still have the right to stop answering at any time until you talk to an attorney. Do you understand?
6. Knowing and understanding your rights as I have explained them to you, are you willing to answer my questions without an attorney present?<

Source: Cartoon © Mark Parisi, Printed with permission. www.offthemark.com

Activity: Legal Registers Game

Come to class with five to seven sets of three to five legal synonyms or synonym phrases in multiple registers. The class will be divided into two teams. A member of Team 1 will approach the board as a member of Team 2 calls out the words in his or her set. The Team 1 player will put the words in descending order from *highest to lowest* then identify who would be a typical user of each *and* what would be a typical context for each.

Model: If the first set is "stir," "correctional facility," and "prison," the contestant might *write*:
correctional facility (and *say* "institutional jargon used by staff")
prison (and *say* "generic term used by general population")
stir (and *say* "jailhouse slang used by prisoners")

(Practice now by matching each of the following to the preceding group that is most likely to use them: "con," "offender," "inmate.")

Rules and scoring: Teammates can argue cases though the instructor will have final say on valid answers. Each set is worth one point for the team; an entire set must be played correctly to score. For fairness, each set may *not* include *only* upper registers or jargon. Sets may be in *English or Spanish*; for advanced play, sets may be in English *and* Spanish (mixed). Play until a predetermined time or until all sets have been read out.

INFER TRANSLATION'S ROLE: LEGAL

Research and define the role translation plays in each of the following text types. Who are the primary participants (commissioner and addressee or user)? What special difficulties does the translator of each text type face? Bring an example and discuss any differences in format or content.

1. Legal briefs
2. Lease agreements
3. Legal codes
4. Witness statements
5. Trial transcripts

Groups report to the class on a respective domain assigned from those listed.

Tasks

1. a. Discover more about *translation and national security*. Connect with your **Manual** Web site to find the link to the National Virtual Translation Center Web site.
   b. Shortfalls of translation and interpretation, and unreadiness in languages critical to national security, are persistent. Search news archives for stories on backlogs of untranslated Arabic intercepts at the national level.
   c. Read up on the scandals involving Pentagon dismissals of language specialists after 9/11.
2. a. Define "derivative work" in a legal sense. Are translations legally considered "derivative work"?
   b. Search "translation without permission." Survey the legal restrictions you find.
   c. Search "A.A. literature translation policy." Summarize Alcoholics Anonymous' policy on translation.
3. What *complaint forms* can you find in English and Spanish? (Hints: Concentrate your efforts in the areas of scams against Hispanics, law enforcement, wage claims, immigration fraud, predatory lending, car sales, and do-not-call registries.) Why do you think Hispanics tend to underreport fraud?
4. The Spanish-language form library for the U.S. Copyright Office (connect with your **Manual** Web site to find the link) posts a disclaimer that their "[*circulares y hojas informativas son] un trabajo en curso y no una traducción exacta de la información en inglés de nuestro sitio. . . .*" Compare.

Did you know that in many places in the United States, if leases or certain sales agreements are negotiated in Spanish, the seller/lessor must provide a Spanish translation of the contract before signing?

TRANSLATION TEASER

What is a "translation disclaimer" usually used for? See, for example, the homepage for the city of Raleigh, North Carolina. Connect with your **Manual** Web site to find the link.

CULTURAL NOTE

Language Protections

The Civil Rights Act of 1964 (Title VI) was designed to protect people with limited English. It reads in part (Section 601): "No person in the United States shall, on the ground of race, color, or national origin be excluded from participation in, be denied the benefits of, or be subjected to discrimination under any program or activity receiving Federal financial assistance." On the world scale, the United Nations International Covenant on Civil and Political Rights mandates the assistance of an interpreter for any defendant needing one in a criminal trial.

Research

1. Make a chart of the differences between the *common law* system and the *civil law* system. Use a graphic organizer (Venn diagram, network tree, KWL(H), concept map, comparison matrix, double cell diagram, or spider map).
2. What are the most common names in Spanish for *criminal law, case law, civil law,* and *common law*? (Be careful of false cognates.)

3. Connect with your **Manual** Web site to find the link to the ProZ.com Web site.
   a. Research into the discrepancies surrounding the Spanish terms for *tort law*. What accounts for all the variation?
   b. Follow the link to Holly Mikkelson's article, "On the Horns of a Dilemma: Accuracy vs. Brevity in the Use of Legal Terms by Court Interpreters." Write a one-paragraph essay on how culture affects the conception and expression of taking another person's life.
4. Find reliable full-text sources of international law in the original language. How accessible are they? Divide into groups to find specific subdomains (e.g., intellectual property, trade, constitutions).
5. In the published Spanish translation of the U.S. Department of Justice's *Guide to Disability Rights Laws* (August 2004, 13), an entry begins "*La Ley de Registro Nacional del Votante de 1993, también conocida como la 'Ley del Votante de Motor' hace mucho más*

fácil que los estadounidenses ejerciten su derecho fundamental del voto." In English, what law is this attempting to describe?

In pairs, translate the following text >es for the reverse side of the ticket.

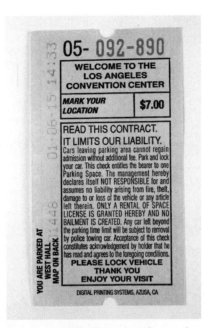

Contracts are everywhere—you need them to use a software demo, to get married, to make calls on your cell phone, to publish a textbook, to transfer ownership of real property, to resolve labor and management disputes, to remove snow from the roadway (a service contract), and even sometimes to park.

Source: Spencer Grant/PhotoEdit Inc.

CASE STUDY: LEGAL TEXT TYPE—CONTRACTS

Read the following text and answer the questions that follow.

El que suscribe............ autoriza a .... para que en nombre y representación de la sociedad, siendo las facultades aquí señaladas enunciativas pero no limitativas, firmar los documentos y emitir votos, hacer declaraciones de voluntad, firmar finiquitos, y tener cuantos poderes fueren necesarios en el ejercicio del mandato en la asamblea de partes convocada el 8 de junio de 2012.

En conformidad de lo antedicho, ante Notario Público cumplo con la legalización de mi firma

> *Firma....................................*
>
> *DNI......................................*
>
> *Huella Digital*

1. What text type is this a *modelo* (template) of? Can you find a parallel text close to this in English?
2. Give the main idea of the text in your own words: What is this form establishing?

Follow-Up

1. Your instructor may wish to give you various documents for identification (a labor contract, an *acta de constitución de asociación*, etc.) for you to familiarize yourself with their language.
2. Brainstorm in small groups the general characteristics of legal language. For example, the use of archaic compounds such as *hereintofore*. If necessary, induce from examples of contracts and other documents.

It has been said that *law is language*. What do you think that means? Consider what law makes happen and the different functions that language accomplishes. For example, in speech act theory, the pragmatics of legal language is revealed in **commissives** and **directives**. Find out what these categories reveal about law.

TRANSLATION TIP

Invest in Byran A. Garner's *The Elements of Legal Style* or his *Dictionary of Modern Legal Usage*, both from Oxford University Press.

Source: CORBIS All Rights Reserved

AMERICAN EXPRESS WORD LIST TASK

Assume you were hired into a work team of terminologists who are responsible for creating a standardized term bank of American Express products in English and Spanish.

Task

Make an Excel spreadsheet with en<>es terms (alphabetized in both directions) for the fine print, the *condiciones generales de utilización*: Connect with your **Manual** Web site to find the link. The text comprises the conditions of use in a Spanish application. The more extensive your glossary, the better it will be. Distinguish, however, between "vocabulary words" (e.g., *día laboral*) and terms (e.g., *Establecimientos Afiliados*), the latter of which are specific to a domain, an industry, or a company and are mapped one to one to a concept. Include multiword strings where appropriate.

Discuss

1. How can terminology be used to differentiate companies (e.g., consider AmEx's unique English term for "*Titular*")?
2. Compare your list with your classmates' in small groups in rotation. What difficulties do you see in the dynamics of standardizing terms?

Note the pragmatic criteria (following Cabré 1999, 48) that differentiate specialized communication from general communication. Whereas the latter values "expression, variety, and originality," specialized communication strives for: first, *concision*, which reduces distortion; second, *precision*, which allows specialists to understand one another; and third, *suitability*, which reflects the appropriate adjustment of register or redundancy depending on the user's understanding. Standardized terminology is crucial to attaining these three criteria.

Follow-Up

1. Can you find variant terminology in Spanish for similar AmEx texts? How do you account for that?
2. What can you determine about the "*casticidad*" of the Spanish terms? Do they appear calqued? Are they in general use in other Spanish institutions? Can you suggest at least one term that in North (or South) American Spanish might be different?
3. How is terminology stored and disseminated?
   a. Make word frequency lists (see corpora section in Chapter 3) of the English and Spanish terms and conditions of the same product.
   b. Go to the Political Database of the Americas and do the same for the *Constitución de 1787* (U.S. Constitution). Determine the 20 most important terms in each case.

PRESS RELEASES

1. What is a **press release**?
   a. Describe at least five of its invariable *stylistic features* as a text type.
   b. Describe as many of its *purposes* as you can.
   c. Focus for a moment on legal press releases. Who writes these, and why?
2. Who is its audience? Pick an example and identify.
3. What does "###" mean?
4. What other domains use press releases besides those listed in question 6? For what purposes are they used? Even if their intent is similar, how is an advertisement different rhetorically or discursively from a press release?

5. Why might press releases be translated? What transformations in audience might they undergo?
6. Find and compare examples of press releases in the following domains: law, marketing, public relations, and entertainment. What do they have in common? What differences do they have?
7. Find a translated press release and infer its brief.
8. What is a **press kit**? In what circumstances are they translated, and in what domains do they tend to appear?
9. What is a **mat release**? Find a company that translates its mat release monthly or quarterly.

10. a. What are **public service announcements** (PSAs) and how do they differ from press releases? What formats do PSAs take?
    b. Connect with your **Manual** Web site to find the link to the Centers for Disease Control and Prevention site. Then follow the link to the "Screen for Life" program. Examine the materials offered in Spanish.
11. Bookmark and compare the source text press releases to the translations at the Hispanic PR Wire site. Connect with your **Manual** Web site to find the link.

FEDERAL COURT INTERPRETER CERTIFICATION EXAMINATION TEXTS

The Federal Court Interpreter Certification Examination (FCICE) contains a written phase and an oral phase. Two texts for sight translation follow. Get a sense of the required level.

FCICE - Practice Sight Translation Spanish

Expediente: D 220124

María del Carmen Pérez de López, de generales conocidas en autos que cito al margen superior derecho, ante usted señor juez respetuosamente comparezco y expongo:

Ratifico en todos sus puntos la contestación de demanda que hice con anterioridad y la cual va agregada al expediente.

Con respecto a la documentación que recibí por vía aérea certificada, contesto que efectivamente no existen hijos menores dentro del matrimonio civil que tengo celebrado con mi cónyuge Víctor Manuel López García. Cabe hacer notar a su señoría que en el formulario número 1281, al dorso, me refiero al punto 5 que se contesta. La ahora demandada hace saber a este Hon. Tribunal que el actor miente y crea con ello un estado de falsedad en el contenido de este punto, en virtud de que en realidad sí existen bienes muebles e inmuebles y también existen obligaciones por parte del actor pendientes de cumplir.

Por lo expuesto, pido:

Único. Que se me tenga compareciendo por escrito, ya que no tengo los recursos económicos suficientes para comparecer personalmente, por encontrarme en pleno abandono de mi esposo y por sufragar los gastos necesarios para la manutención del hogar solamente la suscrita.

Declaro que me opongo rotundamente al procedimiento que se sigue en su instancia, por resultar incompetente para conocer dicho negocio.

Atentamente,

Atotonileo Alto, Jalisco, diciembre 8/00

María del Carmen Pérez de López

FCICE - Practice Sight Translation English

Your Honor, if it please the court, the Government would establish that Mr. Jorge Domínguez was a citizen of the Dominican Republic, having been born there in 1970. He initially entered the United States legally with his parents and siblings on an immigrant visa in 1985. He was subsequently deported from the United States on January 15, 1993 following his conviction and resultant incarceration in New York State the preceding year for the sale of a controlled substance, namely cocaine. On October 24th of last year, Mr. Domínguez was arrested and detained in Wilmington, Delaware where he was charged with the sale of heroin to an undercover state trooper. INS then proceeded to compare his fingerprints, through FBI data banks, with those of the individual who had been deported in 1993, and it was confirmed that they were one and the same person. INS obtained his immigration file and established that he was in fact born in the Dominican Republic. Furthermore, they confirmed his 1985 legal entry into the U.S., his 1992 conviction for an aggravated felony, and the deportation arising from that conviction. The INS would further prove that he had neither submitted an application for nor been granted permission to reenter the United States.

(*Source:* Reprinted by permission of The Administrative Office of the United States Courts. <http://www.ncsconline.org/d_research/fcice_exam/oralpracexamTake1.htm> Accessed March 13, 2009)

CULTURAL NOTE

The Jones Act of 1917

Puerto Rico is an *estado libre asociado*, or "free associated state" (commonwealth); essentially, a colony. The Jones Act (48 U.S.C. § 864), in addition to granting citizenship rights to Puerto Ricans, stipulates that all federal court proceedings be conducted in English; by extension, all oral and written materials must be submitted into evidence with an English translation accompanying the source documents.

What kinds of implications, or complications, has this presented for trial in Puerto Rico or involving Puerto Ricans (see, for example, *State v. Rivera-Rosario et al.*, 2000, or *United States of America v. Morales-Madera*)?

TRANSLATING RACE AND HISTORY: ART CAPTIONS

Many historical terms for racial categories have fallen out of use or taken on other, sometimes racist, connotations. How, then, to approach the important task of translating something as sensitive as Latin America's own conception of racial mixing for a completely different audience today?

Read the legends on the well-known late-eighteenth-century Mexican painting, *Cuadro de castas*, that follow. The 16 "castes," ordered by race, were intended as instructions to officials on how to categorize colonial subjects. What kind of political comment do you think the painter was making, particularly judging by the names he uses in the bottom row? How does this ordering strike you today? Do earlier times' naïve or oppressive ideas about race discount the value of researching and translating them?

Many possible commissions could exist for translating this work—from educational materials to scholarly research into *mestizaje* to government projects. Governments themselves could—and do—show interest in translating such cultural artifacts for various uses. Museums would be another natural patron. Suppose, for our purposes, that archivists are doing comparative work on the *cuadro de castas* genre of art in Colonial times, particularly Mexico, and want a translation available in a digital environment for other scholars. They offer to pay you by the hour for the research involved (so clock your time spent researching this task).

What strategy would you take for translating these 16 captions? (For example, will you choose a documental approach, leaving the Spanish alongside your English?) Where can you search for more information on the genre? Are *castas* in this usage what we would call castes today?

Translate the captions and compare your research and solutions with your classmates'.

Source: "Human Races (Las Castas)", 18th century, oil on canvas, 1.04 x 1.48 m. Museo Nacional del Virreinato, Tepotzotlan, Mexico. Schalkwijk/Art Resource, NY

Here they are listed clearly (note that some variants of this list have #16 not as *Torna atrás* but as *Ahí te estás*; hint: keep an eye out for g>j and b>v):

1. *Español con India: Mestizo*
2. *Mestizo con Española: Castizo*
3. *Castizo con Española: Español*
4. *Español con Mora: Mulato*
5. *Mulato con Española: Morisco*
6. *Morisco con Española: Chino*

7. *Chino con India: Salta atrás*
8. *Salta atrás con Mulata: Lobo*
9. *Lobo con China: Gíbaro*
10. *Gíbaro con Mulata: Albarazado*
11. *Albarazado con Negra: Cambujo*

12. *Cambujo con India: Sambaigo*
13. *Sambaigo con Loba: Calpamulato*
14. *Calpamulato con Cambuja: Tente en el aire*
15. *Tente en el aire con Mulata: No te entiendo*
16. *No te entiendo con India: Torna atrás*

CASE STUDY: LIFE HISTORIES OF WOMEN WORKERS IN MEXICO'S ASSEMBLY INDUSTRY

The following are background descriptions and excerpts from the narrative and testimonials included in the book, *La flor más bella de la maquiladora*, by Norma Iglesias Prieto (1985). The work recounts the processes, conditions, and economic strategies of the *maquila* industry, including why management has hired predominantly young women ages 16 to 24. The women recount their origins and tell of the bosses' means of control of the workers and the unpromising prospects for the women to organize. The tone of the book captures the endurance of continued hardship and the painful process of consciousness raising and serves to draw attention to their complex problems (few safety measures, repetitive strain, physical health problems—diagnosed and undiagnosed, sexual favoritism and exploitation, little creative outlet, and anxiety from reprimands). The work portrays and analyzes a group of women through their own words and from relevant data collected from 1972 to 1982 in the factories of Tijuana, B.C. (a prime location for this type of plant in that it lies in the *zona libre*, or duty-free zone, and abounds in conditions favoring employers).

Imagine that you are given a preliminary translation exam by a press interested in publishing this book in English for a general readership, perhaps with a view to also having it used on campuses in introductory Women's Studies, Border Studies, or Area Studies classes that focus on the political, economic, and social issues leading up to and since the advent of NAFTA. The following passages are chosen as representative of different "voices" in the work—both fact-based reporting and the exposé style of the narrator's contextualizations and the women's own frustrations and tribulations in their candid interviews. The passages are numbered. Read the passages through; translate with the preceding brief in mind. Be very aware of register (the workers are not highly educated women), tone, coherence, and punctuation. One slight manipulation of these authentic texts has been made—the elimination of an author's footnote explaining a word used by a speaker, the meaning of which you will have to discover on your own. Do as a timed translation in class.

① "Condiciones de trabajo" (excerpto)

Las plantas maquiladoras encierran una serie de secretos difíciles de observar a primera vista. Las fábricas, desde la calle, tienen un aire inofensivo; esos edificios bajos y viejos no se diferencian del resto del paisaje, sin embargo, basta entrar para que cuatro cosas llamen inevitablemente la atención e inviten a reflexionar sobre los daños que causan a la salud de las trabajadoras. Cala el olor picante que producen los químicos y la soldadura quemada; el ruido de las máquinas se mezcla infernalmente con la música de los radio que cada una lleva, o con la que pone la empresa a fin de elevar la productividad; humo, vapores y pelusas vuelven gris el ambiente y aquella mancha verde, azul o amarilla de las batas que visten las obreras para proteger, y no contaminar, el material de trabajo. Ironías de la vida. Por algún momento pensé que las batas y mascarillas eran para proteger al trabajador; pero no, son para proteger el material, que ha de estar completamente limpio para pasar el control de calidad. (p. 49 cap. II)

② Entrevista con Alma (excerpto)

—Es que nos tienen atrapados por el cuello —aclara Alma en un tono fuerte, reflejando su gran enojo—, ¿en cuántas maquiladoras no dicen los empresarios a las muchachas que no hagan huelga porque salen perdiendo los trabajadores?, ¿en cuántas maquiladoras no les dicen que tienen que cooperar porque es la fuente de trabajo de muchas personas? Luego luego se ve cómo Conciliación y Arbitraje está por la empresa y no les importan los trabajadores. Además, a las que alegamos siempre nos han dicho "mitoteras", "revoltosas" y nos barrían las demás muchachas. Así nunca puede haber reunión. (pp. 58-9, cap. II)

③ Entrevista con Elena, Margarita, y Cristina (excerpto)

—Hubo un tiempo —continuó Elena, después de una respiración profunda para calmar su risa—, que en la fábrica no querían gorditas. Decían que las gordas no tenían el mismo rendimiento en el calor, quién sabe si sea cierto. Ellas querían muchachas curiositas y que se vistieran bien, si ibas mal arreglada no te daban el trabajo. . . .

—Las maquiladoras nos han dado trabajo a muchas muchachas que lo necesitamos, y si no fuera por esta clase de empresas, no sé en qué podríamos trabajar. Estas fábricas nos dan trabajo a muchas. Yo creo —me dice Cristina en el tono juvenil de quien apenas tiene 18 años—, que desde que se establecerion aquí en Tijuana hay menos vagas. (p. 74, cap. IV)

(*Source:* Iglesias Prieto, Norma. La flor más bella de la maquiladora: historias de vida de la mujer obrera en Tijuana, B.C.N. Mexico City: Secretaría de Educación Pública, Centro de Estudios Fronterizos, 1985.)

A student in the class can volunteer to lead the workshop or discussion of issues the translation raised.

TRANSLATING HUMAN RIGHTS

The citations denoted in this section are from Garre 1999.

Human rights texts fall into the following general categories (47):

1. Legislative instruments (e.g., conventions, declarations);
2. Enforceable case law (e.g., decisions from competent bodies);
3. General literature (e.g. articles, press releases, textbooks).

"In international human rights law, the official languages are specified in each convention. Since there is often more than one official language, translation between at least two official languages is required" (198). Many international organizations have their own translation units in various languages, and thus the time spent translating between two languages and the time spent between 11 may be similar (201).

"[I]nternational human rights law is based on the assumptions that human rights are fundamental and universal, that human rights as they are formulated in the international legislative texts must be protected in all countries around the world and that the fundamental idea of human rights can be applied and understood globally" (48).

How do these assumptions reconcile with the idea of cultural difference? Can differences in worldviews and language—to say nothing of variances in translations even within a single language—allow for something to be textual and universal? Because each nation is responsible for translating conventions and documents into its own national tongue (195), what determines the success of a translation, and how could its relevance be weighed, apart from reference to the document's role in its own national dialogue or legal sphere? How could discrepancies of text interpretation be solved for texts of this sort?

See also Tosi 2003.

Tasks

1. Connect with your **Manual** Web site to find the link to the UN's Office of the High Commissioner for Human Rights homepage. Compare the Spanish and the English. What are some submission requirements for translators? If you have access to an alignment tool, choose a few clauses and set up a basic English>Spanish memory.
2. Connect with your **Manual** Web site to find the link to the Human Rights Watch's site. Notice how many of the features linked there (testimonies, press releases, letters, audio clips) have versions in other languages. These versions are localized with the hyperlinked name of the language *in* the language in question (e.g., "Also available in Español/Português/Deutsch"). Compare where you are taken when you click options on the upper right menu of languages (try them all). Are you linked to the same content for each language? Discuss. Click on "other" as well—how many of these language names do you recognize? What happens when you click on them? Do the characters display or do you see "??????" If the latter, how do you fix that? (Hint: The solution lies in *character encoding*.)

TRANSLATION TIP

Acronyms

Technically, acronyms (*acrónimos*) are abbreviations that are pronounced not as individual letters but as words; for example, UNESCO. Abbreviations (*siglas*) such as M.B.A. are different. In practice, the distinction is often conflated.

In most instances, both change between Spanish and English. NATO (North Atlantic Treaty Organization), for example, is known as OTAN (Organización del Tratado del Atlántico Norte) in Spanish. Sometimes—not always—the letters imply reverse left to right in translation. Other times they are completely different. Note that acronyms in phone numbers are usually not retained in translation.

Translators use two formulas when keeping the original abbreviation: "*por sus siglas en inglés*" or "*por su sigla en inglés*" (into Spanish) and "by its Spanish acronym" (into English). Frequently the target language acronym or name is given first; viz., "*La Administración para Control de Drogas (DEA por sus siglas en inglés) fue demandada…*"

Be well aware that acronyms are often shared—"ALCA" may refer to the Área de Libre Comercio de las Américas, the Apostolic Lutheran Church of America, and the Australian Lactation Consultants Association Ltd.

HINT Find some good es<>en acronym and abbreviation lists online and bookmark them.

GISTING TASK: LEGAL HISTORY/HUMAN RIGHTS

For the full index of studies in which this text* appeared, connect with your **Manual** Web site to find the link to the Desaparecidos Web site. The text appears as Chapter 12.

---

*I am indebted to my former student, Rick Whitmore, for bringing this text to my attention.

Task

Write a *gist translation* of each paragraph as you read.

HINT   Try to hold on to the logic of the text as your guide to meaning, and read deeply in English on the "Dirty War" in Argentina for your key terms.

The text, *"El Tribunal militar se niega a juzgar a sus pares" (Extracto)*, deals with the aftermath and accountability for acts of repression committed by the military during this era of torture and disappearances of leftist dissenters. Gist from *"A partir de esta pieza, quedó claro que el plan elucubrado..."*down to *"justifica en última instancia, la existencia de los tribunales militares"* (Asociación Americana de Juristas 1988).

Imagine that an international human rights organization such as Human Rights Watch has commissioned this translation for an English-language study it is conducting on the democratization processes that follow military dictatorships; the study will be used to educate legislators worldwide. The audience for this text, and its new readers, are subject specialists.

What is the difference ideologically between las Malvinas and the Falkland Islands? Is it a simple matter of substitution in a politicized text of this sort?

LINGUISTIC NOTE

The infinitive "to disappear" used transitively—for example, *to disappear someone*—has carried over from Spanish's use of the cognate to describe a familiar tactic of repressive regimes. Translators, accordingly, should take care not to use "he disappeared" for "he was disappeared." Often the noun *desaparecido* passes untranslated into many different languages.

WORKSHOP #6: POLITICAL SCIENCE

Translate for an international newswire service as if the event reported were a current event and you were working in 2002. Because your English may be carried by a number of different publications, you know only that it must conform to an international English without either obvious Britishisms or Americanisms.

22 de agosto del 2002

Cumbre Mundial de Desarrollo Sostenible

Osvaldo León

Servicio Informativo "alai-amlatina"

En Johannesburgo (Sudáfrica), del 26 de agosto al 4 de septiembre, se realizará la Cumbre Mundial sobre Desarrollo Sustentable para pasar revista al cumplimiento de los compromisos adquiridos hace diez años en la Cumbre de Río de Janeiro y definir nuevos derroteros para la superación de la pobreza crónica y la preservación del planeta.

El evento se anuncia espectacular, tanto por el número de jefes de Estado y de gobierno que han comprometido su asistencia, como por la presencia de alrededor de 60 mil participantes de organizaciones no gubernamentales, de 180 países, que se congregarán en un foro paralelo, en la zona de Gallagher.

El concepto de "desarrollo sustentable" se consagró en la Cumbre sobre Medio Ambiente y Desarrollo, celebrada en Río de Janeiro del 3 al 14 de junio de 1992. En términos de la ONU se define como "el desarrollo que satisface las necesidades del presente sin comprometer la capacidad de las generaciones futuras para satisfacer las suyas", cuyos parámetros centrales son: crecimiento económico y equidad, conservación de recursos naturales y desarrollo social. Propósito que apela a la aplicación de tres principios: la precaución preventiva, la solidaridad intergeneracional y entre pueblos del mundo, y la participación social en los mecanismos de decisión.

Una agenda incumplida

La cita de Johannesburgo se propone evaluar el cumplimiento de los compromisos adquiridos en la Cumbre de Rio-92, que como programa de acción se acuerpó en la Agenda 21. Según la ONU, se trata de un programa bueno, pero débilmente aplicado. Las medidas existentes para preservar el medio ambiente— cada vez más frágil— pecan por insuficiencia. Los buenos propósitos de reducción de la pobreza adoptados en múltiples foros mundiales y regionales se han reducido a nada, pues la lógica de la globalización neoliberal imperante conlleva a una cada vez mayor concentración de la riqueza. Y es así que, se han desvanecido los esfuerzos para impulsar el desarrollo humano y frenar el deterioro del medio ambiente.

Los balances realizados en una multiplicidad de espacios no gubernamentales, tanto en la esfera nacional como internacional, casi sin excepción coinciden en señalar que la aplicación de tal agenda ha sido mínima o nula. Pero también hay quienes destacan que, al menos en el plano formal, hay logros de importancia a no perder de vista, tal el caso de varios tratados internacionales que son producto de Rio-92.

Tan es así que en la agenda de Johannesburgo consta la ratificación de una serie de estos tratados: el Protocolo de Kioto sobre la emisión de gases invernaderos, el Protocolo de Cartagena sobre Bioseguridad, el Tratado Internacional sobre Recursos Genéticos de Plantas para la Alimentación y la Agricultura, el Convenio de Estocolmo sobre Contaminantes Orgánicos y Persistentes (COP), el Convenio de Rotterdam sobre consentimiento previo informado antes de exportar ciertos productos químicos peligrosos y plaguicidas, el acuerdo de la ONU sobre recursos pesqueros que incluye varios planes de la FAO y el Convenio de Basilea sobre el transporte de residuos tóxicos. Como se sabe, varios de estos tratados han sido impugnados por Estados Unidos. Queda por ver si sus presiones lograrán impedir que se concreten las ratificaciones esperadas.

Las negociaciones previas sobre la declaración política oficial y el consiguiente plan de acción, no se anuncian muy alentadoras. Nitin Desai, secretario general de la Cumbre (WSSD, por sus siglas en ingles), anticipó que "el 73 por ciento del texto está listo, pero el 27 por ciento restante corresponde a los temas más importantes como globalización y mecanismos de implementación, en los que se trata el comercio y las finanzas".

Como quien dice, con la retórica no hay problema, pero sí con las decisiones sustantivas.

La cumbre de Johannesburgo se presenta muy compleja, aunque tiene el mérito anticipado de que no pasará inadvertida, como sucedió con la Cumbre contra el Racismo realizada el año pasado en ese mismo país, Sudáfrica. Y decimos que es compleja porque nada más ni nada menos se refiere a la supervivencia planetaria.

No sólo en el sentido de sobre vivencia, sino en la perspectiva de "tener una mejor calidad de vida, basada en valores éticos, culturales y espirituales, y no sólo económicos", como acertadamente señala la declaración de los pueblos indígenas mexicanos reunidos en Toluca el pasado 27 de julio.

(*Source:* Osvaldo León, Director, Agencia Latinoamericana de Información – ALAI. www.alainet.org)

Word count: 717

Work in groups, dividing the labor as you see fit.

8

Medical Translation

MEDICAL TRANSLATION TEXT TYPES

Medical translators face a great number of text types. The list that follows is only partial, but it includes many of the most common ones.

Patient education brochures

Medical articles, news, research papers, and abstracts

Package inserts and product specifications

Investigational new drug applications (INDs)

New drug applications (NDAs)

Publicity and marketing/Product launches

Research questionnaires

Clinical studies

Medical instruction manuals

Patient consent forms (informed consent)

Insurance claims

Patients rights declarations

Hospital in-take questionnaires

Hospital discharge summaries

Patient histories

Medical charts

Medical subject headings

Documentation for medical devices

Activity: Text Types

Each class member will be assigned a text type from the list. Produce (1) a definition of the text type's purpose, the identification of its typical users, and its name in Spanish; followed by (2) a half-page summary of each text type's most common textual features (to turn in); then (3) attach an example of your assigned text type in English and Spanish, whether Rosetta stones or different texts. Make sure your examples represent what you claim about their features.

EN<>ES MEDICAL TERMS COMMON IN TRANSLATION AND INTERPRETING

(Adapted and expanded from Van Hoof 1999)

active phase (of a disease)	*fase evolutiva/activa (de una enfermedad)*
attending physician/ general practitioner (GP)	*médico de cabecera*
autopsy	*autopsia, examen post mortem*
clinical features	*manifestaciones clínicas*
c. history	*antecedentes clínicos*
c. picture	*cuadro clínico*
complaint	*dolencia, síntoma*
condition	*estado, afección*
course	*tratamiento, seguimiento, evolución*
disorder	*alteración, trastorno*
dosage	*posología*
dosage schedule	*esquema posológico*
dullness	*matidez*
early stage (of a disease)	*fase inicial (de una enfermedad)*
effective	*activo, eficaz*
examination	*examen, reconocimiento*
failure	*crisis, ataque, fallo, fracaso, insuficiencia*
fit, attack, spell, seizure	*acceso, ataque, crisis*
follow-up	*seguimiento*
harmful	*nocivo, perjudicial, dañino*
harmlessness	*inocuidad*
health care facilities	*instalaciones médicas*
health care practitioner	*profesional de la salud*
history	*anamnesis, historial, antecedentes*
inpatient	*paciente hospitalizado*
involvement	*afección, daño, ataque*
malaise	*malestar*
mild	*benigno, discreto, leve*
occupational therapy	*ergoterapia*
onset	*principio, instalación, aparición*
outpatient	*paciente de consulta externa, ambulatorio*
present with symptoms	*presentar síntomas*
primary care services	*servicios de cabecera*
procedure	*acción, intervención*
proneness to	*predisposición a*
responsiveness	*reactividad, sensibilidad*

route of administration	*vía de administración*
oral route	*vía oral*
screening	*detección, screening*
silent (or asymptomatic)	*asintomático*
spell	*acceso (de)*
tenderness*	*sensibilidad a la presión*
tightness	*constricción, opresión*
workup	*examen físico, valoración*

*Note: not "ternura"!

Sample Output (Terms and Notes) on Medtrad's *medtradiario*: Keywords = *Screening* and *Double Blind*

Read and determine: What are some of the factors a translator must weigh in deciding on a suitable English for each term?

screening

cribado1,2,3,4 [2074] [2076] [2078] [2079]

detección [sistemática]3,4 [2076] [2079]

selección4 [2076] [2080]

tamizaje [2076]

tamizado4 [2076]

pesquisa[je]4 [-]

rastreo4 [-]

encuesta4 [-]

averiguación4 [-]

escrutinio4,5 [-] [*jur.*]

"*Screening* was defined in 1951 by the US Commission on Chronic Illness as 'The presumptive identification of unrecognized disease or defect by the application of tests, examinations or other procedures which can be applied rapidly. Screening tests sort out apparently well persons who probably have a disease from those who probably do not. A screening test is not intended to be diagnostic. Persons with positive or suspicious findings must be referred to their physicians for diagnosis and necessary treatment." [2079] En: Last JM, *A dictionary of epidemiology,* 4ª ed., Oxford Univ. Press, CIUDAD, 2001.

"The concept of *screening* usually refers to laboratory tests, physical examination or radiologic tests performed on asymptomatic patients in the hope of discovering subclinical disease. In general, a positive result of a screening intervention leads to further diagnostic workup . . ." En: The Medical Clinics of North America, Nov, 1999. [2079]

"*Screening*: Estimation or testing of a group of individuals to separate those who are well from those who have an undiagnosed disease or defect or who are at high risk." En: *Diccionario médico Dorland.* [2079]

"To screen. Examination of a group of usually asymptomatic individuals to detect those with a high probability of having a given disease, typically by means of an inexpensive diagnostic test." En: *Stedman's electronic medical dictionary.* [2079]

1. F. Navarro, *Traducción y lenguaje en medicina,* Fundación Dr. Antonio Esteve, Barcelona, 1997.
2. Medicina Clínica 1999; 112 (18): 40: *cribado serológico.*
3. «El lenguaje médico», *Manual de estilo,* Doyma, p. 197.
4. Lebende Sprachen, n.° 4/97, p. 176.
5. *Puntoycoma,* n.° 60. Víctor González Martínez: Jurid. Def. «The analytical examination of the acquis [. . .] *los negociadores comunitarios analizan minuciosa y rigurosamente la transposición real del Derecho comunitario en cada uno de los sectores, labor que en lengua inglesa denominan abreviadamente* screening. *Si la traducción de la expresión extensa no plantea ningún problema, sí lo supone la traducción de la expresión abreviada* screening. *En nuestra unidad hemos decidido acomodarnos al original, traducir también la primera vez la definición del concepto y denominar después con una sola palabra, escrutinio, el término* screening. *Creemos que esta solución respeta plenamente tanto el significado (escrutinio: examen y averiguación exacta y diligente que se hace de una cosa para formar juicio de ella; DRAE, primera acepción) y permite crear una correspondencia exacta para designar este proceso de control estricto de la homologación jurídica de los países candidatos de la UE.»*

N. de C.: el término cribado *es muy frecuente en las publicaciones médicas de España, pero parece estar menos difundido en Hispanoamérica.*

double blind study

ensayo con doble enmascaramiento [1889]

estudio con ocultación doble [1867] [1889]

estudio bienmascarado [-]

estudio biencubierto [-]

estudio en/con doble anonimato [-]

estudio de doble ciego [-]

«Double blind. *[Est.] Evítese el anglicismo* doble ciego. *Si un objeto, además de mucho dinero, me cuesta tiempo o salud, no diré de él que es* doble caro, *sino doblemente caro. Para calificar un adjetivo como* ciego, *no se puede utilizar en español otro adjetivo (doble), sino un adverbio (doblemente). En cuanto a la incorrección de traducir* blind *por* ciego, *véase* blind study.» [1867]

[*Sobre* doble anonimato] «*Esto es a mi juicio una mala traducción de* double blind *porque no es que no se sepa quién está en el estudio; tanto de los pacientes como de los controles (o testigos [. . .]) se sabe la identidad.*» [1872] [1889]

[*Sobre* bienmascarado] «*Tampoco me gusta lo del ensayo enmascarado (monoenmascarado, bienmascarado, etcétera), porque el ensayo no se enmascara (oculta) a nadie, ni una vez, ni dos veces.*

Lo que se oculta es la identidad de la sustancia administrada (placebo o medicación de estudio), ya al paciente (single blind) *ya a ambos a dos, paciente y observador* (double blind). *[. . .] Cualquiera de estas posibilidades me parece mucho más pertinente: ensayo con enmascaramiento* (single blind), *ensayo con doble enmascaramiento* (double blind), *que no difiere mucho de una de las propuestas de Fernando, es decir, la de* ensayo con ocultación única o doble *(en su* Traducción y lenguaje en medicina).» [1889] [1898]

«*Si el autor desconocido de una obra puede ser* anónimo, *una cosa sin nombre (para el médico y el paciente) no puede serlo menos, aunque el* DRAE *no registre todavía esa acepción.*» [1895]

«*A las cosas sin nombre yo les llamaría* innominadas, *mejor que anónimas. [. . .] Además, en el caso que nos ocupa, las cosas tienen nombres (fármaco activo, el que sea, y placebo) y ambos (médico y paciente) los conocen. Lo que no saben es cuál de los dos están administrando o tomando. En cuanto a los ciegos/enmascarados [. . .] hay autoridades que, también en inglés, recomiendan* masked *en vez de* blind *[. . .]. Por ejemplo, en Lang TA, Secic M,* How to report statistics in medicine. Annotated guidelines for authors, editors, and reviewers. *Filadelfia, Filadelfia, American College of Physicians, 1997, se puede leer:*

[. . .] "Masking (the term is preferred to blinding) . . ." (p. 16)» [1897]

«*[Respecto al comentario anterior del mensaje 1897] no solo en Lang sino también en el* Clinical trials terminology, terminology and usage recommendations *de Curtis L. Meinert (School of Hygiene and Public Health, Center for Clinical Trials) donde puede leerse:*

"mask, masked, adj: of, relating to, or being a procedure in a study, especially an experiment or trial, which a person or class of persons (e.g., patients, treaters, or readers in a trial) is not informed of or is denied access to information known to or made available to others represented in the study or experiment. See single-mask, double-mask, and triple-mask in relation to treatment assignment in trials. Syn: blind **(not recommended; see blind for reasons)** Usage note: preferred to blind because of negative connotations and **ambiguities** associated with **blind**. Blind carries a connotation of **mindlessness** or stupidity in some everyday usages, eg, blind luck or blind stupidity. The term **mask** has greater utility across a wider class of trials and settings than blind (e.g., blind can be confusing in vision trials with blind treatment administration and with blindness as an outcome measure) and is a better descriptor of the operational process implied."» [1911]

«. . . innominado *(que no tiene nombre) y* anónimo *(que lo tiene, pero no se conoce).*» [1901]

N. de C.: el traductor debe saber que la traducción más difundida de double blind study *es* estudio de doble ciego. *Véase* anonimato *en el* DRAE.

(*Source:* MedTrad, Foro de Medicina y Traducción, <http://www.medtrad.org/ escaparate/medtradiario. html>. With special thanks to María Luisa Clark, Adriana Cruz, Martha Daza, María José Hernández Weigand, Ana María Giordano, Paz Gómez Polledo, Laura Munoa, Olga Mutis de la Serna, Consuelo Pascau, Cristina Pruna, Mirta Pryluka, María Verónica Saladrigas, Barbara Shapiro and Elisa Villaret.)

CULTURAL NOTE

Register, Literacy, and Medicine

Everyone knows the story of the Hispanic outpatient who died after taking *11* pills for something that was prescribed to be taken "ONCE" (i.e., one time) daily. Some pharmacies are using bilingual

(Continued)

pharmacists, translation software, or term bases for translating labels to prevent overdosage and other traumas.

The reality of literacy levels is daunting: The *Journal of the American Medical Association* determined that more than 60% of Spanish speakers had difficulties understanding directions on prescription labels, whereas another study found that the mean reading level of Spanish-speaking Medicaid recipients is third grade (Cornelio 2002, 24–8). Translators and interpreters thus must be *extremely* aware of audience in medical environments. Remember: People who struggle to read in their own language have a monumental educational barrier to learning to read English, despite valiant efforts.

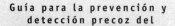

Guía para la prevención y
detección precoz del

Cáncer del SENO

Esta guía se ha diseñado con el
propósito de darle una visión general de
los factores de riesgo asociados con el
cáncer del seno, su detección precoz y
técnicas de diagnostico. También como
su estilo de vida puede afectar el riesgo
de desarrollar cáncer del seno.

Patient education brochure
Source: Bill Aron/PhotoEdit Inc.

LINGUISTIC NOTE

A CLINICAL TRIAL CASE STUDY

 Connect with your **Manual** Web site and use the link to find the McElroy Translation site. Read what was involved in the 530,000-word medical translation job. Some of the source files were even handwritten!

Learn what the word *teletranslation* means.

TRANSLATION TIP

Form Libraries

Find a *medical form library* with many of the forms you need in bilingual format. Bookmark and download multiple variations.

Discussion

How ethical is it for a medical service provider to simply run its products through the Google translator or a similar online program, archive the translation for free downloading, and then issue a disclaimer that the translation is flawed but "for information only"? Is it a good idea to have rough—or extremely rough—medical translations? Is a terrible translation better than none? Try to see exceptions to whatever your point of view happens to be.

••

Tasks

1. Find the same medical insurance application form in English and Spanish. List sets of 10 terms and phrases that you suspect would be standard for the text type (i.e., used on other similar forms).
2. Determine what impact the Health Insurance Portability and Accountability Act (HIPAA) has on translation. What does compliance involve, and what does translation have to do with it?
3. To what extent are the medical textbooks in use in Spain and Latin America translations from the English? Verify. Can you discover how this work is sourced out (from the publisher, through agencies, etc.)?

••

TRANSLATION TIP

Plain Language

Translators need to know about the push toward the use of **plain language**. Advocates of plain language stress the usability and comprehensibility of clear writing, whether for a specialized or lay audience. The legal profession is another important constituency with this goal.

 Connect with your **Manual** Web site and use the link to read "Clear and to the Point: Guidelines for Using Plain Language at NIH" (National Institutes of Health).

EVALUATING PARALLEL TEXTS: *EL RESUMEN CLÍNICO*

The following text is an excerpt from a *resumen clínico*. What textual markers make this a readily identifiable text type? Who uses this type of text? Invent a scenario for the text that follows: Who wrote it? Why is it being translated? For whom? Where?

Task

 Search sites online that could conceivably help in translating the text on page 232. Retrieve 10 to 15 for closer analysis; list the Web addresses of the top 5.

••

Resumen Clínico

Nombre: GRM

Edad: 61

Sexo: Fem.

Estado civil: Casada

Ocupación: Hogar

Escolaridad: Analfabeta

Lugar de Origen: Puebla

Lugar de residencia: Puebla

Fecha realización Historia Clínica: 26 Enero 2004

Expediente: 04:0261

AHF. Negativos para oncológicos.

APNP. Tabaquismo y alcoholismo negativo.

APP. Quirúrgicos, alérgicos, transfusionales, traumáticos y crónico-degenerativos negativos.

AGO: Menarca a los 13 años, ritmo 30x3, FUM. 45 años. IVS 15 años, parejas sexuales 2, G:13 P:12 C:0 A:1 EPP. 18 años, EUP. 37 años. Hormonales negativos. DOCMA: Nunca. Papanicolau. Nunca.

Padecimiento Actual. Paciente la cual refiere un mes de evolución con sangrado transvaginal en moderada cantidad, intermitente, sin ninguna otra sintomatología; por lo que acude al servicio de colposcopía de donde es enviada a nuestra unidad.

Exploración Física

T/A 110/70 Fc. 80Xx' Fr. 22x' Temperatura 36.5°c. Karnofsky 100%

ECOG 0

Paciente consciente orientada, de edad aparente igual a la cronológica, íntegra, bien conformada, constitución endomórfica, sin movimientos anormales y marcha normal.

Cráneo normocéfalo, sin exostosis ni hundimientos, conjuntivas pálidas +, mucosas bien hidratadas, boca con edentulia parcial, cuello sin adenopatías, tórax con mamas simétricas, sin alteraciones. Ruidos cardiacos rítmicos sin agregados, campos pulmonares sin alteraciones. Abdomen globoso a expensas de panículo adiposo, sin tumoraciones ni visceromegalias, peristalsis normal. Extremidades inferiores con insuficiencia venosa superficial. Laboratorio, gabinete y evolución se comentarán en la sesión.

(*Source:* Courtesy of Armando Fernández Orozco, MD, Sociedad Mexicana de Oncología, A.C.)

Follow-Up

1. How many of the abbreviations could be found in parallel texts? If some could not, where would be your second recourse to look for them?

2. Identify what your parallel texts with the most potential have in common. Are they similar in authority? How do you know? Are they adhering to the same established format or content?

3. Brainstorm ways to tell if a Web site is presenting trustworthy information. What critical thinking skills can you apply to information to ascertain its reliability?

Task: Outreach Spanish ("Med Ed")

In pairs, produce a rough translation into Spanish of the text on the topic of smoking cessation (your instructor will provide it to you). Imagine that you are providing the information for a Spanish speaker who does not read English. If you and your partner do not know a term, underline it and during the follow-up, search online. Verify the terms you did use. Take turns sight translating; you can help and make suggestions to one another as you go.

Follow-Up

1. Verify your terms and fix your trouble spots. Find parallel texts, glossaries, translator's forums, and other resources.
2. What different ways of rendering "second-hand smoking" can you find? Rank them in descending order from the highest register to the lowest. Which do you think is most appropriate here? Was this a written assignment for patient outreach?

HINT If you have a cell phone handy in class, see if you can have any translation questions answered by a bilingual operator who has access to similar materials. Try the National Alliance for Hispanic Health's Indoor Air Quality Helpline at 1-800-SALUD-12 (1-800-725-8312) or the Su Familia Helpline 1 (866) SU-FAMILIA. See if the American Lung Association® at 1-800-LUNGUSA has Spanish-speaking operators or can provide parallel texts. As always, be mindful of others' time.

Tasks

1. Write an essay on the Mayo Clinic's use of multilingual materials. You may wish to focus on text type, workflow and editing procedures, project management, or resource pooling and archiving.

2. Connect with your **Manual** Web site and use the link to find the Sound Partners site; listen to the bilingual public service announcement (PSA) on the dangers of second-hand smoke. Using this as an example, in pairs, find a medical topic, write the script, and *record* a PSA in the opposite language. The PSA is played for the class as they follow along on copies of the printed source script. Have a feedback session for each pair's work.

Waiting room in Boriken Neighborhood Health Center, East Harlem, New York City
Source: Ken Karp/Pearson Education/PH College

TRANSLATING GOVERNMENT NUTRITION POLICY AND PROMOTION MATERIALS

The United States Department of Agriculture (USDA) has revamped the old nutrition pyramid in favor of a more customized approach. MyPyramid reflects some of the changes, including the recommendation that physical activity be incorporated into one's lifestyle.

Tasks

Read "Anatomy of MyPyramid" (shown next). Think in terms of audience: Who might be reading a text of this sort, whether in English or Spanish, and in what contexts? (Hint: Consider all age groups of people.) Are there any words or phrases that would diverge for different regional audiences? Which? How would you approach them for a translation of this material for a Web site or educational poster? What educational level should you aim for in terms of diction?

As a group, consider possibilities for the phrases "a healthier you" and "One size doesn't fit all" in this context.

Sight translate. When you have done a version as a class, comment on some of the possibilities generated and offer alternatives.

Your instructor will now give you the published Spanish of "Anatomy of MyPyramid." Comment.

Now go to the following page of the pyramid, which lists grains, vegetables, fruits, milk, and meat and beans. Under each of the headings, there are brief slogans (e.g., "Make half your grains whole").

As a group, discuss strategies and solutions for these. Share as a class.

1. In your groups, gloss the rest of that page en>es as if in preparation for a translation of it.
2. Make a brief convincing argument to a potential patron, or the rights holder or author, about why and for whom this material should be translated. (If you were offered the job, could you also handle the formatting? Do you have health [nutrition] subject knowledge? Do you have a competent proofreader among your contacts?)

Anatomy of MyPyramid

One size doesn't fit all
USDA's new MyPyramid symbolizes a personalized approach to healthy eating and physical activity. The symbol has been designed to be simple. It has been developed to remind consumers to make healthy food choices and to be active every day. The different parts of the symbol are described below.

Activity
Activity is represented by the steps and the person climbing them, as a reminder of the importance of daily physical activity.

Moderation
Moderation is represented by the narrowing of each food group from bottom to top. The wider base stands for foods with little or no solid fats or added sugars. These should be selected more often. The narrower top area stands for foods containing more added sugars and solid fats. The more active you are, the more of these foods can fit into your diet.

Personalization
Personalization is shown by the person on the steps, the slogan, and the URL. Find the kinds and amounts of food to eat each day at MyPyramid.gov.

MyPyramid.gov
STEPS TO A HEALTHIER YOU

Proportionality
Proportionality is shown by the different widths of the food group bands. The widths suggest how much food a person should choose from each group. The widths are just a general guide, not exact proportions. Check the Web site for how much is right for you.

Variety
Variety is symbolized by the 6 color bands representing the 5 food groups of the Pyramid and oils. This illustrates that foods from all groups are needed each day for good health.

Gradual Improvement
Gradual improvement is encouraged by the slogan. It suggests that individuals can benefit from taking small steps to improve their diet and lifestyle each day.

USDA U.S. Department of Agriculture
Center for Nutrition Policy and Promotion
April 2005 CNPP-16

USDA is an equal opportunity provider and employer.

GRAINS	VEGETABLES	FRUITS	OILS	MILK	MEAT & BEANS

GRAINS Make half your grains whole	VEGETABLES Vary your veggies	FRUITS Focus on fruits	MILK Get your calcium-rich foods	MEAT & BEANS Go lean with protein
Eat at least 3 oz. of whole-grain cereals, breads, crackers, rice, or pasta every day 1 oz. is about 1 slice of bread, about 1 cup of breakfast cereal, or ½ cup of cooked rice, cereal, or pasta	Eat more dark-green veggies like broccoli, spinach, and other dark leafy greens Eat more orange vegetables like carrots and sweetpotatoes Eat more dry beans and peas like pinto beans, kidney beans, and lentils	Eat a variety of fruit Choose fresh, frozen, canned, or dried fruit Go easy on fruit juices	Go low-fat or fat-free when you choose milk, yogurt, and other milk products If you don't or can't consume milk, choose lactose-free products or other calcium sources such as fortified foods and beverages	Choose low-fat or lean meats and poultry Bake it, broil it, or grill it Vary your protein routine — choose more fish, beans, peas, nuts, and seeds

For a 2,000-calorie diet, you need the amounts below from each food group. To find the amounts that are right for you, go to MyPyramid.gov.

Eat 6 oz. every day	Eat 2½ cups every day	Eat 2 cups every day	Get 3 cups every day; for kids aged 2 to 8, it's 2	Eat 5½ oz. every day

Find your balance between food and physical activity
- Be sure to stay within your daily calorie needs.
- Be physically active for at least 30 minutes most days of the week.
- About 60 minutes a day of physical activity may be needed to prevent weight gain.
- For sustaining weight loss, at least 60 to 90 minutes a day of physical activity may be required.
- Children and teenagers should be physically active for 60 minutes every day, or most days.

Know the limits on fats, sugars, and salt (sodium)
- Make most of your fat sources from fish, nuts, and vegetable oils.
- Limit solid fats like butter, margarine, shortening, and lard, as well as foods that contain these.
- Check the Nutrition Facts label to keep saturated fats, *trans* fats, and sodium low.
- Choose food and beverages low in added sugars. Added sugars contribute calories with few, if any, nutrients.

MyPyramid.gov
STEPS TO A HEALTHIER YOU

U.S. Department of Agriculture
Center for Nutrition Policy and Promotion
April 2005
CNPP-15

USDA is an equal opportunity provider and employer.

Quiz Text: Guided Translation

Choose the letter of the word or phrase that best renders the corresponding unit of meaning in bold. You may write in your own version. Discuss why you made the choice, including why the other options were not satisfactory. Focus on cognates, collocations, and frequency and naturalness of expression. Here are the situational features of this text: function of source text: to warn about quarantined goods; addressees: Spanish-speaking travelers; time of reception: c. June 2003; place of reception: customs, San Juan, PR; medium of transmission: written flyers; motive for production: public awareness to reduce agricultural risk.
ST:

*Efectivo inmediatamente está **prohibida** (1) la entrada de **los gandules** (2) (gandures) **en vaina** (3) o **desgranados** (4) procedentes de Puerto Rico y la República Dominicana hacia los Estados Unidos debido a cambios en **la reglamentación vigente** (5), entiéndase la cuarentena 7CFR318.58. Este cambio en la reglamentación **obedece a** (6) la presencia en ambos países de **la plaga** (7) conocida como Melanagromyza obtusa, o mosca de la vaina de los gandules. Esta plaga es altamente agresiva y **representa** (8) un alto riesgo para las cosechas de gandules y por ende para la economía agrícola.*

*El Departamento de Agricultura de los Estados Unidos tiene como uno de sus objetivos el proteger **los cultivos** (9) y asegurar a los consumidores el que obtengan alimentos de la mejor calidad. Los gandules que se encuentren en el equipaje de los pasajeros viajando hacia los Estados Unidos serán inspeccionados, **incautados** (10), y destruídos.* (USDA-APHIS-PPQ, Puerto Rico and US Virgin Islands Public Awareness Committee)

1. *prohibida*
   a. prohibited
   b. banned
   c. forbidden
   d. _____

2. *los gandules*
   a. chick peas
   b. pigeon peas
   c. lazy people
   d. _____

3. *en vaina*
   a. in the shell
   b. in the pod
   c. shucked
   d. _____

4. *desgranados*
   a. chaffed
   b. threshed
   c. shelled
   d. _____

5. *la reglamentación vigente*
   a. prevailing orders
   b. current law
   c. rules in force
   d. _____

6. *obedece a*
   a. obeys
   b. is due to
   c. responds to
   d. _____

7. *la plaga*
   a. the plague
   b. the scourge
   c. the pest
   d. _____

8. *representa*
   a. demonstrates
   b. exhibits
   c. poses
   d. _____

9. *los cultivos*
   a. cultivations
   b. crops
   c. cultures
   d. _____

10. *incautados*
   a. enchanted
   b. cauterized
   c. seized
   d. _____

Task: Translating a Hospital Brochure

The text is from a full-color brochure for the Hospital de la Mujer (which, curiously, is no longer for women only, but the name stuck) in downtown San Salvador, El Salvador. (Connect with your **Manual** Web site and use the link to find the hospital Web site.)

The literature is given to visitors and offers an overview of the hospital's services. The terms and phrases are extracted verbatim from the prose used to describe the features of each hospital area. Search and verify:

Unidad de cuidados intensivos

- cubículos independientes con barreras de aislamiento bacteriológico
- sistemas de aire acondicionado con filtros hepa y diferencial de presión positiva
- red de monitores interconectados entre sí e integrados al monitor central ubicado en la estación de enfermería, lo cual permite una vigilancia simultánea total
- Ventiladores Servo-i

Área de Recuperación

- ambiente acogedor, cómodo y favorecedor a la recuperación del paciente de cirugía ambulatoria
- diseño físico que incluye la estadía de un acompañante

División Materno Infantil

- decorado con motivos delicados
- ambiente de asepsia total
- los bebés son recibidos por profesionales comprometidos
- si el bebé lo amerita, contamos con soporte de incubadoras

Unidad de Cuidados Intensivos Neonatales (UCIN)

Equipado con

- Ventiladores Neonatales
- Monitoreo de signos vitales
- Presión arterial y venosa

Salas de Parto

- Modernas salas de parto y expulsión

Areas de Hospitalización

- habitación con camas ergonómicas, colchones anti-escaras, aire acondicionado, servicio de alimentación personalizada

Activity: Patients' Bill of Rights

What would you expect to find in a "patients' bill of rights"?

Now research this type of document. Come to a consensus on the minimum common features it includes. What guarantees does it call for?

Make a glossary of 25 terms and phrases en<>es common to the patients' bill of rights. If there are alternate viable translations for a term or phrase (verified), list them as well.

From your research, answer this: For a translation of a given document of this sort, what percentage would you estimate is boilerplate, extractable almost verbatim from other similar documents? What percentage would have to be produced from scratch?

Identification exercise: Mark the phrases from the following list with an "X" if you think they *conceivably* could be part of a patients' bill of rights in the United States. Each phrase may be part of a longer sentence. If the phrase is inappropriate or highly unlikely in this text type, do not mark it. It is the *meaning*, not the exact wording, that you are being asked about here.

_____ You have a constitutional right to treatment.

_____ You have a right to participate in decisions about your health care treatment.

_____ If you speak another language, assistance may not be provided; you make informed decisions at your own risk.

_____ Patients have the right to considerate, respectful care.

_____ Emergency services are covered wherever acute symptoms are of sufficient severity that a "prudent layperson" could reasonably expect that the absence of medical attention would result in serious risks to health.

_____ *El paciente tiene el derecho de que su proveedor de cuidados de salud le informe acerca del diagnóstico, el curso de tratamiento, las alternativas y los riesgos de su caso.*

_____ *Al paciente de una instalación de cuidados de salud que no entienda o hable inglés, hay que proveerle un intérprete.*

_____ *El derecho a la información antes del tratamiento sobre lo que está cubierto y cuánto hay que pagar.*

_____ *El paciente tiene derecho de una segunda opinión, y en casos excepcionales, una tercera.*

_____ *Ud. tiene derecho de rehusarse a recibir su tratamiento.*

TRANSLATION TIP

Medical Collocations and Other Constructions

Use Simo Merne's *Handbook of Medical English Usage* (1989) to help you with collocations, colligations (for example, a patient presents *with* symptoms, as unusual as that sounds to the layperson), binaries (bedridden vs. ambulatory), morphological information—inflections, derivations, and compounds—(e.g., compromise, immunocompromise), mass nouns and count nouns (anaplasia, anaplasm), and near-synonyms.

Activity: Living Wills

What follows are descriptions of a living will—first, the source text in English, then the Spanish translation. Terms and phrases are omitted. Use the brainstorm list that follows to fill in both texts to create the best possible translation in terms of semantic and terminological accuracy (brief: patient information, U.S. audience). If a better term or phrase occurs to you that is not among those offered, use it. Added twists are that some terms and phrase options may not appear at all for a given blank (whether in English or Spanish, or both). In one case, two different terms are possible solutions; in another, a term is used more than once. Then leverage the verified terminology from the living will descriptions to help you translate the living will statement (shown next) en>es.

Living Will

A Living Will is a written directive issued by a person regarding the treatment he or she wishes to receive in the event of mortal illness, and is unable to communicate his or her desire to the attending _____.

In this document the patient designates a _____ person or guardian to make decisions in his/her regard. It is the duty of the health care institution or provider to carry out the wishes of the patient who has filed and made a Living Will, following legal advice.

The Living Will is effective only when the person is unable to communicate his or her own health care decisions in the event of _____.

1. The wish and desire not to have his/her life artificially prolonged just to receive _____.
2. The patient has the doctors decide if he or she has an incurable, terminal condition, or in a vegetative state, and to provide only the necessary care to keep comfortable.
3. The patient refuses cardiopulmonary resuscitation, electric shock, drugs, artificial breathing or food and fluids artificially administered, and to avoid _____ a hospital.
4. In case of a pregnant woman, the patient requests to be provided with life-sustaining treatment if the embryo/fetus is _____ to the point of live birth.
5. The patient requires all the medical care necessary until the doctors determine that his/her _____ is terminal, with a persistent vegetative state.
6. The patient simply states to want all medical treatment necessary to be kept alive as long as possible.

Un/a _____ es un documento de autorización por escrito del tratamiento que una persona desea recibir en caso de sufrir una enfermedad terminal o condición mortal, y se encuentre impedida de poder comunicar sus últimos deseos _____. El paciente en este documento designa a un _____ o guardián a la cual autoriza para tomar las decisiones necesarias en su lugar. La institución de salud tiene el deber de llevar a cabo la voluntad expresada por el/la paciente en el/la _____ registrado/a legalmente en su expediente.

El Testamento en Vida es efectivo únicamente si la persona se encuentra incapacitada para comunicar las decisiones a seguir si se encuentra en peligro de muerte.

1. Expresa la voluntad de no prolongar su vida artificialmente y de sólo recibir _____.
2. Es la voluntad del/de la paciente que los médicos decidan si su estado es terminal o vegetativo, y que sólo le proporcionen un cuidado paliativo para evitar sufrimiento.
3. Rehusa recibir resucitación cardiopulmonar, choque eléctrico, drogas o respiración artificial, y que eviten _____ un hospital.
4. En el caso de la paciente estar embarazada, su voluntad es de recibir tratamiento si el embrión/feto es _____ hasta el momento de su nacimiento.
5. Requiere todo el cuidado médico necesario hasta que los médicos determinen que su _____ es terminal y su estado es vegetativo persistente.

6. El/la paciente declara su voluntad de recibir todo el tratamiento médico necesario para prolongar su vida lo más posible.

Brainstorm term and phrase list

a los asistentes de salud profesionales	*health care providers*
a los facultativos que le asisten	*incapacitation*
being confined to	*palliative care*
being taken to	su tranferencia a
capaz de sobrevivir	su traslado a
comfort care	suplente
condición	*surrogate*
condition	última declaración voluntaria en vida
cuidado confort	un cuidado que provea alivio
directiva a los médicos y familia	*viable* (Eng.)
en vida	vital
estado	vivo

Living Will Statement

Choice determined by the patient: _____, on her/his own behalf, without assistance by anyone, relative, friend, or any health care professional connected with this case.

1. ___ If I have a terminal condition I do not wish that my life be artificially prolonged, I desire only comfort care.
2. ___ If my doctors decide that I am in irreversible or permanent coma, a terminal condition, or an unchangeable vegetative state, I wish to have only the medical treatment necessary to provide care that would keep me comfortable. I do not want the following:
   a. Cardiopulmonary resuscitation, use of drugs, electric shock and artificial breathing or any means to prolong my life.
   b. Artificially administered food and fluids.
   c. To be taken to a hospital if at all avoidable.
3. ___ In the event that I am pregnant, I do not want life-sustaining treatment withheld or withdrawn if it is at all possible that the embryo/fetus can develop to the point of live birth.
4. ___ Until my doctors conclude after carefully studying my case that it is terminal, or I am in a persistent vegetative state, I desire to have the use of all medical care necessary to treat my condition.
5. ___ I want all the medical treatment necessary to keep me alive as long as possible.

Signature of patient: _____

_____ _____ _____
Location City   State   Date

_____ _____
Name and Signature of Witness   Date

(*Source:* Herrera McElroy, Onyria, and Lola L. Grabb. *Spanish-English, English-Spanish Medical Dictionary = Diccionario médico español-inglés, inglés-español.* 3rd ed. Philadelphia: Lippincott Williams & Wilkins, 2005. Reprinted with permission.)

What is the most comprehensive, advanced health care directive package available in Spanish on the market today? Find one that includes a Do Not Resuscitate (DNR) form.

· ·

Activity: Medical Prefixes and Suffixes

Compile a personal term list of 30 of the most common *prefixes, suffixes*, and *roots* used in medicine. Choose items that you have heard or read but whose meaning you didn't know explicitly. Give the meaning of each root, prefix, and suffix you enter. Finally, find the corresponding Spanish and exemplify. To get you started, connect with your **Manual** Web site and use it to find medical prefixes and suffixes. Include in your table both the layman term and specialist term where they both exist. Back in class, meet in small groups and quiz your group mates.

· ·

Quiz: Medical Greek and Latin

Answer 1 through 10 without researching first.

1. A root of *autopsy* (*autopsia*) can be found in the Greek:
   a. atos (horn)
   b. auto (self)
   c. opsis (appearance)
   d. acos (remedy)

2. Thrombosis is most related to which of the following word pairs?
   a. bleeding/bruising
   b. spasm/nerve
   c. rupture/hemorrhage
   d. clot/embolism

3. If I'm suffering a myocardial infarct, I should be worried about what part of my heart?
   _____

4. *Pneuma* refers to your:
   a. aura
   b. tires
   c. lungs
   d. breath
   e. both a and b
   f. both c and d
   g. none of the above

5. This Greek root is used as a prefix indicating numbness (*entumecimiento*):
   _____

6. Endemic deafmutism occurs in individuals living where *goiter* is prevalent, and stems from severe thyroid deficiency.
   a. What is goiter, then, and what is its relationship to the thyroid?
   b. Where is your thyroid?

   c. What is the Spanish for "goiter"?

   _____

   _____

7. Words such as *pepsin, peptic, Pepsi, eupeptic,* and *dyspepsia* refer to:
   a. energy
   b. gastrointestinal function
   c. salvation of the immortal soul
   d. carboxypeptidase inhibition

8. Circle the nonexistent neologisms (there are three):

choriotomy	neuropath	emetology
hypotrophy	neuralgia	phlebotomy
osteomyolitis	stigmatosis	esophophagus
cystitis	sclerotic	nephritis
neuralgia	dyspnea	pyrexia
periosteal	rheumatic	encephalatrophy
stomata	adenoidal	melancolitis
algedonic		

9. Circle the valid or standard en<>es pairings from the following options; all should be assumed to be found in medical contexts (assume at least one context where the pairing is possible)*:

en		es
a. abatement	< >	*disminución*
b. condition	< >	*enfermedad*
c. renovascular	< >	*renovascular*
d. generic name	< >	*denominación común*
e. fluoroscopy	< >	*radioscopia*

10. Judging only from context, give the meaning of the underlined word in this passage:

> **Periodic arthralgia [is]** "a condition in which pain and swelling of one or more joints, most commonly the knee, occurs at regular intervals; there is sometimes abdominal pain, purpura, or <u>oedema</u>" (Biology-Online.org. Scientific American Partner Network).

· ·

Activity: Medline Plus® Interactive Health Tutorials

The U.S. National Library of Medicine and the National Institutes of Health have created a health resource with animated graphics and sound to educate the general public. Connect with your **Manual** Web site and use it to find these sites. As a group, listen to and watch predetermined tutorials from the choices offered. Make a brief en>es glossary. Listen to the English first, then to the corresponding Spanish. (Click on the yellow tab reading "español.") Lay your glossary out in two columns; in a third column, verify the translation shown with the URL of another reputable site, or offer valid variations based on what you find elsewhere. Proofread your glossary by replaying and reviewing the tutorials in both languages. When you have finished verifying, regroup. Then as a class, create a master glossary, coordinating your term databases. Discuss any complications such as regional

---

* Based on Segura 1999.

usage, polysemy, ambiguity, register, and others. Critique problems found on the site's Spanish or English.

Your instructor may give you another text on the topic for which you've created a glossary.

· ·

Activity: Prescription Instruction Background Research and Boilerplate

Imagine that you are doing the research for a translator working into Spanish on a prescription instruction sheet for propoxyphene. Answer questions 1 through 10 in pairs. Some of the translator's questions have to do with general terms and strategies for this text type.

1. Find the line on a prescription reading "common name."
   a. What does "common name" contrast with? What textual markers distinguish this type of drugs from its counterpart?
   b. What is the Spanish for "common name"? Find all possible renderings and verify.
2. In what class of drugs is "acetaminophen"?
3. Find MedicineNet. What kind of information can be found there?
4. What are substrates, inhibitors, and inducers? Find the Spanish for these three terms.
5. What are the most reliable drug interaction sites? What leads you to believe in their reliability?
6. Under the subheading "Before Using This Medicine," there is mention of "drowsiness-causing drugs." What is the most frequent rendering of this phrase for this text type? What is meant by "misused" in the line "Fatalities have occurred in patients when this medication was misused"? Does Spanish have an unambiguous term or phrase for this? What is "over-the-counter" medicine in Spanish? What is ritonavir primarily used for? How would this term best be rendered in Spanish? What class of drug is it? How should "breast-feeding" be rendered in Spanish in the following context: "Inform your doctor of any medical conditions, allergies, or breast-feeding"? What is the difference between *lactación* and *lactancia*? Is *dar de pecho* ever used in this kind of text type?
7. What is "patient information leaflet" usually called in Spanish?
8. Under "Cautions," how would you render "habit-forming"? What preposition in Spanish is most often used when taking something "for" pain?
9. How do parallel texts render "cold, clammy skin" ("overdose")?
10. Find examples of differences in format or organization, cultural content, or other differences es<>en for this text type of which the translator should be cognizant.

· ·

CASE STUDY: MEDICAL DOCUMENTATION IN THE MCGILL PAIN QUESTIONNAIRE

1. What are pain questionnaires (pain scales)? Connect with your **Manual** Web site and use the link to find the McGill Pain Questionnaire. Consider how the instrument organizes the descriptors, that is, each of the category boxes and the rank values (e.g., flickering, quivering, pulsing, throbbing, beating, pounding). Do you think this is effective for all patients? Explain.
2. Kinds of pain scales in use for pain management include the FLACC and the NIPS. For what audiences (patients) are these each intended?
3. Can you find another, simplified pain scale, one even more widely used than the McGill? Find it in Spanish as well. In what sense are the target audiences for these

Drug Facts

Active ingredients (in each tsp=5 mL)   Purpose
Aluminum hydroxide
(equiv. to dried gel, USP) 200 mg.............................Antacid
Magnesium hydroxide 200 mg.................................Antacid
Simethicone 20 mg...Antigas

Uses relieves   ■ heartburn   ■ sour stomach   ■ gas
■ acid indigestion   ■ upset stomach due to these symptoms

Warnings
Ask a doctor before use if you have kidney disease

Ask a doctor or pharmacist before use if you are presently
taking a prescription drug. Antacids may interact with
certain prescription drugs.

When using this product do not exceed 24 tsp (120 mL) in a
24-hour period or use the maximum dosage for more than 2 weeks

Stop use and ask a doctor if symptoms last for more than 2 weeks

If pregnant or breast-feeding, ask a health professional before use.
Keep out of reach of children.

Directions   ■ shake well before use
■ take 2-4 tsp (10-20 mL) between meals
  and at bedtime

Inactive ingredients butylparaben,
carboxymethylcellulose sodium, flavor,
hydroxypropyl methylcellulose, microcrystalline
cellulose, propylparaben, purified water, sorbitol

Store at room temperature tightly closed.
CAP SEALED WITH BREAKAWAY
BAND FOR YOUR PROTECTION

Antacid label with ingredients, warnings, and directions. Increasingly, labels for medication (including OTM or "over-the-counter" medications) need to be translated and so do patient information leaflets (sheets). Many pharmacists have translation-enabled dispensing software; some even develop their own. Inttranews reports that translated prescriptions could prevent 98,000 deaths a year.

Source: Jonathan Nourok/PhotoEdit Inc.

texts different? Who administers these texts, and how? Do people in Hispanic cultures express themselves in these terms? How would you find out if you don't know? Can you find studies (called *performance tests*) on the McGill Questionnaire conducted with Spanish-speaking patients?

Task

Make a template of the key terms that a translator would need for the above text (labeled 'Drug Facts'); include abbreviations. Use the most common terms and phrases.

Activity: Buzz Groups for Informed Consent Forms

"Buzz groups" are small student teams that meet in the pretranslation phase of a task to debate aspects, identify problems, and propose solutions (Kelly 2005, 101). For this activity, each group will be "deputized" to find and share with the class an assigned portion of the information needed to gain an understanding of this text type. Team members of each buzz group can research at home and organize their information in the first minutes of class before presenting.

Team 1. Find out what **informed consent** is legally. Who requires these forms? Who signs them, and why? Find out the *range* of informed consent forms—all the possible circumstances for which different consent forms may be used. Compare, contrast, and summarize this information.

▸ **HINT** ◂ Search keywords: template + "informed consent" or *"modelo"* + *"consentimiento informado"*

Team 2. What are the minimal features of informed consent forms, both on the word level and on the global semantic level? What are their most typical reused clauses (boilerplate), and what varies?

Team 3. Your task is to answer the following questions about the *structures* involved in the translation solutions en>es for a specific text (which your instructor will supply) and for this text type in general.

1. "You are being asked to participate in a research study." Should this be rendered into the passive voice in Spanish? Propose the most standard structure for this line. For the other passive structures in the source, propose target solutions.

2. Identify at least four procedural operations of any sort (e.g., supplements, recastings, recategorizations, etc.) that you would need in translating this text and the instances where they would be needed.

3. Identify the potentially difficult language that a classmate who is sight reading this text may need. List variants if you find valid ones. Find the legal collocations (e.g., "reasonably foreseeable risks") in a verifiable Spanish.

4. Each buzz group presents in order. Team 3 should volunteer a sight reading of this text. Teams 1 and 2 can offer variants. Your instructor will distribute the published translation of the chosen text, if available, for comment.

¿?

What Spanish solutions or strategies will you need for this text type (or similar legal texts) in the future? How flexible or inflexible are the standard structures for this text type—in other words, how free or how constrained is the translator of informed consent forms, relative to your perception of other text types with which you are familiar?

TRANSLATION TIP

Read *Caduceus: A Publication of the Medical Division of the American Translators Association*. It comes out quarterly and is full of relevant terminological and vocational information.

TRANSLATION TIP

Medical Term Searches: Register

When searching on the Internet, try "scientific name" as part of your keyword string; for example:

1. "Whooping cough" + "scientific name" ➞ pertu**ss**is (Lat.) [so by inference ➞ *pertu**s**is* (Sp.)]
2. Now that you have the Latinate version, you can quickly see if there are common names for it by searching *"pertusis"* + *"tos"* ➞
3. = *tos convulsiva / tos ferina*

Activity: Health Brochures

Read page 9 of the English and Spanish brochures produced separately by the National Center of Birth Defects and Developmental Disabilities (see later) of the Centers for Disease Control and Prevention (CDC). Answer the following questions, researching where necessary.

1. What is the connection among migrant women, folic acid, and birth defects?
2. In the target text, why are the vitamin nutrition facts left in English?
3. In the target text, why is the name of the organization translated to Spanish?
4. Are all the addresses different in translation? Comment on the implications for feedback.
5. In what collocations is *sano* more appropriate than *saludable*, or are they interchangeable?
6. Think for a moment about the phraseology *"salir embarazada."* What tone or undertone is potentially present in the expression? How would that come across were it translated back into English?
7. Visit the two Web sites listed in the addresses section. Compare and comment.

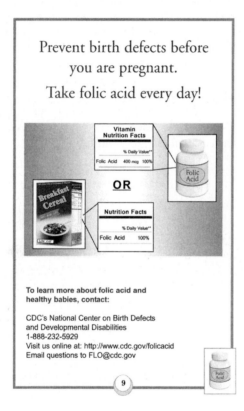
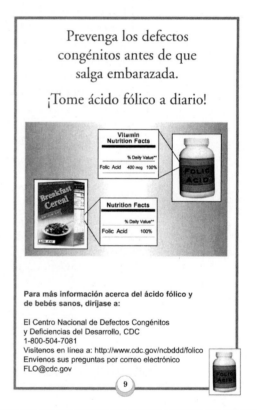

Activity: Medical Abstracts

Connect with your **Manual** Web site and use the persistent link at EBSCOhost to find the MedicLatina database, a collection of full-text articles and abstracts from nearly 120 Latin American and Spanish journals. A Spanish interface and translation software are available free to EBSCOhost subscribers. You can use the free trial for the task that follows if your school does not subscribe.

Task

Evaluate an abstract in the database on an article of interest to you. Edit the author's translation into English and then make a summary of the edits you would recommend. Do a "round-robin edit," with students given several abstracts and a fixed time for each in turn; each student edits the same passage or starts from where the previous student left off until all abstracts are satisfactorily edited.

Follow-Up

What are the distinct sections included in medical and scientific research papers? Does it seem, from your perusal of several examples, that the abstracts contain the same content in the same order? (For example: Are conclusions always stated explicitly?)

Discussion

Why does it seem that so many errors appear in translated abstracts? Finally, study how abstracts make claims. What kind of rhetorical stance do they use to assert hypotheses or findings, and how is this represented (tentatively, assuredly, etc.)? Can you see patterns of such abstract writing strategies in a given journal or field? Can you see differences across languages?

As an option, write a medical abstract from a medical study in the subfield of your choice. Translate it. Hot link the terms in the translation to sites, authenticating your term choices.

> Did you know that many abstracts are translated by the source language authors into their nonnative tongue, whereas other abstracts are translated professionally? Abstracts are a genre that is frequently read *instead of* the source text (i.e., the whole research article)—they are a way of saving time for the specialist who cannot read every development in his or her field. Here is a case, then, in which the translation often replaces the original rather than complementing it.

Activity: Medical Article and Chapter Reviews

The following are some ideas for article or chapter reviews. Each student will be assigned one reading to critique and present main ideas to the class. Other readings, including on Hispanic health issues, may be assigned.

NOTE   The last title listed here offers an overview of the protocol and ethics of community interpreting.

- "Translation, the Great Pollinator of Science: A Brief Flashback on Medical Translation." *Scientific and Technical Translation.* Fischbach, Henry, ed. New York and Amsterdam: John Benjamins, 1993.
- "c. 13 Health and Illness in Hispanic American Communities." *Cultural Diversity in Health and Illness.* Spector, Rachel. Upper Saddle River, NJ: Prentice Hall Health, 2000.

Chong, Nilda. *The Latino Patient: A Cultural Guide for Health Care Providers.* Yarmouth, ME: Intercultural Press, 2002.

"Legal Issues in the Translation of Healthcare Documents." Cornelio, Maria. *ATAChronicle*, Aug. 2002.

"Medical Terminology Management." *Handbook of Terminology Management.* Lynch, Clove. Sue Ellen Wright and G. Budin, eds. Amsterdam; Philadelphia: John Benjamins, 1997–2001.

"Online Medical Terminology Resources." Lynch, Clove. *Translation and Medicine.* H. Fischbach, ed. Amsterdam; Philadelphia: John Benjamins, 1998. 147–162.

Excerpts from Vázquez y del Árbol, E. *Propuesta de un análisis comparado de cien textos biomédicos (español e inglés) desde la perspectiva del género.* Granada: Universidad, 2002.

Excerpts from *Medical Translation Step By Step: Learning by Drafting.* Vicent Montalt and Maria Gonzalez Davis. St. Jerome, 2008.

Lessons and exercises from *Bridging the Gap* interpreting manual: for example, 1, Roles; 2, Code of Ethics; 5, Being a Clarifier; 7, Intervening; 8, Sight Translation; 9, Health Care System Overview.

WORKSHOP #7: VACCINES (ACADEMIC STUDY)

This week's workshop is entitled *"El desarrollo de nuevas vacunas: generación de información para la toma de decisiones"* from the *Revista Panamericana de Salud Pública/Pan American Journal of Public Health* (Castillo-Solórzano et al. 2004). Assume an audience of educated readers who are not, however, specialists in the region. The translation would be subject to peer review by an editorial board of doctors and medical writers. Translate the second paragraph (*En la actualidad ... la síntesis peptídica.*), and the fourth paragraph, (*Aproximadamente 20% ...*) through the first sentence of the seventh paragraph (*En el contexto... vigilancia epidemiológica de rotavirus.*). Time permitting, other parts of the text may be selected on the day of the workshop for sight reading, with selected terms provided. Read the article all the way through before translating the text. In the workshop, general possibilities will be discussed. At an assigned deadline, you will turn in a revision attached to your first draft (annotated in the workshop).

Connect with your **Manual** Web site and use it to find the link to the text; register for free and download the pdf.

TRANSLATION TIP

Connect with your **Manual** Web site and use it to find the bilingual glossary, AIDS*info* Translation Tool. A sample entry follows:

English term	Término en español
Immunocompromised	***Inmunodeficiente***
Unable to mount a normal immune response because of an impaired immune system	*Que no puede presentar una respuesta inmunitaria normal debido al deterioro del sistema inmunitario*

Such bilingual glossaries do much toward standardizing terminology involved in diagnosis and treatment. Who do you think are the primary users of this tool?

See the pdfs of the glossaries and the other resources on the page, including materials on cultural competency in health care.

Medical Wrap-Up: Documentation and Professional Practice

Fill in the blank with a word or phrase that appropriately completes each sentence.

1. An example of handwritten medical writing is _____.
2. Medical symbols are used in _____.
3. An interpreters' resource that translators may find useful is _____.
4. A medical product manufacturer needs translation for the following text types: _____.
5. *Readability testing* involves _____.
6. If you are translating regulatory documentation, the subject content likely will include such features as _____.
7. According to the organization Hablamos Juntos, a deciding factor on whether or not a given document should be translated is _____.
8. One of the most authoritative terminological resources for biomedicine I can find online is _____.
9. The Unified Medical Language System (UMLS) metathesaurus provides the following information: _____.
10. A need for translation of product licensing in the health care industry arises, for example, when someone _____.
11. Two health organizations with in-house translation departments are _____ and _____.
12. A health questionnaire that is culturally relevant to Latinos might include _____.
13. When a "back translation team" in health care translation carries out a back translation, the purpose is thought to be to _____ _____.

TRANSLATION TIP

Reference Works

Learn to recognize the key names in medical reference: Merck, Dorland, Mosby, Stedman, and others. Connect with your **Manual** Web site and use it to find a medical translation resource page.

9

Scientific and Technical Translation

WHAT DISTINGUISHES SCIENTIFIC TRANSLATION FROM TECHNICAL TRANSLATION?

In essence the distinction lies in that **science** is a collection of theoretical knowledge, and **technology** is the application of this knowledge to industrial exploitation, or the exploitation of the soil (Gamero Pérez 2001, 26). Furthermore, the scientist writes to disseminate knowledge (e.g., the research article), whereas the technician writes to fulfill certain legal requirements (e.g., patents, instruction manuals) or to market products (e.g., the informational brochure) (Pinchuck 1977). Fittingly, in scientific texts argumentation and description prevail, whereas in technical texts description and exhortation are predominant (Borja Albi, Gamero Pérez, and Ruíz Anton 1998). Gommlich (1993) distinguishes "transtextual" and "transbehavioural."

Activity: Typology

Give the English name for each of the following technical translation text types (source for the Spanish: Gamero Pérez 2001, 65–7); each student should bring in an example in Spanish of an item from the list—preferably written originally in Spanish—to pass around in class so students gain familiarity with as many types as possible:

Acta de reunión técnica

_____

Anuncio en medio especializado

_____

Anuncio técnico en medio general

_____

Artículo comercial

_____

Artículo divulgativo

_____

Carta técnica

_____

Certificado técnico

Comunicación interna de empresa

Descripción técnica

Enciclopedia técnica

Folleto informativo publicitario

Informe técnico

Instrucciones de trabajo

Listado de piezas

Manual de instrucciones especializado

Manual de instrucciones general

Manual técnico

Memoria anual

Monografía divulgativa

Norma laboral

Norma técnica

Patente

Plan de estudios

Plan de producción

Pliego de condiciones

Prospecto de medicamento

Proyecto técnico

_____

Publirreportaje

_____

Solicitud de desarrollo del producto

_____

1. Can you find genre conventions that may not be the same es<>en for any of the categories? For example, is a *publirreportaje* a common text in print media, or is it more common in another media? Find a Rosetta stone in print or online for a text type of your choice and try to find en<>es divergences, whether in format or content.
2. Find the UNESCO classifications of technical fields. What two broad fields of science do the classifications use? Invent plausible scenarios for particular technologies listed where translation would occur en<>es.
3. What are the most common science-technology subfields offered on en<>es ProZ profiles? How do they match up with the most in-demand expertise listed on Aquarius and other job sites?

TECHNICAL TRANSLATION: "EST" REGISTERS

The English language, as we saw in the section on register, can be classified into five stylistic levels: **frozen**, **formal**, **consultative**, **casual**, and **intimate**. English for science and technology (EST), a subcategory of English for special purposes (ESP), falls into the frozen and formal levels. In the recent decade, the terms *EST* and *ESP* have appeared frequently in literature relating to the teaching of English and translation studies. The main technical registers are enumerated next:

2.3.3 register (terminology)

Description: Classification indicating the relative level of language individually assigned to a lexeme or term or to a text type.

Note: In some regions and terminology management environments (for instance, family-planning medicine), the categorization of terms according to register can be critical.

Permissible Instances: Types of register qualifiers that can be relevant in terminology work include:

a. neutral register

Admitted Name: standard register

Description: The register appropriate to general texts or discourse.

b. technical register

Description: The register appropriate to scientific texts or special languages.

c. in-house register

Description: The register of terms that are company-specific and not readily recognized outside the environment.
Example: In-house usage at one automotive company for the automotive tuning characteristic gear rattle is crowds.

Note: In-house terminology is not necessarily equivalent to bench-level terminology, inasmuch as the former can thrive at very high levels of research and development. In-house terminology is frequently the source of new technical terminology that eventually gains widespread acceptance on a broader scale.

d. bench-level register

Admitted Name: shop term

Description: The register of terms used in applications-oriented as opposed to theoretical or academic levels of language.

Example: The retrieval end of a broach is commonly called a puller in bench-level usage.

e. slang register

Description: An extremely informal register of a word, term, or text that is used in spoken and everyday language and less commonly in documents.

Example: In aviation, the phrase *fly by the seat of your pants* is slang for the more formal *fly without instruments*.

f. vulgar register

Description: The register of a term or text type that can be characterized as profane or socially unacceptable.

Note: Although vulgar register is avoided in formal technical terminology, languages with broad distribution such as English or Spanish require the documentation of problematic terms that vary in register from region to region.

Note: In-house terminology is not necessarily equivalent to bench-level terminology, inasmuch as the former thrive at very high levels of research and development. In-house terminology is frequently the source of new technical terminology that eventually gains widespread acceptance on a broader scale.

(*Source:* <www.ttt.org>, 2000, Accessed December 17, 2008)

Task

Find five terms in English and five in Spanish that have three different registers each. Label them.

Model:
gypsum wallboard	= technical
sheetrock	= in-house
rock	= bench

LINGUISTIC NOTE

VERNACULAR OR TECHNICAL? TWO SIDES OF A DEBATE

Proponents of the use of ordinary language in scientific writing argue that simplified words—"honeybee" instead of "*Apis mellifera*" or "windpipe" over "trachea"—can convey meanings better, and to more people, in a language familiar to them regardless of their native tongue. Those arguing the other side claim that scientific nomenclature is more descriptive, more precise, and free of affective meanings.

(Continued)

In addition, they maintain that technical terms offer translation proofing in that they pass in and out of every language unchanged. Many scientists, for example, see Latin as stable because it is a dead language (Nybakken 1959, 9–29).

Can you think of, or find, examples that offer support for either side? Do you find a paradox in using dead languages for their stability? (Don't those reanimated parts then behave as living language does with all its inherent drawbacks?)

TRANSLATION TEASER

Language Awareness

How closely do you pay attention to wording? Let's experiment. Without researching, try translating this 404 error message text, es>en, phrasing it exactly as it would appear as if sent from a server:

¡Objeto no encontrado! El enlace en la página referente parece tener algún error o ha expirado. Por favor comunique al autor de la página el error. Si usted proporcionó el enlace de manera manual le solicitamos que por favor revise los datos e inténtelo de nuevo.

Now verify the exact standard wording in English. You see that we can look at texts many times without really reading them. But read them we must to become competent translators.

By the way, this kind of "static," standard phrasing reused verbatim, which you learned is called boilerplate language, or simply **boilerplate**, is common not only in the legal domain but in technical texts and the commercial field as well. Be on the lookout for boilerplate, from short collocations to entire paragraphs or longer.

TECHNICAL WRITING

Technical writing is most often associated with online help and user manuals; however, there are other forms of technical content created by technical writers, including:*

Alarm-clearing procedures	Procedures
Application programming interface programmers' guides	Proposals
	Reference documents
Certification and accreditation activities	Release notes
Corporate disclaimers	Reports
Hardware maintenance and repair Procedures	Requirements documentation
	Scientific reports
Installation guides	Site preparation guides
Magazine articles	Specifications
Network administrators' guides	Technical papers
Network configuration guides	Training materials
Network recovery guides	Troubleshooting guides
Policies and procedures	User guides
Presentations	White papers

---

* This list was from http://www.fortechnicalcommunicators.com/; however, the domain name was deleted on April 2007.

Areas of Technical Writing

Byrne (2006, 48), following the National Writers' Union's delineations, claims three broad areas for technical writing:

> *Technology education*: for nonspecialists
>
> *Traditional technical writing*: for a specialist audience
>
> *Technology marketing* ("marcom"): for an audience equally specialized

Tasks

1. Find out about the parallels and overlap between technical writing and translation: In what sense is there mutual awareness between technical writers and translators, and what form does the interaction take? What role do technical writers have in the ultimate success of a translation? Is there such thing as multilingual technical writing? Discuss. You'll want to read *The Global English Style Guide: Writing Clear, Translatable Documentation for a Global Market* by John R. Kohl (2008).

2. Read Inger Lassen, "Appendix: Survey of Writing Style in Technical Manuals," in *Accessibility and Acceptability in Technical Manuals: A Survey of Style and Grammatical Metaphor* (2003, 175–77).

Activity: Group Translation of an Electric Shaver Product Instructions

For this task you will produce a "group sight translation" for an internationally distributed handheld electric shaver. By turns, you will sight translate and orally edit one another as you go. The text will be distributed by your instructor. As each person finishes his or her passage (approximately three minutes), others can offer solutions until the best ones are decided upon as a group. All should participate and take notes during the edits and maintain terminological consistency with the group when their respective turns arise. If you have a laptop or desktop computer available, a volunteer can enter the text.

Discussion

1. To what extent does having experience with similar products help one translate a text of this sort? Can you conclude anything about experience as part of the translator's toolbox? Can research totally compensate for a lack of experience on a given job? Discuss.

2. How would you describe the language of manuals? Give concrete examples of textual characteristics of a manual. Is the language of manuals *legal* language? What prompts you to think so?

3. Find examples of manual boilerplate in English and Spanish (e.g., from landscaping tools, computers, home appliances, industrial machinery, exercise equipment, do-it-yourself kits, toys, and gadgets). Start a collection.

4. Read Julio Cortázar's short parody of the language of manuals, "Instrucciones para subir escaleras", available online. Why is "manualspeak" appropriate to one environment and comedically inappropriate to others?

5. Find examples of the phrase "Act of God" in warranties. What situations does this describe? What parallel concept (term or terms) does Spanish use?

LINGUISTIC NOTE

ICONICITY

A good principle to be aware of when translating manuals, or any technical instructions, is that of **iconicity**. Iconicity posits that language should reflect the order in which the real-life process is carried out. When temporal sequences are reversed in this text type, the mind has a harder time processing information intended to be performative or directive. Note the following "dos" and "don'ts":

NO	"Before setting the potentiometer, unplug device from power source."
NO	"Unplug device after placing on a flat surface."
YES	"Place device on flat surface. Unplug."
YES	"Unplug device from power source. Set potentiometer."

CASE STUDY: EMPLOYEE TRAINING MATERIALS FOR PESTICIDES

Employee training materials can take the form of videos, factsheets, workbooks, posters, comic books, flipcharts, handbooks, manuals, carrying cards, flyers, audio tapes, slides, or other kinds of media and formats. Not only are they often legally mandated (see the Worker Protection Standard), employee training materials are vital to reducing workplace accidents and illness and to creating community and an efficient work culture.

What employee training materials have you personally used or come across? How technical was the material? What sort of tone was used? Are training manuals materials to be read and reread, skimmed, or consulted? What industries do you think are particularly needful of translations for personnel? Speculate briefly on the advantages or appropriateness of one presentation format for training materials versus another—which types of information would be best presented in which format?

In pairs, brainstorm the expected features of an employee training manual. What translation issues do you think translators face with this text type? Do you think a translated document of this text type would have legal weight in a dispute? Discuss.

Find a *recruitment video* for a technical firm. Discuss its features.

NOTE Safety information, training manuals, and company handbooks may be classifed as *human resources translation*, which intersects with legal and economic translation.

Some examples of employee training materials on the handling of pesticides and other safety issues (Frisk 2000):

Video: *Chasing the Sun/Siguiendo el Sol* (National Center for Farmworker Health), English/Spanish (Farmworkers)

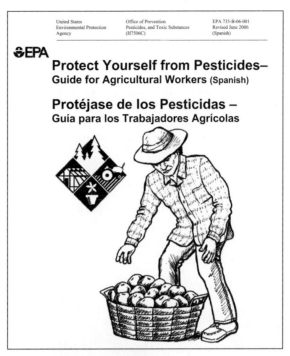

Occupational safety brochure
Source: Reprinted by permission of the National Center for Farmworker Health, Inc.

Cassette: *Radio Pesticida: A Program for Pesticide Safety Education with Hispanic Agricultural Workers*, English/Spanish

Manual: *Recognition and Management of Pesticide Poisonings/Reconocimiento y manejo de los envenamientos por pesticidas*, English/Spanish (Health care providers/Migrant centers)

Pamphlet: *Dora Evelia* (Farmworkers)

Notice that the next one is targeted primarily at *growers*, not their employees; however, a Spanish translation might be needed for such texts:

Pamphlet: *The Worker Protection Standard: Farms and Agricultural Businesses* (Agricultural employers)

Task

1. Find a copy of the Environmental Protection Agency's (EPA) *Worker Protection Standard for Agricultural Pesticides—How to Comply: What Employers Need to Know*. Rewrite/translate into Spanish for two different audiences: the children of agricultural workers and the workers themselves. You may divide the class into groups so that each executes their texts in different formats: pamphlet, safety sheet, video, and so on. Another group can translate intralingually (en>en) for an English as a Second Language (ESL) for farm workers classroom workbook activity. Watch the register.

2. Connect with your **Manual** Web site and use it to find the link to the Migrant Clinician Network and read the education materials there. Do you think these materials were conceived in Spanish? What clues do you have that they were or were not? If they

were produced only in Spanish, can you think of reasons why having at least a gloss in English might be needed and for whom? What risks of terminological inconsistency exist in this area?

3. Find training manuals in Spanish. How many different industries are represented? Find out who funds the translations. For starters, two community education tools from the Migrant Clinician Network mentioned earlier include the comic book, "Aunque cerca . . . sano" by the National Children's Center for Rural and Agricultural Health and Safety with funding by the National Institute for Occupational Safety and Health, and the "Aunque cerca . . . sano" *Training Manual* (English).

TRANSLATING HOW-TO BOOKLETS

The home improvement industry is expanding abroad at a dizzying pace, and in North America it is now commonplace to find signage and brochures in Spanish for the burgeoning Latino consumer market.

Lowe's® Home Improvement Warehouse typifies this trend. At left is "Step 5: Let's paint" from a brochure for a line of paint the company carries in its stores. Imagine that the corporate office needs this material made available in Spanish in certain regions of the country as part of a copromotion, including in-store events such as a clinic. Suppose that the region involved includes Arizona, southern California, Colorado, and New Mexico. When you are given the job and you ask about in-house terminology, you are told only to check its Web site and to stay consistent with whatever is used there.

1. Use painter's tape to mask off any areas not being painted.
   - Cover furniture and floors with drop cloths.
   - Stir paint thoroughly throughout the painting process.
   - If using multiple cans of the same color, mix together for the best uniform color, also called "boxing your paint."

2. Prime the area to promote hide and adhesion.
   - See page 3 for primer information.

3. Paint the ceiling first.
   - Brush a 3" border. (Called "cutting-in")
   - Begin in a corner and roll across the ceiling in 3-foot sections.
   - Finish with long, even roller strokes across the entire ceiling.

4. Paint the walls next.
   - Paint only one wall at a time.
   - Brush a 3" border around the ceiling, floor, trim, and corners.
   - Always maintain a wet edge.

5. Working in a 3'x 3' area, roll a large "W" onto the surface.
   - Fill in the "W".
   - Work horizontally across the room, moving from side to side.
   - Continue pattern across the wall.

6. Paint the trim.
   - Use a 1"– 2" brush for sashes, moldings and woodwork.
   - Leave windows open one hour to prevent sticking to newly painted sills.

For more help, visit www.valspar.com

Source: Reprinted by permission of The Valspar Corporation

Task

In pairs, read the pamphlet excerpt from the Valspar interior paint project guide, "Step 5: Let's paint". Your task is severalfold:

1. Make a list of terms, and sort them by registers (see "EST" registers).
2. Produce a bilingual glossary.
3. When finished, each pair meets with another pair to compare glossaries. What other features of the text would propose a challenge? Discuss them.
4. Then regroup as a class to discuss and to compare the published Spanish version (Instructor's Resource Manual).
5. Finally, compare resources used.

¿?

Can you mine language for a company's translation using a competitor's Web site?

Follow-Up

Find a technical text online that uses multiple registers; copy it and color code the registers. What do you think accounts for a hybrid of registers in a text?

TEXT FOR PREP: SEMITECHNICAL

Virus borra los archivos de Kazaa

Kazaa se ha considerado como el reemplazo de Napster en muchos sentidos y en particular por la posibilidad de descargar todo tipo de archivos. Esta posibilidad también incluye virus.

Aunque en realidad los virus para sistemas de intercambio de archivos de par a par o P2P ya existían desde hace algún tiempo, ninguno ha resultado tan peligroso como un nuevo archivo que se ha disfrazado de "Skin" o piel del programa para ingresar en el sistema del usuario y borrarle todos los archivos bajados desde Kazaa.

Como muchos otros programas, las pieles permiten personalizar y darle una apariencia diferente a la apariencia de la interfaz. Pero en este caso, el usuario al descargar la piel denominada Eightball, lo que obtiene es permitirle al virus ingresar para iniciar su proceso de borrado.

El virus viene con la presentación de un archivo comprimido llamado eightball2.zip, el cual al descomprimirse le presenta al usuario una ventana preguntándole si desea ver algo de magia, luego de cerrar esta ventana aparecen otras cinco con un conteo regresivo las cuales, después de ser cerradas, le dan inicio al proceso de borrado, el cual incluye las raíces del sistema operativo y otros archivos de Windows que terminan por hacer que el sistema se bloquee definitivamente.

Cabe aclarar que para fortuna de muchos usuarios que no se han actualizado, este virus sólo se activa sobre el sistema operativo Windows XP, para lo cual utiliza una característica propia de este sistema. En otros sistemas operativos previos el usuario podrá cerrar las ventanas y descubrir al final que aparece un mensaje de error que anuncia la falta de un archivo .DLL para ejecutar la operación.

La única manera de evitar el contagio, es evitar abrir la opción de descargar el archivo, el cual aprovecha estar en la plataforma de intercambio de par a par para presentarse como una opción poco peligrosa.

De todas formas, conociendo los antecedentes de los sistemas de intercambio de archivos, se recomienda revisar con detenimiento todos los archivos descargados bajo este tipo de mecanismo, así como mantener actualizado su programa de seguridad y antivirus.

(*Source:* Rodríguez, John. "Virus borra archivos de Kazaa." Reprinted by permission of IDG Latin America)

Follow-Up

In a story on a similar topic, "Los pájaros le tiran a las escopetas," the same author writes that "*[c]uando parecía que la estrategia de bloquear los sitios de intercambio de archivos de música era una buena idea de las casas discográficas, Kazaa, una de las 'afectadas' responde con una demanda por violación de patentes*" (Rodríguez n.d.). How could the title be rendered in English, given the context?

CASE STUDY: TECH ADS FOR MICROSOFT AND APPLE

1. a. Research Microsoft's history with translation and localization, especially the latter. What provisions in terms of personnel has it made for translation? Are there departments of translation or localization? Is the work outsourced? Are the internationalization/globalization goals defined specifically anywhere, or somehow apparent in its business model or products?
    b. What is Microsoft® Content Management Server (MCMS) 2002, and what is it used for?
    c. Compare in detail Microsoft's home page with several versions of its page in other Spanish-speaking countries (connect with your **Manual** Web site and use it to find the link). What content and design differences appear?
    d. Try to find Microsoft product advertisements for consumption abroad that differ considerably in some way, whether in graphics, ad copy, medium, context in which the ad appears or some other factor.
2. Your instructor will give you English-language print ads for translation; your target audiences are Spanish American general interest news magazines. Focus on terminology. Use a Spanish-speaking informant in computer science, parallel texts, or an online newsgroup to clarify terms. Don't forget retail sites as another source.

Glossary Task: How to Fire a Cannon

1. Read the text that follows and determine its likely audience.
2. Discuss as a class—in what context would you expect to find such a text and how would you classify it? Do you suppose it always had the same audience (i.e., that it was written with one specific audience in mind)?
3. In pairs, make an es>en glossary of the terminology in the following text.
4. Define the English-language terms, documenting and validating your sources.

Cómo disparar un cañón

(Castillo de San Felipe del Morro, Bahía de San Juan, Puerto Rico)

Mueva el cañón a una yarda de la pared.
Limpie el ánima con la lanada mojada.
Inserte el cartucho en el ánima y atáquelo hacia la recámara con el atacador.
Inserte la aguja dentro del oído y rompa el saquete de pólvora.
Mueva el cañón a la tronera.
Apunte el cañón utilizando las palancas y las cuñas de puntería.
Utilice el gato para buscar rasgaduras en el ánima.
Utilice el cucharón para extraer el cartucho no disparado.
Remueva la aguja y reemplácela con un cebo.
Déle fuego al cebo con la mecha del botafuego.
Rézele a Santa Barbara.

Source: National Park Service, San Juan National Historic Site 2000

5. Now compare any illustrations (diagrams, blueprints, sketches) you found. Do any contain a majority of the terms you need? Discuss how visual information helps in the term extraction process.

6. Combine two groups of two and create an es>en glossary of five terms in which your two groups coincide. Create a glossary of terms that differ between the two groups. Compare sources. Can some consensus be reached, or can further research resolve any terminological discrepancies?

7. Compare your versions as a class. Is consensus possible? Attempt a team version on the board.

Activity: Tech Term Scavenger Hunt

Following is a list of stitch types and sewing machine parts you are responsible for translating en>es for a packing list. The client is in the business of import-export (industrial goods) and wants to export the goods to Mexico and to label items, or what the items are used for, accordingly.

The twist here is that you will not be translating these terms but getting a *definition* of each English term first from an expert. For our purposes, an expert will be someone who sells, repairs, makes, or practices the operation or item in question. You must understand each term and be able to explain it in your own words (what it is, what it looks like, what it does, and/or where it is). Document your calls, emails, or meetings. Remember not to be a drain on anyone's time; be scrupulously polite and explain your purpose; don't run up telephone bills in the process. Your task is to make the best use of your time and find the best informants for this job—the Internet is off limits for this task.

encroaching satin stitch	bobbin winder spindle
fly stitch	feed dog
stem stitch	hand wheel
lazy daisy	thumb screw
even weave fabric	needle plate

Follow-Up

Put these other resources in descending order (1–8) based on how useful you think they would be were you given the full source text (text only, with no illustrations) described earlier and then discuss the following:

_____ A bilingual glossary
_____ A parallel text (Spanish-language parts list)
_____ Monolingual (English and Spanish) specialized dictionaries (textiles)
_____ A bilingual technical dictionary
_____ Labeled "Rosetta stone" diagrams (the same diagram found in both English and Spanish)
_____ A Spanish-labeled diagram (without the English one)
_____ The Real Academia de la Lengua online dictionary
_____ A sewing chatroom

Terminology Activity: *Taladros*

1. Connect with your **Manual** Web site and use it to find the link to the Dewalt sites. In teams of two, make a 40-word bilingual glossary on the following drill and accessories: D25900K (*martillo electroneumático*) and DW502 (*taladro percusión*). Do a 20-word glossary from the specifications. Select terms that you deem useful for future in-house or general use in this domain. You may find splitting the screen to be a useful work technique.

2. a. Now use your glossary to gloss the FAQs on *taladros*. Connect with your **Manual** Web site and use it to find the site. Go back now and add any terms that did not appear in your original glossary.

   b. Test a few glossary entries with the Google "Images" feature; do the same in Spanish from the Chilean Google page (connect with your **Manual** Web site and use it to find the site). While on your **Manual** Web site find the Babelplex page, which searches for English terms from the Spanish keyword.

   c. Compare features, product line and layouts, or other user interfaces of the two Web sites. Do the same products exist in both countries? What about other Spanish-speaking countries?

3. Pick two competing companies (note that Black & Decker owns Dewalt) and test your glossary on similar products. What conclusions can you begin to draw about product-specific vs. industry-specific terminology for this particular domain?

Follow-Up

Use any of Dewalt's existing Spanish-language Web pages to find the following terms from its category Product Catalog>Drills>**Spade Handle**. You may also find the online technical dictionary useful. Connect with your **Manual** Web site and use it to find the following terms:

Amps	
Capacity in Steel (Hole Saw)	Gear Reduction
Capacity in Steel (Twist Bit)	Max Watts Out
Capacity in Wood (Hole Saw)	No Load Speed

Capacity in Wood (Self-Feed)	Shipping Weight
Capacity in Wood (Spade Bit)	Specifications
Chuck Size	Tool Weight

HARNESSING PARALLEL TEXTS: THE BEAUFORT WIND SCALE

Over two centuries old, the Beaufort scale is still used to help estimate wind speeds and has been translated into many languages. The language used is a curious mixture of meteorological precision and lyricism.

Beaufort Scale: Specifications and Equivalent Speeds for Use at Sea

Force	Equivalent Speed 10 m above ground miles/hour	knots	Description	Specifications for Use at Sea
0	0–1	0–1	Calm	Sea like a mirror
1	1–3	1–3	Light air	Ripples with the appearance of scales are formed, but without foam crests.
2	4–7	4–6	Light Breeze	Small wavelets, still short, but more pronounced. Crests have a glassy appearance and do not break.
3	8–12	7–10	Gentle Breeze	Large wavelets. Crests begin to break. Foam of glassy appearance. Perhaps scattered white horses.
4	13–18	11–16	Moderate Breeze	Small waves, becoming larger; fairly frequent white horses.
5	19–24	17–21	Fresh Breeze	Moderate waves, taking a more pronounced long form; many white horses are formed. Chance of some spray.
6	25–31	22–27	Strong Breeze	Large waves begin to form; the white foam crests are more extensive everywhere. Probably some spray.
7	32–38	28–33	Near Gale	Sea heaps up and white foam from breaking waves begins to be blown in streaks along the direction of the wind.
8	39–46	34–40	Gale	Moderately high waves of greater length; edges of crests begin to break into spindrift. The foam is blown in well-marked streaks along the direction of the wind.

(Continued)

Force Equivalent Speed 10 m above ground miles/hour knots			Description	Specifications for Use at Sea
9	47–54	41–47	Severe Gale	High waves. Dense streaks of foam along the direction of the wind. Crests of waves begin to topple, tumble and roll over. Spray may affect visibility.
10	55–63	48–55	Storm	Very high waves with long over-hanging crests. The resulting foam, in great patches, is blown in dense white streaks along the direction of the wind. On the whole the surface of the sea takes on a white appearance. The 'tumbling' of the sea become heavy and shock-like. Visibility affected.
11	64–72	56–63	Violent Storm	Exceptionally high waves (small and medium-size ships might be for a time lost to view behind the waves). The sea is completely cov-ered with long white patches of foam lying along the direction of the wind. Everywhere the edges of the wave crests are blown into froth. Visibility affected.
12	73–83	64–71	Hurricane	The air is filled with foam and spray. Sea completely white with driving spray; visibility very seri-ously affected.

Source: Observers Handbook, Met Office 1999. Adapted from British Crown Copyright data supplied by the Met Office.

Tasks

1. Study the Spanish-language parallel texts of the scale online. Learn the language com-monly used for the descriptions and specifications (see two columns to the right, in the scale). Assume that you are going to do a long project with this vocabulary or will do mul-tiple assignments using it. Learn the terms well enough to put the Spanish descriptions in order when you return to class from researching. They will be handed out to you as *fichas* for you to place in the proper squares. You must become familiar with variant sets, because your instructor may give you any one, without announcing which.

2. The second task you will complete is based on the specifications. Your instructor will give them to you in Spanish translation with *blank spaces* in several passages. Fill in the gaps. No notes may be used—you can learn the language of this circumscribed field well enough to do this task unaided.

TRANSLATION TEASER

What devices or processes related to translation or interpreting currently are patented or have patents pending?

Editing Task: Technical Data Sheets

Connect with your **Manual** Web site and use it to find the link to Absorbentes Españoles, S.L. Go to >*Producto* and download the pdf ("ver la Ficha Técnica de Petresorb").

Read over the text. What can you instinctively determine about this text type's function? Is this a "material safety data sheet" or a "technical data sheet," or both? (Connect with your **Manual** Web site and use it to find the Meridian Engineering & Technology site. The site may prove to be of interest.) What is a *ficha técnica* in all its possible meanings? Which do you think applies here? Give the gist of the information on this data sheet in a single English sentence.

Print the Spanish source text. Now suppose the client simply ran it through an open source statistical machine translation (SMT) program. For the English version, use Google Translate, then identify the most serious errors in translation by circling them. Verify using parallel texts. Propose fixes for the errors in a two-column chart.

What kinds of errors do machines make that a human, even a nonnative speaker, probably would not? To what extent do the errors impede communication? Would it be easier to edit the English entirely or to do your own translation from scratch? Discuss.

TRANSLATION TIP

Make a short list of newsgroups and discussion groups dedicated to es<>en technical translation. Connect with your **Manual** Web site and use it to find the link to scientific/technical glossary posts such as GlossPost.

Follow-up: Your instructor may wish to assign part of a technical glossary or dictionary for translation or assign a text to be translated with the aid of parallel glossaries available online.

Terminology Activity: The Flavor Wheel

Find the "coffee taster's flavor wheel" online. Who uses a text of this sort? Suppose you were a project manager (PM) and had to create two glossaries for this text, one of en>es terms and one of es>en terms. (Think: Why might an es>en glossary be useful for the Spanish-speaking end user?)

Brief: As part of a promotional package for her clients (coffee roasters and "cuppers"), a woman's multinational coffee company, Aroma Her Own, has contacted you to translate this text. It is to be rendered into Spanish for a new market—the Southern Cone—where she seeks to begin international market penetration. She has tasked you, the freelancer, with producing a prototype of the wheel with her company name on the back. It will be used in the promotional campaign, at trade fairs, in an online e-newsletter for "industry people," and at tasting events.

1. Identify terms that depend absolutely on the whole textual context—the other terms—for their meaning, particularly those elements of the series with multiple meanings (e.g., "hard").
2. What terms would potentially be most problematic en>es? What would you do with "mellow," "acidy," "winey," and "soury"?
3. In what type of format would you ask this to be sent to you for you to produce a three-dimensional wheel prototype for the client? What other tools (software) would you use for image manipulation?

Activity: On-Board Diagnostics: E-Check Brochure

Prepare a bilingual glossary for the following text.

My vehicle didn't pass. Now what should I do?

✓ If the emissions malfunction indicator won't light, the bulb and/or circuitry must be repaired. Take your vehicle to a service technician.

✓ If the emissions malfunction light is on when the engine is on, the OBD II system has found a problem that needs to be fixed. Take your vehicle to a service technician.

✓ If the required readiness monitors are not set, talk to your service technician.

✓ Review the "Repairing a Failed Vehicle" brochure and the "Repair Facility List" you received from the inspector.

My vehicle didn't fail, but my readiness monitors are not set. How can I set them?

There are many reasons the monitors could be reset or *not ready*. Usually this is caused during routine maintenance. For example, if the battery is disconnected for any reason, the monitors of most vehicles are reset. Also, a service technician may have to reset them as part of a repair process.

As mentioned earlier, the vehicle must be driven for a certain period of time and under certain conditions to set the monitors. Some owner's manuals explain driving procedures while others do not. The vehicle manufacturer or a qualified service technician is the best source for this information.

For directions to the E✓Check station nearest you, call the Ohio E✓Check hotline at
1-800-CAR-TEST
or, visit the E✓Check website at
www.epa.state.oh.us/dapc/mobile.html

Ohio E✓Check
Vehicle Emissions Testing Program

What is OBD II?

On-board diagnostics (OBD II) is a complex computer package installed on 1996 and newer cars and light trucks, and 1997 and newer diesel vehicles. This sophisticated system serves as an advanced warning to alert vehicle owners and auto technicians of potentially high emissions. OBD II is now being used by auto emissions testing facilities.

How is the driver notified about an emissions problem?

There is a special light on the dash that is reserved for emissions control and monitor systems. The light is turned on when OBD finds a fault or error that could cause emissions to exceed standards.

What does the light look like?

Automobiles and light trucks use a variety of warning lights to notify drivers of different conditions. However, in the case of emissions malfunctions, the driver will see either the phrase "service engine soon" or "check engine," or a standard engine-shaped light as in the following examples:

What does it mean if the light is on?

The vehicle's OBD II computer turns the "check engine" light on when it finds a fault that may cause high engine or evaporative emissions. In some cases, it means that immediate service is needed to prevent expensive damage and high emissions.

If the light is flashing, immediate service is recommended. Expensive damage may result if the problem is left unattended.

How is the OBD II inspection performed?

There are two basic steps to the OBD II inspection:

1. With the engine off, an inspector turns the key on to verify that the emissions malfunction light works. The inspector then turns the engine on. If the malfunction light stays on, the vehicle will not pass the E✓Check test.

2. If the malfunction light does not come on with the engine on, the inspector plugs an OBD II hand-held reader device into the vehicle's on-board computer port to check the OBD II system status.

The OBD II hand-held reader device plugs directly into a vehicle's on-board computer to quickly check the status of the emissions system.

What does the OBD II hand-held reader device check?

Three pieces of information are downloaded from the vehicle:

1. Is the emissions malfunction command on or off?

2. What is the readiness monitor status?

3. Which, if any, fault codes are stored?

What are readiness monitors?

The vehicle's readiness monitors indicate if individual emissions components have been fully evaluated by the vehicle's OBD II system. The most common reasons for unset readiness codes are a recent vehicle battery disconnect, a low or dead battery. Also, a service technician may have to reset them as part of a repair process.

The presence of unset readiness codes does not mean that a vehicle has failed the OBD test. Unset readiness codes indicate that the vehicle cannot be fully OBD tested because the information needed to make a pass/fail determination is not available in the vehicle's computer.

To set the monitors to *ready*, the vehicle must be driven through a drive cycle; the length of time and driving conditions necessary to reset the readiness monitors vary from one vehicle model to another. Check your owner's manual or contact the vehicle manufacturer or qualified service technician for more information. It is possible that up to three weeks of driving may be necessary to reset the readiness monitors.

What are fault codes?

Fault codes are stored in the vehicle's computer. They indicate which system or component might be causing the problem. Even though this is helpful to the repair technician, additional diagnosis by the repair technician will generally be needed to isolate the problem and identify the proper repair.

How does my vehicle pass the OBD II emissions inspection?

Four things must be satisfied to pass the inspection:

1. The emissions malfunction light must illuminate with the key on and engine off. This simply tells the inspector that the bulb is not broken or burnt out.

2. The emissions malfunction light must be commanded off by the OBD II system. In other words, when the engine is turned on, the light must go off.

3. The required readiness monitors must be complete. This will show if the vehicle is ready to test.

4. No fault codes are set.

Source: Reprinted by permission of Ohio EPA/Ohio E-Check

TRANSLATION TEASER

Which End Is Up?

 A cardboard box arrived at the house with the following inscriptions. Fix the flawed Spanish, and explain what conditions or procedures led to it going wrong.

Handle with care.	*Dirija con cuidado.*
Do not stack more than 3 high.	*No apile mas de 3 altos.*
Handle from this side./	*Manija de este lado. /*
Handle from the other side.	*Manija del otro lado.*
Table bottom	*Fondo de la tabla*
Table top	*Tapa de la tabla*
This side up./This side down.	*Este costado arriba. / Este costado abajo.*

WORKSHOP #8A (EN>ES): MONTEREY BAY AQUARIUM

Rocky Shore Exhibits, Monterey Canyon, and the Deep Sea

This week you will be working either >en or >es. The texts that follow were featured on the Monterey Bay Aquarium's (MBA) Web site early in the 2000s. In teams, you will be translating the texts for Web site and print materials (patron education) for the MBA's Spanish links.

Realize that the aquarium is interactive and family-friendly; carefully consider the register that is used. It will be helpful for you to have a visual of the flora and fauna referenced. Document the locations where you find your terms. Underlined ST terms are hyperlinks.

ST:

On the rocky edge of the bay, tides and waves rule life along the crowded shores. In zones from high and dry to low and wet, creatures live where they best can cope. Periwinkles and <u>limpets</u> cling to life in the highest zone, a world of sun and air: more land than sea.

<u>Mussels</u>, <u>barnacles</u>, <u>shore crabs</u> and rockweeds thrive in the rich middle zone between land and sea, where tides rise to cover the rocks more often than not.

<u>Sponges</u> and <u>tunicates</u> stick to the low zone, full of life and only rarely exposed by ebbing tides.

The secret lives of those who live on the bay's edge open to all in the Rocky Shore gallery.

Here, <u>monkeyface-eels</u> wriggle between rocks where gaudy <u>nudibranchs</u> lay spirals of eggs.

<u>Surfperches</u>, at home in the perpetual motion of surge channels, turn to face currents you create with a hand-turned crank.

When you visit, you can take the controls of our <u>tide pool video camera</u> (or see the view through our online live feed and go eye-to-eye with <u>hermit crabs</u> and fishes as you explore our tide pool exhibits.

On our outer decks, mechanical waves bring the aquarium's tide pools to life. Every forty seconds, a reservoir upstairs sends water crashing down a pipe to the tide pools below.

Enthralled by the world captured in these exhibits, aquarium explorers lean close, finding something new in each pool.

Nearby, <u>sea stars</u> and <u>crabs</u> prowl the floor of the Great tide Pool, and exhibit enclosed by rocks so natural-looking few realize they're artificial.

Here, where visitors watch as baby otters learn to hunt and shorebirds comb the rocks for <u>limpets</u> and <u>snails</u>, bay and aquarium truly meet.

Come explore with us . . .

<u>Rocky Shore in the wild</u>

Life in the Deep Interactive - Take a Virtual Dive into Monterey Canyon

Take a trip into the deep sea off Monterey Bay and explore its three distinctive habitats—sheer, vertical canyon walls, the endless midwater and the sediment-buried seafloor.

As you explore this dark mysterious world, you'll encounter unusual creatures such as primitive hagfish, predatory tunicates, spotted ratfish, giant siphonophores and light-producing cockeyed squid. The video was taken with cameras on MBARI's remotely-operated vehicles (ROVs).

(*Source:* © 2003, Monterey Bay Aquarium Foundation)

Follow-Up

What educational materials has the Monterey Bay Aquarium translated into Spanish? Has it translated a hard-copy field guide for its exhibits? The captions on the exhibits themselves? What parts of its Web site are *not* in Spanish? Who apart from patrons might use the Spanish-language information on its Web site? Are its aquarium maps translated? How could this terminology most easily be leveraged for use in the future (assuming you had an implied agreement with the aquarium), and for what kinds of other texts foreseeably?

Connect with your **Manual** Web site and use it to find the link to the Monterey Bay Aquarium site.

WORKSHOP #8B (ES>EN): ACADEMIC RESEARCH (*LAS CÉLULAS MADRE EMBRIONARIAS*)

The other workshop text for this chapter is on genetic engineering. Find the full text online and determine its purpose (summative? informative? innovative?), its audience, and what concessions, if any, for a new audience would have to be made. Determine if most of the research in this field is done in English, and what implications this has for translation (look particularly at bibliographies). Your text for translation appears next, beginning under 3.1.1 and is contained within these symbols: ꙮ. Other text, including the initial outline, appear for context.

Índice:

1.   Células madre: conceptos básicos
2.   Células madre humanas
2.1   Células madre embrionarias y germinales
2.2   Células madre de adulto
2.2.1   Biología básica de las células madre de adulto
2.2.2   Papel en la renovación celular del organismo
2.2.3   La plasticidad de las células madre de adultos (transdiferenciación)
3.   Terapias con células madre
3.1   Terapias celulares y trasplantes
3.1.1   Perspectivas con las células madre embrionarias (ES)
3.1.2   Perspectivas con células madre de adultos
3.1.3   ¿Reprogramación directa de células somáticas?
3.1.4   Algunos ejemplos de terapias experimentales con células madre
3.2   Células madre para terapia génica somática
4.   ¿Hacia la reconstrucción de órganos y tejidos?
...

3.1   Terapias celulares y trasplantes

La esperanza terapéutica principal que se tiene en las células madre es que se puedan emplear para terapias celulares y trasplantes de tejidos, sin los problemas actuales ligados a los aloinjertos: escasez de donantes histocompatibles, necesidad de administrar drogas inmunosupresoras (ciclosporina, corticoides) con sus efectos secundarios (riesgo de infecciones, de cáncer, nefropatías, etc.). Lo ideal sería derivar tejido con la identidad histológica del propio paciente para hacer autotrasplantes.

Se está abriendo el campo de la Ingeniería Celular, que en definición de Bernat Soria es "un nuevo campo interdisciplinar que aplica los principios de la ingeniería y de las ciencias de la vida a la obtención de sustitutos biológicos para restaurar, mantener o mejorar la función tisular".

⸙ 3.1.1   Perspectivas con las células madre embrionarias (ES)

El uso que más ha llamado la atención sería el empleo de células diferenciadas a partir de células madre embrionarias para terapias celulares o incluso reparación de tejidos dañados.

Una posibilidad sería tipificar muchas líneas diferentes de ES, con diferentes sistemas MHC (HLA), pero la diversidad de los haplotipos HLA es enorme. Una alternativa sería manipular por ingeniería genética las ES para crear líneas con diferentes haplotipos del HLA, de manera que se obtuvieran bancos de células apropiados para diferentes receptores de trasplantes. De todas formas, aunque se lograran células con HLA similar al paciente, quedarían otros sistemas minoritarios de histocompatibilidad, cuya falta de concordancia con el paciente podría llevar a problemas no siempre controlables.

En cambio, el potencial terapéutico de las ES se pondría de manifiesto sobre todo empleando ES derivadas del propio paciente, ya que no habría problemas de rechazo de injertos: estaríamos ante un autotrasplante. Pero ¿cómo es posible esto en un individuo ya nacido, si por definición estas células proceden de embriones? Aquí es donde entraría el método de transferencia de núcleo de célula somática (la llamada clonación terapéutica): el paciente suministra células somáticas, se transfiere núcleo a ovocito desnucleado, se crea un "embrión artificial" (embrión somático), hasta la fase de blastocisto; se toman las células de su masa interna, se cultivan como células madre, y finalmente se diferenciarían al tipo de célula o tejido para la terapia celular o el injerto, sin los problemas del rechazo (autotrasplante). Según algunos, es muy probable que en las próximas décadas seamos capaces de derivar células madre autólogas para todos los que las necesiten. ⸙

El 21 de noviembre de 2001, la empresa ACT (Robert Lanza, Michael West en J. Regenerat. Med.) comunicó que había logrado la primera clonación de un embrión humano mediante este sistema. Muy debatido científicamente: 57 óvulos maduros de 7 mujeres. Con la mitad, partenogénesis. Sólo lograron mantener 6 durante 7 días, pero sin células madre (NO es embrión). Otros 17 óvulos fueron desnucleados, y se les transfirió núcleos de adulto. Sólo 6 se dividieron hasta 4 o 6 células, y no progresaron. ¿Embriones de verdad?

Los científicos del Instituto Roslin han propuesto a las autoridades británicas un proyecto consistente en obtener "bancos de células madre clonadas" por transferencia de núcleos de células pluripotentes de cordón umbilical de los recién nacidos. Cada cultivo quedaría conservado en previsión de la necesidad ulterior de diferenciarlo hacia tipos celulares requeridos para autotrasplantes del individuo donante.

⸙ Pero los retos técnicos de este enfoque son formidables, incluso dejando aparte los derivados de la transferencia de núcleos a ovocitos.

Las células ES de ratón (y quizá las humanas) son tumorigénicas: si se inyectan a un animal adulto originan teratomas y teratocarcinomas. Por lo tanto, un tema de seguridad será asegurarse de que en un cultivo diferenciado a partir de ES no quedan estas células troncales, o bien disponer de métodos fiables de separación y purificación de las células diferenciadas de interés respecto de las ES.

Para ello habrá que avanzar en estudios de marcadores (al estilo de los CD de las células inmunes) para caracterizar todas las fases intermedias de cada ruta de diferenciación.

En general, la obtención de poblaciones celulares puras exige el empleo de técnicas eficaces de selección clonal: p. ej., el uso del FACS (citómetro de flujo activado por fluorescencia, que discrimina poblaciones en función de marcadores de superficie). Alternativamente, marcadores genéticos fácilmente seleccionables en el cultivo.

Alternativamente, se puede introducir por ingeniería genética en el genoma donante un bloque de genes que permita simultáneamente la selección de las células diferenciadas y un sistema suicida que garantice la autodestrucción de las células que no se hayan diferenciado.

¿Podremos forzar a las células madre embrionarias a diferenciarse en líneas celulares concretas? Aún tenemos una idea muy pobre de la biología básica de las señales y factores implicados en el desarrollo y diferenciación del embrión humano, pero se espera que este campo avance con rapidez.

Otras cuestiones de seguridad para asegurar la salud a largo plazo de las células a trasplantar.

Hay que asegurar la no introducción de mutaciones lesivas, que se pueden haber acumulado en el núcleo somático donante durante la vida del individuo. Será esencial garantizar que tales mutaciones no aumentan el potencial cancerígeno.

Igualmente está la muy debatida cuestión de la "edad biológica" de las células. Mientras algunos informes hablan de mayor edad, otros dicen que el propio proceso de transferencia de núcleo somático "rejuvenece" las células y estimula a la telomerasa.

Habrá que aclarar la eventual implicación de las alteraciones de la impronta genética sobre las células ES y sus derivadas, logradas tras transferencia nuclear. ╡

(*Source:* Reprinted by permission of Fundación Don Roberto Fernández Viña)

10

Literary Translation

A FEW ISSUES IN LITERARY TRANSLATION ES>EN

Before we look at specific challenges in literary translation, here are a few general issues to consider:

1. Relative "trade imbalance": Spanish translates from English much more than vice versa. Two related phenomena help explain why: "usurpation of authority" and "resistance to translation," in André Lefevere's terms.
2. Homogenization and repetition of the same authors, canons, genres; stagnation also due to rights holders (and publishers) refusing retranslation.
3. Editorial streamlining ("rationalization") of an author's unique voice in order to fit in comfortably into the polysystem.
4. Lack of uniformity or sound criteria in determining what "good" translation is or in training qualified translators.
5. Power differential. A postcolonial concern is: Is it appropriate to translate a Third World writer for First World consumption? Doug Robinson (2003) writes of *translatio studii et imperii* ("translation of learning and empire")—the westerly movement of civilization and power, here understood as *assimilative* translation. Some take issue, furthermore, with the terms "World Literature" and "World Music" (e.g., Macondo vs. "McOndo").
6. Aesthetic differential. Spanish-American poetry is much more vocative, politicized; the United States tends toward the confessional, the antirhetorical. Spanish-speaking countries have a long tradition of the *baroque*; the United States favors spareness of speech.
7. Ethical differential. One example is how to translate sexist speech (partial answer: Some feminists have used prefacing, footnoting, and supplementing); another example is translating Roman Catholicism for a Protestant country.
8. Prosodic differential. For example, in poetry, metric feet (English) vs. syllabification (Spanish). There is an abundance of end-rhymes in Romance languages *(-ión, -dad, -or)*; English is rhyme-poor.
9. U.S. readership is not trained to read translations *as* translations or to buy them or to value them. Reviewers invariably want *transparency* for the text and *invisibility* for the translator.
10. One major result: pragmatic differential. U.S. translators have the tendency to *domesticate* (more on domestication later in this chapter).

Source: Christophe Vorlet

Ask a toad what beauty is, absolute beauty, the *to kalon*. He'll tell you that it's his female with two big round eyes popping out of her little head. . . .

Ask the devil: he'll tell you that beauty is a pair of horns, four claws, and a tail. . . .

I went to a play one day with a philosopher. "That is really beautiful!" he said. . . . We took a trip to England and saw the same play, perfectly translated; it made the audience yawn. "Oh! Oh," he said, "the *to kalon* is not the same for the English as for the French." He concluded, after much deliberation, that beauty is very relative, in that what is decent in Japan is indecent in Rome, and what is fashionable in Paris isn't fashionable in Peking; and he spared himself the trouble of composing a long treatise on "beauty."

(Voltaire 1764)

There is no Majesty and there is no Might save in Allah the Glorious, the Great!

Passage from Sir Richard Burton's translation of *The Arabian Nights*
(*"The Fisherman and the Jinni"*)

There is no strength nor power but in God, the High, the Great!

Edward Lane's translation of the same passage

Yahweh and Allah Battle

Title of Allen Ginsberg poem

TRANSLATION TIP

Style Is More Than Information

Richard Pevear: "You could tell people what is portrayed in Rembrandt's 'Return of the Prodigal Son' and move them deeply. But the telling would have little to do with the experience of looking at the unique disposition of color, light, space, scale, line, texture, brushwork in Rembrandt's painting", which depicts the same subject but much more expressively. It is the same, the author suggests, with words. (Jones 2007)

DOMESTICATION AND FOREIGNIZATION

To **domesticate** is to translate by "bringing the text to the reader"; to **foreignize** is the opposite, or leading the reader to the text. Domestication makes the strange *familiar*; foreignization keeps the "strangeness" strange.

Following are two versions of a passage from the Russian novel, *One Day in the Life of Ivan Denisovich* by Alexander Solzhenitsyn. Read them comparatively and answer the questions that follow. (Activity based on the discussion in Hofstadter (1997), *Le Ton Beau de Marot: In Praise of the Music of Language*.)

TT1: And he pulled the thin, dirty blanket over his face and didn't hear the guys from the other half of the barracks who were crowding around the bunks waiting to be checked.

Shukhov went to sleep, and he was very happy. He'd had a lot of luck today. They hadn't put him in the cooler. The gang hadn't been chased out to work in the Socialist Community Development. He'd finagled an extra bowl of mush at noon. The boss had gotten them good rates for their work. He'd felt good making that wall. They hadn't found that piece of steel in the frisk. Caesar had paid him off in the evening. He'd bought some tobacco. And he'd gotten over that sickness.

Nothing had spoiled the day and it had been almost happy.

There were three thousand six hundred and fifty-three days like this in his sentence, from reveille to lights out.

The three extra ones were because of the leap years . . .

(Tr. Hayward and Hingley)

TT2: And he buried his head in the thin, unwashed blanket, deaf now to the crowd of zeks from the other half as they jostled between the bunk frames, waiting to be counted.

Shukhov went to sleep fully content. He'd had many strokes of luck that day: they hadn't put him in the cells; they hadn't sent his squad to the settlement; he'd swiped a bowl of kasha at dinner; the squad leader had fixed the rates well; he'd built a wall and enjoyed doing it; he'd smuggled that bit of hacksaw blade through; he'd earned a favor from Tsezar that evening; he'd bought that tobacco. And he hadn't fallen ill. He'd got over it.

A day without a dark cloud. Almost a happy day.

There were three thousand six hundred and fifty-three days like that in his stretch. From the first clang of the rail to the last clang of the rail.

Three thousand six-hundred and fifty-three days.

The three extra days were for leap years.

(Tr. Ralph Parker)

Discussion

1. What differences in *general* translation strategy do you notice? How are these strategies evidenced specifically in each text?
2. a. What passage is the most "Russian"? Discuss what effect the Russianness has on comprehension and on the literary effect created.

b. Which passage is Americanized? What effect does this have on tone? What differences in *pacing* exist, and how do differences in punctuation contribute? Which passage makes more demands of the reader?

3. Which passage do you think is most successful? On what basis? Do you think multiple translations should be read to see which is "best," or for other reasons?

LINGUISTIC NOTE

FORMATTING FOR TRANSLATIONS: A QUESTION OF VISIBILITY

For translations, the source language name of a work is left out of the Modern Language Association (MLA) format and citation guidelines. This, in some small measure, creates the domesticating effect that the target text displaces the original, and it can be disorienting: When source and target titles do not appear frequently together, as they should in bibliographies and in booklist advertising, it is harder for the public to associate them as the intimately related works that they are.

If you are a reader of translations, at some point you will read a translation without realizing you may have read the work in translation before under a vastly different title. Or maybe you read a work in high school—say, *Im Westen Nichts Neues*—but you knew it only as *All Quiet on the Western Front*, its problems of translation passed over.

Did you know that translators have fought to have their names on the covers of translations, and now this right is even part of many contracts? And yet translations still appear all the time with all traces of their translational origins erased. Connect with your **Manual** Web site to have a look at the prescribed title page and copyright page for translations, according to MLA Style.

"TRIANGULATING" TRANSLATIONS: THE SPIRIT FROM THE LETTER

If you don't know the language of a source text, you can gain insight into its inner workings (and into translation) by "triangulating": comparing translations into languages that you do know. Read the first teaching of the *Tao Teh Ching* by Laotzu in an English translation and a Spanish translation (e.g., Witter Bynner's *The Way of Life According to Lao Tzu*, and *El libro del Tao* by Iñaki Preciado Idoeta).

Task

In pairs, try to determine the "essence" of the original Chinese. Next, based on these versions, think about if you could make a version (in any language but Chinese) that "captures" the Chinese better, even without knowing the text. Would seeing other versions help or complicate the task? Can you tell if one or the other text is divergent from the Chinese, and if so, in what ways? How can you tell (intuitively, logically, linguistically, culturally)? Do all translators work directly from the Chinese to translate this work?

THE MOST TRANSLATED WRITERS IN THE WORLD

Following is a list from the Index Translationum of the most translated writers in the world.

Author and Number of Translations

Author	Translations	Author	Translations
Disney (Walt) Productions	9,181	Stevenson, Robert Louis	1,803
Christie, Agatha	6,543	Dickens, Charles	1,787
Verne, Jules	4,185	Stine, Robert L.	1,762
Lenin, Vladimir Il'ic	3,516	Roberts, Nora	1,751
Shakespeare, William	3,603	Holt, Victoria	1,572
Blyton, Enid	3,495	Marx, Karl	1,496
Cartland, Barbara	3,403	Steiner, Rudolf	1,481
Steel, Danielle	2,858	Wilde, Oscar	1,480
Andersen, Hans Christian	2,811	Sheldon, Sidney	1,385
King, Stephen	2,696	Hemingway, Ernest	1,377
Grimm, Jakob	2,448	Hesse, Hermann	1,367
Grimm, Wilhelm	2,438	Maclean, Alistair	1,352
Bible, NT	2,274	Balzac, Honoré de	1,313
Twain, Mark	2,081	Engels, Friedrich	1,261
Simenon, Georges	2,046	Ludlum, Robert	1,250
Asimov, Isaac	2,012	Chase, James Hadley	1,241
Doyle, Arthur Conan	1,980	Clark, Mary Higgins	1,234
Joannes Paulus II, Pope	1,961	Tolkien, John Ronald Reuel	1,229
London, Jack	1,928	Poe, Edgar Allan	1,227
Dostoyevsky, Fedor	1,926	Chekhov, Anton Pavlovic	1,222
Dumas, Alexandre	1,923	Dahl, Roald	1,218
Goscinny, Rene	1,923	Kafka, Franz	1,212
Lindgren, Astrid	1,817	Plato	1,211
Bible	1,815	Rendell, Ruth	1,205
Tolstoy, Lev Nikolaevic	1,808	Bible, OT	1,201

(*Source:* United Nations Educational, Scientific and Cultural Organization, "Top 50 authors", © UNESCO <http://databases.unesco.org/xtrans/stat/xTransStat.a?VL1=A&top=50&lg=0>Accessed June 14, 2009)

Task

Study the names appearing on the preceding list of most translated authors. How many of them are familiar to you? What do you think accounts for their status as the most translated authors? Are any of them relatively unknown in North America? What role, as far as you can determine, has translation played in their reputation? Give an example in detail.

Finally, offer some economic, cultural, and ideological reasons why this list might have been quite different even a half century ago. What writer(s) do you think were ranked highest then? Why?

Translation tidbit: The most translated author from a Spanish-speaking country has been Gabriel García Márquez, who ranked at number 55 in the 1994 survey.

> Guy: Yo, I never knew Dean Koontz wrote books in Spanish.
> He's mad smart! And Bill Clinton too!
> —Anonymous, <www.overheardinnewyork.com>, Barnes & Noble, *Libros en español* section, Union Square, New York

TRANSLATION TEASER

The most prolific writer in the Spanish language was Corín Tellado (1927–2009), who has published more than 4,000 books and sold over 400 million copies. She worked in the genre of the *novela rosa* (romance). Because such writers as Barbara Cartland and Danielle Steel thrive in Spanish, one would suppose that someone so well-known and popular as Corín Tellado would break through into English and other languages. Can you find evidence that translations of her work exist in English? (Caution: She has a series of works that *masquerade* as translations—their titles were registered in English—but the books were written in Spanish.)

To what extent do you think this genre's conventions translate?

Task: Listening in on Literature

In groups of three, join and "eavesdrop" on a translators' discussion list or forum dealing with literary and cultural texts. Cull 8 to 10 of the threads you find most interesting and present them in summary to the class. Take sides in any debates that arise, inviting your classmates' responses as well; include discussion about solutions to *specific* textual problems >en or >es. Write up some issues of translation practice (vocational, procedural, ethical, etc.) in the form of "hypotheticals" and pass out for discussion. See if your classmates reason as the professionals do. Give at least some kind of handout so your class members (and your instructor) can see the texts under discussion.

Translator Profile: Suzanne Jill Levine

A translator who has taken on great challenges in literary translation is Suzanne Jill Levine. Levine has always been drawn to writers with great verbal flair, punsters, parodists, and multilingual artists of the word who have demanded a translator who pushes the boundaries between new creation and re-creation. As much as any translator of her generation (coinciding with the Boom and post-Boom writers and continuing to today), she has explored the ludic dimension of translation, the element of *play*. In her works, many of them chronicled in the essential reading *The Subversive Scribe* (1991), Levine has looked to relationships with her authors—co-conspirators—as collaborations, opportunities to take the text further, to unleash the playful, and critical, possibilities inherent in translation. *Subversive Scribe* recounts her instructive, and unique, correspondence with major authors such as Manuel Puig, Severo Sarduy, Guillermo Cabrera Infante, and others. Part memoir and part metalinguistic meditation on the mysteries and felicities of the art, *Scribe* does much to recover the creative in translation—against all notions of translation as a subservient, secondary activity.

TRANSLATION TEASER

Not What It Can But What It Must

The project was undertaken by a panel of experts to translate alphabet soup into Chinese. Among them were linguists, culinary artists, calligraphers, nutritionists, and editors.

"The most important thing is semantics," said one linguist. "We can't have people eating incoherent food."

A fight broke out among the linguists. "And how do you propose we work that morphosyntactically? And what characters will be given preference over others?"

The chefs spoke up. "The translation must be *flavorful*, first and foremost. We don't want this to smack of translation."

"*Form* is all," retorted the calligrapher. "People want beauty in their translations. Sell them the illusion. Make them happy."

"No, no," objected the nutritionist. "Without quality ingredients, no one will believe it's as good as the original stuff. Forget the appearance. If the label says it's good for them they'll buy it."

The philosopher had the floor. "No," he said. "It must be good unto itself, without needless comparisons."

"It must reflect the kingdom of Heaven," said the clergyman.

"It must fit in a can," said the typesetter.

"It must reach the heart by way of the stomach," said the Romantic.

"It must be machine-made to insure objectivity," said the computer scientist.

"It must use simplified characters, not fattening full ones," said the dietician.

"It must sound good when you slurp it," said the poet.

"It must account for dialects and regionalects," said the dialectitian-regionalectition.

"It must be done yesterday, and come in under budget (or maybe I'll just have my secretary do it)," said the client.

"It must seem like even I could have done it," said the consumer.

"It must include bibliography," said the critic.

"*Stop*!" cried a hysterical little man, jumping up on the table.

It was the original inventor.

"It must be *faithful* to my invention, and *only* that!"

And the translation was never completed.

(K. Washbourne)

TRANSLATION TEASER

What **translation hoaxes** have been perpetrated? What constitutes a translation hoax? What is pseudotranslation? How does the literary establishment look upon this practice?

What if you found out that a favorite translation of a deceased author was not a translation at all but an original work passed off as a translation? What if you found an exciting new foreign author in English translation who turned out not to exist at all but was the figment of a translator's imagination?

Task: "Voices from the Field"

In pairs, brainstorm a set of interview questions to ask a working translator. Each student will interview an established translator by email and write a profile on him or her using the comments gathered. Use the set of core questions, but allow your subjects to express themselves naturally, even divergently, and use follow-up questions or clarifications if needed. As a class you should have representation from a variety of subspecializations in the language industry, such as terminologists, localizers, technical translators, legal translators, project managers, translator-interpreters, translation teachers, and editors. Set aside a few days for everyone to present their interactions to the whole class in a formal presentation. Be sure to remember protocol and to respect the professionals' time commitments. If you can, include practitioners working in other countries in order for the class to compare working conditions and experiences. Each group should interview a different professional.

As a follow-up, arrange as a class to have one or two local practitioners come to class as invited speakers, logistics permitting. A class member could even make the arrangements on behalf of the class.

Task: Translators' Introductions

Translators' introductions give crucial information about strategies, author background, and even the individual translators' philosophies of translation. Go into the stacks in your campus library and peruse the Latin American and Spanish literature sections, housed just past the PQ 6000 range.

1. Where are translations shelved relative to the authors' source-language works? (i.e., after each respective source text, after all the authors' works, after the criticism of the authors' works?)
2. Cull a stack of translations with fairly substantial translators' introductions.
3. Peruse them.
4. Now make a list of typical inclusions you find. Do the translators discuss microstrategies? Do they disparage previous translations (however tactfully) or give justification for a new one? Are there any other aids in understanding the work that translators include?
5. Choose a text with an extensive translation *apparatus*, as it is called (the whole paratextual framework of notes, introduction, afterward, etc., that a translator uses). Does a large translation apparatus limit the works' appeal? Discuss.

Activity: Class Debate

Make a case for or against the use of *footnotes* in translations of fiction and poetry. Does anyone in the class feel they are always a burden? Does anyone feel that footnotes should be used as liberally as possible? Who takes the middle road? Who can make an argument that there are circumstances for which they are appropriate and others for which they are not? If you are *for* translator's notes (footnotes or endnotes), prescribe what they should or should not include.

Follow-Up

1. What would determine what you include in a translator's introduction? Would you insist on writing one if the option were not offered? Why or why not?
2. Do you have a *philosophy of translation* at this point in your understanding of the art? Or more realistically, a partial philosophy or set of principles or norms? Would your philosophy apply to other text types as well?

3. What is the most important function of the translator's introduction from what you have seen? Do you think literary criticism happens in a translation proper or only in a work's metadiscourse (writing that helps the reader make sense of the material at hand, for example, the introduction)?

4. What *tone* should the translator's introduction strike? Should the translator sound humble, apologetic, defeated, subservient? Conquering? Reverential? Tentative? Can you make a general strategy of what the introduction should be, or will different texts necessitate varying approaches? If so, how so?

5. How would you react to a translator's introduction that declared, in so many words, that many liberties were taken, and that the work had to be reimagined entirely to make it at all appealing to modern sympathies, including an updating of the vernacular into current slang and even the addition of pop culture references?

6. Debate the truth or falsity (of all parts and the whole) of this statement: "A translator's text should be measured only against what his or her stated goals are in the translator's introduction; any measure outside of that is an unfair and irrelevant absolute."

7. What variances in a translator's brief for literary works do you think can exist? Do you think a translator's brief for literature is relevant? That is, does literature "function" or have a purpose the way nonliterary texts do?

TRANSLATION TIP

Proofread Out Loud

Proofread your literary translations out loud. You can enhance your translation's effects on the "mind's ear" of a potential silent reader if you attune your lines with actual sound, not simply the word on the flat page.

Chaucer's line, "the lyfe so short, the craft so long to lerne" (translating Horace's famous precept, "Ars longa, vita brevis," in turn a translation from the Greek), may be periphrastic and have shifted the emphasis of the Latin, but no one can deny its rhythm. Try it aloud.

One of the best-known poems in the Spanish language is José Asunción Silva's "Nocturno (III)" (95–100), which works both visually (it re-creates the languorous movements of the lovers and the narrator's obsessive thoughts) and acoustically (its syncopations recall those of Edgar Allan Poe's most haunting poems). Notice next how the English is heightened by maintaining strict rhythms of four-"beat" measures (or their multiples), by using internal rhyme, and by creating trapped echoes—long "o" and "u" assonances. The lines are the poem's opening, when the reminiscing narrator recounts the shadow-lovers' embraces before his beloved's death. Notice how the Spanish has the distinct advantage of *sombra* being a feminine noun.

Connect with the **Manual** Web site to find a link to the Spanish source text.

TT:

One night
one night full of perfumes, whispers, music of wings

   One night
in which fantastic fireflies burned in the humid nuptial gloom,
slowly, pressing closely at my side, and wholly,

   hushed and pallid
as if foretasting bitternesses measureless,
to your most secret depths it shook you, every fiber of your frame,
down the lane through the budding plain

(Continued)

> you walked,
>
> and the full moon
> through endless heavens, blue-imbued and deep, was strewing its white light.
>
> ---
>
> Translation by K. Washbourne

PHONEMIC TRANSLATION

Phonemic translation strives for the reproduction of the source text's *sound*. Some phonemic translations can achieve synergy of sound and content, evoking the required mood. Read *aloud* the opening paragraph of Miguel Ángel Asturias' classic novel, *El señor presidente* (1946), then do the same with the translation by Frances Partridge (1963).

I

En El Portal Del Señor

ALUMBRA, lumbre de alumbre, Luzbel de piedralumbre! Como zumbido de oídos persistía el rumor de las campanas a la oración, maldoblestar de la luz en la sombra, de la sombra en la luz. ¡Alumbra, lumbre de alumbre, Luzbel de piedralumbre, sobre la podredumbre! ¡Alumbra, lumbre de alumbre, sobre la podredumbre, Luzbel de piedralumbre! Alumbra, alumbra, lumbre de alumbre ..., alumbre ..., alumbre ..., alumbra, lumbre de alumbre ..., alumbra, alumbre ...

(*Source:* Asturias, Miguel Ángel. *El señor presidente.* Buenos Aires: Editorial Losada, 1946.)

Chapter I

In the Cathedral Porch

"Boom, bloom, alum-bright, Lucifer of alunite!" The sound of the church bells summoning people to prayer lingered on, like a humming in the ears, an uneasy transition from brightness to gloom, from gloom to brightness. "Boom, bloom, alum-bright, Lucifer of alunite, over the somber tomb! Bloom, alum-bright, over the tomb, Lucifer of alunite! Boom, boom, alum-bright ... bloom ... alum-bright ... bloom, alum-bright ... bloom, boom."

(*Source:* Asturias, Miguel Ángel. *El señor presidente.* Trans. Frances Partridge. New York: Atheneum, 1963.)

Discussion

1. In what sense do the sound and the theme work together in these passages? How would you describe the tone?
2. Critique the translator's choices. Can she sustain the effect? Compare especially the second sentences of the source and target. Try a version of that sentence in which the long "o" sounds are preserved. Even if you produce a somewhat "freer" version, see how the sounds help the overall mood of the English passage.

3. Would the title *El señor presidente* work if left in Spanish for the English translation's title? What does it connote, if anything? Read a synopsis of the work, check what the English-language translator actually used, and see if you can devise a better title if you think one is necessary.

- -

TRANSLATION TIP

Conventions for Titles of Translated Books

The standard is to *bracket* "[ ]" and *not* italicize the English translation title if it is a translation of only the title and does not reference an actual *published* translation. In other words, italicize only real books. Some publications use parentheses instead of brackets; others use quotation marks instead of brackets. Some examples follow (other publishing information is left out here for the sake of simplicity):

Published translation:

Canto cósmico [*Cosmic Canticle*, tr. John Lyons] by Ernesto Cardenal

Unpublished translation:

20 poemas para leer en el tranvía [Twenty Poems to Be Read on the Streetcar] by Oliverio Girondo

Nonexistent translations should never be made to appear as if they exist. Note too that with unpublished translations, translators have the leeway to account for different possibilities in a title by offering more than one, separated by "or": *Amistad funesta* [Doomed Friendship, or, Terrible Ties of Friendship] by José Martí.

Titles are often modulated, amplified, explicitated, or otherwise "metonymized" (anecdotal evidence suggests that it is less common that translation will contract or implicitate titles): for example, *El mundo alucinante* (Reinaldo Arenas) >> *Hallucinations: or, The Ill-fated Peregrinations of Fray Servando* (tr. Andrew Hurley).

Names of translators should always appear when an actual title is mentioned in either the text or the bibliography.

TRANSLATION TIP

Connect with your **Manual** Web site and use it to find a sampling of literary e-journals and print magazines.

SEMANTIC FIELDS

Semantic fields are abstractions that help organize the words used within a concept, an area of human experience, or a practice. For example, the semantic field of *cooking* may include all the words with the same semantic marker (shared component): "sauce," "roast," "recipe," "to boil," "al dente," "fillet," "bouillon," "stock," "yield," "sherry." Semantic field theory claims that the meanings of words must be understood, in part, in relation to other words that articulate a given domain (subject) and that stand in relation of affinity and contrast to the word(s) in question (Kittay and Lehrer 1992, 3). Or more simply, semantic field theory postulates that *words gain their meaning from their position alongside other words in a system.* This is closely related to the idea of *context.* Moreover, *the challenge posed by polysemy can be met by focusing on semantic fields.*

Between languages, semantic field differences can occur as *lexical gaps* or *partial overlap.* For example, not every language has the same number of color terms or the same ones, nor do they divide them at the same places. The relevance of semantic fields for the translator is this: One must understand where in the semantic field a word lies in order to see how it is producing meaning. Of course, words may belong to multiple fields at once, particularly in highly charged language such as poetry. Yet attention to the unifying field(s) of a source text aids a translation's *cohesiveness*, how it "hangs together." An error in reading semantic fields seldom occurs in isolation; further, it may introduce an error of tone, an improper referent, or an infelicitous connotation. In fact, ignoring the organizing cohesion of semantic fields can lead to whole strings of meaning errors.

Prereading activities with semantic fields—"semantic fieldwork"—has advantages over merely translating imagery in that it focuses on the *how* rather than the *what*. In the exercises that follow we are going to focus on specific models and variations that will heighten your awareness of semantic fields and the semantic aspects of coherence (leaving aside, for the moment, phonological patterning and other issues), and help you develop tools to make you a stronger reader of source texts. Semantic fields are best learned with literary or highly expressive texts, though the fields are by no means always easy to see. As a rule of thumb, *assume the unity of a work and translate into unity*.

Activity

1. a. **Discordant fields** ("howlers"):
   "Howlers" are outrageously funny or surpassingly bad translation blunders that make the reader howl with glee or scorn, although the name may suggest language itself in pain, or perhaps calling attention noisily to itself. Many translators collect and post them, pretending they only happen to other translators.

   One of the most infamous in Spanish to English translation was W. S. Merwin's rendering of the line "La noche está estrellada . . ." from Neruda's "Poema XX" as "The night is shattered. . . ."

   b. **Overinterpretive translations** ("Overexplicitation" of the field)
   "Her skeleton was small and **spare**; perhaps that was why what would have been merely plumpness in another was obesity in her. She looked bloated, like a **body** long submerged in **motionless** water, and of that pallid hue" (Faulkner 1930, 169, "A Rose for Emily").
   1944 translation: "*Su osamento era menudo y* **frágil**. *Quizá por eso, lo que en otra mujer no hubiera sido sino robustez, en ella era obesidad. Parecía inflada, como si fuera un* **cadáver** *que hubiera permanecido demasiado tiempo en un agua* **estancada**, *y hasta tenía la tez* **lívida**" (305).*
   Discuss intensifications of the grotesque in the TTs. Retranslate the passage.

2. a. **Semantic fields and intertexts**. In the following poem by Rubén Darío (1991, 159), identify the semantic field of the boldface word "*potro*," and defend your choice with other elements from the field presented in the poem.
   b. What intertext do you see in "*he robado el fuego*"? What connection is there between this intertext and the semantic field you identified?

   ### En las constelaciones
   En las constelaciones Pitágoras leía,
   yo en las constelaciones pitagóricas leo;
   pero se han confundido dentro del alma mía
   el alma de Pitágoras con el alma de Orfeo.
   Sé que soy, desde el tiempo del Paraíso, reo;
   sé que he robado el fuego y robé la armonía;

---

* Boldface added to passages; example from *In Search of the Latin American Faulkner*.

que es abismo mi alma y huracán mi deseo;
que sorbo el infinito y quiero todavía . . .
    Pero ¿qué voy a hacer, si estoy atado al **potro**
en que, ganado el premio, siempre quiero ser otro,
y en que, dos en mí mismo, triunfa uno de los dos?
    En la arena me enseña la tortuga de oro
hacia dónde conduce de las musas el coro
y en dónde triunfa, augusta, la voluntad de Dios.

3. Fill in the blanks in the next exercises, noting (a) the semantic field(s) of each word or words in bold in the context of the passage, (b) a conceivable translation, and (c) what clues to the semantic field appear in the passage.
    *"Cuando por fin se retiraban, quedaba atrás una **estela** de esperanza que perduraba muchos días en el aire, como el recuerdo magnífico de un cometa"* (Allende 1990, 17).
    a. semantic field = _____
    b. *estela* ≈> _____
    c. indication of field from the passage: _____
    _____

4. "[Just as individuals had to] rise from the bondage of myths and half-truths to the **unfettered** realm of creative analysis and objective appraisal, we must we see the need for nonviolent gadflies to create the kind of tension in society that will help men rise from the dark depths of prejudice and racism. . . ." (King, Jr. 1995).
    a. semantic field = _____
    b. *unfettered* ≈> _____
    c. indication of field from the passage: _____

5. "[José Martí] murió físicamente para volver a nacer convertido en ideas. . ., no sólo impedir a tiempo que Cuba fuese parte de una fuerza que cayera sobre los pueblos de América, sino para que ella fuese trinchera de ideas e **inexpugnable fortaleza** frente al enemigo de los pueblos latinoamericanos. . . ." (Castro 2001).
    a. semantic field = _____
    b. *inexpugnable fortaleza* ≈> _____
    c. indication of field from the passage: _____

6. "The universal language of cinema now gave way to **the Tower of Babel**. . . ." (King 1998, 463).
    a. semantic field (intertext) = _____
    b. *the Tower of Babel* ≈> _____
    c. indication of field from the passage:
    _____

7. Search online for the poem by Jorge Luis Borges (1960), "Arte poética," from *El hacedor.* Consider the following verse contained therein, particularly the word in bold, and supply the information below:

    *Que pasa y queda y es **cristal** de un mismo*

    a. semantic field(s) =
    _____

    b. *cristal* ≈>
    _____

    c. indication of field(s) from the passage:
    _____

    d. Explain the allusion to *Heráclito* in context:
    _____

8. Map these polyvalent titles across the language pair; use a graphic organizer to show multiple senses:

    Light in August
    The Cask of Amontillado
    Finnegan's Wake

9. Find and read the poem "Yo en el fondo del mar" by Alfonsina Storni (1997) and answer the questions that follow.

    Consider the *tone* of the poem. If you were translating this poem, would you be more inclined to use "sirens" or "mermaids" for "*las sirenas*"? Research each word thoroughly for denotation and connotation, taking notes for a discussion of semantic fields and the (in)appropriateness of each. Defend your answer in small groups first, then as a class.

....

> ### TRANSLATION TIP
>
> **Ambiguity Is a Value in Literature**
> Preserve ambiguity in literary translation. Don't "solve for X" or impose a limiting interpretation on a text—let the target readers do the meaning-producing work that the source text intends them to do. A translator's overcommitting reduces the expressive possibilities of a text.

DIACHRONIC TRANSLATION: JORGE MANRIQUE'S *COPLAS A LA MUERTE DE SU PADRE*

If it is true that "the past is a foreign country," then diachronic translation—translation across time—poses a double challenge to the translator.

What decisions does a translator have to make about how to render a work from centuries past?

Have you ever seen a modernization on stage or read a modern version of an Old English (e.g., Heaney's *Beowulf*) or of medieval work? How did you respond? Could you, realistically, reproduce the speech of an earlier era? If yes, what if you were asked, for the sake of devil's advocacy, if you had rendered accurate Victorian speech (for example), or "merely" the *impression* of Victorian speech from our modern point of view? Could such a reproduction still be defensible in your view? Could a "timeless" language be found (or created) for a translation?

What do you make of a translation that in turn has dated? Perhaps the one you are about to read next will seem unnatural to you, or perhaps you will find it ingenious. Spanish poet Jorge Manrique's *coplas* (fifteenth century) were "Englished" in the nineteenth century by Henry Wadsworth Longfellow, at one time the most popular U.S. poet. Discuss his translation. Would it be acceptable if done today? If not, what does that say about the status of a translation from the past? Can it only be valued *as* a translation from the past? Does it influence our judgment that Longfellow was a great in his own right apart from his translations?

Connect with your **Manual** Web site to compare the first three stanzas of both Manrique and Longfellow's versions.

> ### Discussion

1. Describe Longfellow's approach and how successful you deem his translation. Is it rather a "version"? If he takes liberties, are they in the spirit of the source text, or are they impositions?

2. What appreciable difference exists between *el morir* (III l. 3) and *la muerte*? Why might a translator decide to preserve that nuance in the context of this poem?

3. What do you think has led to the waning of the popularity of rhyming poetry ("formal verse")? (Many journals today will reject almost outright any submissions of rhyming translations.) Would your first instinct be to try a version of a rhymed poem by using rhymes in English?

4. To what extent do you think retranslation is collaborative, in the sense that any new translation cannot help but be a response to—even an edit of—the old?

5. Retranslate using a contemporary poetic idiom for a twenty-first century audience. Produce a translation, however, not a version.

▶ **HINT** ▷ Be spare where Longfellow embroiders.

··

TRANSLATION TEASER

Find a poem from a language of which you don't speak a single word. "Translate" quickly based on what impressions the words make on you. (This is a good remedy for writer's block.)

Diachronic Translation Activity En>Es: "Songs Of Ourselves"

> I am the poet of the Body and I am the poet of the Soul,
> The pleasures of heaven are with me and the pains of hell are with me,
> The first I graft and increase upon myself, the latter I translate into new tongue.
>
> —Whitman 1860

This activity centers on the first 13 lines of an often-translated major work, *Leaves of Grass*. First, connect with your **Manual** Web site and use it to find the link and read online about poet Walt Whitman and the poem "Song of Myself" if you have little or no experience with it. Next, read the first 618 lines of the poem (red numbers are the editor's footnotes). Pay close attention to diction, rhythm, and thematics. Then come back to the opening 13 lines:

1. I celebrate myself, and sing myself,
2. And what I assume you shall assume,
3. For every atom belonging to me as good belongs to you.
4. I loafe and invite my soul,
5. I lean and loafe at my ease observing a spear of summer grass.
6. My tongue, every atom of my blood, form'd from this soil, this air,
7. Born here of parents born here from parents the same, and their parents the same,
8. I, now thirty-seven years old in perfect health begin,
9. Hoping to cease not till death.
10. Creeds and schools in abeyance,
11. Retiring back a while suffced at what they are, but never forgotten,
12. I harbor for good or bad, I permit to speak at every hazard,
13. Nature without check with original energy.

··

Task

1. Find the following words in the *Oxford English Dictionary* (OED)—online, in print, or CD-ROM—in the context(s) in which Whitman uses them. Consider also if Whitman is extending the conventional meaning(s) of the word.

assume	line 2
schools	l. 10
sufficed	l. 11
hazard	l. 12
original	l. 13
check	l. 13

2. List in descending order the possible meanings you would consider in a translation out of English. Do the dictionary entries prepare one adequately for nuances, overlap, and ideolect (a writer or speaker's particular or distinguishably unique use of language)?
3. Connect with your **Manual** Web site to find the link to the site where you can read these two translations en>es of *Canto I*: first, Leon Felipe's version, and the second, Leandro Wolfson's version in *Hojas de hierba* (publisher: Longseller), which can be found in Google Books. Both translators are from Argentina; the first was published in the 1940s, the second in 2002. Note the differences and similarities. What complementarities do you notice; that is, what interpretive junctures of the poem open it into different possible readings (meanings)? What differences in phrasing do you see? Comment on the two versions.
4. Point out an example of a choice that either translator, or both translators, made that works against the unity of the poem in some way or fails to capture something of Whitman's English. Provide a better solution if you can.
5. For a fascinating roundtable on translating Whitman, see "Whitman in Translation" (1996, 1–58).

Walt Whitman

Source: Courtesy of the Library of Congress

TRANSLATION TIPS

Submitting to Literary Translation Journals

Follow submission policies *to the letter*—if the review board wants no more than four poems per submission, don't send more than four. Don't send electronic submissions if the journal doesn't accept them; increasingly, electronic submissions are preferred but not always.

Use self-addressed stamped envelopes if sending paper submissions.

Read back issues of the journal to which you are submitting. A huge percentage of pieces are rejected simply because of poor "fit." You should not submit blindly. Read several of the most recent issues, and take note of editor preferences and trends.

Peruse calls for submissions carefully for announcements of issues devoted to special themes. Correlate matches from your eligible pool of work to these themes.

Journals will either require permissions to be in hand when you submit or as a condition of acceptance. They often will advise about copyright issues, but it's wishful thinking to expect editors to clear copyrights for you.

Keep a careful log of submissions you have out, that are returned, and that are published.

Remember etiquette—send a *brief* cover letter with a biography describing your credentials and a biography of the writer. You may mention something about the journal or recent work you read there to personalize the contact. For more on submission etiquette, consult *Writer's Market*, which publishes yearly in September.

Be aware of the practice of *simultaneous submissions*, which many in the writing world frown upon. This consists of a submitter sending the same pieces to more than one potential outlet at a time. If you wish to engage in this, make absolutely certain that the journals where you are submitting accept simultaneous submissions.

New journals are often very open to submissions by new translators, even though often they are in competition with established translators for the same page space.

No matter how much experience you have in the field, rejection is a basic fact of the writing business. Neither ignore rejection nor be undone by it—learn from it where you can. Rejection frequently is given unceremoniously and without feedback.

 Connect with your **Manual** Web site to find the link to the site where you can read "ALTA Guides to Literary Translation: Breaking Into Print" before submitting.

Activity: Children's Literature

Research what general issues dominate the translation of children's literature. Survey them, and rank them in the order you feel would be most important.

The Scholastic en español imprint publishes many children's titles. Are these original works or translations? Find out more about this company's operations vis-à-vis translation.

What role do children's books play in the rise of multiculturalism? Give specific examples of works or authors that have brought greater inclusivity to the themes and characters written for children.

Discussion

1. Many children's books today are bilingual. What effect do you think this has on language acquisition? On a child's self-image? (See Dale's [2003] *Bilingual Children's Books In English and Spanish: An Annotated Bibliography, 1942 Through 2001*.)

2. Do you think children want foreignness or familiarity in their books? On the linguistic level, should characters in children's books speak "American"?

3. Do you think a censored translation of a foreign children's book is ever justified? Discuss.

4. Do you think children's books are really written for children, or for their parents? Or for both?

5. Find canonical works of foreign literature adapted for children (sometimes called "retellings") via translation. What transformations have the works undergone? What goals seem to have guided the adaptations?

   For research on children's literature, consult: *The Translation of Children's Literature: A Reader* (Lathey 2006).

TRANSLATION TEASER

Here's a real puzzler for you. As a child, did you find it odd that Cinderella should wear a *glass* slipper? Some say she really wore a *fur* slipper because the French *verre* (glass) and *vair* (fur) were confused in translation. What can you uncover on this?

Consider these questions: What did the earliest illustrations of Cinderella in France show on her feet? Do French children today who watch Disney versions of the tale expect the slipper to be fur?

¿?

Here are some works of literature for children and young adults you may have read in translation. Can you think of others or works you read in Spanish from non-English languages?

Grimm's Fairy Tales (German)

The 1001 Nights ("*Sinbad,*" "*Alladin,*" "*Ali Baba and the Forty Thieves*") (Arabic)

The Neverending Story (German)

The Little Prince (French)

Pippi Longstocking (Swedish)

Tales of Hans Christian Andersen ("*The Little Mermaid,*" "*The Little Match Girl*") (Danish)

Tales of Charles Perrault (*Tales of Mother Goose*) (French)

The Story of Babar (French)

The Three Musketeers (adapted) (French)

The Adventures of Pinocchio (Italian)

The novels of Jules Verne (*Around the World in Eighty Days*, etc.) (French)

Tales of E.T.A. Hoffman ("*The Sandman,*" "*Nutcracker*") (German)

Platero and I (Spanish)

Don Quixote (adapted) (Spanish)

TRANSLATION TIP

Royalties and Copyright Ownership

Royalties, advances on royalties, and subsidiary rights are not something to count on in literary translation, because translations don't typically sell more than 2,000 copies, unless they are adopted for classroom use, gain wide critical attention, or are made into a film. Increasingly, however, royalties can be negotiated. They tend to range from 1 percent to 10 percent, most commonly 2 percent to 6 percent.

According to the PEN American Center, in recent years, U.S. publishers have copyrighted more literary translations in the translator's name as well, affording more protections for translators. International copyright law, as it applies to translators and their rights as authors, is exceedingly complicated.

 Connect with your **Manual** Web site and use it to find the link to the PEN American Center site and see "A Translator's Model Contract," a template for legal arrangements between book publishers and literary translators.

Familiarize yourself with the concept of *public domain*. How many years after an author's death do rights enter public domain in the countries of your language pair?

Activity: *Like Water for Chocolate* Translation Comparison

1. Find out about the decisions made behind the scenes of the translation of Laura Esquivel's (1993) *Como agua para chocolate*. When did points of contention arose with the publishers, and around what lexical issue did they tend to revolve?

2. Go over the translation of Chapter 1 ("*Preparación*") of *Como agua para chocolate* passage by passage, comparing the target closely with the source. Mark up the English and take copious notes. Be conscious of the size of *segmenting* you do as you compare—the size of text "chunks" you tend to compare. How large or small do they tend to be?

3. What shifts occur that you would challenge as an editor? Explain your reasons. What culture-bound difficulties arise? How do the translators cope with them in general? Give an example or two of a choice they make that reflects their larger approach or strategy. Would you say that the translation tends toward domestication or toward foreignizing? What impact do the translators' choices seem to have?

4. Show points where meaning loss may have occurred; where you point out these passages, you may try to offer an alternative, improved version. For this task, you may find pages 98–104 of Hervey, Higgins, and Haywood, *Thinking Spanish Translation*, to offer a useful framework: a discussion of different types of connotative meaning, including *associative, affective, reflected, collocative,* and *allusive*. Otherwise you can discuss translation strategies, pragmatic or otherwise. How successful would you judge this work? How was it received in the United States? In what measure can that be attributed to the translation? Could its reception have anything to do with market conditions at the time, or expectations of Spanish American literature? How did reviewers receive the translation?

5. What does the title refer to in Spanish? Do you think the English does this justice? Try for an improved title if you know the book.

6. Read both the Spanish and English novellas. Write up a book review in English, giving heavy coverage to the translation as a translation and what voice comes across.

> **CULTURAL NOTE**
>
> ### The Reading Walk
>
> **Tibbon, Judah Ben** (twelfth century)—translator of Judah Halevi's Book on the Khazars from Arabic into Hebrew. The translation appeared in 1167, and there are two explanations for its unevenness: that later, printed versions were castrated in the hands of the Christian Inquisition, and that the whole thing depended not just on Tibbon, but on circumstances.
>
> The translation was faithful when ben Tibbon was in love with his betrothed, good when he was angry, wordy if the winds blew, profound in winter, expository and paraphrased if it rained, and wrong if he was happy.
>
> When he finished a chapter, Tibbon would do as the ancient Alexandrian translators of the Bible had done—he would have someone read him the translation while walking away from him, and Tibbon would stand still and listen. With distance, parts of the text were lost in the wind and around corners, the rest echoing back through the bushes and trees; screened by doors and railings, it shed nouns and vowels, tripped on stairs, and finally, having begun as a male voice, would end its journey as a female voice, with only verbs and numbers still audible in the distance. Then, when the reader returned, the entire process would be reversed, and Tibbon would correct the translation on the basis of the impressions he had derived from this reading walk.
>
> (Pavic 1988)

> **TRANSLATION TIP**
>
> ### "Has This Been Translated Before?"
>
> Information on Publication Status of Translations†
>
> *RLIN* [Research Libraries Information Network, a computerized catalog of holdings at major research libraries.]
>
> *Books in Print* (New York: Bowker, 1948–)
>
> *British Museum Catalog* [lists all books published in Great Britain]
>
> *Humanities Index* (New York: Wilson, 1974–)
>
> *Index Translationum* (Paris: UNESCO, 1949–)
>
> *Library of Congress Catalog* (Ann Arbor, MI: Edwards, 1950–)
>
> *National Union Catalog* (Chicago: American Library Association, 1968–)
>
> *OCLC* (On-line College Library Center, a bibliographic database)
>
> † "For informative articles on the subject of OCLC and the newer bibliographic utilities EPIC (which provides subject access to the OCLC database) and RLIN, see Larry Stephen Perry's two-part "Lost in Translation: A Guide to Finding Literary Translation," in *Translation Review* 28 (1988) pp. 7-9; and "A Supplemental Guide to Locating Translations," in *Translation Review* 38/39 (1992), pp. 3-6."
>
> (PEN American Center)
>
> Finding an untranslated work is a bit like courtship—you may have rivals for the object of your affections. Although it is perhaps unrealistic to strive at first to publish the latest bestselling author in English, occasionally an author has lesser or less visible gems (e.g., short stories) that can be mined. If you go back further in time, you often find even major works that have been missed or passed over. Find out about foreign rights before investing major amounts of time translating. Still, odds are that at least once in your career you'll finish something only to find another translator beat you to publication.

¿?

In general, there are three typical project initiators in literary translation: a translator, an author, or a publisher. Cooperation between the three is the ideal once the project is contracted and underway. Which type of project (translator initiated, author initiated, or publisher initiated) do you think has the best chances for success? Discuss.

TRANSLATION TIP

Contacting Authors

Authors may be contacted through the author's publisher (or agent) or directly, via their email, often their work affiliation (e.g., a university). There are other channels, but these are perhaps the two most common. Don't make unsolicited phone calls to authors' home telephones.

Here is another, lesser known way to establish contact: Get in touch with the author's leading critic or biographer, who will usually be happy to contribute to translation efforts and will be flattered at being consulted about the subject of his or her expertise. They may even smooth the way for you.

LITERARY TRANSLATION: SUGGESTED READINGS (BACKGROUND AND ARTICLES FOR CRITIQUE)

"A Rose by Any Other Name." Eco, Umberto. Translated by William Weaver. *Guardian Weekly*, January 16, 1994, http://www.themodernword.com/eco/eco_guardian94. html

"Missing Out on the World of Scholarship." Schiffrin, André. *The Chronicle of Higher Education*, October 6, 2000.

"Translation: Its Genealogy in the West," in *Translation, History, and Culture*. Susan Bassnett and André Lefevere, eds. London/NY: Pinter, 1990, 14–27.

"Words Cannot Express . . . The Translation of Cultures." Rabassa, Gregory. *Voiceovers: Translation and Latin American Literature*. Daniel Balderston and Marcy E. Schwartz, eds. Albany: State University of New York Press, 2002.

"No Two Snowflakes Are Alike: Translation as Metaphor." Rabassa, Gregory. *The Craft of Translation*. J. Biguenet and R. Schulte, eds. Chicago and London: University of Chicago Press, 1989, 1–12.

"Decisions at the Outset." Landers, Clifford E. *Literary Translation: A Practical Guide*. Clevedon/Buffalo/Toronto/Sydney: Multilingual Matters, Ltd., 2001, 49–71.

"Latin American Poetry in Spanish." *Oxford Guide to Literature in English Translation*. Peter France, ed. Oxford and New York: Oxford University Press, 2000, 430–37.

"Transplanting the Seed: Poetry and Translation." Bassnett, Susan. *Constructing Cultures*. Clevedon/Buffalo/Toronto/Sydney: Multilingual Matters, Ltd., 1998, 57–75.

"Interview with Octavio Paz." Edwin Honig, ed. *The Poet's Other Voice*. Amherst: University of Massachusetts Press. 151–63.

"Translation and the Trials of the Foreign." Berman, Antoine. *The Translation Studies Reader*. L. Venuti, ed. London and New York: Routledge, 2000. 284–97.

"Borges on Translation." Kristal, Efraín. *Invisible Work: Borges and Translation*. Nashville, TN: Vanderbilt University Press, 2002, 1–18; 30–5.

"The Homeric Versions." Borges, Jorge Luis. *Voiceovers: Translation and Latin American Literature*. Daniel Balderston and Marcy E. Schwartz, eds. Albany: State University of New York Press, 2002, 15–20.

"Translation and the Formation of Cultural Identities." Venuti, Lawrence. *Cultural Functions of Translation*. Christina Schaffner and Helen Kelly-Holmes, eds. Clevedon, UK; Bristol, PA: Multilingual Matters Ltd., 1995, 9–25.

"Gender and the Metaphorics of Translation." Chamberlain, Lori. *Rethinking Translation: Discourse, Subjectivity, Ideology*. L. Venuti, ed. New York: Routledge, 1992, 56–74.

WORKSHOP #9: PROSE FICTION

The literary workshop for this chapter is an excerpt from a contemporary work of historical fiction, *Santa Evita*, by Tomás Eloy Martínez. Before beginning, brainstorm about what you know about Evita Perón, both historically and in fictional representations. Are there unresolved contradictions in these portrayals? Vested interests at work (myth-making or demythifying)? Research especially Evita's relationship to the *descamisados*. Next, identify terms in the source text borrowed from other domains (architecture, religion, horticulture). Reflect on the "hybrid" nature of other literary works you know—quite frequently one finds that a work of literature includes specialized knowledge from a great many subject areas. *Moby-Dick*, for example, has adventure scenes interspersed with vast stretches of highly technical whaling jargon and anatomical digressions. As part of your pretranslation research, find a historian's description of Evita's postmortem period and compare tone, details, and chronological and factual similarities. Your instructor may wish to divide these different tasks into groups for presentations. You may read the Spanish novel up to the passage selected if you wish.

> Evita murió y su cuerpo fue velado durante doce días bajo la cúpula de jirafa de la Secretaría de Trabajo, donde se había desangrado atendiendo las súplicas de las multitudes. Medio millón de personas besó el ataúd. Algunos tuvieron que ser arrancados a la fuerza porque trataban de suicidarse a los pies del cadáver con navajas y cápsulas de veneno. Alrededor del edificio funerario se colgaron dieciocho mil coronas de flores: había otras tantas en las capillas ardientes alzadas en las capitales de provincia y en las ciudades cabeceras de distrito, donde la difunta estaba representada por fotografías de tres metros de altura. El Coronel asistió al velorio con los veintidós edecanes que la habían servido, llevando el obligatorio crespón de luto. Permaneció diez minutos de pie, rezó una plegaria y se retiró con la cabeza baja. La mañana del entierro se quedó en cama y siguió los movimientos del cortejo fúnebre por las descripciones de la radio. El ataúd fue colocado sobre una cureña de guerra y tirado por una tropilla de treinta y cinco representantes sindicales en mangas de camisa. Diecisiete mil soldados se apostaron en las calles para rendir honores. Desde los balcones fueron arrojados un millón y medio de rosas amarillas, alhelíes de los Andes, claveles blancos, orquídeas del Amazonas, alverjillas del lago Nahuel Huapí y crisantemos enviados por el emperador del Japón en aviones de guerra. ‹‹Números››, dijo el Coronel. ‹‹Ya esa mujer no tiene más ancla con la realidad que los números››.
>
> Pasaron los meses y la realidad, sin embargo, siguió ocupándose de ella. Para satisfacer la súplica de que no la olvidaran, Perón ordenó embalsamar el

cuerpo. El trabajo fue encomendado a Pedro Ara, un anatomista español, céle-bre por haber conservado las manos de Manuel de Falla como si aún estuvieran tocando «El amor brujo». En el segundo piso de la Confederación General del Trabajo, se construyó un laboratorio aislado por las más rigurosas precauciones de seguridad.

Aunque nadie podía ver el cadáver, la gente lo imaginaba yaciendo allí, en el sigilo de una capilla, y acudía los domingos a rezar el rosario y a llevarle flores. Poco a poco, Evita fue convirtiéndose en un relato que, antes de termi-nar, encendía otro. Dejó de ser lo que dijo y lo que hizo para ser lo que dicen que dijo y lo que dicen que hizo.

. . .

Murió joven, como los otros grandes mitos argentinos del siglo: a los treinta y tres años. [. . .] Los descamisados adivinan su luz, oyen tremolar su vestido, reconocen el murmullo de su voz ronca y agitada, descubren la servidumbre de sus luces en el más allá y los trajines de sus nervios y, mientras encienden velas de promesa en el sitio donde tendría que haber reposado su catafalco, la interrogan sobre el porvenir. Ella responde con elipsis, variaciones de negro, nublamientos de la luz, anunciando que los tiempos futuros serán sombríos. Como siempre han sido sombríos, la credulidad de los devotos está asegurada. Evita es infalible.

(*Source:* Martínez, Tomás Eloy. Santa Evita. New York: Random House, 1995.)

Word count: 498

Activity: De-Briefing in Literary Translation

1. Very, very few people make a living exclusively through literary translation. It does, however, afford tremendous personal satisfaction and is a lifeline of cultural exchange. What appeal do you think literary translation will hold for you in the future? Why?
2. Do you think, having now done literary and nonliterary translations, that the distinc-tion is valid? What differentiates the two? What core competences do the two share? Contrast how each tends, in general, to view ambiguity.
3. Quite a few translators—students and practicing translators alike—are intimidated by literary translation and perpetuate a widespread belief that literary translation is the most difficult kind. Is this an objective truth, do you think, or does it have more to do with one's own comfort level and experience with literature?

Do you think that a translator of poetry must be a poet? Discuss. Do you think a strong creative writer can also be an expert translator without overpowering the source author's voice? Discuss.

Task

1. Find at least one untranslated text or at least identify an author that interests you to translate es>en at some future date. Which tack appeals to you more—finding a new, unproven or emerging author or finding a forgotten gem by an established writer? (Both are valid.) Would you like to work with a living author or work on a writer from the past? What pros and cons can you see with each?
2. Do you think writers should have the last word on how their work is translated? Do you think *they* think that? Test your suppositions by checking interviews with authors who have collaborated in translations of their own work. What insights does the process tend to give them? Do such collaborations tend to be fruitful? Describe.
3. Find at least five online journals that publish literature from Spanish regularly. Compare their submission policies.
4. Why do you think certain writers are translated before others? What factors do you think come into play for a writer to be brought out in translation?
5. Find a self-translating writer or a writer who collaborates closely with translators. How does this writer see translation in relation to his or her writing?

Why do you think that it is said that retranslations of the classics should occur at least every generation? Do you know of a translation that may have been well done but has aged badly?

Follow-Up

1. Compare a screen version of a film to the English translation of the Spanish (e.g., Manual Puig's *The Kiss of the Spider Woman*). What intersemiotic translation elements and cultural substitutions appear in the film that do not appear in the book? Why do you think?
2. Study the life's work of a single master translator (es>en), for example, Margaret Seyers Peden, Helen Lane, Gregory Rabassa, or Edith Grossman.
3. Subscribe to and read *Translation Review*.
4. Find the official Web sites of Spanish-language authors you admire. If they have not been translated/localized, assess the difficulties and size of such a job.
5. Read and discuss a novelization of a translator's life or a novel featuring an interpreter or translator. Alternatively, see biographies, such as the exciting ones on Captain Sir Richard Burton, the Victorian-era polyglot adventurer.

11

Cultural and Consumer-Oriented Translation

FILM DUBBING AND SUBTITLING

Most movie-going crowds are unappreciative of the fine art of subtitling, which requires the dexterity of a juggler, the incisiveness of a surgeon, and the timing of a pyrotechnic artist. Ask three people on the street to word-associate when you say "subtitles" or "dubbing": Who doesn't have strong opinions on self-dubbed Hong Kong kung fu movies or white-on-white titles that blow a scene?

Subtitling is usually an underfunded afterthought. Frequently, subtitlers don't even get a chance to see the film they are titling. In addition, they must work at an unbelievable pace and anonymously. Subtitlers must compress—and omit—a great deal of information into a readable space. Characters in film speak faster than moviegoers read, so cuts, overlaps, and other "directorial" choices have to be made. It is arguably at the level of the entire text—the film—that the subtitler works, not each utterance. Or as Henrik Gottlieb (1998, 247) notes, in subtitling, the pragmatic dimension—intentions and effects—takes precedence over isolated elements of a script. The challenge of accounting for intonation, emotion, irony, verbal qualities, and idiosyncrasies are formidable.

Subtitling is seen by many to be preferable to **dubbing**, which is far more expensive, among other drawbacks. Whichever format is used, subtitlers and dubbers can have a major impact on the overall aesthetic experience. Poor titles are enough to ruin a movie. Bad dubbing is enough to make a movie unintentionally funny.

Subtitlers work comparatively rarely into English. Americans, statistically, don't like reading—at home and away from home, but especially not at the movies. (At recent showings of *Pan's Labyrinth*—the title of which is, uncharacteristically, more literary than the Spanish original—audiences audibly groaned when they realized they would be reading subtitles.) It is no surprise that less than 3 percent of foreign films make it into the U.S. movie and TV market (Germann 2004, 93). Germann argues that a "market censorship" is in place that "prevents content from other cultural origins, except the one dominating the market, to reach mass audiences. These mass audiences, in turn, are denied the right to freely choose contents from other cultural origins than the one dominating their market because another no longer exists" (93). The author also argues that mass audiences have developed consumption habits of preferring works originally created in English. He suspects that although "local languages will always find a niche in their respective home markets, the demand for contents in original languages of countries other than English will decrease, and, in the worst case, fully disappear" (93). Many screenwriters, songwriters, novelists, and others are essentially opting into the world markets by opting out of their own language.

Jorge Luis Borges's essay "Sobre el doblaje" (283–4) likens dubbing to a monstrous process of recombination like the one that wrought the Chimera (an incongruous mythological beast with a lion's head, a goat's body, and a dragon's tail). Borges speculates that the process will be perfected when not only voices but faces are "usurped"—replaced (118n). That era may be upon us. A more insidious and troubling process was begun in the 1980s and 1990s, when marketers and producers would run trailers for foreign films that hid the films' foreign origins, a deception that fed Americans' "imperial normativity"—the assumption that the whole world shares our values and point of view, and by extension, language (see "To Read or Not to Read: Subtitles, Trailers, and Monolingualism," by B. Ruby Rich, pp. 154–69, in Egoyan and Balfour's excellent *Subtitles: On the Foreignness of Film*). The Academy Awards reinforces this view with its separate but unequal category, Best Foreign Language Film.

For further reading, see Zatlin (2005, Chapter 6, 123–49).

Dubbing or titling?
Which do you think is more of a foreignizing strategy, dubbing or subtitling? Which is more domesticating? Which do you think is preferable, and by what criteria?

Think about all the different stakeholders involved in both operations—which do you think is preferable to each of them?

What gaffes and shortcomings tend to appear in subtitles? Why is this so?

Research

1. The bibliography on film subtitling—and multimedia translation in general—is growing apace. Find specific *constraints*—technical, linguistic, temporal, cultural, economic—that subtitlers have to work under, and how they have dealt with them. As part of your background research, form a realistic assessment of the work prospects (>en) in this area by checking translator forum archives or querying same. (Consider: How many subtitled films make it to your local multiplex?)
2. Where are academic courses in multimedia translation offered? What do they cover?
3. Find out what voiceover work is available, how voice talent is contracted, what connections to the language industry it has. Report to the class.
4. What about closed captions? Are they used only in the deaf community, or is there a connection to bilingual broadcasting?
5. Find out the types and features of subtitling software on the market today. Do a "Consumer Reports"-style presentation of the best value, most popular, etc.
6. Some countries are "dubbing countries" and others are "subtitling countries." Try to determine what accounts for the different preferences.

Activity: Group Experiments

1. As a group, watch a dubbed segment of a film and then a subtitled version of the same segment. Compare.

2. Record and transcribe sections from a Spanish-language *telenovela*. Half the class transcribes; the other half translates into subtitles (using the industry average of 35-character maximum line lengths). The transcribers act out the Spanish script; the subtitle translators then act out the scene using the English subtitles. As a group, compare the effect. Discussion: Are subtitles "performable" or are they merely shorthand, suggestive of something performable? Consider a reception issue: Are subtitles intended to be read "stereo-optically," that is, comparatively, against the source?

CULTURAL NOTE

Secondary Audio Programming

Secondary Audio Programming (SAP) technology allows many television programs to be simulcast with Spanish audio or closed captions, for which most new TVs are equipped. SAP works from scripted material—translations—except in the case of live telecasts such as sports and the nightly news (which is simultaneously interpreted in some markets).

The "extreme sport" of media interpreting is working the Academy Awards out of English. The Spanish audio feed is on a mere seconds-long time delay, the interpreter must negotiate an onslaught of in-jokes, culturally bound humor, sight gags, risqué innuendo, titles and song lyrics, unintelligible asides, foreign names, and the wild emotions of Oscar® night. Academy Award interpreters usually have no advanced script to work from—they "fly without a net." Unsympathetic editorial writers savage them year after year in newspapers around the world, blaming them for the "dead air" and mumbled defeat that is their lot. More than one unfortunate soul has been heard to interpret resignedly (in Spanish): "The host is telling a joke about something, and the audience finds it quite funny. . . ."

Follow-Up: If you are reading this near the award ceremony's airing (late February/early March), watch from the point of view of an interpreter. Take notes. If you have access to Spanish programming, listen in to see how the interpreter is faring.

TELEVISION AND TRANSLATION/LOCALIZATION

Television programming is part of the matrix of intercultural flows that some theorists have seen in terms of a battle between globalizing forces, which homogenize, and "tribalizing" forces, which entrench local worldviews.

TV shows are often retooled—remade—for audiences abroad. Can you think of some examples? Think, too, about your perception of foreign shows—for example, shows that are relatively foreign to North American sensibilities. Do you think differences are embraced in our media markets, or is there a cultural filter in place that enforces norms?

Tasks

1. Research the globalization of the children's television program *Sesame Street*. What are some of the localizing issues that were dealt with? What specifically linguistic issues arose? What cultural issues? Report on the most dramatic transculturations. Use primary and secondary sources. You may find the documentary on this topic, *The World According to Sesame Street*, to be well worth a look.

2. Suppose you were hired as a language consultant for a breakout new Latin American video channel. Research VH1 and MTV in their various Spanish-language Web pages. Decide the features (8–10) you want to compare head to head and make a chart of them.

3. Imagine that you were writing an online article on adapting media for foreign markets. Suppose that, via email, you were going to interview a professional who has worked in creating localized content of foreign programming, mostly for TV. In pairs, come up with the 10 best questions most likely to elicit responses that would help produce the article you need, which focuses on the *why* and the *how* of this subfield. As with any interviewing, this will require some research beforehand. Also remember that interviews do not always follow a question-and-answer format—the interviewers can also make statements or observations and follow up with questions premised on them.

Activity: Translating Songs

For this mini-workshop, you will be translating a song. It can be in any genre (traditional, children's, pop, folk, etc.). Here is the extensive brief for the task:

The source should be a song.

The text should be one page minimum, with several stanzas, up to two to three pages.

The text should be chosen that makes linguistic and cultural negotiations necessary.

You may work in either direction (en>es or es>en).

Format the texts in bitext columns.

You will make a formal *presentation* of 7 to 10 minutes, in English or Spanish, of your source and target texts (define the genre), followed by 3 to 5 minutes of *analysis* in which you discuss your macrostrategy, difficulties encountered, and how you solved them. Make some mention of skopos (a new setting, new genre, new era? Are listener expectations different? Have you accentuated the refrain to remake the song into one of protest? etc.). The presentation should have a handout. Make copies for each member of the class and your instructor. You may bring the written score, play music or video, sing, dance, recruit classmates to sing the chorus, and so on. You also may simply read it as you would a poem.

You should strive to be attentive to the following criteria:

1. Song selection
2. Creativity/artistry of the translation
3. Resourcefulness in problem solving
4. Analytical insight
5. Performability

Performability means that the song must still be a song to be *sung*, actually or potentially, not read on the page. Appropriate *rhythms* and/or *rhyme* should be in place.

HINT Avoid slant rhymes (forced quasi-rhymes)—"sea" doesn't rhyme with "tranquility," try as you might. Remember that vowels are more sing-able than consonants.

Try rhyming dictionaries online (connect with your **Manual** Web site to find the link) or in print (*The Oxford Rhyming Dictionary*).

1. Find well-known songs and compare their (in some cases multiple) translations and adaptations; for example: "De Colores," "Guantanamera," or "Fortune Presents Gifts Not According to the Book" (vocal duo Dead Can Dance's version of Luis de Góngora's *letrilla* [XIII]).
2. Study the interplay of languages in code-switching songs: "Hotel California" (Gipsy Kings' version in Spanglish), the bilingual "Colores" (Mocedades with Donovan).
3. Scavenger hunt: A prize for the tango or milonga lyrics that sound corniest in English.

Source: Page from sheet music to 1919 Spanish-language version of "The Star-Spangled Banner," commissioned by the U.S. Bureau of Education

CULTURAL NOTE

Real-Time Translation at the Opera

Operagoers tend to prefer songs sung in the original. How, then, do they follow the plot, short of learning the language? Librettos are often translated, synopses are given, but a third—controversial—option has emerged: the **surtitle** or **supertitle**. They are prepared in advance and only *appear* in real time (sometimes with regrettable comic timing). Supertitles are projected *above* the stage, in contrast with **subtitles**, which appear below, and are more common in TV and film. (Subtitles are also what the printed dialogue in silent movies were called—now these are termed **intertitles**, which are commonly translated, usually in a different font or color.) An even more recent innovation—a tiny screen on the seat back in front of each patron—is in the experimental phase. Either way, some critics decry the use of titles as distracting from the action. What do *you* think about reading titles at a performance?

TRANSLATION TEASER

Traductor, No Hay Traducción, Se Hace Traducción Al Traducir

"Cantares" is a well-known poem by Antonio Machado, later made even more famous worldwide in J. M. Serrat's song using Machado's lyrics. The part of the chorus featuring the line "*caminante, no hay camino,*" is instantly recognizable.

Find the Machado/Serrat poem in its entirety. In small groups, discuss the meanings. Then try a version in English of the chorus. (Hint: Be cognizant of words that have their stress on the last versus the penultimate syllable, and in what patterns they fall.)

As an option, do the whole poem.

Activity: Adaptation

> With the Lorca poem ["Pequeño vals vienés"], the translation took 150 hours, just to get it into English that resembled—I would never presume to say duplicated—the greatness of Lorca's poem. It was a long, drawn-out affair, and the only reason I would even attempt it is my love for Lorca.
> Leonard Cohen, interview in *Your Flesh* magazine, 1992

Adaptation may take many forms: from a script or a novel to the stage, from a poem to a film, or from a poem in one language to a poem in another. Read Canadian singer-songwriter Leonard Cohen's version of Federico García Lorca's "Pequeño vals vienés," and reread it. Then in groups, discuss:

1. Why may this be considered an adaptation and not a translation? (A more conservative stance might be to call this an *imitation*.) What interpretations that go beyond the implicit appear explicitly in Cohen's Lorca? Make a chart of specific images, passages, or lines that strike you. Comment on them from the point of view of a translator—what transformations does the poem undergo and how does Cohen craft the changes? What purpose or strategy seems to be visible to you as you read the English? What does Cohen do with the *format* of the poem? What about *rhythms*?
2. How successful does the translation strike you? What criterion or criteria are you using for your judgment? If you know other works by Lorca, what about the English would you call distinctively Lorquian?
3. Connect to the **Manual** Web site to find a link to a video of Leonard Cohen's "Take This Waltz". Listen in class as you read along. How does the listening change your perception, if indeed it does?

4. Try Cohen's approach to a Lorca poem or passages from a Lorca poem. Try for a new poem that can be sung.

5. Try a version of Lorca's poem, taking licenses that stay true to Lorca's voice while giving the poem the highest personal resonance for you. Test your final rendering by seeing if you can waltz to it.

●●●

Research

Explore the boundaries between a *translation*, a *version*, an *adaptation*, and an *imitation*. Compare how writers and theorists have demarcated these terms, and how different eras define and value each.

●●●

Activity: Translating Titles

Consider each of the title translations that follow (as listed in *Dictionary of Translated Names and Titles* by Adrian Room [1985]). With a partner, enumerate the strategies used. List specific examples of why you think certain choices were made; where you think the translation is improvable, try to improve on it. Comment specifically on both disparities and successful solutions. Recall what you learned about particularization, generalization, and overlap. The English title is the first of each pair; the actual Spanish translation used is the second. Reflect on the following: Do any unwanted associations creep in? Do any reveal "too much"? Do any seem more successful to you than in the source? Do any seem less successful? Why? Is there a place for literalism and "non-translation" in translating titles? Finally, come to a consensus about what constitutes a successful title.

Literature	***Literatura***
All Quiet on the Western Front (Remarque, 1927)	*Sin novedad en el frente*
All God's Chillun Got Wings (O'Neill, 1924)	*Todos los hijos de Dios tienen alas*
The Bed Bug (Mayakovsky, 1929)	*La pulga*
The Call of the Wild (London, 1903)	*La llamada de la selva*
The Day of the Locust (West, 1939)	*El día de la langosta*
Film	***Cine***
Belle de Jour (Buñuel, 1967)	*Belle de jour*
The Big Sleep (Hawks, 1946)	*El sueño eterno*
Billy the Kid (Vidor, 1930)	*Billy, el niño*
Blackboard Jungle, The (Brooks, 1955)	*Semilla de maldad*
Blow-up (Antonioni, 1966)	*Blow up*
Bonnie and Clyde (Penn, 1967)	*Bonnie y Clyde*
Breakfast at Tiffany's (Edwards, 1961)	*Desayuno con diamantes*
Breathless (Godard, 1959)	*Al final de la escapada*

Butch Cassidy and the Sundance Kid (Hill, 1969)	Dos hombres y un destino
Cat on a Hot Tin Roof (Williams, 1955)	La gata sobre el tejado de zinc
A Clockwork Orange (Burgess, 1962)	La naranja mecánica
Close Encounters of the Third Kind (Spielberg, 1977)	Encuentros íntimos de tercera clase (original translation)
	Encuentros cercanos del tercer tipo (subsequent translation)
Dr. Strangelove (Kubrick, 1964)	¿Teléfono rojo? Volamos hacia Moscú
Double Indemnity (Wilder, 1944)	Perdición
The Empire Strikes Back (Kershner, 1980)	El imperio contraataca
Fantasia (Disney, 1940)	Fantasía
Five Easy Pieces (Rafelson, 1970)	Mi vida es mi vida
Jesus Christ Superstar (Webber & Rice, 1969)	Jesus Christ Superstar (unchanged in every major language)
Rear Window (Hitchcock, 1954)	La ventana indiscreta
Rosemary's Baby (Polanski, 1968)	La semilla del diablo
Seven Samurai (Kurosawa, 1954)	Los siete valientes
The Sound of Music (Wise, 1965)	Sonrisas y lágrimas
Sunset Boulevard (Wilder, 1950)	El crepúsculo de los dioses
Those Magnificent Men in Their Flying Machines (Annakin, 1965)	Aquellos chalados en sus locos cacharros

Spanish into English	*Del español al inglés*
¡Átame! (Almodóvar, 1990)	Tie Me Up! Tie Me Down!
El amor brujo (Saura, 1986)	Love, the Magician
	A Love Bewitched
Mujeres al borde de un ataque de nervios (Almodóvar, 1988)	Women on the Verge of a Nervous Breakdown

Now try some of your own. If you can, do at least two versions of each, employing different strategies for each. Do research on the film if you need to, but avoid finding Spanish titles until you have finished. Discuss.

Fargo	O, Brother, Where Art Thou?
_____	_____
_____	_____
Goodfellas	The Shawshank Redemption
_____	_____
_____	_____
The Green Mile	Toy Story
_____	_____
_____	_____

King Kong   *The Matrix*

_____   _____

_____   _____

Now see if you can find published titles in Spanish for the movies listed or those you chose. Compare. Give your translated titles to classmates for them to guess the originals. Then translate other movie titles and quiz people with them.

● ●

CASE STUDY: TITLES IN NEWARK PUBLIC LIBRARY SPANISH-LANGUAGE READING LIST ON ILLNESS AND BEREAVEMENT

Self-help (psychology, spirituality, relationships, etc.) is a category of nonfiction that does billion-dollar business around the world, much of it generated from the work of U.S.-based writers.

Compare the titles that follow and discuss: What do you think prompted the obvious shifts? Do you prefer an enigmatic title or a functional one that explains exactly what the book contains? Which do you think is more appropriate for this text type? Who do you think are the audiences for these books? In what ways might the Spanish-speaking audiences differ from the original intended Anglo readership? (Note that many of the titles were published in Spain, where a great deal of translation, and translator-training, work is happening.)

Many translators agree that titles should be translated last, after the main text. Why do you think this is so? Note: Publishers frequently will suggest, alter, or insist on certain titles; titles are often a joint effort or do not involve the translator—perhaps more than providing a way of identifying a book, titles are part of marketing strategies.

S155.937 F325mo

Feinstein, David, and Peg Elliott Mayo. *Sobre el vivir y el morir: un programa de afirmación de vida para enfrentarse a la muerte.* Translation of *Mortal Acts.* Madrid, Spain: EDAF, 1994.

S155.937 K95oc

Kübler-Ross, Elisabeth. *Una luz que se apaga.* Translation of *On Children and Death.* Mexico City: Editorial Pax Mexico, 1985.

S155.937 K95de

Kübler-Ross, Elisabeth. *Morir es de vital importancia.* Translation of *Death Is of Vital Importance.* Barcelona, Spain: Luciérnaga, 1995.

S155.937 L5113go

Lee, Carol. *La muerte de los seres queridos.* Translation of *Good Grief.* Barcelona, Spain: Plaza & Janes, 1995.

S155.937 D343

Sherr, Lorraine. *Agonía, muerte y duelo.* Translation of *Death, Dying and Bereavement.* Mexico City: Editorial El manual moderno, 1992.

What translation-related efforts are community, school, and national libraries involved in? Consider not just research tools but also programming and other outreach initiatives.

● ●

TRANSLATING SACRED TEXTS

The translation of sacred texts was the most formative influence in shaping modern translation theory. Many of the issues involved are the same ones that have characterized the secular traditions: debates over word-for-word versus sense-for-sense translation, content "versus" form, gender, the sacredness of the source material, the role of relay translation (translating not from the original sources but from translations), the elusiveness of the source text(s), the implications of translation by committee, and the politicization and ideology of translations, to name only a few.

WICLIF WRITING.

John Wycliffe translating the Bible into English, 1300s
Source: North Wind Picture Archives

Discussion

Discuss the issue of audience in translating sacred texts. Why do you think so many versions of certain canonical works exist? What motivates retranslation? Do you think contemporaneity is justified for a text type of this sort—that is, should an ancient devotional text sound like it was just written?

What do you think is the single most important factor in translating sacred texts? How high should the literary qualities of the target text rank versus its literal (verbatim) accuracy?

Research

1. Research how translators have had to communicate across vast cultural divides—what is sometimes called "radical translation." Are the images in a religious text changed wholesale to accommodate new audiences, for instance? Give examples.
2. What accounted for the tremendous resistance among the ancients about translating sacred texts? Look in particular at the issues of the use of vernacular tongues, the restricted access (by class or other privilege) to the source text, and the all-important belief in the divinity of a given source text. (Do a study in the field of comparative religion, examining these factors for more than one tradition.)

3. Many sacred texts were set down in writing, though emerged from, and for, largely oral cultures. What challenges does this fact pose for translation?

4. Trace how translations of sacred texts have influenced the general language of a population or the writing of a particular author.

Did you know that translators have been burned at the stake? Find out why. Also, find out what modern-day translators have been persecuted and why.

TRANSLATING TOURISM

The translation of tourism texts frequently involves negotiation of local cultural realities. What expectations do English-language readers have of such texts? What tends to characterize this language?

Tourism in Peru

Connect now to your **Manual** Web site to find the link to the Santuario Histórico Machu Picchu.

Individually, read the entire document, pages 1-5. Then in pairs, assuming a translation brief that directs you to translate for a well-educated, monolingual foreign traveler to the Peruvian ruins who is accessing the text online, circle all the words or phrases in the list that follows that you would use in producing your translation. You are not obligated to use any in a given set of options. Finally, compare in larger groups the words your pair chose. Remember to survey parallel texts; again, non-translated texts are most useful for this purpose.

four-eyed bear	channels
myopic bear	canals
Peru's national bird	permanent pluvial precipitations
rock hen	year-round rainfall
tunki	watchtower
Inca Highway	surveillance towers
Inka Royal Road	lookouts
Inca Trail	guardposts
pudú	pebbles
dwarf deer	boulders
agricultural terraces	disappearing species
stations	species in extinction
terraced fields	bromelias
sarunas	bromeliaceae

Debriefing

1. What would account for the differences in technical detail and functional tenor (what purpose language is meant to accomplish) in texts about Machu Picchu?

2. What accounts for the multiple spellings of "Machu Picchu" that exist?

3. Brainstorm with your partner about what special tasks and considerations might be involved in tourism and hospitality translation (e.g., translating for hotels, airlines, etc.). After generating a list, complement it by following up with searches of Web sites of agencies specializing in this domain.

Tourism in the United States

Recently, translators were commissioned by The Constitutional Foundation, Inc., in Philadelphia to translate materials out of English for its tours. Connect with your **Manual** Web site and use it to find the link to the foundation's site. The Constitutional™ Walking Tour of Philadelphia is described on the Web site as follows:

> The Constitutional Walking Tour of Philadelphia takes visitors on a walking journey through Independence National Historical Park, "Where Every Day is Independence Day!"™ Located in Center City Philadelphia, The Constitutional includes many sites within Historic Philadelphia, which is home to the Liberty Bell and Independence Hall. Since Philadelphia is best seen by foot, The Constitutional is the best way to explore America's Birthplace, taking you behind the scenes to the places where other tours cannot venture. Get up close with a High-Definition Historical Experience™ and see more than 20 historic sites in 75 minutes on a 1.25 mile outdoor walking adventure. Come see where The Declaration of Independence and The United States Constitution were created. The Constitutional is one of Philadelphia's "Top 25 Tourist Attractions" as ranked by the Philadelphia Business Journal and one of the leading providers of School Field Trips of Historic Philadelphia. Visitors can experience The Constitutional: 1) on their own as a free, self-guided walking tour, 2) with a lively tour guide for a fee, or 3) with the Philly MP3 Audio Tour. For more information on The Constitutional Walking Tour's various offerings, please visit www.TheConstitutional.com.

Task

Read the descriptions of six stops on this self-guided tour. As you read, consider the following: What skills or knowledge would the ideal translator for this job possess? What Spanish-speaking audiences could be expected to visit an attraction like this in Philadelphia? Where could you find out this information if you don't know? How would you describe the type and level of discourse of these texts? When you are through reading carefully, answer in pairs the questions that follow, and finally regroup to perform the class activities.

Source: Jonathan H. Bari for The Constitutional Walking Tour of Philadelphia

For our purposes, assume that the Spanish translation you produce would be used in audio *and* group tour scripts. Let's also assume that your contact gives you no further information about what Hispanophone countries the visitors are from (a logical premise because the tour is relatively new); you must deduce your likely audience.

Independence Hall Independence Hall, the birthplace of America, was built in 1732 as the Pennsylvania State House. Within this hallowed hall, the Second Continental Congress met in May 1775, and The Declaration of Independence was adopted on July 4, 1776. Independence Hall is also where the Constitutional Convention met to draft, debate and then sign The United States Constitution on September 17, 1787. **Note:** Every visitor to Independence Hall will need a free timed ticket, which you can get at the Independence Visitor Center on the morning of your visit, on a first-come, first-served basis. To reserve your tickets in advance for a small processing fee, call 800.967.2283 or log onto **http://reservations.nps.gov**.

Source: Jonathan H. Bari for The Constitutional Walking Tour of Philadelphia

The American Philosophical Society The American Philosophical Society was founded in 1743 as a home for thinkers about nature, machines, industry and governance. It was founded through the outgrowth of an idea fostered by Benjamin Franklin, and it is the oldest learned society in the United States. Today, the Society continues as an eminent scholarly organization of world-wide reputation, renowned for its excellence in scholarly research and publications, its library, its exhibitions and its international roster of elected members who make up a veritable "Who's Who" of outstanding individuals in the arts, humanities and the sciences. The Museum in Philosophical Hall

Source: Jonathan H. Bari for The Constitutional Walking Tour of Philadelphia

presents exhibitions and programs based on the Society's rich collection of art and artifacts. The museum is free and open to the public.

The Tomb of the Unknown Soldier The Tomb of the Unknown Soldier lies within Washington Square, one of the five public parks drawn up by William Penn in his 1682 blueprint for Philadelphia. In 1954, the Washington Square Planning Committee decided to erect a memorial that honored both George Washington and an unknown soldier from the Revolutionary War.

Source: Jonathan H. Bari for The Constitutional Walking Tour of Philadelphia

The Merchants' Exchange The Merchants' Exchange, designed by William Strickland in 1831, is the oldest stock exchange building in the United States. During President Andrew Jackson's first term in office, Philadelphia, along with the rest of America, was in the midst of an economic boom, and the building was a hub for financial and commercial activities.

Source: Jonathan H. Bari for The Constitutional Walking Tour of Philadelphia

The First Bank of the United States The First Bank of the United States was chartered by Congress and President Washington in 1791 under the direction of the Treasury Secretary, Alexander Hamilton. Architecturally, the First Bank of the United States building won wide acclaim upon its completion in 1797, and it is believed to be one of the first examples of Classical monumental design. The constitutionality of the First Bank of the United States sparked the first great debate between "strict constructionalists" and "loose constructionalists" regarding the interpretation of The United States Constitution.

Source: Jonathan H. Bari for The Constitutional Walking Tour of Philadelphia

The Bourse Building The Bourse Building, opened in 1895, was the first Commodities Exchange in the United States. The Bourse Building was the first in the world to simultaneously house a stock exchange, maritime exchange and grain-trading center. Be sure to visit The Bourse's souvenir shops and food court, which serves everything from cappuccino to world-famous Philadelphia cheesesteaks.

What general, recurrent issues for translation would be most pressing to solve for these short texts (e.g., how to deal with "x")?

What differences, if any, would you make in your translation for an audio translation (using MP3 software) of these texts versus a hard-copy brochure and map that the visitor carries?

Answer the translation questions that your instructor will now pose to you, or perform the assigned task. Depending on time constraints, the instructor may wish to have you do any of the following activities:

1. Gloss the text for problematic terms or passages
2. Translate a passage or two as a group
3. Discuss the strategies of translating certain terms ("Philadelphia cheesesteaks")
4. Focus on coherence, collocations, or "tourist boilerplate" in Spanish ("free and open to the public")
5. Prepare and then do sight translations in turns
6. Translate the whole text, workshop it, and do a revision

Research

What provisions has the Disney Corporation made for Spanish speakers in its customer relations?

Identify text types in the tourist industry that would need translation. (Are maps of any kind translated?)

Brochure for a restaurant in Puerto Vallarta, Mexico. Try a timed translation of this text unassisted by electronic or paper resources.

Source: Publicom, Inc.

Follow-Up

Find a menu posted online in Spanish; produce a bilingual menu, including appropriate formatting.

CULTURAL NOTE

Bilingual Toys

According to John Yunker, author of *Beyond Borders: Web Globalization Strategies*, toys have gone dual language: Fisher-Price® has brought out Dora the Explorer™ and Go, Diego, Go!™ talking toys that comment in English and Spanish. Vtech's ® Pink Nitro Notebook has Spanish activities for young readers (Connect with your **Manual** Web site and use it to find the link to the Going Global site.)

Magnetic Poetry®, to give another example, has a kit with words in Spanish on one side of magnetic tiles and English on the other.

Design a bilingual toy for any age group that would help prepare a future translator.

CASE STUDY: COLOR TERMS

Languages divide color names up differently, and perhaps even "see" them differently. (What do you think? Do more terms mean a greater discrimination of nuance? Or just a greater penchant for naming?) Not only are color boundaries different between languages, some languages have no names for somewhat basic colors common in other languages.

Modern European languages have more words than earlier, nonindustrial societies. Lehrer and Kittay, citing a study by Berlin and Kay, note that the cultural and technological advancement of a society determines the degree of evolution of its color terminology to a great extent, and that cultures evolve languages in order: black and white (which all cultures have); if they have a third color, it will be red; if a fourth, yellow or green; languages with five will have both; blue comes sixth, brown seventh; if eight or more, purple, pink, orange, and gray (1992, 153).

In addition to these issues, color terms are loaded with *connotations*. (Think of some examples in English and Spanish.)

Task: Translating Crayolas

Suppose that the executives at Crayola have hired you. They want to produce a commemorative series of their crayons using all the names their most famous product has had over the years (connect with your **Manual** Web site to find the link). Imagine that the crayons have not yet appeared in translation in more than 80 countries as they have; Mexico is to be among the test markets. Consider the names carefully. Render your assessment about the prospects for this job to the executives. Think about what *transcultural problems* this assignment poses. Use the language of the layperson to explain why this job has complications the initiators could not foresee. Propose examples of solutions on the micro and macro levels. (Don't forget to address issues of *coherence*: In many ways, the names constitute a *text*, among other reasons, for their semantic structure—how they relate to one another, and what experience the names reflect.) Finally, consider how a translation strategy might differ for a U.S. Latino market segment relative to a foreign market.

Did you consider issues of racial sensitivity?

Source and Target Gap Task: Board Game Instructions

1. Connect with your **Manual** Web site and use it to find the instructions to Scrabble®. Identify strategic issues for translation.
2. Then connect with your **Manual** Web site and use it to look at the rules to a Spanish edition of Scrabble®. (Does the Spanish edition of a board game have English-language instructions?)
3. Read through the two texts together: contents, word formation, scoring, how to win, and so on. Compare the issues you identified with the solutions given in the Spanish. What do you find?
4. Discuss in particular the issues involved in translating the word formation and scoring examples. Think in terms of what the pragmatic function of this section is. How were these sections handled in Spanish?

PERFORMANCE TESTING (EVERYDAY STRETCHES)

One of the ways that translations are tested is by seeing if the information they contain is *functional*; that is, that it can be translated into the intended action. This kind of evaluation is called **performance testing**.

What kinds of source texts do you think are best suited for performance testing?

One reason this sort of text is important to see is that it reminds you that *translation is involved in the physical world*, not just the plane of discourse. Texts become actions. Witness "Everyday Stretches" (see pages 314 and 315). This text is one of the most popular on the subject of basic stretches. It was produced as a poster for use in public places such as offices and gymnasiums. It is not intended for specialists. A Spanish translation actually exists but is not readily available.

Task

This activity is good fun. One person will be chosen as the volunteer. Qualifications: He or she should have no compunction about performing stretches in front of the group, have a good understanding of spoken Spanish, and have a sense of humor. Groups of three students each will be assigned selected stretches to prepare for a translation into Spanish. One person in each group will be group spokesperson/sight-translator. After preparations, the volunteer will perform the assigned stretches in turn according to each group's sight-translated instructions in Spanish. (Consider using a small blanket in class or go outside in the grass.) *The volunteer should only perform what is read and not interpret or helpfully supply movements in any way.* This will reveal any needed cohesion problems, for which the sight reader should adjust on the spot. The other groups will judge the effectiveness of each stretch (or its adequacy to the brief, which is to produce a translation for a poster of these stretches for nonspecialists in a U.S. public gymnasium). The volunteer may participate in the preparation phase or, alternatively, may be isolated until called on to perform the stretches sight unseen.

Everyday Stretches

For a free catalog of Stretching Inc. publications/products, contact: P.O. Box 767, Palmer Lake CO 80133-0767 or call 1-800-333-1307 fax (719)481-9058 or visit our website at www.stretching.com

Stretching can be done before and after activity or whenever you feel like it.

Note: If you have had any recent surgery, muscle or joint problem, please consult your personal health care professional before starting a stretching or exercise program.

How to Stretch:

Stretching should be done slowly without bouncing. Stretch to where you feel a slight, easy stretch. Hold this feeling for 5-20 seconds. As you hold this stretch, the feeling of tension should diminish. If it doesn't, just ease off slightly into a more comfortable stretch. The easy stretch reduces tension and readies the tissues for the developmental stretch.

After holding the easy stretch move a fraction of an inch farther into the stretch until you feel mild tension again. This is the developmental stretch which should be held for 5-20 seconds. This feeling of stretch tension should also slightly diminish or stay the same. If the tension increases or becomes painful, you are over-stretching. Ease off a bit to a comfortable stretch. The developmental stretch reduces tension and will safely increase flexibility.

Hold only stretch tensions that feel good to you. The key to stretching is to be relaxed while you concentrate on the area being stretched. Your breathing should be slow, deep and rhythmical. Don't worry about how far you can stretch. Stretch relaxed and limberness will become just one of the many by-products of regular stretching.

Do a light warm-up of walking or jogging for several minutes prior to stretching.

The dotted areas are those areas of the body where you will most likely feel the stretch.

1 Relax with your knees bent and the soles of your feet together. This comfortable position will stretch your groin. Hold this stretch for 30 seconds. For comfort, place a small pillow under your neck and head.

2 Interlace your fingers behind your head and rest your arms on the floor. Using the power of your arms, slowly bring your head and shoulders forward until you feel a slight stretch in the neck and upper back area. Think of elbows going toward mid-thighs. Hold an easy stretch for 5 seconds. Repeat three times. Do not over-stretch.

3 Shoulder Blade Pinch: From the bent-knee position, pull your shoulder blades together to create tension in the upper back area. (As you do this your chest should move upward.) Hold this controlled tension for 4-5 seconds, then relax and gently pull your head forward as shown in stretch #2. This will help release tension and allow the neck to be stretched effectively. Think of creating tension, relaxing the same area, then stretching the back of the neck to help keep the muscles of the neck free to move without tightness. Repeat 3-4 times.

4 With your head resting on the floor or mat, put one arm above your head (palm up) and the other arm down along your side (palm down). Reach in opposite directions at the same time to create a stretch for 8-10 seconds. Do both sides at least twice. Keep your lower back relaxed and flat. Do not hold your breath.

5 From a bent knee position, interlace your fingers behind your head and lift the left leg over the right leg. From here, use your left leg to pull your right leg toward the floor until you feel a good stretch. Stretch and relax. Keep the upper back, shoulders, and elbows flat on the floor. The idea is not to touch the floor with your right knee, but to stretch within your limits. Hold for 15-20 seconds. Repeat stretch for other side.

6 Next, straighten both legs and relax, then pull your left leg toward your chest. For this stretch keep the back of your head down, if possible, but don't strain. Hold an easy stretch for 30 seconds. Repeat, pulling your right leg toward your chest. Stretches hip and upper hamstrings. Breathe while stretching.

7 Bend your leg and with opposite hand, pull that bent leg up and over your other leg as shown above. Turn your head to look toward the hand of the arm that is straight (head should be resting on the floor). Make sure the back of your shoulders are kept flat on the ground. Now, using your hand on your thigh (resting just above the knee), pull your bent leg down toward the floor until you get the right stretch feeling in your lower back and side of hip. Keep feet and ankles relaxed. Hold a comfortable stretch for 15-20 seconds, each side. Do not hold your breath.

8 Straighten out your arms and legs. Point your fingers and toes as you stretch as far as you can. Stretch and then relax. This is a good stretch for the entire body. Hold for 5 seconds. Breathe.

9 Repeat stretch #1

10 Put the soles of your feet together with your heels a comfortable distance from your groin. With your hands around your feet slowly contract your abdominals to assist you in flexing forward until you feel an easy stretch in the groin. Make your movement forward by bending from the hips and not from the shoulders. If possible, keep your elbows on the outside of your lower legs for greater stability during the stretch. Hold a comfortable stretch for 20-30 seconds.

11 With your right leg straight put your left foot flat on the ground on the other side of your right knee. Reach over your left leg with your right arm so that your elbow is on the outside of your left leg. With your left hand resting on the ground behind you, slowly turn your head to look over your left shoulder, and at the same time, turn your upper body (but not your hips) toward your left hand and arm. Be sure to keep your right elbow and to gently push it against your bent leg. This will help create and stabilize the stretch. Hold for 5-15 seconds for each side. Stretches the outside of your upper leg and lower back.

12 To stretch the upper hamstrings and hip, hold on to the outside of your ankle with one hand, with your other hand and forearm around your bent knee. Gently pull the leg as one unit toward your chest until you feel an easy stretch in the back of the upper leg. (Make sure the leg is pulled as one unit so that stress is not put on the knee.) You may want to do this stretch while you rest your back against something for support. Hold for 15-20 seconds.

13 Lie on your left side and rest the side of your head in the palm of your left hand. Hold the top of your right foot with your right hand between the toes and ankle joint. Now move the front of your right hip forward by contracting the right butt (gluteus) muscles as you push your right foot into your right hand. This should stretch the front of your thigh. Hold an easy stretch for 10 seconds. Keep your body in a straight line.

14 Repeat stretches #12-14 for other leg.

15 Sitting, straighten your right leg, the sole of your left foot resting next to the inside of your straightened leg. Lean slightly forward from the hips and stretch the hamstrings of your right leg. Find an easy stretch and relax. If you can't touch your toes comfortably, use a towel to help you stretch. Hold for 20 seconds. Do not lock your knee. Your right quadriceps should be soft and relaxed during the stretch. Keep your right foot upright with the ankle and toes relaxed. Breathe relaxed.

Reproduced from the 22 1/2" x 34" poster. Revised edition ©2001 Robert A. Anderson & Jean E. Anderson. All rights reserved.

Source: EVERYDAY STRETCHES © 2001, by Bob Anderson, illustrated by Jean Anderson, Stretching Inc., Palmer Lake CO USA, www.stretching.com.

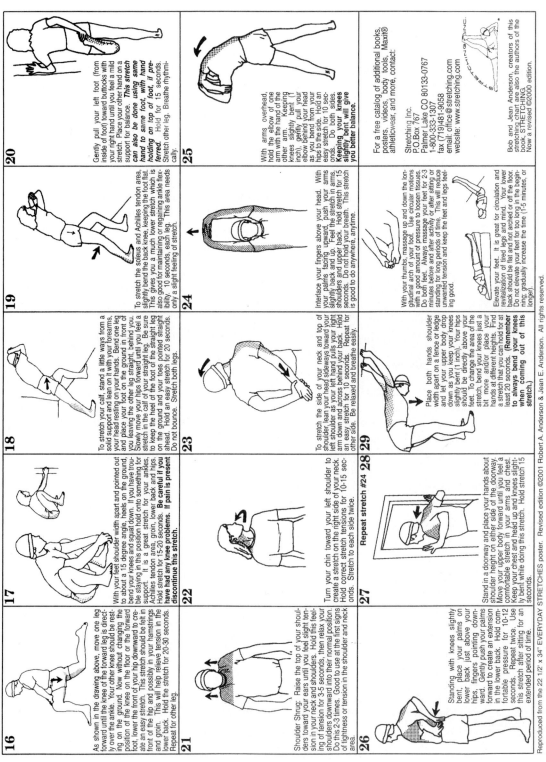

16
As shown in the drawing above, move one leg forward until the knee of the forward leg is directly over the ankle. Your other knee should be resting on the ground. Now without changing the position of the knee on the floor or the forward foot, lower the front of your hip downward to create an easy stretch. This stretch should be felt in front of the hip and possibly in your hamstrings and groin. This will help relieve tension in the lower back. Hold the stretch for 20-30 seconds. Repeat for other leg.

17

18
To stretch your calf, stand a little ways from a solid support and lean on it with your forearms, your head resting on your hands. Bend one leg and place your foot on the ground in front of you leaving the other leg straight, behind you. Slowly move your hips forward until you feel a stretch in the calf of your straight leg. Be sure to keep the heel of your straight leg on the ground and your toes pointed straight ahead. Hold an easy stretch for 20 seconds. Do not bounce. Stretch both legs.

19

20
Gently pull your left foot (from inside of foot) toward buttocks with your right hand until you feel a mild stretch. Place your other hand on a support for balance. *This stretch can also be done using same hand to same foot, with hand holding on top of foot, if preferred.* Hold for 15 seconds. Stretch other leg. Breathe rhythmically.

21
With your feet shoulder width apart and pointed out to about a 15 degree angle, heels on the ground, bend your knees and squat down. If you have trouble staying in this position hold onto something for support. It is a great stretch for your ankles, Achilles tendon area, groin, lower back and hips. Hold stretch for 15-20 seconds. **Be careful if you have had any knee problems. If pain is present discontinue this stretch.**

22
Shoulder Shrug: Raise the top of your shoulders toward your ears until you feel slight tension in your neck and shoulders. Hold this feeling of tension for 3-5 seconds, then relax your shoulders downward into their normal position. Do this 2-3 times. Good to use at the first signs of tightness or tension in the shoulder and neck area.

23
To stretch the side of your neck and top of shoulder, lean your head sideways toward your left shoulder as your left hand pulls your right arm down and across behind your back. Hold an easy stretch for 10 seconds. Repeat for other side. Be relaxed and breathe easily.

24
Interlace your fingers above your head. With your palms facing upward, push your arms slightly back and up. Feel the stretch in arms, shoulders and upper back. Hold stretch for 15 seconds. Do not hold your breath. This stretch is good to do anywhere, anytime.

25
With arms overhead, hold the elbow of one arm with the hand of the other arm. Keeping knees slightly bent (1 inch), gently pull your elbow behind your head as you bend from your hips to the side. Hold an easy stretch for 10 seconds. Do both sides. **Keeping your knees slightly bent will give you better balance.**

26
Standing with knees slightly bent, place your palms on lower back just above your hips, fingers pointing downward. Gently push your palms forward to create an extension in the lower back. Hold comfortable pressure for 10-12 seconds. Repeat twice. Use this stretch after sitting for an extended period of time.

27
Turn your chin toward your left shoulder to create a stretch on the right side of your neck. Hold correct stretch tensions for 10-15 seconds. Stretch to each side twice.

Repeat stretch #24 **28**

29
Place both hands shoulder width apart on a fence or ledge and let your upper body drop down as you keep your knees slightly bent (1 inch). Your hips should be directly above your feet. To change the area of the stretch, bend your knees just a bit more and/or place your hands at different heights. Find a stretch that you can hold for at least 20 seconds. **(Remember to always bend your knees when coming out of this stretch.)**

With your thumbs, massage up and down the longitudinal arch of your foot. Use circular motions with a good amount of pressure to loosen tissues. Do both feet. Always massage your feet for 2-3 minutes before and after activity or after sitting or standing for long periods of time. This will reduce unwanted tension and keep the feet and legs feeling good.

Elevate your feet. It is great for circulation and revitalization of tired legs and mind. Your lower back should be flat and not arched or off the floor. Do not elevate your feet for too long in the beginning; gradually increase the time (1-5 minutes, or longer).

To stretch the soleus and Achilles tendon area, slightly bend the back knee, keeping the foot flat. This gives you a much lower stretch which is also good for maintaining or regaining ankle flexibility. 10 seconds, each leg. This area needs only a slight feeling of stretch.

For a free catalog of additional books, posters, videos, body tools, Maxit® athleticwear, and more, contact:

Stretching Inc.
P.O. Box 767
Palmer Lake CO 80133-0767
1-800-333-1307
fax (719)481-9058
email: office@stretching.com
website: www.stretching.com

Bob and Jean Anderson, creators of this stretching chart are also the authors of the book STRETCHING. Now a revised ©2000 edition.

Reproduced from the 22 1/2" x 34" EVERYDAY STRETCHES poster.   Revised edition ©2001 Robert A. Anderson & Jean E. Anderson. All rights reserved.

Source: EVERYDAY STRETCHES © 2001, by Bob Anderson, illustrated by Jean Anderson, Stretching Inc., Palmer Lake CO USA, www.stretching.com.

Activity: Short Takes

1. Translate en>es the text "Congratulations! It's a boy!" and "Congratulations! It's a girl!" for a Texas retail chain's line of greeting cards and baby announcement novelties for sale in the San Antonio, Laredo, and Brownville areas.
2. Find 10 traffic signs, industrial safety signs, or street signs in Spanish (e.g., versions of Don't Be a Litterbug, No U-Turn). Sight translate them. Can you find at least one with no English-language equivalent?
3. As a project manager, you have been sent a poorly labeled and wayward file containing only the short text: "*Advertencia: peligro de asfixia.*" What kind of project could this text correspond to and what keywords in English would you search to find its matching English source text on your hard drive?
4. You've bid on Job #22366 posted on a site you frequent. The job is related to video games for a big agency (Bite the Wax Tadpole Translation Solutions). Its client needs the following three bits of dialogue retranslated immediately for licensing in Spain (the test audience did not react as hoped to the first versions done by another professional). Decide if they can be done without reference to the storylines, and whether you'd need to see the first drafts.

    a. "I'll use this voodoo cannonball to send my significant other to the significant *otherworld*!" (from Curse of Monkey Island)
    b. "Sonic Boom!" (from Street Fighter 2)
    c. "D'ya like haggis?" Dwarven demo-team (from Warcraft II)

    (InThe90s Web site)

5. You are working as an interpreter (who often have to work from scripts, sight read from forms, etc.); a health care practitioner has the results of an X-ray for a young deaf international student from Matamoros, Mexico, and wishes to communicate the following: "It looks like your wrist is not broken, only sprained. But let's have you immobilize it and stay off the computer for two weeks." Write out this medical advice to send in Spanish over the TDD/TTY to the patient, who is not present for the results.
6. An executive hires you to translate the in-store directory en>es for the entryway to a new local department store, Bricken Morter, in Chicago, Illinois. Here are the departments listed in the text:

Activewear	Juniors
Appliances	Lawn and Garden
Automotive	Men's Apparel
Baby	Outerwear
Clothing	Plus Sizes
Crafts and Scrapbooking	Sleepwear
Dorm Accessories	Tailgaiting
Fitness and Sports	Toddler
Home Accents	Underwear
Housewares	Wellness and Health

    a. Identify culture-bound terms. What is the likelihood they would be relevant outside the United States or have near-equivalents? Discuss. For U.S. Latino consumers, what degree of assimilation would be required for these terms or concepts to be meaningful in English or Spanish?

b. In groups, translate the directory, finding parallel texts where possible. One set of groups should translate for a U.S. Latino audience; the other, for a predetermined Spanish-speaking country. C316ompare versions. Would you argue that certain categories would simply not exist in certain foreign markets? Discuss.

WORKSHOP #10: PHILOSOPHY: *ENSIMISMAMIENTO Y ALTERACIÓN*

José Ortega y Gasset (1883–1955) was one of Spain's great philosophers of the twentieth century. Many of his books have been translated into English. Some of his best-known works in the English-speaking world include *Invertebrate Spain*, *The Dehumanization of Art*, *The Revolt of the Masses*, and *The Modern Theme*, and he is known for the idea that "Man has no nature," accepted as an Existentialist precept.

For this task we will look closely at parts of an essay, originally given as a *curso* (lecture), from 1939, and published in book form as *Ensimismamiento y alteración*. It has not appeared in English. After reading the passages, you will have a clearer idea of what the title refers to, though its translation will take some ingenuity. In the passages selected, Ortega is discussing the difference between human beings and *"nuestros primos, los monos"* to point up the two states alluded to in his title, and concludes with the idea of human existence as personal responsibility, as Becoming.

Brief: Translate for a book fair brochure, Web site, and exhibition catalogue on this philosopher, held in New York in 2010, 55 years after the author's death. The translation is for these commemorative publications, will represent a summary of the work, and thus will appear as an excerpt. You also would like to use the translation as part of a prospectus to gauge publisher interest in your translating the whole work.

NOTE These are all hypothetical events.

… La bestia, en efecto, vive en perpetuo miedo del mundo, y a la vez en perpetuo apetito de las cosas que en él hay y que en él aparecen, un apetito indomable que se dispara también sin freno ni inhibición posibles, lo mismo que el pavor. En uno y otro caso son los objetos y acaecimientos del contorno quienes gobiernan la vida del animal, le traen y le llevan como una marioneta. El no rige su existencia, no vive desde *sí mismo* sino desde *lo otro*, traído y llevado y tiranizado por *lo otro*, equivale a decir que el animal vive siempre alterado, enajenado, que su vida es constitutiva *alteración*.

… [E]l hombre puede, de cuando en cuando, suspende su ocupación directa con las cosas, desasirse de su derredor, desentenderse de él, y sometiendo su facultad de atender, a una torsión radical—incomprensible zoológicamente—, volverse, por decirlo así, de espaldas al mundo y meterse dentro de sí, atender a su propia intimidad o, lo que es igual, ocuparse de sí mismo y no de *lo otro*, de las cosas.

Con palabras, que de puro haber sido usadas, como viejas monedas, no logran ya decirnos con vigor lo que pretenden, solemos llamar a esa operación: pensar, meditar. Pero estas expresiones ocultan lo que hay de más sorprendente en ese hecho: el poder que el hombre tiene de retirarse virtual y provisoriamente del mundo, y meterse dentro de sí o dicho con un espléndido vocablo, que sólo existe en nuestro idioma: que el hombre puede *ensimismarse*.

... El animal es pura alteración. No puede ensimismarse. Por eso, cuando las cosas dejan de amenazarle o acariciarle; cuando le permiten una vacación; en suma, cuando deja de moverle y manejarle *lo otro* que él, el pobre animal tiene que dejar virtualmente de existir, esto es: se duerme. De aquí la enorme capacidad de somnolencia que manifiesta el animal, la modorra infrahumana, que continúa en parte en el hombre primitivo y, opuestamente, el insomnio creciente del hombre civilizado, la casi permanente vigilia—a veces, terrible, indomable—que aqueja a los hombres de intensa vida interior. No hace muchos años, mi grande amigo Scheler—una de las mentes más fértiles de nuestro tiempo, que vivía en incesante irradiación de ideas—, se murió de no poder dormir.

... Bien entendido, que esas dos cosas, el poder que el hombre tiene que sustraerse al mundo y el poder ensimismarse, no son dones hechos al hombre. Me importa subrayar esto para aquellos de entre ustedes que se ocupan de filosofía: no son dones hechos al hombre. *Nada que sea sustantivo ha sido regalado al hombre.* Todo tiene que hacérselo él.

(*Source:* Ortega y Gasset, José. Ensimismamiento y alteración, Meditación de la técnica. Buenos Aires/México: Espasa-Calpe Argentina, 1939.)

Word count: 442

Follow-Up

How would you characterize Ortega y Gasset's style? How could you tell his work apart from that of other philosophers you might have read?

Research

1. What have translators of Ortega y Gasset's work had to say about the challenges his work presents? Read some introductions and some translations of his long works and compare your impressions. Can you identify translator strategies that appear to be unique to philosophical texts?
2. What treatment has Ortega y Gasset's older contemporary, Miguel de Unamuno, received in English translation? In general, how soon after they published their Spanish texts was the translation "lag time"? Can one deduce more about the writer or about the age upon knowing how long before an author was translated?

Revising, Editing, and Proofreading

WORKFLOW AND REVISION

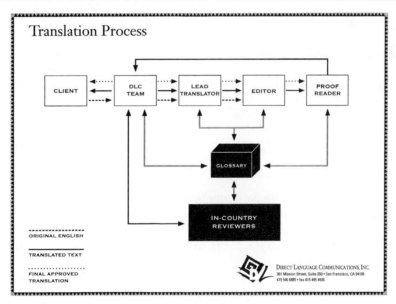

Source: Courtesy of Direct Language Communications

Remember our discussion of translation workflow in Chapter 1? Now let's revisit it from the point of view of proofreading and reviewing.

Study the graph of one organization's translation process. Follow the steps. See if you can visualize them better by acting out roles with your classmates, physically simulating the process.

QUALITY ASSESSMENT, QUALITY ASSURANCE, AND QUALITY CONTROL

Some key terms, as defined by Brian Mossop:

quality assessment: "A check of selected parts of a translation, often after delivery to the client, by someone other than the translator, to determine the degree to which professional standards . . . were met with respect to one or more *parameters*. No corrections are made. The result of the assessment may be quantified for such purposes as employee performance assessment and selection of freelances.

quality assurance: The whole of procedures applied before, during and after the translation production process, by all members of a translating organization, to ensure that quality objectives important to clients are being met. Objectives may pertain to quality of service (deadlines met, interaction with translation unit pleasant), quality of the physical product (layout, electronic form), and quality of the text (style suited to user and use, terminology, language quality).

quality control: Same as revision; checking all of a translation, or only part of it." (Mossop 2007, 168–9)

Do you think supervisors of translations need to be translators themselves?

Discuss what qualifies a person to judge a translation's merits.

Do you think editors and proofreaders should be bound by certain ethical principles? Discuss.

Task

Give a summary of the editing tools most commonly in use in the language industry today. See if you can evaluate the relative advantages and disadvantages of their features and for what kinds of jobs each is useful. You may wish to contact a translation editor for this task.

TESTING TRANSLATIONS

Larson (1984, 489) enumerates **five ways of testing a translation**:

1. *Comparison with the source text* (passage by passage probably best)
2. *Back-translation* (translating from the target to the source language)
3. *Comprehension checks* (others recount content or answer questions on it)
4. *Naturalness and readability testing* (reviewers check style, information load)
5. *Consistency checks* (terms, formatting, punctuation)

Task

1. Can you think of other ways, or an effective combination of any of these five, to test translations? What do you think is the most effective test of these five?
2. Assuming that you don't always have the testers, reviewers, and consultants to take part in the testing scenarios Larson describes (488), do you think there is a single best way to test any translation on your own (a self-check)?
3. For the sake of argument, could you critique one of these testing methods, pointing out its potential limitations or flaws?
4. What do you think the relationship (the order performed, importance, and thoroughness) of these three tasks is?

   - Thoroughly comparing the target to the source
   - "Spot checking" the target to the source
   - Reading the target without the source

Discuss as a class the degree to which these procedures are helpful. From your experience thus far, did it occur to you to read the target without comparing? What advantage did that bring? Is it detrimental to *only* proofread the target without comparing? What risks do you take in only checking this way? Bear these issues in mind for the next workshop text; take notes on which checks you use.

5. What does *functionality testing* in localization typically consist of?

6. Find a sampling of the Myers-Briggs personality test (or similar instrument) in English and Spanish and take it or administer it to a bilingual person. Compare the results. What might any discrepancies suggest? How could you determine a margin of error?

LINGUISTIC NOTE

READABILITY TESTING AND USABILITY TESTING

Two translation quality checks are **readability testing**, as Larson (1984) notes (see preceding), and **usability testing**. Readability testing is a metric of the difficulty level, concision, and amount of "fog" or confusing writing in a text. Usability testing is an index of the "ease with which users (readers) can access and assimilate information and then use it to complete their intended tasks . . ." (Byrne 2006, 92–4). Examples of domains where these checks are especially prevalent include software user guides, patient information materials (pharmaceuticals), and Web site localization.

TRANSLATION TEASER

Some Assembly Required

Find a somewhat complicated object with assembly required (10–15 steps). As a class, translate the directions into English from Spanish. A volunteer from outside the class (a random, unsuspecting victim passing down the hall; for example, an authority figure) can be brought in to follow the class's translated directions. For optimal suspense, don't show or tell your subject what he or she is assembling. Fun for almost everyone!

EVALUATING TRANSLATION QUALITY

Read the following source text, which is excerpted from an undergraduate textbook for U.S. students on Latin American civilization. Two translations (see next) are produced; their respective authors are in competition for a contract to do a book translation of the same work for undergraduate nonmajors.

ST:

Se cree que el carácter latinoamericano varía más por razones sociales, culturales y económicas que étnicas. Se pueden señalar, sin embargo, algunos rasgos muy extendidos: decencia, personalismo, machismo, compadrazgo [y otros].

La «decencia» o el temor al «qué dirán» se deriva del antiguo honor español. Las gentes de los sectores medios y altos de la sociedad se preocupan mucho por el grado de estimación y respeto que les tienen sus iguales y

superiores de la escala social. La obsesión por la decencia lleva a muchos a tener obstinadamente un nivel de vida superior al de sus medios económicos. La ambición de muchos para escalar posición social comienza con la imitación de los aspectos externos de la manera de vivir y de comportarse de la clase social inmediatamente superior. A veces la falsa interpretación de la decencia conduce a algunos a adoptar los aspectos más llamativos, decorativos y externos del estrato social considerado ideal.

El personalismo es el respeto o la admiración que el latinoamericano le tiene al individuo por su honor, valentía, liderazgo y otras cualidades espirituales propias que defiende a todo trance, aunque sea sacrificándose. Es una exaltación del «yo» que con orgullo el individuo defiende y los demás respetan.

Machismo es el culto a la concepción latinoamericana del macho: el hombre atrevido, con confianza en sí mismo, resoluto, de gran capacidad y actividad física y sexual. Se ha dicho que no todos los machos son caudillos pero eso sí, todos los caudillos deben ser machos.

Compadrazgo, como lo veremos más adelante, es la especial relación y obligación que se tienen los compadres (padres y padrinos del hijo de aquél) y los padrinos con sus ahijados. Es una extensión de los lazos sanguíneos y políticos para incluir a los que mediante el sacramento del bautismo ahora pertenecen al clan. El compadrazgo a veces se convierte en arma del ambicioso que desea escalar posiciones sociales, económicas y políticas. Se vale de su beneficio el que tiene menos. Lo usa más el que ambiciona más. Hay quienes creen que cuando se cierran las puertas de la justicia hay que empujar las puertas del compadrazgo. (Chang-Rodríguez 1991, 28–9)

Now, read TT1, a translation of the segment in bold, paying close attention to general strategy: How does the translator handle culture-bound, Spanish-language words? How does he or she handle tone? How accurate is the rendering? (Check line by line against the source.) How natural is the expression? Mark the text, summarizing your impressions.

TT1:
«Decency» or the fear of «what they will say» derives from the old Spanish honor. The peoples from medium and high sectors of society worry a lot about the grade of estimation and respect that they have for their equals and superiors of the social staircase. The obsession for the decency carries many to have obstinately a level of life superior to that of their economic means. The ambition of many to scale a social position begins with the imitation of the external aspects of the way of living of the immediately superior social class. Sometimes the false interpretation of decency leads some to adopt the most attractive, decorative and external aspects of the social stratus considered ideal.

Now read TT2, comparing against TT1 and the ST. Consider idiomaticity (naturalness of expression), accuracy, tone, comprehensibility. Write down your impressions.

TT2:
"*Decencia*", or respectability—the fear of "what the neighbors will say"—is rooted in the Spanish honor of old. People in the middle class and upper echelon of society are highly concerned about how well-thought-of and how respected they are in the eyes of their equals and betters in the social order. The obsession with respectability leads many to stubbornly enjoy a standard of living beyond their means. Many people's ambition to gain status begins by their imitating the outward appearances of the dress and behavior of the social class just above their own. Oftentimes a misunderstanding of *decencia* drives people to embrace the flashier, showier, superficial aspects of the social rank they hold as ideal.

Follow-Up

1. Which translation would you choose? Why? Make a final, formal recommendation about the two translators' work as if you were a consultant or acquisitions editor "vetting" it (appraising or checking it for accuracy). Be as specific as you can about strengths and weaknesses. Consider the notions of documental and instrumental.
2. How could you test the quality of each translator's work, assuming there were some questions in your mind about which translator to hire?
3. If you were to continue the strategy used in TT2, how would you handle *personalismo*, *machismo*, and *compadrazgo*, in context?
4. As a class, compare and contrast specific choices the TT1 and TT2 translators made. What would you do to improve TT2? TT1?
5. Given the brief, could any of the following expressions fit anywhere in the TT?: "to move up in the world"; "the pecking order"; "the totem pole"; "social hierarchy"; "status-seeking"; "social climbing"; "lifestyle"; "the high life"; "aping"; "idealize". Discuss each.

Activities

1. Do a gist translation of the whole passage provided (not simply the translation segment) as a single PowerPoint slide, as if you were going to present this information in summary to study-abroad candidates.
2. Do three translations of the last line of the passage under study (*"Hay quienes creen que cuando se cierran . . ."*), one keeping the image of the door in the TT, one modulating it, and one de-metaphorizing it (translating meaning with nonfigurative language). Discuss.

LINGUISTIC NOTE

THE PERSISTENT MYTH OF BACK TRANSLATION

Back translation as a classroom exercise surely has its proponents, as quite likely certain text-specific processes are laid bare and offer learning opportunities; in the field, however, back translation can present inaccurate views of translation quality whether used as a line of first or last defense.

Terminologist Sue Ellen Wright (2006) notes: "The new ASTM standard on translation quality, which is currently in ballot, has this to say about back translation: '3.1.3 *back translation*, *n*—retranslation of a translated text back into its source language.; 3.1.3.1 *Discussion—*A back translation will not result in a text that is identical to the source text, and furthermore, a back translation is not necessarily a good indicator of the quality of the translation.'" She concludes: "The one place that back translation is useful is when playing with poor-quality machine translation programs—it's really good for a laugh. . . . Clients who foolishly request it need to be educated."

Indeed if the translation were flawless, and the back translation monstrously poor, how would an unsuspecting client discover where the fault lay? Surely there are better ways to assess quality! Also, the *regressus infinitum* implied by back translation is inescapable: Will the back translation in turn be assessed? And then the back-back-translation?

In what other field would a product be tested by adding an unstable variable? To determine if a subject bears a likeness to a photograph, would you paint a portrait based on the photograph and then verify the portrait against the subject? Of course you wouldn't.

(Continued)

In sociological research methods, back translation is used as a matter of course, particularly with cross-cultural surveys and questionnaires. One alternative to back translations is the *multiple-forward translation* method, whereby more than one translation is made, and then the results triangulated and discussed. This methodology may prove equally burdensome but is more procedurally sound.

There is arguably one limited scenario in which back translation is unavoidable: as an information-only guideline for anyone in the document chain who has no knowledge of the source language (e.g., the front office in a country outside the language combination). In that event, back translations should be heavily annotated, particularly where choices are not obvious.

 A client has just asked you to back-translate a 10-page health questionnaire. With a partner, assume the roles of translator and uninformed client and discuss the implications of the assignment, and, if the client is amenable, possible alternatives. (Be aware that some clients have back translations performed as part of their standard procedure, even instituting back-translation teams.)

TRANSLATION TEASER

Punctuation

Two "Gestalt" puzzles that have made the rounds recently appear next; each reader will punctuate the phrases as he or she sees them. See what initial reading you give to each; when you finish, try to see them another way:

a woman without her man is nothing

señor muerto esta tarde llegamos

We resolve ambiguities according to our own mindset. What differences are there between how you punctuated the sentences and how your classmates did? Is there a difference between how the male students in the class saw the first one versus how the female students saw it? What context did you imagine for the second one? Can you see how others read these lines differently?

Translation Exercise: Punctuation

Punctuate the following source text (from an introductory study on grammatical analysis) grammatically and coherently; remember to place accents appropriately:

existen muchas definiciones del lenguaje pero casi todas pecan de unilaterales limitadas parciales pretenden definir y caracterizar el lenguaje basandose en alguno de sus muchos caracteres nada mas inutil el lenguaje por su propia naturaleza es una realidad muy compleja
(Onieva Morales 1985)

Now, translate the passage for an introductory text. Pay particular attention to cohesion: What clarifications or additions have to be made? Have you avoided false cognates and unreliable cognates?

Summarize the key differences in Spanish and English punctuation. In what domains do these differences weigh heaviest? Discuss: should punctuation always disambiguate?

Editing Interlanguage

Edit the personal correspondence below from "Ramón," who is not a native speaker of English. Use a familiar tone, assume a present-day receiver, and strive for idiomaticity (natural syntax and diction). After rewriting the English, translate the letter into Spanish so Ramón can see the interference and learn from his mistakes.

> My esteemed friend:
>
> It is to be lamented that it should not be possible for us to encounter ourselves. The truth is that I don't give any more with one thing and another.
>
> In the past proximate week I have engaged in the tramitations to put a little society of limited responsibility with a friend. Something modest, you understand, in the line of importation, with a little section in which we will occupy ourselves with properties. If it runs it will be something good.
>
> The secretary I have called by the phone several times. Disgracefully every time I have arranged to encounter myself with her I have had to do. The other day I told her to make herself presentable and I would take her to eat someplace. What do you think—my watch wasn't well and I arrived a little retraced—three hours, I think.
>
> Until soon, Ramón

(*Source:* Child, Jack. Lesson 16 supplemental exercises to *Introduction to Spanish Translation* [unpublished ms., 2001]. Lanham, Md.: University Press of America, 1992. Reprinted by permission of Jack Child.)

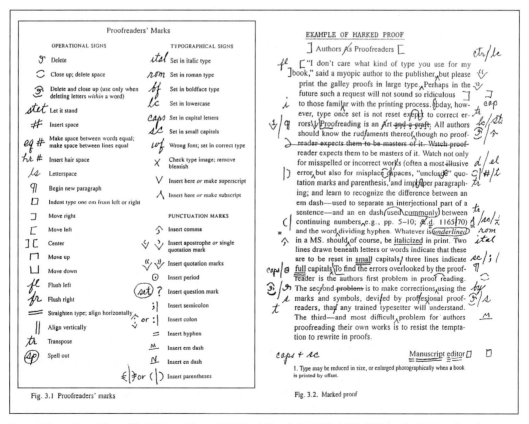

Fig. 3.1 Proofreaders' marks

Fig. 3.2. Marked proof

Source: Reproduced from *The Chicago Manual of Style*, 14th ed. (c) 1969, 1982, 1993 by the University of Chicago Press.

TRANSLATION TEASER

Evaluate the Spanish version of the New York State Department of Motor Vehicles Web site (connect with your **Manual** Web site to find the link). Once logged on, go to: >español, then > Continúe en español.

Editing Task: Nobel Prize Toast

For this task, you will be editing the English translation of a Nobel Prize toast slated to appear in an English-language newspaper in Mexico City for an upcoming special Sunday feature on the author of the piece, Octavio Paz (1914–1998). The audience is to be primarily U.S. expatriates. These were Paz's words to the Academy on December 10, 1990, upon receipt of the Nobel Prize in Literature. Pay special attention to errors in the English—they may include coherence, intratextual or intertextual referents, collocations or another type of usage problem, and syntax. Edit using proofreading symbols, and mark directly on the target text itself. Assume that the text will be returned to the original translator. Because other versions exist—for example, the one published in *Vuelta* magazine, be sure that the translator has worked from the same authoritative source text (see later).

ST:

Seré breve, sin embargo, como el tiempo es elástico, ustedes tendrán que oírme durante ciento ochenta largos segundos.

Vivimos no sólo el fin de un siglo, sino de un período histórico. ¿Qué nacerá del derrumbe de las ideologías?

¿Amanece una era de concordia universal y de libertad para todos o regresarán las idolatrías tribales y los fanatismos religiosos, con su cauda de discordias y tiranías? Las poderosas democracias que han conquistado la abundancia en la libertad ¿serán menos egoístas y más comprensivas con las naciones desposeídas? ¿Aprenderán éstas a desconfiar de los doctrinarios violentos que las han llevado al fracaso? En esa parte del mundo que es la mía, América Latina y especialmente México, mi patria: ¿alcanzaremos al fin la verdadera modernidad, que no es únicamente democracia política, prosperidad económica y justicia social, sino reconciliación con nuestra tradición y con nosotros mismos?

Imposible saberlo. El pasado reciente nos enseña que nadie tiene las llaves de la historia. El siglo se cierra con muchas interrogaciones. Algo sabemos, sin embargo; la vida en nuestro planeta corre graves riesgos. Nuestro irreflexivo culto al progreso y los avances mismos de nuestra lucha por dominar a la naturaleza se han convertido en una carrera suicida. En el momento en que comenzamos a descifrar los secretos de las galaxias y las partículas atómicas, los enigmas de la biología molecular y los del origen de la vida, hemos herido en su centro a la naturaleza. Por esto, cualesquiera que sean las formas de organización política y social que adopten las naciones, la cuestión más inmediata y apremiante es la supervivencia del medio natural. Defender a la naturaleza es defender a los hombres.

Al finalizar el siglo, hemos descubierto que somos parte de un inmenso sistema —o conjunto de sistemas— que va de las plantas y los animales a las células, las moléculas, los átomos y las estrellas. Somos un eslabón de "la cadena del ser", como llamaban los antiguos filósofos al universo. Uno de los gestos más antiguos del hombre —un gesto que desde el comienzo, repetimos diariamente— es alzar la cabeza y contemplar, con asombro, el cielo estrellado. Casi siempre esa contemplación termina con un sentimiento de fraternidad con el universo. Hace años, una noche en el campo mientras contemplaba un cielo puro y rico de estrellas, oí entre las hierbas oscuras el son metálico de los élitros de un grillo. Había una extraña correspondencia entre la palpitación nocturna del firmamento y la musiquilla del insecto. Escribí estas líneas:

> Es grande el cielo
> y arriba siembran mundos.
> Imperturbable,
> prosigue en tanta noche
> el grillo berbiquí.

Estrellas, colinas, nubes, árboles, pájaros, grillos, hombres: cada uno en su mundo, cada uno un mundo —y no obstante todos esos mundos se corresponden. Sólo si renace entre nosotros el sentimiento de hermandad con la naturaleza, podremos defender a la vida. No es imposible: fraternidad es una palabra que pertenece por igual a la tradición liberal y a la socialista, a la científica y a la religiosa.

Alzo mi copa —otro antiguo gesto de fraternidad— y brindo por la salud, la ventura y la prosperidad de Sus Majestades y del noble, gran y pacífico pueblo sueco.

(*Source: Les Prix Nobel. The Nobel Prizes 1990*, Editor Tore Frängsmyr, [Nobel Foundation], Stockholm, 1991, Octavio Paz's speech at the Nobel Banquet. © The Nobel Prize Foundation 1990.)

TT:

Your Majesties, Ladies and Gentlemen:

I profoundly, though not fearlessly, appreciate that I have been entrusted with the difficult task of speaking before you this evening. I will attempt to be brief, and not waste these precious moments with circumlocutions that serve no end.

We are living not only the end of a century but of an historical period. What will be born of the collapse of ideologies? Will we see the dawning of a new age of universal harmony and freedom for all, or will tribal idolatries and religious fanaticism return, in all their abundant discord and tyranny? The powerful democracies who have won abundance in freedom, will they be less self-possessed and more understanding toward the disposed nations? Will the latter learn to distrust violent doctrines that have led them to failure? And in that part of the world that I call my own, Latin America, and especially in Mexico, my country, we will finally achieve true modernity, which is not only political democracy, economic prosperity and social justice, but reconciliation with our tradition and with ourselves? Impossible to know. The recent past has taught us that no one holds the keys to history. This century comes to a clothes with many question marks.

However, this much we do know: life on our planet is running serious risks. Our thoughtless cult of progress and the very advancements in our struggle to master nature have become a suicide run. The moment we begin to unravel the secrets of the galaxies and atomic particles, the riddles of molecular biology and those of the origin of species, we have wounded the very heart of nature. Therefore, whatever forms of political and social organization nations may have adopted, the most immediate and pressing issue is the survival of the natural setting. To defend the natural setting is to defend human beings.

In the final years of this century we have discovered that we are part of a vast system—or a totality of systems—that run from the plants and animals to the cells, molecules, atoms and stars. We are a link in "the Network to Be", as the philosophers of old used to call the Universe. One of the oldest gestures known to man—a gesture which, from the beginning, we repeat daily—is to raise our eyes a loft and, in wonderment, contemplate the starry havens. Nearly always this contemplation ends in a feeling a fraternity with the university. Years ago, one night in the country, while I was contemplating a clear and star-spangled sky I heard among the dark grass the cricketing of cricket wings. There was a strange correspondence between the nocturnal palpitation of the heavens and the insect's little music. I wrote these lines:

> Es grande el cielo
> y arriba siembran mundos.
> Imperturbable,
> prosigue en tanta noche
> el grillo berbiquí.

Stars, hills, clouds, trees, birds, crickets, men: each one in his world, each one a world—and there is a two-way street of sympathy between all those worlds. If only the feeling of brotherhood with nature is reborn among us, we defend life. It is not impossible: brotherhood with nature is reborn a word that belongs equally to the liberal and the socialist traditions, to the scientific and the religious.

I lift up my glass—another ancient gesture of fraternity—and toast to the health, happiness and prosperity of Your Lord and Ladyships and the noble, grand and peace-loving people of Switzerland.

TRANSLATION TIP

Many editors will use a "?" after a suggestion in the margin—not to show uncertainty, but as a convention for offering an improvement.

TRANSLATION TIP

Parataxis and Hypotaxis

Leland Wright notes (2006, 12–13): "Aside from the lexicon/terminology and certain grammatical conventions, one major difference between Spanish and English is the way that ideas are commonly joined to form sentences and paragraphs. English speakers tend to state a point directly and then develop it with *parataxis*, that is, loose joining of simple clauses with coordinating conjunctions and sentence adverbials. Spanish speakers, however, tend toward a less abrupt start and prefer to link ideas through *hypotaxis*, i.e., embedded clauses with subordinating conjunctions. For example, compare the following examples of an English sentence followed by two Spanish counterparts. The first of these is fully grammatical but sounds/reads like a less typical Spanish utterance than the second one with hypotaxis.

English: We must quickly find means of coordination and cooperation in trade policy, or many countries will face new, insurmountable difficulties.

Spanish 1: Debemos encontrar pronto medios de coordinación y cooperación en políticas de intercambio, o muchos países enfrentarán nuevas e insuperables dificultades.

Spanish 2: Si no encontramos pronto medios de coordinación y cooperación en lo que a políticas de intercambio se refiere, muchos países enfrentarán nuevas e insuperables dificultades."

What other discourse features distinguish Spanish from English?

(*Source:* Text courtesy of Dr. Leland Wright)

¿?

Have you ever stopped to consider how gender agreement in Spanish helps create coherence? Consider:

ST: *Hay tumbas debajo de los palacios, las cuales fueron saqueadas antiguamente.*

TT: Tombs lie under the palaces, which were sacked in former times.
The ST is clear—the tombs were sacked, not the palaces. In the TT, it is difficult with this construction to make "which" refer to "tombs." Thus the relative disadvantage of English—antecedents cannot be clarified with number and gender as they can in Spanish. Solution? Recast:

TT2: Under the palaces lie tombs, which were sacked in former times.
Can you offer another recasting that would work?

TEXTURE: COHESION AND COHERENCE

Texture (Halliday and Hasan 1976, 2) comprises **cohesion** and **coherence**, two qualities of a text that allow it to "hang together" and make sense. Cohesion—"cohesive markers"—may take the form of sound patterns, semantic relations, lexical items, anaphora and other repetitions, conjunctions (include cause and effect expressions), and constitute intertextuality and *intra*textuality that organize a text (Malmkjær 2005, 139). We have already looked at collocation (in Chapter 3), one type of cohesive tie across one text or many.

Task

Malmkjær (2005, 139) gives a helpful example of a text extract that uses many cohesive ties. To take it one step further, let's present the text out of order. Even further, we'll break certain sentences down into clauses. Following is your task:

1. Put the text back in order, sequencing the passages by number in the order they should be read.
2. Identify how the cohesive ties led you to arrive at the proper sequencing.
3. Discuss what patterns of cohesion might differ in Spanish translation, or at least what resources Spanish has to maintain coherence while avoiding redundancy.

You may find it easiest to work this task out on scratch paper.

HINT Read it out loud.

1. —and this will take time.
2. which we shall not be in a position to understand until we have examined some problems about definition in general,
3. and that is one of the things we shall endeavor to do in this chapter.
4. But the term 'philosophy' cannot be defined as easily as 'chemistry', 'biology', or 'sociology'.
5. It will be preferable to show, in the course of our investigations,
6. that should first be weighed as carefully as possible.
7. even conflicting, definitions of the term;

8. At the beginning of any systematic discussion one is expected to define terms,
9. and if we presented a definition at the outset,
10. are special difficulties about the definition,
11. *why* scholars in the field have suggested different definitions
12. and our principal term is 'philosophy'.
13. For one thing, people working in the field they call philosophy have offered very different,
14. we would be running the great risk of making a premature judgment on a matter
15. Second, and more important,

Text passages in order: ____ ____ ____ ____ ____ ____ ____ ____ ____ ____ ____ ____ ____ ____ ____

(Malmkjaer 2005; Hospers 1967; Halliday and Hasan 1976)

Activity: Mastering from Two Versions

Read the following pairs of translations of selected passages from the *multifuncionales wireless* article. First locate the ST passages; then discuss translation "chunks" that are likely misreadings for the context given; use process of elimination. Continue comparing and editing the versions into one, *forming a master version from the two*. OJO: You are not obligated to use any segments of either translation, nor are you being asked to choose between them. Brief: *Advertising Age*, U.S. audience, present year.

Connect with your **Manual** Web site to find the article ("Multifuncionales: el boom del todo en uno").

TT1: In addition to their easy usability, it can be said in their defense that they are eco-friendly—paperless—thus saving trees from being felled, and also space for storing hard copies. Taking nothing away from these important considerations, the printer market enjoys excellent health and grows apace.

TT2: In addition to their affordability, they do not use paper, thus saving trees, and also the space that would be needed for storing the printouts. These arguments, while important, have not stood in the way of the booming printer market.

TT3: They have been embraced quickly as it has penetrated the market, since the printers have kept up their quality, but have notoriously augmented their performance. And this has allowed them to make texts, data sheets, presentations, all while printing photographs for the same price as before.

TT4: The printers have quickly overcrowded the market, since their resolution is still the same, but famously, their features on offer are as well. Thus you can do text files, spreadsheets, presentations, and still print pictures for the same low price.

TT5: In October, HP has just rolled out its new line of image and printing products for home-based consumers and small and medium enterprise. The new printers that have been launched include models for clients' different needs:

from the simple and easy-to-use for the customer that merely wants to print, to photographic-quality printers for a more knowledgeable public.

TT6: HP brought out its new home-based-consumer-centric portfolio of image and printing products that is also for small and medium-sized business solutions in October. Among the new printers are models for different customer needs: from the simple and user-friendly for the customer who merely wants to meet his printing needs, to photo-quality printers for a more sophisticated clientele.

TRANSLATION TRAP

Differing Conventions for Citations

In American culture, citation of sources tends to be both more thorough and more codified than in some other cultures, where in some cases it is common for the author's name to be given, and a quote, but no other source. Translators should be on guard against accepting work—book translations—that may require extensive bibliographic sourcing, correcting, or supplementing of missing or inaccurate data—this can be extremely time-consuming.

Editing: Various

1. a. Come up with editorial policies for the translation of block quotes (indented long quotes) in a piece of writing. When should they be translated, when not, in what kinds of texts, for what readerships?

   b. Now read the following passage from literary critic Leo Spitzer's "Linguistics and Literary History" (1948); the bracketed comment is a subsequent note from his editors. Read, discuss, and assess Spitzer's strategy of nontranslation and his editors' addition; critique from the point of view of your policy (see earlier). Spitzer first notes that his many untranslated foreign language quotations may prove difficult for the English-language reader but offers the defense that he wishes to consider the poets' exact wording, and because the

   > convincingness and rigor of my stylistic conclusions depends entirely upon the minute linguistic detail of the original texts, it was impossible to offer translations. [Since the linguistic range of readers of literary criticism is not always as great as Spitzer's, the editors of this volume decided to provide translations.] (Apter 2004)

2. Connect with your **Manual** Web site to find the Spanish Web site for eXpansys (XPS), an online multinational retailer of portable communications. (Note that the Mexican office is based in Bloomington, Illinois!) Once there, choose a product; on the menu bar reading "*Página principal,*" "*Descripción,*" "*Accesorios,*" "*Ofertas,*" *y* "*Foro,*" click on "*Descripción*" and copy the specs. Then, click on eXpansy's UK site. Find the same

product and repeat the procedure. Print the product description on separate pages and bring them to class.

With a partner in class, you are going to challenge your classmate to sight read the text (en>es) with new information you provide, with the catch that he or she has to recognize where in the target text the updates go. The new information—which may be updated functions, numbers, features, and such—will be provided before the sight reading *only in the target language* by you, in the role of the translation initiator. The updater "spot checks" as the translator sight reads; at no point should the sight translator see the target text. Naturally, in preparation for this activity, each partner should have read the sites carefully to become current with this technology.

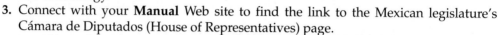

3. Connect with your **Manual** Web site to find the link to the Mexican legislature's Cámara de Diputados (House of Representatives) page.

Your client has asked you to run a diagnostic check of the site's monolingual glossary against a translator's bilingual glossary (both shown later). The information will be used to create a parallel corpus, so the matches must be authenticated. Audience: U.S. jurists and scholars. Fill in missing information, delete any extraneous information, and correct any errors. The English glossary should correspond to these glossary entries only.

es<>en

Pleno <> plenary session; plenary meeting; full membership

Cámara de Dipultos <> Chamber of Deputies

para la integración del quórum <> to constitute a quorum

integrantes <> members

sesionar <> to be in session

competencia <> bailiwick

Comisión <> Committee

elaboración <> elaboration

en su seno <> in the heart of the legislature

dictamen <> ruling

punto de acuerdo <> memorandum of understanding

Minuta <> bill; abstract; minutes; draft

efectos correspondientes <> effects

promulgación [de una minuta] <> promulgating [of a bill]

Follow-Up

1. Evaluate the English pages of the *Cámara de Diputados* site, including the glossary. Edit.

2. After doing the task yourself, imagine that you're an agency representative scouting for a qualified freelance translator, a specialist, who, let's suppose, you might want to hire for future work in this area. Time your search, and defend your choice to your classmates. Balance these criteria as you judge them in each candidate: cost, quality, and translator reliability, expertise, and professionalism.

STYLE SHEETS AND STYLE GUIDES

Style sheets and style guides are used in agencies, international organizations, and publishing houses.

Task

Research several examples of these important documents and answer the following questions:

1. What are style sheets used for in this industry? Who develops them? Who uses them? Are they the same across languages?
2. What might a style sheet include? List at least 10 important features.
3. Does a style guide prescribe *specific* choices when several obvious ones exist?
4. What published style guides (e.g., *APA*, *Chicago Manual of Style*) take precedence in journal and book publishing and in what respective fields?
5. Is "writing for translation" a category in any style guides that you can find? What domains does this writing technique seem to most concern?
6. Find out where *writing for translation* is being done, what it is exactly, who is doing it, and why. Check in your library's electronic databases as well.

CASE STUDY: WORLD BANK TRANSLATION STYLE GUIDE

Connect with your **Manual** Web site to find the link to the World Bank site and answer the following:

1. What does the disclaimer on World Bank documents say about which document is in force if there is an inconsistency between the English and the translation?
2. For press releases, what does the "Embargoed" header mean?
3. Can footnote references go in the middle of a sentence?

Now substitute the word "Spanish" in the Web address, download the file, and answer the following:

1. Should translated letters beginning "Dear Governor" read "*Estimado Gobernador:*"?
2. Should the report entitled *Las condiciones para la inversión y el Grupo del Banco Mundial* appear in all capitals?
3. Does the guide distinguish between *siglas* and acronyms, or are they the same?
4. What's the difference between *1.000 millones* and *un billón*? (Note: This is *very* important for a translator.)
5. Is it still all right to use *países en vías de desarrollo* as a polite term for "developing countries"?

NOTE   The European Commission has a style guide that may be of interest to students. Connect with your **Manual** Web site to find the link to its site.

Inferencing Task

Find a professional translation on any topic, at least 20 to 30 pages in length. Inferring back to a hypothetical style guide, give 10 to 15 guidelines that must have governed the translation.

Mission Statement Task

Translate the World Bank mission statement that follows en>es (20 minutes). Then compare the Spanish pdf and annotate for comment in class.

Mission Statement

Our dream is a world free of poverty.

Our Mission

To fight poverty with passion and professionalism for lasting results.

To help people help themselves and their environment by providing resources, sharing knowledge, building capacity, and forging partnerships in the public and private sectors.

To be an excellent institution able to attract, excite, and nurture diverse and committed staff with exceptional skills who know how to listen and learn.

Our Principles

Client centered, working in partnership, accountable for quality results, dedicated to financial integrity and cost-effectiveness, inspired and innovative.

Our Values

Personal honesty, integrity, commitment; working together in teams—with openness and trust; empowering others and respecting differences; encouraging risk-taking and responsibility; enjoying our work and our families.

(*Source:* Text courtesy of the World Bank)

Editing Exercises: Scientific Style*

According to Woodford (1986), four rules (guidelines) in writing, (self-)editing, and translating scientific prose are:

1. Be simple, concise, and jargon-free wherever you can.

   For example: "In studies pertaining to the identification of phenolic derivatives, drying of the paper gives less satisfactory visualization." ->>>

   "Phenolic derivatives are more easily seen and identified if the paper is left wet."

2. Make sure of the meaning of every word; clarify grammar.

   Pitfalls: Dangling participles:

   Unobjectionable: "The experiment was performed using redistilled solvents."

   Misleading: "Chromatography fractions were sampled, followed by UV measurement, and dried."

   Ludicrous: "After closing the incision, the animal was placed in a restraining cage."

   Dangling infinitives:

   "The flask was flushed with nitrogen to remove ozone." (Implied subject of "remove" is the experimenter, not "flask".) Solution: ->>>> Insert a true subject: "We flushed the flask with nitrogen (in order) to remove excess ozone."

---

* Modification of Woodford, *Scientific Writing for Graduate Students*. Bethesda, MD: Council of Biology Editors, 1986.

3. Use *verbs* instead of abstract nouns, noun phrases, gerunds, participles.

   For example: "The separation of A from B was effected." ->>>> "A was separated from B."

4. Break up noun clusters and stacked modifiers.

   Watch more than two nouns together or even one modifier of a two-noun cluster.

   OK: "liver disease" (= "disease of the liver")

   Not good: "heavy beef heart mitochondria protein" (which does "heavy" modify—the beef, the heart, the mitochondria, or the protein?)

Your instructor may wish to give you flawed scientific writing to revise. What other tendencies in this kind of writing tend to inhibit communication?

Activity: Translation Portfolio

Find the three or four tasks on which you consider you have done your best work over the semester(s). Include a balance of different domains and text lengths. Reread them. Present them in a translation portfolio that showcases your growing competence.

TRANSLATION MARKETPLACE ANALYSIS

It is fitting now to return to the job search and other vocational issues, which you previewed in Chapter 1. Your instructor will revisit some of the issues involved in order to bring you closer to market readiness.

Activity: Translation Survey

In Chapter 1, you took a self-assessment survey about your skills and propensities as they relate to translation. Your instructor will hand out the same survey now. Without looking back on your responses, fill out the survey again. Compare your answers now to your first answers. With a partner, interview one another about what knowledge and self-knowledge translation has given you, and in what ways your thinking has changed. Talk about your goals in the language industry, what translation may hold for each of you now and in the future.

TRANSLATION TIP

Professionalism

Translation as a human activity is age-old, but as a profession it is still in its formative years. Everyone who joins the field bears some of the responsibility for seeing that translators and their work are valued in the marketplace, that knowledge is passed on, and that clients know as much as possible about what goes into quality translation work. Professional behavior is our obligation to future professionals and to the health of the practice; let's all contribute to the profession's profile by working with integrity.

WORKS CITED

Acuña Ortega, Víctor Hugo. "The Formation of the Urban Middle Sectors in El Salvador, 1910–1944." In *Landscapes of Struggle: Politics, Society and Community in El Salvador*, ed. A. Lauria-Santiago and L. Binford. Pittsburgh, Pa.: University of Pittsburgh Press, 2004.

Administración Federal de Seguridad de Autotransportes. "Excepciones y Exenciones. Operaciones de Campos Petroleros." <http://www.fmcsa.dot.gov/spanish/pdfs/tm_hos_sp_ppt_index.htm>, Accessed April 11, 2009.

Aguilú de Murphy, Raquel. *Los textos dramáticos de Virgilio Piñera y el teatro del absurdo*. Madrid: Pliegos, 1989.

Aixelá, Javier Franco. "Culture-Specific Items in Translation." In *Power, Translation, Subversion*, ed. Román Àlvarez and M. Carmen-Àfrica Vidal. Clevedon, England: Multilingual Matters, 1996.

Allende, Isabel. *Cuentos de Eva Luna*. Buenos Aires: Editorial Sudamericana, 1990.

Alurista. "Address." *Xroads*. American Studies at the University of Virginia. <http://xroads.virginia.edu/~UG01/voss/address.html>, Accessed May 21, 2007.

Alvarez, Antonia. "On Translating Metaphor." *Meta* 38.3 (1993): 479–490.

American Literary Translators Association. "Breaking into Print." Dallas: University of Texas at Dallas, 2007. <http://www.utdallas.edu/alta/resources/breakingintoprint.html>, Accessed May 3, 2009.

Anaya, Rudolfo. *Bless Me, Ultima*. New York: Warner Books, 1994.

Andrés, P., Juan Pablo. "Multifuncionales: el boom del todo en uno." Publimark: Revista de Marketing, Comunicación y Publicidad. Holanda Comunicaciones, S.A. <http://www.publimark.cl/index.asp?id=133&id_edicion=26>, Accessed May 8, 2009.

Apter, Emily S. "Global Translation." In *Debating World Literature*, ed. C. Prendergast, 76–109. London/New York: Verso, 2004.

Asociación Americana de Juristas. "Juicios a los militares: documentos secretos, decretos, leyes y jurisprudencia del juicio a las juntas militares." *Cuadernos* 4 (1988). Published by Equipo Nizkor on the Web de Desaparecidos.

Asturias, Miguel Ángel. *El señor presidente*. Buenos Aires: Editorial Losada, 1946.

———. *El señor presidente*. Trans. Frances Partridge. New York: Atheneum, 1963.

Baker, Mona. *In Other Words: A Coursebook on Translation*. New York: Routledge, 1992.

Baker, Mona, G. Francis, and E. Tognini-Bonelli, eds. "Corpus Linguistics and Translation Studies: Implications and Applications." In *Text and Technology: In Honour of John Sinclair*. Philadelphia: John Benjamins, 1993, 233–50.

Baker, Mona, and Kirsten Malmkjær, eds. *Routledge Encyclopedia of Translation Studies*. New York: Routledge, 1998.

Batchelor, Ron, and Christopher Pountain. *Using Spanish: A Guide to Contemporary Usage*. New York: Cambridge University Press, 2005.

"The Beaufort Wind Scale." Excerpted from the *Observers Handbook*, Met Office. 1999. <http://www.zetnet.co.uk/sigs/weather/Met_Codes/beaufort.htm>, Accessed April 26, 2009.

Beeby Lonsdale, Allison. *Teaching Translation from Spanish to English: Worlds beyond Words*. Ottawa: University of Ottawa Press, 1996.

Belda Medina, José R. *El lenguaje de la informática e Internet y su traducción*. Alicante, Spain: Publicaciones de la Universidad de Alicante, 2003.

Beowulf: A New Verse Translation. Trans. Seamus Heaney. New York: W. W. Norton, 2001.

Berk-Seligson, Susan. *The Bilingual Courtroom: Court Interpreters in the Judicial Process*. Chicago: University of Chicago Press, 2002.

Bilboa, Luis. "Apoyo internacional para Ernesto Villegas" aporrea.org. 2002. February 13, 2004. <http://www.aporrea.org/actualidad/a6839.html>, Accessed June 1, 2009.

Biology-Online.org. Scientific American Partner Network. "Periodic Arthralgia." 2005 Oct. <http://www.biology-online.org/dictionary/Periodic_arthralgia>, Accessed April 25, 2009.

Bloom, B. S. *Taxonomy of Educational Objectives, Handbook 1: The Cognitive Domain*. New York: David McKay, 1956.

Bloom, Benjamin S., and David R. Krathwohl. *Taxonomy of Educational Objectives: The Classification of Educational Goals, by a Committee of College and University Examiners*. New York: Longmans, Green, 1956.

Bohannon, Laura. "Shakespeare in the Bush." In *Culture Shock: A Reader in Modern Cultural Anthropology*, ed. Philip K. Bock. New York: Knopf, 1970.

Bonet, Josep. "Cuestión de perspectivas (I)." In *Antología de 'El trujamán'*, ed. Jaime Nieto and María Pepa

Palomero. Madrid: Centro Virtual Cervantes, 2002, 20–1.

Borges, Jorge Luis. *El Hacedor*. Buenos Aires: Emecé Editores, 1960.

———. "Sobre el doblaje." In *Obras completas 1923–1949*. Buenos Aires: Emecé Editores, 1989, 283–4.

Borja Albi, A., Silvia Gamero Pérez, and J. C. Ruíz Anton. "El laboratorio de traducción como escenario didáctico." *Quaderns. Revista de Traducció* 2 (1998): 143–54.

Bowker, Lynne. *Computer-Aided Translation Technology: A Practical Introduction*. Ottawa: University of Ottawa Press, 2002.

Bülher, Karl. *Sprachtheorie: Die Darstellungsfunktion der Sprache*. Stuttgart: Gustav Fischer, 1934/1965.

Byrne, Jody. *Technical Translation: Usability Strategies for Translating Technical Documentation*. Dordrecht: Springer, 2006.

Cabré, M. Teresa. *Terminology: Theory, Methods, and Applications*. ed. Juan C. Sager; Trans. Janet Ann DeCesaris. Amsterdam/ Philadelphia: John Benjamins, 1999.

Calishain, Tara, and Rael Dornfest. *Google Hacks*. Sebastopol, CA: O'Reilly, 2003.

Crystal, David, ed. *The Cambridge Encyclopedia of Language*. Cambridge: Cambridge University Press, 1997.

Camero, Ysrrael. "La encrucijada de la paradoja azteca." *Analítica.com Venezuela* 30 (June 2000). Analítica Consulting. <http://www.analitica.com/va/hispanica/elecciones_mexico/3920545.asp>, Accessed May 20, 2007.

Candia, Rubén. "The Business Letter in Spanish: A Cultural Perspective." Global Business Languages. 2001. <http://www.krannert.purdue.edu/centers/ciber/publications/gbl/GBL%20-%202001/1i-Candia %20Rub%E9n-134-139.doc>, Accessed June 1, 2009.

Canfield, D. Lincoln. *East Meets West, South of the Border; Essays on Spanish American Life and Attitudes*. Carbondale: Southern Illinois University Press, 1968.

Cantinflas, *El analfabeto*. Directed by Miguel M. Delgado. Posa Films International, S.A., Mexico, 1960.

Carrol, Lewis. *Alice in Wonderland*. New York: Arcadia House, 1950.

Cartagena, Chiqui. *Latino Boom!: Everything You Need to Know to Grow Your Business in the U.S. Hispanic Market*. New York: Random House, 2005.

Castillo-Solórzano, Carlos, Jon Andrus, and Mirta Roses Periago. "El desarrollo de nuevas vacunas: generación de información para la toma de decisiones." *Revista panamericana de salud pública = Pan American Journal of Public Health* 15.1 (2004): 1–3. <http://journal.paho.org/index.php?a_ID=525#xpand3>

Castro, Fidel. "Hoy conmemoramos la aplastante victoria de las fuerzas revolucionarias y la primera derrota del imperialismo en América." Speech delivered on the 40th anniversary of the Bay of Pigs invasion, 19 April 2001. 2000 – 2005, Analítica Consulting 1996 <http://www.analitica.com/BITBLIO/fidel/giron40.asp>, Accessed June 1, 2009.

Celdrán, Pancracio. *Inventario general de insultos*. Madrid: Ediciones del Prado, 1995.

Cervantes Saavedra, Miguel de. *Don Quixote*. Trans. P. A. Motteaux. New York: Dutton, 1954.

Chandler, Raymond. *Trouble Is My Business*. New York: Ballantine Books, 1972.

Chang-Rodríguez, Eugenio. *Latinoamérica: su civilización y su cultura*. 3rd ed. Boston: Heinle & Heinle, 1991.

Chesterman, Andrew. "Teaching Translation Theory: The Significance of Memes." *Teaching Translation and Interpreting 3: New Horizons: Papers from the Third Language International Conference, Elsinore, Denmark, 9–11 June 1995*. Ed. Cay Dollerup and Vibeke Appel. Philadelphia: John Benjamins, 1996, 63-7.

Child, Jack. "Lesson 16 Supplemental Exercises" to *Introduction to Spanish Translation* [Unpublished manuscript, 2001]. Lanham, MD: University Press of America, 1992.

Christie, John S. *Latino Fiction and the Modernist Imagination: Literature of the Borderlands*. New York: Garland, 1998.

Chuang-Tzu. *Basic Writings*. Trans. Burton Watson. New York: Columbia University Press, 1996.

Cisneros, Sandra. *The House on Mango Street*. Houston: Arte Público Press, 1985.

"Comercial De *La Llorona* premiado por sorprendente creatividad." *Hispania News*. Oct. 2002. <http://www.hispanianews.com/archive/2002/10/09/13.htm>, Accessed April 15, 2009.

Committee for Economic Development. *Education for Global Leadership: The Importance of International Studies and Foreign Language Education for U.S. Economic and National Security*. [Research and Policy Committee of the Committee for Economic Development] Washington, D.C.: Author, 2006, 6–7.

Common Medical Prefixes, Common Medical Suffixes. Medical Terminology Web. English Centre. October 20, 2006. <http://ec.hku.hk/mt/dictiona.htm>, Accessed April 25, 2009.

The Constitutional Walking Tour. The Constitutional Guided Walking Tours LLC, 2003–2008. <http://www.theconstitutional.com/index.html>, Accessed May 5, 2009.

Cornelio, Maria. "Legal Issues in the Translation of Healthcare Documents." *ATA Chronicle* (Aug. 2002): 24-8.

Cortázar, Julio."Instrucciones para subir escaleras." *www .literatura.org* <http://www.literatura.org/Cortazar/ Instrucciones.html>, Accessed May 22, 2007.

Cronin, Michael. *Translation and Globalization*. New York: Routledge, 2003.

Cuadrado, Luís Alberto Hernando. *El lenguaje de la publicidad*. Madrid: Editorial Coloquio, 1984.

Cultural Metaphors: Readings, Research Translations, and Commentary. Ed. Martin J. Gannon. Thousand Oaks: Sage Publications, 2001.

Dale, Doris Cruger. *Bilingual Children's Books in English and Spanish: An Annotated Bibliography, 1942 Through 2001*. Jefferson, NC: McFarland, 2003.

Dale, Edgar. *Audio-Visual Methods in Teaching*. 3rd ed. New York: Holt, Rinehart, and Winston, 1969.

Darío, Rubén. *Páginas escogidas*. 8th ed. Edited by Ricardo Gullón. Madrid: Ediciones Cátedra, 1991.

de la Vega, Garcilaso. *Comentarios reales de los incas*. Ed. Aurelio Miró Quesada. Caracas: Biblioteca Ayacucho, 1985.

Delisle, Jean. *L'analyse du discours comme méthode de traduction*. Ottawa: University of Ottawa Press, 1980.

Delisle, Jean. *La traduction raisonnée. Manuel d'initiation à la traduction professionnelle de l'anglais vers le français*, Ottawa: University of Ottawa Press, 1993.

Delisle, Jean, Hannelore Lee-Jahnke, and Monique C. Cormier (eds.). *Terminologie de la Traduction/Translation Terminology/Terminología de la traducción/Terminologie der Übersetzung*. Amsterdam/Philadelphia: John Benjamins, 1999.

Diaz, Junot. *Drown*. New York: Riverhead Books, 1996.

Diccionario Clave de uso del español actual. Ed. Concepción Maldonado. Madrid: Ediciones SM, 1996.

Dictionary of International Trade. Ed. Edward G. Hinkelman. San Rafael, CA: World Trade Press, 1994.

Do You Speak American? Episode 3. Directed by William Cran. Princeton, NJ: Films for the Humanities & Sciences, 2005.

Donne, John. *Poems of John Donne*. Ed. E. K. Chambers. London: Lawrence & Bullen, 1896.

"Double blind," "Screening" [entries]. Medtradiario. Tremédica: Asociación Internacional de Traductores y Redactores de Medicina y Ciencias Afines. 2009–2010. Trimédica, Inc. <http://www.medtrad.org/escaparate/ medtradiario.html>, Accessed April 25, 2009.

Doyle, Michael Scott, T. Bruce Fryer, and Ronald Cere. *Éxito comercial: prácticas administrativas y contextos culturales*. 4th ed. Boston: Thomson Heinle, 2006.

Dreyfus, Hubert L., and Stuart E. Dreyfus. *Mind over Machine: The Power of Human Intuition and Expertise in the Era of the Computer*. Oxford: Blackwell, 1986.

Duff, Alan. *The Third Language*. Oxford; New York: Pergamon Press, 1981.

Durban, Chris. "Translation: Getting It Right." American Translators Association. 2003. <http://www.atanet.org/ docs/Getting_it_right.pdf>, Accessed June 1, 2009.

———. "Translation: Getting It Right" (UK version). American Translators Association. 2006. <http://www.iti .org.uk/pdfs/trans/Translation(UK).pdf>, Accessed June 1, 2009.

Durban, Chris, and Alan Melby. "Translation: Buying a Non-Commodity." 2008. <http://www.atanet.org/ docs/translation_buying_guide.pdf>, Accessed April 10, 2009.

Eco, Umberto. *Mouse or Rat? Translation as Negotiation*. London: Phoenix, 2004.

Edwards, Alicia Betsy. *The Practice of Court Interpreting*. Amsterdam/Philadelphia: John Benjamins, 1995.

Egoyan, Atom, and Ian Balfour, eds. *Subtitles: On the Foreignness of Film*. Cambridge, MA: MIT Press, 2004.

"El Tribunal militar se niega a juzgar a sus pares." *Documentos secretos, decretos, leyes y jurisprudencia del juicio a las juntas militares argentinas*. <http://www .desaparecidos.org/arg/doc/secretos/pares02.htm>, Accessed May 21, 2007.

English Style Guide: A Handbook for Authors and Translators in the European Commission. European Commission Directorate-General for Translation. <http://ec.europa .eu/translation/writing/style_guides/english/ style_guide_en.pdf>, Accessed May 8, 2009.

Espy, Willard R. *An Almanac of Words at Play*. New York: C. N. Potter, 1975.

Esquivel, Laura. *Like Water for Chocolate*. Trans. Carol Christensen and Thomas Christensen. London: Black Swan, 1993.

Esselink, Bert. *A Practical Guide to Localization*. Philadelphia: John Benjamins, 2000.

"Farmworker Pesticide Safety Resources: An Annotated Bibliography of Bilingual (English-Spanish) Resources for Trainers of Farmworkers under the Worker Protection Standard." Comp. Melissa Frisk. Minneapolis, MN: Institute for Agriculture and Trade Policy, 2000.

Fass, Dan. *Processing Metonymy and Metaphor*. Greenwich: Ablex, 1997.

Faulkner, William. *These 13*. New York: J. Cape & H. Smith, 1930.

Fayen, Tanya. *In Search of the Latin American Faulkner*. Lanham, MD: University Press of America, 1995.

Felstiner, John. *Translating Neruda: The Way to Machu Picchu*. Stanford, CA: Stanford University Press, 1980.

Field, John. *Psycholinguistics: The Key Concepts*. London/ New York: Routledge, 2004.

Fonda, Daren. "Selling in Tongues." *Time.com* (Nov. 2001).

Fonseca, José da. *English as She Is Spoke*. New York: D. Appleton & Co., 1883.

Frames, Fields, and Contrasts: New Essays in Semantic and Lexical Organization. Ed. Adrienne Lehrer and Eva Feder Kittay. Hillsdale: L. Erlbaum Associates, 1992.

Francisco, Adriana. "Blog as a Marketing Tool for Freelance Translators and Interpreters." ProZ.com Translation Article Knowledgebase. 1999-2009. <http://www.proz.com/doc/631>, Accessed April 10, 2009.

Frängsmyr, Tore, ed. *Les Prix Nobel. The Nobel Prizes 1990* [Octavio Paz's speech at the Nobel Banquet]. Stockholm: Nobel Foundation, 1991.

Gamero Pérez, Silvia. *La traducción de textos técnicos*. Barcelona: Editorial Ariel, 2001.

García Lorca, Federico. *Selected Verse*. Ed. Christopher Maurer. Trans. Catherine Brown et al. New York: Farrar, Straus and Giroux, 2004.

García-Pelayo y Gross, Ramón, Micheline Durand, Barry Tulett, Alan Biggins, Carol Cockburn, Barbara Penick, and Della Roberts. *Larousse gran diccionario: español/inglés*. México, D.F.: Ediciones Larousse, 1984.

Garner, Bryan A. *Dictionary of Modern Legal Usage*. 2nd ed. New York: Oxford University Press, 1995.

———. *The Elements of Legal Style*. Oxford/New York: Oxford University Press, 2002.

Garre, Marianne. *Human Rights in Translation: Legal Concepts in Different Languages*. Copenhagen: Copenhagen Business School Press, 1999.

Germann, Christophe. "Content Industries and Cultural Diversity: The Case of Motion Pictures." In *Cultural Imperialism: Essays on the Political Economy of Cultural Domination*, ed. Bernd Hamm and Russell Smandych. Peterborough, Ontario, Canada: Broadview Press, 2004, 93–113.

Gerrard, A. Bryson, ed. *Cassell's Colloquial Spanish: A Handbook of Idiomatic Usage Including Latin-American Spanish*. London: Cassell, 1993.

Godayol Nogué, Pilar. "Interviewing Carol Maier: A Woman in Translation." *Quaderns. Revista de traducció* 2 (1998): 155–62. [Interviews from 1995 and 1996] <http://www.bib.uab.es/pub/quaderns/11385790n2p155.pdf>, Accessed July 5, 2007.

Gommlich, Klaus. "Text Typology and Translation-Oriented Text Analysis." In *Scientific and Technical Translation*, ed. Sue Ellen Wright and Leland D. Wright, Jr., Philadelphia: John Benjamins, 1993, 175–183.

González, Julia, and Robert Wagenaar. *Tuning Educational Structures in Europe: Final Report: Phase One*. Bilbao, Spain: Universidad de Deusto. 2003.

González-Davies, Maria. "Minding the Process, Improving the Product: Alternatives to Traditional Translator Training." In *Training for the New Millennium: Pedagogies for Translation and Interpreting*, ed. Martha Tennent. Philadelphia: John Benjamins, 2005, 67-82.

———. *Multiple Voices in the Translation Classroom: Activities, Tasks and Projects*. Philadelphia: John Benjamins, 2004.

González, Eduardo. To Ser or Not to Be: That Is La Cuestión!. *Translation Journal* 10, no. 4. October 2006. <http://accurapid.com/journal/38spanglish.htm>, Accessed August 12, 2008.

Gottlieb, Henrik. "Subtitling." In *Routledge Encyclopedia of Translation Studies*. Edited by Mona Baker and Kirsten Malmkjær. London/New York: Routledge, 1998, 244–48.

Gramley, Stephan, and Kurt-Micheal Pätzold. *A Survey of Modern English*. 2nd ed. New York: Routledge, 2004.

Gregory, Michael, and Susanne Carroll. *Language and Situation: Language Varieties and Their Social Contexts*. Boston: Routledge and Kegan Paul, 1978.

Gullickson, Richard. *Reference Data Sheet on Material Safety Data Sheets*. May 1996. <http://www.meridianeng.com/msds.htm>, Accessed April 26, 2009.

Hall, Ed. *Beyond Culture*. New York: Anchor Press, 1976.

Halliday, M. A. K., and Ruqaiya Hasan. *Cohesion in English*. London: Longman, 1976.

HarperCollins Spanish Unabridged Dictionary. 8th ed. New York: HarperCollins, 2005.

Harvey Ciampi, Tanya. *Search Engine Tricks for Finding Translations on the Internet in Bilingual/Multilingual Glossaries or Parallel texts on the Same Page*. <http://web.ticino.com/multilingual/internet/search_engine_tricks.htm>, Accessed April 10, 2009.

Hasbro.com. *About Scrabble: The Rules of the Game (Game Play)*. 2008. <http://www.hasbro.com/games/adultgames/scrabble/home.cfm?page=About/gameplay>, Accessed May 5, 2009.

Hatim, Basil, and Ian Mason. *The Translator as Communicator*. London: Routledge, 1997.

Hatim, Basil, and Jeremy Munday. *Translation: An Advanced Resource Book*. New York: Routledge, 2004.

Helbich, Carl. "Controlled Authoring: Writing for Re-Use." In *Multilingual. Getting Started Guide: Writing for Translation*, 1998-2009. Sandpoint, ID: MultiLingual Computing, Inc., October/November 2006, 3–6. <http://www.multilingual.com/guides.php>.

Hemingway, Ernest. "A Clean, Well-Lighted Place." *Winner Takes Nothing*. New York: Scribner, 1933.

Hermans, Theo. "Translation and Normativity." *Current Issues in Language and Society* 5, Nos. 1 & 2 (1998): 51–72.

Herrera McElroy, Onyria, and Lola L. Grabb. *Spanish-English, English-Spanish Medical Dictionary = Diccionario médico español-inglés, inglés-español.* 3rd ed. Philadelphia: Lippincott Williams & Wilkins, 2005.

Hervey, Sandor J., Ian Higgins, and Louise M. Haywood. *Thinking Spanish Translation: A Course in Translation Method: Spanish to English.* New York: Routledge, 1995.

Hinkelman, Edward G. *A Short Course in International Trade Documentation: The Documents of Exporting, Importing, Transportation and Banking.* Novato, CA: World Trade Press, 2002.

Hofstadter, Douglas R. *Le ton beau de Marot: In Praise of the Music of Language.* New York: Basic Books, 1997.

Hofstede, Geert. *Culture's Consequences: International Differences in Work Related Values.* Thousand Oaks, CA: Sage, 1980.

———. *Culture's Consequences: Comparing Values, Behaviors, Institutions, and Organizations.* Thousand Oaks, CA: Sage, 2001.

Hospers, John. *An Introduction to Philosophical Analysis.* 2nd ed. London: Routledge & K. Paul, 1967.

House, Juliane. *A Model for Translation Quality Assessment.* Tübingen, Germany: TBL- Verlag Narr, 1977.

Huxley, Aldous. *Brave New World.* New York: Harper & Row, 1969.

Iáñez Pareja, Enrique. "Células madre y clonación terapéutica." Granada, Spain: Departamento de Microbiología e Instituto de Biotecnología, Universidad de Granada. <http://www.ugr.es/~eianez/Biotecnologia/clonembrion.htm>, Accessed June 1, 2009.

IFEMA Trade Fair Calendar [insert]. *Ronda Iberia.* Zeta Gestión de Medios. S.A., Jan. 2005.

Iglesias Prieto, Norma. *La flor más bella de la maquiladora: historias de vida de la mujer obrera en Tijuana, B.C.N.* Mexico City: Secretaría de Educación Pública, Centro de Estudios Fronterizos, 1985.

Interlingual and Intercultural Communication: Discourse and Cognition in Translation and Second Language Acquisition Studies. Ed. Juliane House and Shoshana Blum-Kulka. Tübingen, Germany: G. Narr, 1986.

"Spanish/English Medical Translation Resources." Institute for Applied Linguistics, Kent State University. <http://appling.kent.edu/ResourcePages/Courseware/French MedicalResources/SpanishMedical.htm>, Accessed April 25, 2009.

Ivins, Molly. "Bush's Bracero Program." *Alternet* (14 Jan 2004). Independent Media Institute. <http://www.alternet.org/columnists/story/17561>, Accessed May 21, 2007.

Jacot de Boinod, Adam. *The Meaning of Tingo and Other Extraordinary Words from Around the World.* New York: Penguin Books, 2005.

Jakobson, Roman. "On Linguistic Aspects of Translation." In *The Translation Studies Reader,* ed. Lawrence Venuti. New York: Routledge, 2004.

James, Stuart H., and Jon J. Nordby, eds. *Forensic Science: An Introduction to Scientific and Investigative Techniques.* Boca Raton, FL: CRC Press, 2003.

Jones, Malcolm. "Lost in Translations." *Newsweek* (Oct. 15, 2007) <http://www.newsweek.com/id/42451/page/3>, Accessed April 29, 2009.

Joos, Martin. *The Five Clocks.* Publication 22. Bloomington: Indiana University Research Center in Anthropology, Folklore, and Linguistics, 1962.

Kaplan, Stephen M. *English-Spanish, Spanish-English Electrical and Computer Engineering Dictionary = Diccionario de ingeniería eléctrica y de computadoras inglés/español, español/inglés.* New York: Wiley, 1996.

Kelly, Dorothy. *A Handbook for Translator Trainers: A Guide to Reflective Practice.* Manchester, England/Northampton, MA: St. Jerome, 2005.

Kenny, Dorothy. "CAT Tools in an Academic Environment: What Are They Good For?" *Target* 11.1 (1999): 65-82.

King, John. "Cinema." In *A Cultural History of Latin America: Literature, Music, and the Visual Arts in the 19th and 20th Centuries,* ed. Leslie Bethell. New York: Cambridge University Press, 1998.

King Jr., Martin Luther. "Letter from a Birmingham Jail." In *Voices of Diversity: Perspectives on American Political Ideals and Institutions.* Comp. Pat Andrews. Guilford, CT: Dushkin, 1995.

Kiraly, Donald. *A Social Constructivist Approach to Translator Education: Empowerment from Theory to Practice.* Manchester, UK/ Northampton, MA: St. Jerome, 2000.

Kohl, John. *The Global English Style Guide: Writing Clear, Translatable Documentation for a Global Market.* Cary, NC: SAS Institute, 2008.

Korzenny, Betty Ann, and Felipe Korzenny. *Hispanic Marketing: A Cultural Perspective.* Burlington, MA: Elsevier/Butterworth-Heinemann, 2005.

Lakoff, George, and Mark Johnson. *Metaphors We Live By.* Chicago: University of Chicago Press, 1980.

Lao Zi. *El libro del Tao.* Trans. Iñaki Preciado Idoeta. Madrid: Alfaguara, 1978.

———. *The Way of Life According to Laotzu. An American version by Witter Bynner.* New York: John Day, 1944.

Larson, Mildred. *Meaning-Based Translation: A Guide to Cross-Language Equivalence.* Lanham, MD: University Press of America, 1984.

Larsson, Susan. "Glossary Search Tips." Swedish-English Translation Services. November 5, 1999. <http://home.ncia.com/~slarsson/glosearch.html>, Accessed April 10, 2009.

Lassen, Inger. *Accessibility and Acceptability in Technical Manuals: A Survey of Style and Grammatical Metaphor.* Amsterdam/Philadelphia: John Benjamins, 2003.

Lathey, Gillian. ed. *The Translation of Children's Literature: A Reader.* Multilingual Matters, 2006.

Lawlor, Terry. "Is the Writing on the Wall for Inefficient Translation?" <http://www.gdspublishing.com/ic_pdf/bmus/sdli.pdf> Accessed April 5, 2009.

Laurillard, Diana. *Rethinking University Teaching: A Conversational Framework for the Effective Use of Learning Technologies.* New York: Routledge, 1993.

Laviosa, Sara. *Corpus-Based Translation Studies: Theory, Findings, Applications.* New York: Rodopi, 2002.

Lechado García, José Manuel. *Diccionario de eufemismos y de expresiones eufemísticas del español actual.* Madrid: Editorial Verbum, 2000.

Leech, Geoffrey N. *Semantics.* Harmondsworth, England: Penguin, 1974.

León, Osvaldo. "Cumbre mundial de desarrollo sostenible." *Rebelión.org* (22 Aug 2002). Rebelión. <http://www.rebelion.org/economia/osvaldo220802.htm#>, Accessed May 21, 2007.

Levine, Suzanne Jill. The *Subversive Scribe: Translating Latin American Fiction.* Saint Paul, MN: Graywolf Press, 1991.

Lewis, Nigel. *The Book of Babel: Words and the Way We See Things.* Iowa City: University of Iowa Press, 1994.

Lewis, Oscar. *Big Four: The Story of Huntington, Stanford, Hopkins, and Crocker, and of the Building of the Central Pacific.* New York/London: A. A. Knopf, 1938. <http://skonline.org/courses/la/LW504427000/lessons/50b2-tools.pdf>, Accessed April 10, 2009.

Lipton, Ronnie. *Designing Across Cultures.* Cincinnati, OH: HOW Design Books, 2002.

Llera Llorente, María Teresa. "www.babyviajes.com: Un modelo de negocio basado en la gestión especializada de información y contenidos." In *Proceedings VIII Jornadas de Gestión de la Información*, Madrid, Spain, 2006, 137–45. Reprinted at <http://eprints.rclis.org/7897/>, Accessed April 12, 2009.

Lörscher, Wolfgang. *Translation Performance, Translation Process, and Translation Strategies: A Psycholinguistic Investigation.* Tübingen, Germany: G. Narr, 1991.

Lowry, James, Alex Ulanov, and Thomas Wenrich. *Advancing to the Next Level of Latino Marketing: Strike First, Strike Twice* [online]. BCG Publications, 2003. <http://www.bcg.com/impact_expertise/publications/ publication_list.jsp?pubid=791>, Accessed April 15, 2009.

Maia, Belinda. "Training Translators in Terminology and Information Retrieval Using Comparable and Parallel Corpora." In *Corpora in Translator Education.* Ed.

Federico Zanettin, Silvia Bernardini, and Dominic Stewart. Northampton, MA: St. Jerome, 2003.

Malmkjær, Kirsten, ed. *Translation in Undergraduate Degree Programmes.* Philadelphia: John Benjamins, 2004.

Malmkjær, Kirsten. *Linguistics and the Language of Translation.* Edinburgh: Edinburgh University Press, 2005.

Manrique, Jorge. *Coplas, with Henry Wadsworth Longfellow's Rendering.* New York: R. M. McBride, 1919.

Mañach, Jorge. *Indagación del choteo.* Havana, Cuba: La Verónica, 1940.

Marcus, Erin N. "Cases; When a Patient Is Lost in the Translation." *New York Times* (8 April 2003). The New York Times Company. <http://www.nytimes.com/2003/04/08/health/cases-when-a-patient-is-lost-in-the-translation.html>, Accessed May 20, 2007.

Martí, José. *Traducciones.* La Habana, Cuba: Editorial Trópico, 1945.

———. *Versos sencillos.* La Habana, Cuba: Publicaciones de la Secretaría de Educación, Dirección de Cultura, 1939.

Martínez, Tomás Eloy. *Santa Evita.* New York: Random House, 1995.

———. *Santa Evita.* Trans. Helen Lane. New York: Knopf, 1996.

Mateo, Marta. "The Translation of Irony." *Meta: journal des traducteurs / Meta: Translators' Journal* 40 (1) (1995): 171–8. <http://www.erudit.org/revue/meta/1995/v40/n1/003595ar.pdf>, Accessed April 10, 2009.

Mayoral Asensio, Roberto. *Translating Official Documents.* Northampton, MA: St. Jerome, 2003.

Mengzhi, Fang. "Sci-tech Translation and Its Research in China." *Meta* 44.1 (1999): 185–197.

Merne, Simo. *Handbook of Medical English Usage.* Oxford: Heinemann Professional, 1989.

Mescan, Suzanne. "When a CMS Should Speak More Than Just English…" *CIDM Information Management News* (2006 February). <http://www.infomanagementcenter.com/enewsletter/200602/second.htm>, Accessed April 3, 2009.

Mikkelson, Holly. *The Interpreter's Edge.* Santa Barbara, CA: ACEBO, 1995.

———. "On the Horns of a Dilemma: Accuracy vs. Brevity in the Use of Legal Terms by Court Interpreters." Originally published in *Translation and the Law*, ATA Monograph Series, Vol. 8. Ed. Marshall Morris. Amsterdam/Philadelphia: John Benjamins, 1995. <http://www.acebo.com/papers/HOMICIDE.HTM>, Accessed April 17, 2009.

Molina, Lucía, and Amparo Hurtado Albir. "Translation Techniques Revisited: A Dynamic and Functional Approach." *Meta* 47.4 (2002): 498–512.

"Mission to the Deep." Monterey Bay Aquarium, 1999–2009. <http://www.mbayaq.org/efc/efc_mbh/dsc_about_life.asp>, Accessed April 26, 2009.

Mooij, Marieke K. de. *Global Marketing and Advertising: Understanding Cultural Paradoxes*. Thousand Oaks, CA: Sage, 2005.

Morales, Ed. "The Fine Art of Translation: Overcoming the Pitfalls of Bringing Books from Spanish to English." *Críticas* (1 April 2002). <http://www.libraryjournal.com/article/CA201139.html?display=criticas&pubdate=4%2F1%2F02> Reed Business Information.

Morrison, Patt. "Adios, Rancho Palos Verdes; Hello, Green Sticks Ranch." *Los Angeles Times* (10 June 1998).

Mossop, Brian. *Revising and Editing for Translators*. Manchester, England/Kinderhook, NY: St. Jerome, 2007.

Multimedia Translation: Concepts, Practices, and Research. Ed. Yves Gambier and Henrik Gottlieb. Philadelphia: John Benjamins, 2001.

Munday, Jeremy. *Introducing Translation Studies: Theories and Applications*. New York: Routledge, 2001.

Murphy-Larronde, Suzanne. "Boosting a Flavorful Bean." *Americas* (June 2005): 39.

Neer, Katherine. "How Chupacabras Work." howstuffworks. 1998–2009. HowStuffWorks, Inc. <http://science.howstuffworks.com/chupacabra.htm>, Accessed April 12, 2009.

Neruda, Pablo. *Twenty Love Poems and a Song of Despair*. Trans. W. S. Merwin. New York: Penguin, 2004.

Newmark, Peter. *Approaches to Translation*. New York: Pergamon Press, 1981.

Nord, Christiane. *Translating as a Purposeful Activity: Functionalist Approaches Explained*. Manchester, England: St. Jerome, 1997.

Nybakken, Oscar Edward. *Greek and Latin in Scientific Terminology*. Ames: Iowa State College Press, 1959.

O'Brien, Judith Grunert, Barbara J. Millis, Margaret W. Cohen. *The Course Syllabus: A Learning-Centered Approach*. 2nd ed. San Francisco : Jossey-Bass, 2008.

Onieva Morales, Juan Luís. *Cómo dominar el análisis gramatical: nivel básico: teoría y práctica*. Madrid: Editorial Playor, 1985.

Orlowski, Lawrence, and Florian Lengyel. "The Corner Office in Bangalore." *New York Times* (9 June 2006). <http://www.nytimes.com/2006/06/09/opinion/09orlow.html?ex=1307505600&en=8926f03224ff1d65&ei=5088&partner=rssnyt&emc=rss>, Accessed April 10, 2009.

Ortega y Gasset, José. "Misery and Splendor of Translation." *The Translation Studies Reader*. Ed. Lawrence Venuti. New York: Routledge, 2000.

———. *Ensimismamiento y alteración, Meditación de la técnica*. Buenos Aires/México: Espasa-Calpe Argentina, 1939.

Orwell, George. *1984*. New York: New American Library, 1953.

Pablo Neruda and the U.S. Culture Industry. Ed. Teresa Longo. New York: Routledge, 2002.

"Para entenderse mejor: algunos vocablos del argot nocturno en cinco capitales de Latinoamérica (y en Madrid)." *El País* (21 Nov. 1997). <http://www.udel.edu/ leipzig/texts4/diccio.htm,>, Accessed August 8, 2007.

Pardo, José. "Diez pasos para ahorrar de manera inteligente." March 23, 2008. <http://librefinancieramente.wordpress.com/2008/03/23/diez-pasos-para-ahorrar-de-manera-inteligente/>, Accessed April 11, 2009.

Pavic, Milorad. *Dictionary of the Khazars: A Lexicon Novel in 100,000 Words*. Trans. Christina Pribicevic-Zoric. New York: Knopf, 1988.

Paz, Octavio. *El laberinto de la soledad*. Mexico City: Fondo de Cultura Económica, 1986.

Pazos, Hugo. "El triunfo de la eñe." www.loscuentos.net. *28 May 2006. La Página de los Cuentos*. <http://www.loscuentos.net/cuentos/link/209/209041/print/>, Accessed May 20, 2007.

Pen American Center. "A Translator's Model Contract." 2004–2009. <http://www.pen.org/page.php/prmID/322>, Accessed May 3, 2009.

Pérez Firmat, Gustavo. *Literature and Liminality: Festive Readings in the Hispanic Tradition*. Durham, NC: Duke University Press, 1986.

Pérez-Sabido, Jesús. *Spanish English Handbook for Medical Professionals = Compendio en inglés y español para profesionales de la medicina*. 4th ed. Los Angeles: PMIC, 1994.

Pinchuck, Isadore. *Scientific and Technical Translation*. Boulder, CO: Westview Press, 1977.

Piri, Thomas. *Down These Mean Streets*. New York: Knopf, 1967.

Pounds, J. Alan Martín R. Bustamante, Luis A. Coloma, Jamie A. Consuegra, Michael P.L. Fogden, Pru N. Foster, and Enrique La Marca. "Widespread Amphibian Extinctions from Epidemic Disease Driven by Global Warming." *Nature* (12 Jan 2006): 161–7.

Proetz, Victor. *The Astonishment of Words; an Experiment in the Comparison of Languages*. Foreword by Alastair Reid. Austin: University Texas Press, 1971.

Pym, Anthony. *The Moving Text: Localization, Translation, and Distribution*. Philadelphia: John Benjamins, 2004.

———. *Translation and Text Transfer: An Essay on the Principles of Intercultural Communication.* Frankfurt am Main: Peter Lang, 1992.

Quintana, Alicia. *Guía: Museo del Prado.* Madrid, Spain: Aldeasa, 1994.

Rainof, Alexander. "Dialectal Dialectics and Diatribe." *The ATA Chronicle.* (May 2001): 51-5.

Rabassa, Gregory. *If This Be Treason: Translation and Its Dyscontents: A Memoir.* New York: New Directions Book, 2005.

"Reglamento de Scrabble 2007." Federación Internacional de Scrabble en Español. ReDeLetras.com. 2007. <http://www.redeletras.com/rules/reglamento2007/reglamento2007.pdf>, Accessed May 5, 2009.

Reiss, Katharina. *Texttype und Übersetzungsmethode. Der Operative Text.* Kronberg: Scriptor, 1976.

Reiss, Katharina, and Hans J. Vermeer. *Grundlegung einer allgemeinen Translationstheorie.* Tübingen, Germany: Niemeyer, 1984.

Remarque, Erich Maria. *All Quiet on the Western Front.* Trans. A. W. Wheen. Boston: Little, Brown, and Company, 1929.

Research and Policy Committee of the Committee for Economic Development. "Education for Global Leadership: The Importance of International Studies and Foreign Language Education for U.S. Economic and National Security." Washington, DC: Committee for Economic Development, 2006.

Reyes, Israel. "De-facing Cuba: Translating and Transfiguring Cristina Garcia's The Agüero Sisters." *Voice-overs: Translation and Latin American Literature.* Ed. Daniel Balderston and Marcy Schwartz. Albany: State University of New York Press, 2002, 224–34.

Rich, B. Ruby. "To Read or Not to Read: Subtitles, Trailers, and Monolingualism." In *Subtitles: On the Foreignness of Film*, ed. Atom Egoyan and Ian Balfour. 154–69. Cambridge, MA: MIT Press, 2004.

Ricks, David A. *Big Business Blunders: Mistakes in Multinational Marketing.* Homewood, IL: Dow Jones-Irwin, 1983.

Ricœur, Paul. *The Rule of Metaphor: The Creation of Meaning in Language.* Trans. Robert Czerny, Kathleen McLaughlin, and John Costello. New York: Routledge, 2003.

Rivera, Wilga, Milton Azevedo, and William H. Heflin, Jr. *Teaching Spanish: A Practical Guide.* Lincolnwood, IL: National Textbook Co., 1988.

Roberts, R. P. "Traduction et qualité de la langue." Actes du colloque, *Société des traducteurs du Québec/Conseil de la langue française.* Québec. Editeur official du Québec, 1984, 172-84.

Robinson, Douglas. *Becoming a Translator: An Introduction to the Theory and Practice of Translation.* 2nd ed. London: Routledge, 2003.

Rodale, J. I., ed. *The Word Finder.* Garden City, NY: Garden City Books, 1952.

Rodriguez Araque, Ali. "An Unequal System of Trade: A Better World is Possible." *Vital Speeches of the Day* 72, no. 4 (1 Jan 2006:190).

Rodríguez, John. "Virus borra archivos de Kazaa." *PC World Latin America*, 2000–2009. <http://www.pcwla.com/pcwla2.nsf>, Accessed April 26, 2009.

Room, Adrian. *Dictionary of Translated Names and Titles.* Boston: Routledge & Kegan Paul, 1985.

Rosen, Robert, Patricia Digh, Marshall Singer, and Carl Phillips. *Global Literacies: Lessons on Business Leadership and National Cultures: A Landmark Study of CEOs from 28 Countries.* New York: Simon & Schuster, 2000.

Ross, S. D., "Translation and Similarity." In *Translation Spectrum. Essays in Theory and Practice*, ed. M. G. Rose. 8–22. Albany, NY: SUNY Press, 1981.

Rundell, Mike, "If Only They'd Asked a Linguist," *Humanising Language Teaching* 4, no. 4 (July 2002). <http://www.hltmag.co.uk/jul02/idea.htm>, Accessed July 16, 2007.

Rusk, Matthew. "Preventing Malaria." HTH Worldwide. 1998-2009 Highway to Health, Inc. <http://www.hthtravelinsurance.com/travel_center/general/ne_24.cfm>, Accessed April 12, 2009.

Saint Augustine, *De Doctrina christiana*, II, X, 15. Trans. Stefano Arduini, 2000, 78. <http://isg.urv.es/publicity/masters/sample/macrostrategies.html>, Accessed May 20, 2007.

Samson, Richard. "Computer-Assisted Translation." In *Training for the New Millennium: Pedagogies for Translation and Interpreting*, ed. Martha Tennent. Philadelphia: John Benjamins, 2005, 101–26.

Sánchez, Luis. "Sin pelos en la lengua." coloquio, inc. 1986–2009. <http://coloquio.com/coloquio/496poem.html>, Accessed April 4, 2009.

Sandburg, Donald. *The Legal Guide to Mother Goose.* Los Angeles: Price/Stern/Sloan, 1978.

Santiago, Esmeralda. *When I Was Puerto Rican.* Reading, MA: Addison-Wesley, 1993.

Savery, John R., and Thomas M. Duffy. "Problem Based Learning: An Instructional Model and Its Constructivist Framework." In *Constructivist Learning Environments: Case Studies in Instructional Design*, ed Brent G. Wilson. Englewood Cliffs, NJ: Educational Technology, 1996, 135–48.

Schäffner, Christina. "The Concept of Norms in Translation Studies." In *Translation and Norms*, ed.

Christina Schäffner. Philadelphia: Multilingual Matters, 1999.

Schäffner, Christina, and Uwe Wiesemann. *Annotated Texts for Translation: English- German: Functionalist Approaches Illustrated.* Buffalo: Multilingual Matters, 2001.

Scientific Writing for Graduate Students: A Manual on the Teaching of Scientific Writing. Ed. F. Peter Woodford. Bethesda, MD: Council of Biology Editors, 1986.

Scott-Tennent, Christopher, Maria Gonzalez Davies, and Fernanda Rodriguez Torras. "Translation Strategies and Translation Solutions: Design of a Teaching Prototype and Empirical Study of its Results." In *Investigating Translation: Selected Papers from the 4th International Congress on Translation, Barcelona, 1998,* ed. Allison Beeby, Doris Ensinger, and Marisa Presas. Philadelphia: John Benjamins, 2000, 107-16.

Scars, Olivia E., ed. *Two Lines: A Journal of Translation.* San Francisco: Center for the Art of Translation. <http://www.catranslation.org/translation.html>, Accessed May 8, 2009.

Segura, Jack. "The Spanish Language in Medicine." *Translation Journal* 3, no. 3. (July 1999). <http://www.accurapid.com/journal/09medic1.htm>, Accessed April 25, 2009.

Shah, Indries. *The Thinkers of the East.* London: Arkana, 1991.

Shamaa, Najah. "A Linguistic Analysis of Some Problems of Arabic to English Translation." Diss. University of Oxford, 1978.

Shreve, Gregory. "Integration of Translation and Summarization Processes in Summary Translation." in *TIS: Translation and Interpreting Studies.* Vol. 1, No. 1 (2006): 87–109.

Siegel, Carolyn F. *Internet Marketing: Foundations & Applications.* Boston: Houghton Mifflin, 2006.

Silva, José Asunción. "Nocturno (III)." *An Anthology of Spanish American Modernismo.* Ed. Kelly Washbourne. Trans. by Kelly Washbourne with Sergio Waisman. New York: Modern Language Association of America, 2007, 95–100.

Singh, Nitish, and Arun Pereira. *The Culturally Customized Web Site: Customizing Web Sites for the Global Marketplace.* Burlington, MA: Elsevier Butterworth-Heinemann, 2005.

Smead, Robert N. *Vocabulario Vaquero = Cowboy Talk: A Dictionary of Spanish Terms from the American West.* Norman: University of Oklahoma Press, 2004.

Sociedad Mexicana de Oncología, A.C. "Resumen clínico." <http://www.smeo.org.mx/bajables/ResumenClinico28AbrilCarcinoma.doc>, Accessed December 20, 2007.

Solzhenitsyn, Aleksandr Isaevich. *One Day in the Life of Ivan Denisovich.* Trans. Max Hayward and Ronald Hingley. New York: Praeger, 1963.

———. *One Day in the Life of Ivan Denisovich.* Trans. Ralph Parker. 1963. Alexandria, VA: Time-Life Books, 1981.

Sonesson, Göran. "The Quadrature of the Hermeneutic Circle: The Picture as Text." In *LSP and Theory of Translation. Acts of the XVI Vakki Symposium, Text and Image, Vöjri, February 10–12, 1996.* Vaasa, Finland: 1996, 9–33.

Soto, Moira. "¿Un bledo o un carajo?" 2005. <http://www.pagina12.com.ar/diario/suplementos/las12/9-2043.html>, Accessed May 21, 2007.

Sprague, David. "Leonard Cohen and the Death of Cool." Speaking Cohen—A Tribute to Leonard Cohen and His Words. April 14, 2009. <http://www.webheights.net/speakingcohen/flesh92.htm>, Accessed May 5, 2009.

Sprung, Robert C., ed. *Translating Into Success: Cutting-Edge Strategies for Going Multilingual in a Global Age,* Amsterdam/Philadelphia: John Benjamins, 2000.

Sprung, Robert C., and Alberto Vourvoulias-Bush. "Adapting Time Magazine for Latin America." In *Translating into Success.* Ed. Robert C. Sprung and Simone Jaroniec. Amsterdam; Philadelphia, PA: John Benjamins, 2000, 13–27.

Stevenson, Tom, ed. *Sotheby's World Wine Encyclopedia: A Comprehensive Reference Guide to the Wines of the World.* Boston: Little, Brown, 1988.

Steiner, George. *After Babel: Aspects of Language and Translation.* New York: Oxford UP, 1975.

Stejskal, Jiri. "International Certification Study: ATA's Credential." *The ATA Chronicle.* (July 2003): 15.

"Stocks Basics: How to Read a Stock Table/Quote." Investopedia. 2009. Investopedia ULC. <http://www.investopedia.com/university/stocks/stocks6.asp>, Accessed April 16, 2009.

Storni, Alfonsini. "Yo en el fondo del mar." In *Twentieth Century Latin American Poetry.* Ed. Stephen Tapscott. Austin: University of Texas Press, 1997, 110–11.

The Arabian Nights: Tales from a Thousand and One Nights. Trans. Sir Richard Francis Burton. New York: Modern Library, 2001.

The Arabian Nights' Entertainments; or The Thousand and One Nights. Trans. Edward William Lane. New York: Pickwick, 1927.

The BBI Dictionary of English Word Combinations. Ed. Morton Benson, Evelyn Benson, and Robert Ilson. Philadelphia: John Benjamins, 1997.

"The Most Untranslatable Word in the World." Today Translations. 6 December 2004. <http://www.todaytranslations.com/press-room/most-untranslatable-word/ID/>, Accessed April 12, 2009.

The Oxford Companion to Wine. Ed. Jancis Robinson. New York: Oxford University Press, 2006.

The Prentice-Hall Encyclopedia of World Proverbs: A Treasury of Wit and Wisdom Through the Ages. Comp. Wolfgang Mieder. Englewood Cliffs, NJ: Prentice-Hall, 1986.

Toury, Gideon. "A Handful of Paragraphs on 'Translation' and 'Norms'." *Translation and Norms.* Ed. Christina Schäffner. Philadelphia: Multilingual Matters, 1999, 13.

———. *In Search of a Theory of Translation.* Tel Aviv: Porter Institute for Poetics and Semiotics, Tel Aviv University, 1980.

Tosi, Arturo. *Crossing Barriers and Bridging Cultures: The Challenges of Multilingual Translation for the European Union.* Clevedon, England: Multilingual Matters, 2003.

Translating Into Success: Cutting-Edge Strategies for Going Multilingual in a Global Age. Ed. Robert C. Sprung and Simone Jaroniec. Philadelphia: John Benjamins, 2000.

"Translation Briefs." Basic Building Blocks of Translation. <http://www.hablamosjuntos.org/sm/translation_basics.asp>, Accessed April 10, 2009.

Trilling, Lionel. *The Liberal Imagination: Essays on Literature and Society.* Garden City, NJ: Doubleday, 1950.

ttt.org-CLS Framework. Translation Research Group. 2000 (Updated January 27, 2001). "CLS Framework: ISO 12620 data categories section 022000. <http://www.ttt.org/clsframe/datcats02.html>, Accessed April 26, 2009.

Ugarte García, María del Carmen. "Free es 'libre', no 'gratis'." In *Antología de 'El trujamán'.* Ed. Jaime Nieto and María Pepa Palomero, 184–5. Madrid: Centro Virtual Cervantes, 2002.

Ullmann, Stephen. *The Principles of Semantics.* Glasgow: Jackson, Son & Co., 1957.

United Nations Educational, Scientific and Cultural Organization. "Top 50 Authors." Index Translationum Statistics. 1995–2009. <http://databases.unesco.org/xtrans/stat/xTransStat.a?VL1=A&top=50&lg=0>, Accessed May 3, 2009.

Un Guía [sic] *para las leyes de los derechos de las personas con discapacidades.* Spanish translation of *A Guide to Disability Rights Law.* Washington, DC: U.S. Department of Justice, Civil Rights Division, 2004.

Upton, Clive, and Eben Upton. *The Oxford Rhyming Dictionary.* New York: Oxford University Press, 2004.

U.S. Department of Health and Human Services. "Immunocompromised" [entry]. AIDSinfo. U.S. Department of Health and Human Services. Updated April 24 2009. <http://aidsinfo.nih.gov/Glossary/TransTool.aspx>, Accessed April 25, 2009.

"WMPG PSA on the Dangers of Second-Hand Smoke." Sound Partners for Community Health. A Program of the Benton Foundation. <http://www.soundpartners.org/node/936>, Accessed April 25, 2009.

Valero-Garcés, Carmen. *Languages in Contact: An Introductory Textbook on Translation = manual introductorio a la traducción.* Lanham, MD: University Press of America, 1995.

Van Hoof, Henri. *Manual práctico de traducción médica: Diccionario básico de términos médicos (inglés-francés-español).* Granada, Spain: Comares, 1999.

Van Vranken, Lilian Novas, Cecilia Bohannon, and Terry Hanlen. "The Accreditation Program and Examination: An Informational Presentation." *Proceedings of the 44th Annual Conference of the American Translators Association,* Nov. 5–8, 2003, Phoenix, Arizona. Ed. Scott Brenna, 3–12.

Vanderauwera, Ria. *Dutch Novels Translated into English: The Transformation of a "Minority" Literature.* Atlantic Highlands: Humanities Press, 1985.

Vermeer, Hans. Ein Rahmen fur eine allgemeine Translationtheorie, *Lebende Sprachen* 23, no. 3 (1978): 99–102.

Villarreal, José Antonio. *Pocho.* Garden City, NY: Doubleday, 1959.

Voltaire. *Philosophical Dictionary.* Ed. and trans. Theodore Besterman. New York: Penguin Books, 1972.

White, Stephen. "Translation and Teaching: Dangers of Representing Latin America for Students in the United States." *Voice-overs: Translation and Latin American Literature.* Ed. Daniel Balderston and Marcy Schwartz. Albany: State University of New York Press, 2002.

Whitman, Janet. "Song of Myself." In *Leaves of Grass.* Philadelphia: David McKay, 1891–1892. Ian Lancashire and the University of Toronto. 2009.<http://rpo.library.utoronto.ca/ poem/2288.html#49>, Accessed May 3, 2009.

———. "Translated Ads Can Miss the Point." *The Wall Street Journal* (18 Sept 2003). Transperfect Translations, Inc. <http://www.transperfect.com/tp/eng/wsj0918.html>, Accessed May 21, 2007.

Whitman, Walt. *Leaves of Grass.* Boston: Thayer and Eldridge, 1860.

———. *Canto a mí mismo.* Trans. Leon Felipe. Buenos Aires: Editorial Losada, 1950.

———. "Canto de mí mismo." In *Hojas de hierba.* 1950. Trans. Leon Felipe. A Media Voz. <http://amediavoz.com/whitman.htm>, Accessed May 3, 2009.

———. "Canto de mí mismo." In *Hojas de hierba.* Trans. Leonardo Wolfson. Buenos Aires: Ediciones Librería Fausto, 1976.

———. "Slang in America." In *Imagining Language.* Ed. Jed Rasula and Steve McCaffery. Cambridge, MA: MIT Press, 1998, 77–8.

"Whitman in Translation." *Walt Whitman Quarterly Review* 13.1–2 (1996): 1–97.

Whorf, Benjamin Lee. "Linguistic Relativity and the Relation of Linguistic Processes to Perception and Cognition." In *Psycholinguistics; A Book of Readings*. Ed. Sol Saporta. New York: Holt, Rinehart, and Winston, 1961, 464–5.

Will, George F. "Bilingual Ballots Won't Serve New Citizens." *Seattlepi.com*. 28 May 2006. *Seattle Post-Intelligencer*. <http://seattlepi.nwsource.com/opinion/271640_will26.html>, Accessed May 21, 2007.

Willis, Jane R. "Perspectives on Task-based Instruction: Understanding Our Practices, Acknowledging Different Practitioners." In *Task-Based Instruction in Foreign Language Education: Practices and Programs*, ed. Betty Lou Leaver and Jane R. Willis. Washington, DC: Georgetown University Press, 2004, 3–44.

Wilss, Wolfram. *Knowledge and Skills in Translator Behavior*. Philadelphia: John Benjamins, 1996.

Wolfson, Leandro. "A 10-Year Retrospective on a Distance Revision Course: Most Frequent Translation Problems (Part II)." Trans. Alicia Marshall. *ATA Chronicle*. (Jan 2005): 30.

Woodford, Peter. *Scientific Writing for Graduate Students*. Bethesda, MD: Council of Biology Editors, 1986.

World Bank. *The World Bank Translation Style Guide: English Edition*. International Bank for Reconstruction and Development, Translation Division. 2004. <http://siteresources.worldbank.org/TRANSLATIONSERVICESEXT/Resources/Translation_Style_Guide_English.pdf>, Accessed May 8, 2009.

Wright, Leland Jr. Essays on Translation [Unpublished manuscript]. 2006.

Wright, Sue Ellen. TranslationTeacher@yahoogroups.com, Digest #38. 27 February 2006.

Young, Jeffrey. "Online Education's Drawbacks Include Misunderstood E-Mail Messages, Panelists Say." *Chronicle of Higher Education*, June 12, 2002. <http://chronicle.com/free/2002/06/2002061101u.htm>, Accessed April 10, 2009.

Yunker, John, *Beyond Borders: Web Globalization Strategies*. Indianapolis, IN: New Riders, 2003.

———. "Does Your Website Speak Spanish?" *CCaps Newsletter* 10 (Nov 2004). <http://www.ccaps.net/newsletter/11-04/art_3en.htm>, Accessed April 15, 2009.

———. "¿Habla español?" Byte Level Research. 2000–2009 Byte Level Research LLC. <http://www.bytelevel.com/global/es/, Accessed April 15, 2009.

———. "Trend #2: Bilingual Toys." Going Global. 4 November 2006. <http://goingglobal.corante.com/archives/2006/11/04/happy_bilingual_holidays.php>, Accessed May 5, 2009.

Zatlin, Phyllis. *Theatrical Translation and Film Adaptation: A Practitioner's View*. Clevedon, England/Buffalo, NY: Multilingual Matters, 2005.

Zetzsche, Jost. "Navigating the Translation Environment Tool Market." *ATA Chronicle* (March 2006).

INDEX